HISTORY
ARCHAEOLOGY
AND
CHRISTIAN
HUMANISM

HISTORY
ARCHAEOLOGY
AND
CHRISTIAN
HUMANISM

William Foxwell Albright

McGRAW-HILL BOOK COMPANY

NEW YORK   TORONTO   LONDON

To my wife
in memory of a fortnight
in Killarney
(August, 1959)

Preface

This is the first of a series of volumes planned to cover areas of the author's research which have been inadequately represented in his past publications. The first volume includes fifteen selected lectures, essays, and review articles, the first three of which have not hitherto appeared anywhere. While these fifteen chapters only skim the author's shorter publications of more general nature, it has seemed best not to include any more such material here.

The first chapter, "Toward a Theistic Humanism," strikes the keynote; the remaining fourteen chapters are supplementary and illustrative. Actually, nearly half the content has not appeared before in print, and the rest has been thoroughly revised, annotated, and indexed. The book is in no sense a repetition of what has already appeared in previously published volumes (e.g., *From the Stone Age to Christianity*), though it does supplement them in many respects.

Special acknowledgments and bibliographical data will be found in the first note in each chapter. All translations are the author's except when otherwise stated.

According to present plans, the second volume in the same McGraw-Hill series will deal with the intellectual revolution of the seventh-fifth centuries B.C., under the provisional title, *Experience in Quest of Reason: Phoenicia, Israel, and Ionia*. The third volume, as now planned, will describe the history of ancient Syria and Palestine, with special reference to currents of civilization. While the third volume reflects his primary interest during most of his scholarly life, the second is largely based on the author's research since 1960.

The author wishes to express his special thanks to the *ad hoc* advisory committee, consisting of G. Ernest Wright, Frank M. Cross, Jr., David Noel Freedman, and David H. Scott, for initiating and guiding the project.

The author also owes hearty thanks to friends who have read or listened to parts of the book, especially to Paul F. Bloomhardt (who entered the Oriental Seminary of the Johns Hopkins University in the same year, 1913), and to his son Hugh (Brother E. Alban of La Salle College in Philadelphia). Herbert B. Huffmon, his research assistant, has helped in a multitude of ways; the book has gained immensely from his patient collaboration. The author is also profoundly indebted to the dedicated ophthalmologists who have saved his vision, threatened since 1960 by glaucoma.

Above all, however, he must express his gratitude to his wife for her care during the difficult years after retirement (1958), when he was in constant danger of breaking down under the heady effect of freedom from academic routine (with consequent temptation to overexert in all directions). Between 1959 and 1962 she must have read well over a hundred books to him as he lay in bed with drops in his eyes, or recovering from attacks of nervous exhaustion. As an inadequate token of affection this book has been dedicated to her.

The Author

August, 1963

Contents

PART ONE

GENERAL SURVEYS

Chapter 1

Toward a theistic humanism[1]

Three main types of humanism

The word "humanism" has been so misused that one may hesitate to employ it at all, conscious of the grave danger of being completely misunderstood.[2] There is, however, a great tradition behind this word, and any ambiguity can generally be removed by prefixing the proper adjective. Whatever affects mankind is important to us as human beings, but it is only *sub specie aeternitatis* that it can be seen in its true perspective and acquire full meaning. We may distinguish three main types of humanism: the classical humanism of the Renaissance and of *litterae humaniores;* modern atheistic humanism, often called "hominism" by its foes; theistic humanism.[3]

[1] This is a greatly expanded and completely revised form of the Wimmer Lecture given at St. Vincent Archabbey, Latrobe, Pennsylvania, Dec. 14, 1952 (No. 6 in the series). It is a great pleasure to thank the Benedictine Fathers for their kind hospitality. Special thanks are also due my wife for reading the text; I owe a great deal to her criticisms. I wish also to thank the Reverend Maximilian G. Duncan, O.S.B., president of St. Vincent College, for giving permission to publish this lecture here instead of in the regular Wimmer series.

[2] The best definition I have seen is that of Christopher Dawson in his paper, "Christianity and the Humanist Tradition,"*Dublin Review*, 1952, p. 3: "Humanism is a tradition of culture and ethics founded on the study of humane letters." For the history of the term "humanism" and a clear account of Renaissance humanism see P. O. Kristeller, *Renaissance Thought: The Classic, Scholastic and Humanist Strains*, New York, 1961.

[3] After this lecture had been given, there appeared an extremely interesting symposium on "Christian Humanism" by six distinguished American Catholic

A fourth type, deistic humanism, in the manner of Voltaire, has been extinct for generations.

CLASSICAL HUMANISM

There is no need to dwell at length on the extraordinary phenomenon of the Renaissance, when Europeans rediscovered the treasures of classical antiquity, and through this rediscovery were stimulated to branch out into the unknown in all directions. It is unnecessary to insist that the Renaissance would have been impossible without the two great centuries which preceded it, when the imposing structure of scholastic philosophy unified all knowledge in coherent and comprehensive form, and when the flowering of Gothic architecture was followed by the birth of Italian art and the rebirth of national literatures. Nor need one stress the debt owed by the West to mediating Arab and Jewish scholars, who introduced Aristotle and Galen in translation to the West. Scarcely had the Renaissance begun when Constantinople fell, on May 29, 1453, over five centuries ago, and the flood of Greek manuscripts and teachers flowed westward in earnest.

In the fifteenth century, men of letters rediscovered Greco-Roman culture and were astonished to find that it had formed an organic whole of imposing dimensions and of even more remarkable luxuriance in detail. Small wonder that many of them abandoned their medieval heritage and tried to reverse the transformation of *Romanitas* into *Christianitas* which had taken place a thousand years before![4] The new humanism had pagan overtones, and it has been said with reason that we are still experiencing the effects of the wave of secularism which swept over the educated circles of Europe in the fifteenth century. And yet the world's gain was much greater

---

thinkers (*Social Order*, May-June, 1953, pp. 193-288); I wish to thank the Reverend Frederick L. Moriarty, S.J., for calling my attention to it and procuring me a copy. The contributions to this symposium are without exception excellent, and since they are almost entirely devoted to philosophical and humanitarian rather than to historical aspects of theistic humanism, they form a welcome complement and corrective to the emphases in this lecture. It goes without saying that the subject cannot be exhausted in a whole series of volumes.

[4] On this subject see the superb treatment by C. N. Cochrane, *Christianity and Classical Culture*, rev. ed., 1944.

than its loss: the wealth of knowledge and beauty accumulated by the Mediterranean world before the barbarian irruptions was now assimilated and digested, and men were enabled to move out toward the conquest of regions never reached by the Greeks.

In the late fifteenth and sixteenth centuries the development of printing made it possible to circulate handbooks and manuals on the sciences and arts, incorporating all available classical material. Most important—but rarely understood—was the fact that the sound common sense of Christian Europeans began to discard the mass of enveloping superstition in which Greek science had foundered after the second century B.C. During the following centuries Stoics, Neo-Pythagorean *Physiologoi*, Neo-Platonists, and Hermeticists had vied with one another in creating vast corpora of pseudo-science. Only Hero of Alexandria, in the first century A.D.,[5] and Ptolemy and Galen in the second, had been able to penetrate this undergrowth and to accomplish notable scientific work along the best Hellenistic lines. The often-expressed view that Christianity was somehow responsible for the downfall of Greek science has absolutely no justification; the "science" against which the early Christians reacted unfavorably was a farrago of unscientific accretions hiding an often tiny nucleus of sound observation and inference.[6]

Keen competition in recovering lost works of the past and the fame acquired by successful searchers brought more and more scholars into the arena of humanism in the course of the sixteenth century. Since philologians trained in the best methods of that day were required for publication, translation (from Greek into Latin), and organization of the new material, philology became the queen of the sciences. Humanistic emphasis was divided between recovery of the past, utilization of the recovered data for new syntheses, and cultivation of new literary and artistic tastes. These interests reached a climax in such talented scholars as Erasmus and Scaliger.

[5] The date of Hero has been notoriously uncertain, but O. Neugebauer seems to have fixed it astronomically in the reign of Nero; see his discussions in *Kgl. Danske Vidensk. Selskab, Hist.-fil. Med.*, XXVI/2, 1938, pp. 21-24; *The Exact Sciences in Antiquity*, 2d ed., 1957, p. 178.
[6] See the excellent survey of Greco-Roman science by T. B. Jones, *The Silver-Plated Age*, Sandoval, N. M., 1962, pp. 162-182, and his analysis of its downfall, pp. 183 ff.: "a gigantic log-jam . . . blown to bits by Christian dynamite."

However, the new learning speedily became organized into an academic structure which tended to freeze knowledge, and before the end of the seventeenth century the famous "quarrel between Ancients and Moderns" brought to a focus the rapid progress of natural science. Compared to what was being done by Galileo and Kepler, Boyle and Newton, the achievements of philology and history seemed very pale. Though the *litterae humaniores* survived into the twentieth century, their domination was really broken in the eighteenth century, just as Aristotelianism had been two centuries before.

MODERN ATHEISTIC HUMANISM

Disregarding the crudities of some extreme representatives of the Enlightenment, and the pallid deism of many distinguished scholars and literary figures of the eighteenth century, we may trace the real origins of modern atheistic humanism back to the early nineteenth century.[7] Auguste Comte tried to create a "Religion of Humanity," and his younger contemporary, Ernest Renan (1823-1892), made atheistic humanism respectable among historians and men of letters. Renan was, indeed, a humanist of a new type, combining classical tradition with an atheistic attitude which he made artistically attractive through the beauty of his French prose.[8] Britain had a similar though less prominent figure in Gilbert Murray (1866-1957), whose atheistic humanism is not so well known because of his lesser stature as a literary figure.[9] In America we find in James Henry Breasted (1865-1935) one of its most learned representatives. In his *Dawn of Conscience* (1933) Breasted stressed the view that man is the creator of his own achievements, possessing boundless capacity for self-improvement.[10]

[7] On this general subject see H. de Lubac, *Le drame de l'humanisme athée*, Paris, 1945, (Eng. trans., *The Drama of Atheistic Humanism*, New York, 1950). In this paper I am not dealing with Marxism at all, since its dialectical materialism is not a humanism of any kind.

[8] On Renan see the masterly survey of his scholarly career by René Dussaud: *L'oeuvre scientifique d'Ernest Renan*, Paris, 1951.

[9] Gilbert Murray combined a completely anti-theistic attitude with an extraordinary high-mindedness, devoting himself in later life to such worthy causes as internationalism. It is, incidentally, no accident that several members of his immediate family joined Christian churches.

[10] See below, Chapter 9, for my discussion of Breasted's point of view.

Passing over the rather ephemeral "new humanism" of Irving Babbitt (1865-1933), which was comparatively easy to bring into some sort of accord with Christianity, as attempted by Paul Elmer More (1864-1937), we come to the self-styled humanists of today. The "Humanist Manifesto" of 1933 was an uncompromising denial of any superhuman control of man's life or values and an unequivocal affirmation of man's ability to improve the "common good." Their chief periodical organ is *The Humanist*, which generally limits itself to polemics against all forms of Christianity. Their leading protagonists were until recently nearly all naturalistic philosophers like the late Max Otto and Roy W. Sellars, as well as ultraliberal Unitarian clergymen. Only twenty years after the original Manifesto, there appeared in *The Humanist* a retrospect,[11] unintentionally highlighting the widespread defection within their own ranks brought about by the second thoughts of some signers and by the stern realities of the Second World War, which have hardly favored such optimistic meliorism and have made both "humanity" and "science" appear as something less than beneficent abstractions.[12]

Among American thinkers closest to the humanists, and indeed a signer of the Manifesto, was John Dewey (1859-1952). He shared with them a conviction that man is the sole creator of his own future and that the past should be forgotten as rapidly as practicable. This dislike of history avenged itself within Dewey's lifetime, since the essays on contemporary events which he contributed to various journals during the period between the Wars, are already singularly antiquated. How shortsighted seem his optimistic predictions about

[11] For the text of the original statement and a survey of the views of all the original signers who were then living and felt able to reply, see *The Humanist*, 13, 1953, pp. 58-71. It is an exceedingly instructive document.

[12] Several years ago there was a reorganization of the American Humanist Association under the previous editor, Edwin H. Wilson, who became executive head. The new board of editors (1959 ——) included some eminent scientists: Chauncey D. Leake, physiologist, pharmacologist, and historian of science (who later withdrew); Winfred Overholser, psychiatrist; Sir Julian Huxley, biologist and publicist. Occasional contributions now appeared from Hermann J. Muller, Nobel prize winner in genetics and bitter opponent of what he calls "spiritualism"; Hudson Hoagland, physiologist; G. G. Simpson (eminent paleontologist and authority on evolution); and Linus Pauling (Nobel prize winner in chemistry and peace). In general the editorial policy still seems to be characterized by disregard of unwelcome evidence.

the Chinese Republic and its "democratic" future, written thirty years ago![13] Incidentally, it may be observed that Dewey's experimental pragmatism had a remarkable affinity for Confucian empirical wisdom, and that his ideas spread like wildfire among Chinese intellectuals, many of whom also became prominent in the Communist party.[14]

Dewey's knowledge of the history of his own subject was rather inadequate; for instance, he once pictured the Sage of Königsberg as a nonparticipant in the "vital intellectual currents and issues of his own day."[15] Actually, Kant was one of the best-informed men of his day, intensely interested in current events and movements. The reason for this downgrading of Kant was, of course, that the latter's epistemological approach was profoundly antipathetic to Dewey's own pragmatism, which led Dewey to exalt what he called "first-hand" intellectual participation at the expense of the remoteness from current reality which allegedly characterized Kant.

The experimental humanism of Dewey was doomed to failure from the outset because of the short perspective in which it set human activities. There is no known scientific method of determining whether a given change of an existing institution or a modification of social organization is justified by its effects unless we allow ample time for the change in question to operate. As a rule, at least a generation is required before the effect of change can be adequately measured,[16] and even then it is usually so complicated by concurrent changes that no clear case can be made for or against its

[13] See Dewey's collected papers on China in *Characters and Events,* ed. Joseph Ratner, New York, 1929, Vol. I, pp. 193-323 (essays originally published in 1920-1925). Of course, there are also correct and acute observations.

[14] The best known of Dewey's Chinese disciples was Hu Shih (1891-1962), whose writings were saturated with instrumentalist philosophy. That he was stoutly anticommunist himself should not blind us to the fact that the majority of his educated compatriots on the Chinese mainland—many of whom studied at Columbia—turned to Communism partly because a materialistic experimentalism had displaced both traditional philosophies and Christian attitudes. On his career, Dewey's influence on it, and the bitter opposition of the Communists to his views, see the excellent survey by Ch'en Shou-Yi, *Yearbook, American Philosophical Society,* 1962, pp. 135-143.

[15] See his article "Kant after Two Hundred Years" in the *New Republic,* 38, April 30, 1924, pp. 254-256.

[16] A very instructive example of the length of time required to measure the simplest of all types of change—the physical—is found in the article by Bentley Glass, "The Genetics of the Dunkers," *Scientific American,* August, 1953, pp.

value. Such operational thinking loses all justification when it cannot be controlled mathematically or by experiment. In short, Dewey's philosophy is antipodal to the whole idea of classical humanism, and it places man at the center only to treat him as a subject for detached experimentation on the part of a scientific elite.

His undoubted influence on education his been directly—though not entirely—responsible for the decline of formal discipline and intellectual content in our contemporary school curricula. "Progressive" education has proved to be as much regress as progress, in spite of some needed liberalizing in educational methods. (We shall return to John Dewey later, in connection with our remarks on functionalism.)

RECENT THEISTIC HUMANISM

It is hard to define the movement toward theistic and Christian humanism now taking shape. The classical tradition has gradually lost its strength, and yet our knowledge of antiquity has been greatly extended at the same time that specialization has notably reduced the proportion of broadly trained intellectuals uniting knowledge of history and philosophy or combining philology with literary background. Moreover, the exponents af the various movements toward atheistic humanism, sketched above, have by their habitual contempt for history brought about general confusion of humanism with naturalism. It is, accordingly, doubtful whether any two contemporary thinkers would agree on what is meant by humanism, much less on the names of the leading theistic humanists of our time.

Again it is necessary to insist on the impossibility of separating any

---

76 ff. Psychological changes are much too elusive to furnish useful clues to the effect of such "experiments" in social organization and institutional practice as might be instituted in democratic societies. The careful sociologist and political scientist can find plenty of material for observation in the effects of Communism and similar large-scale experiments without being influenced in any respect by Dewey's philosophy. Archaeology is already proving one of the most valuable laboratories, through which it is possible to study the capacity of various groups to develop high cultures even when they are cut off entirely or almost entirely from more advanced cultures. The Middle American and Peruvian situation is well known; less known are the high cultures of West and Southeast Africa during the millennium which preceded their destruction by Moslem and Christian slave trade. See Basil Davidson, *The Lost Cities of Africa*, 1959, with my review in the *New York Herald Tribune*, Nov. 15, 1959.

form of classical humanism from history. From my point of view, theistic humanism is the study and cultivation of our higher cultural heritage in the light of Judeo-Christian religious tradition.[17] Since the term "higher culture" includes the accumulation of knowledge and art from the past, which vastly exceeds the additions of the present, this definition involves historically-centered consideration of our cultural heritage in the light of our religion, and conversely. The theistic humanist cannot be a mere historian, but must also be a philosopher; besides, he must be something of an artist in his sensitivity to cultural forms.

Among the scholarly and literary figures who incorporate this ideal of theistic humanism, one may name the British historians Christopher Dawson (1889 ——), Arnold J. Toynbee (1889 ——), and Herbert Butterfield (1900 ——). Dawson is easily first in this group, since his books have consistently presented a Christian view of history, combining historical, philosophical, and literary competence in an aesthetically satisfying whole. His Catholicism is informed by a broad spirit of humanity which prevents him from ever descending to the depths of national and social prejudice that prevented Hilaire Belloc from being counted among Christian humanists—regardless of his undoubted brilliance. Toynbee's twelve-volume *A Study of History* (1934-1961), supplemented by *An Historian's Approach to Religion* (1956), indicates a gradual shift from a theistic (though Platonic) philosophy toward Jungian psychologism and Indic pantheism. His aversion for the uncompromising monotheism of the Old Testament and traditional Christian thought is so great that it is increasingly doubtful whether he can be labeled as a theistic humanist at all. One may quote different utterances of his in support of almost every shade of theism and pantheism.[18] Butterfield's point of view is quite different; his studies in Christian philosophy of history justify the hope that he will continue to apply his talents as historian of politics, ideas, and science to the task of constructing a theistic humanism for our time.[19]

Turning to France, one finds several outstanding scholars and

[17] Cf. Dawson's definition, n. 2, above.
[18] See my discussion of Toynbee below, Chapter 11.
[19] See esp. his *Christianity and History*, London, 1950, which is easily the best volume of its kind to appear for many years. It may be recommended as a thoroughly intelligent and well-informed approach to such problems as the

thinkers—all Catholic—who merit particular notice for the role they are playing in the development of theistic humanism. Etienne Gilson (1884 ——) is by far the most distinguished humanist in the classical sense among Neo-Thomists, and two Jesuits, Jean Daniélou[20] and Henri de Lubac, are easily the ablest men in the combined fields of historical theology, history of ideas, and philosophy. Writing with ease and brilliance, these three scholars already exert great influence in Europe, and are becoming equally well known in America. Bypassing old boundaries between orthodoxy and modernism, they enrich both with new insights which, if not balanced, might have led to rationalistic or even pantheistic tendencies (as in the case of Loisy and to a certain extent in the earlier writings of Baron von Hügel).

Germany and America seem to be absent from my survey. In part this may be traceable to certain predilections of my own. Much more than this is, however, involved. In Germany, professional specialization has been carried so far in the universities that a man who undertakes to cross boundaries is suspect. A philosopher or theologian is not supposed to be also a *Fachmann* in history; no Collingwood has arisen in recent Germany, combining distinction as an archaeologist with eminence as a philosopher. Leopold von Ranke (1795-1886) and Eduard Meyer (1855-1930) were universal historians, admitted by all competent judges to be great, but they deliberately remained historians. Similarly, German philosophers remain primarily metaphysicians, dealing frequently with historical and scientific topics but almost exclusively for philosophical purposes. Moreover, the vast majority of nineteenth- and earlier twentieth-century German thinkers were philosophical idealists who seldom paid more than lip service to theism. Hegel's quasi-pantheistic system was far from traditional Christianity and invariably led

---

nature of historical man and the bearing of history on theodicy. Of great interest is also his lecture on "History and Man's Attitude toward the Past" (lecture at the University of London, 1961). His Johns Hopkins lectures on the development of historical method (1963) have not yet been published, but they fit into the same broad canvas.

[20] See esp. his *Essai sur le mystère de l'histoire*, translated as *The Lord of History*, London, 1958. While this is a volume of lectures with dominantly theological interest, it may be heartily recommended for breadth of historical outlook.

those historians who adopted it into neutral or anti-Christian positions. Such philosophical idealists as Wilhelm Dilthey (1833-1911)
and Ernst Cassirer (1874-1946) could not be called humanists in the
West European sense, and they were certainly not theists. Both of
them approach historical questions from an idealistic point of view,
one as a disciple of Schleiermacher, the other as a Neo-Kantian.
Essentially the same is true of the leading German philosopher of
our day, Karl Jaspers (1883 ——), whose existentialism developed
from an attempt to solve problems underlying psychiatry with the
aid of metaphysics. His best known book, *Vom Ursprung und Ziel
der Geschichte* (1949), is neither historical nor theistic in its approach. It is not necessary to dwell here on the arbitrary constructions of the romanticist Spengler (1880-1936) nor on the pseudo-
religion of the anthroposophist Ludwig Steiner (1861-1925), which
is definitely not humanism, whatever else it may or may not be.[21]

In America we have not as yet been able to develop a consistent
approach to the tradition of classical Christian humanism, owing
chiefly to the strong influence of two opposite tendencies. Until
very recently American Catholicism was intellectually undeveloped
and under strong direct European influence. American Protestants
were swept away by liberal schools of thought in which history was
either left out entirely or comfortably adapted to their purposes,
while theology was dismissed as irrelevant to the new world of
today. Naïve belief in social and cultural evolution replaced traditional Christianity, and process theology became popular, under
the influence of Dewey's experimentalism. Instead of historical
revelation, evolutionary meliorism became the watchword. In the
new America history was dismissed as worthless or at best as essentially irrelevant to a rapidly advancing culture.

The Second World War and the advent of the Nuclear Age have
swept away much of the easy confidence with which men used to
face the future, and we have begun to realize that we remain under
the yoke of our common humanity, which begins to weigh heavily
on us whenever we try to break away from our human heritage. It is
not at all surprising that there has been a swing away from "liberal"

---

[21] We must not fail to mention Eric Voegelin, whose work, *Order and History*,
has been appearing in successive volumes since 1956. Though inspired mainly
by German thought, the execution has clearly been influenced by his many
years in America. For a discussion of his approach see below, Chapter 12.

Christianity toward various forms of neo-orthodoxy and existential-ism. All of these tendencies, so opposed in some ways to evolution-ary liberalism, are German in final inspiration, going back through Søren Kierkegaard (1813-1855) or Karl Barth (1886 ——) to earlier German thinkers. Dominant figures in the arena of American historico-philosophical theology are Reinhold Niebuhr (1892 ——) and Paul Tillich (1886 ——), to whom we must add the disciples of Rudolf Bultmann.

In Niebuhr's *Faith and History* (1949) he comes to grips with the problem of history, as he sees it. This book is difficult to un-derstand because of its unusual approach. "History" is used in two main—and quite refractory—meanings: (1) *Heilsgeschichte*, in the Lutheran-Reformed sense; (2) history in the sense in which it is used by the philosophical idealists Dilthey and Collingwood. Niebuhr's *Heilsgeschichte* is not the history of Judeo-Christian faith as de-scribed in the Bible; it has little to do with ancient religious, cul-tural, political, or social developments. It is rather a kind of sum-mation of the eloquent analysis of Christian theology presented at length in the two volumes of his Gifford lectures on *The Nature and Destiny of Man* (1941-1943). (In these lectures he already in-terpreted history theologically, with existentialist overtones, but there is no obvious influence of Dilthey or Collingwood.) As a philosophical heir of Schleiermacher, Dilthey was actually such a strong subjectivist as to be quite outside the pale of traditional Christian realism, while Collingwood was an avowed Neo-Hegelian, though also influenced by Dilthey's variety of relativism.[22] Nie-buhr's opposition to historical realism is manifested in his sharp re-jection of Maurice Mandelbaum's effort to free history from the relativistic approach by distinguishing between different types of judgment in the field of history.[23] In general, recent philosophical idealists and historical relativists distinguish sharply between "his-torical" and "scientific" thinking, designating the former as *Geisteswissenschaft* and the latter as *Naturwissenschaft*, which al-legedly exhibit basically different methods and structures. Niebuhr appears to weaken his theological approach, which is neither relative

[22] See below, pp. 28 n., 249.
[23] See *Faith and History*, pp. 116 ff., and for the writer's development of Man-delbaum's classification of types of historical judgment see now the discussion below, pp. 23-27.

nor idealistic, by accepting some of the subjective postulates used by Schleiermacher in his day and Bultmann in ours.[24]

In contrast to Niebuhr, his long-time colleague at Union, Paul Tillich represents a variety of philosophical idealism in which even the Neo-Hegelian practice of dissolving history into philosophy and the Schleiermacher tradition of volatilizing theology into ontology are bypassed. This particular idealism is substantially that of Schelling, Hegel's younger contemporary, as Tillich himself has stressed repeatedly.[25] (As is well known, Schelling himself went through successive phases under the influence of Fichte and Schleiermacher; an unusually strong vein of Neo-Platonism also runs through his work.) Tillich's view of the successive manifestations of God as pure Being, structured Being, and created Being or Existence, is a simplification of Schelling going back to Plato through Plotinus. Tillich sometimes accepts and sometimes rejects Schelling's *Identitätsprinzip*, i.e., the identity of opposites in absolute being, where matter and spirit, subject and object, etc., coalesce. On this protean substructure have been superimposed strong influence from Jung,[26] less from Freud, and an increasing use of existentialist ideas and terminology. There is no place for history in such a system, and Tillich himself, followed even more obviously

[24] See below, Chapter 13.

[25] E.g., in his paper in the *Journal of Philosophy*, 53, 1956, pp. 739-748.

[26] Since Tillich, after a period in the late 1940s during which he was an admirer of Jung's analytical psychology, has apparently abandoned it (both statements based on conversations between him and the writer), it may be well to mention such passages as the following: "In our terminology we could say that the angels are concrete-poetic symbols of the structure . . . of being. They are not beings but participate in everything that is. . . . Their rediscovery from the psychological [i.e., Jungian] side as archetypes of the collective unconscious and the new interpretation of the demonic in theology and literature have contributed to the understanding of these powers of being, which are not beings, but structures." (*Systematic Theology*, Vol. I, p. 260, and n. 1.) The volumes abound in similar Neo-Gnostic ideas. It is significant that G. Quispel in his illuminating little book, *Gnosis als Weltreligion*, Zurich, 1951, p. 46, calls Jungian psychology "die wichtigste Gnosis unseres Jahrhunderts . . . Das aber hinter dieser Psychologie ein Typus gnostischer Einstellung steckt, ist ein Geheimnis, das wohl den wenigsten verborgen blieb." Jung himself considered Gnosticism as the most useful of all forms of religion for the light it sheds on the human unconscious, and he regarded the closely related Neo-Pythagorean system of philosophical alchemy as the most valuable speculative corpus extant because of the psychological symbolism he found in it.

by his pupils, shows the same indifference toward history as is shown by other idealistic and existentialist thinkers in America. It must also be stressed that there is exceedingly little *Heilsgeschichte* in his most ambitious work (*Systematic Theology*, Vols. I-II, University of Chicago Press, 1951-1957), where it is replaced by a kind of "correlation" between "existential questions and theological answers in mutual interdependence" (*ibid.*, Vol. I, p. 60). It has, however, proved impossible to reduce Tillich's vague and often contradictory ideas to any system,[27] since theology is largely dissolved into existential judgments—which are too often nothing but introspective psychological constructs without any experimental basis whatsoever. The revelation of God in history is replaced by direct intuition of God as "ultimate concern" and of one's current aesthetic preference as "ultimate reality."[28]

As a result of the increasing influence of Bultmannism in America, Heidegger's existentialism is steadily gaining ground among religious thinkers; I shall have occasion below to show how antipathetic this is to any form of theistic humanism.[29] In particular it is quite impossible to correlate Bultmann's views with Judeo-Christian tradition, let alone with any form of orthodox Christian theology. This is scarcely surprising: existentialism is just as impossible a basis for historical inference as Husserl's phenomenology, from which it arose, is for the establishment or confirmation of data in natural

[27] Through his career he has shifted philosophical and theological notions and terms in a most bewildering fashion. A good example may be found in his *Systematic Theology*, Vol. I, p. 9, where he states that the key ideas of ten heterogeneous philosophical systems from the Scholastics to Brightman are all based on immediate intuitive experience "of something ultimate in value and being." In all systems ("empirical and metaphysical") there is an a priori "mystical experience" which "directs the induction and the deduction." Again, "the theological concepts of both idealists and naturalists are rooted in a 'mystical a priori' . . . that transcends the cleavage between subject and object." Since Tillich has repeatedly stated that he does not accept Schelling's "principle of identity," it is obvious that he is inconsistent in this, as in many other instances. No amount of philosophical prestidigitation can reduce mutually exclusive systems to a common denominator. Nor can any such verbal pyrotechnics as the famous statement of Tillich, "It is more atheistic to affirm the existence of God than it is to deny it" (where *existere* is treated as a synonym of *creatura esse* instead of *esse* alone with the Scholastics), clarify anything. It is, in short, impossible to erect a system where there is such fluidity of concepts and definitions, dissolving almost as fast as the thinker moves in any direction

science. Pure ontology is always too much hampered by the verbalism in which it must be stated, to have any independent probative value; in this respect it is entirely different from mathematics and symbolic logic.

The expansion of historical horizons

It was Breasted who first called effective attention to the parallel between the Renaissance and our own time in respect to the conquest of vast new areas of history.[30] In the fifteenth century man's knowledge was extended by recovering the whole then accessible area of classical culture. During the past century we have seen our knowledge of the sources of our own higher culture pushed back to include pre-Hellenic ages, at the same time that new historical horizons have opened up throughout the world. So recent has been this expansion of knowledge that Toynbee's *A Study of History* could not have been written a decade or two earlier. In the early Renaissance the sudden expansion of horizons by including the Greco-Roman world had led inevitably to a resurgence of pagan ways of thinking and a cult of Hellenism which often stood in direct opposition to Christianity. Similarly, Breasted summoned our new knowledge of antiquity to the aid of philosophical naturalism and meliorism, labeling his approach "the new humanism" in independent competition with the school of Babbitt and More. His adoption of the label was no more successful than theirs and was indeed generally disregarded, since he had no reasoned philosophy to present.

The very same data on which Breasted based his challenge to Christian faith, multiplied several times over by using all the evidence from the ancient East now available, are of the greatest possible value in giving world history a new theistic perspective, one

---

from his momentary base of operations. This is not "sustained reasoning" but kaleidoscopic shifting of pattern; it cannot serve as a foundation for analysis of either *Heilsgeschichte* or Christian experience—let alone any field of research in the non-religious humanities.

[28] Both these ubiquitous concepts of Tillich come from Schelling.

[29] See Chapter 13.

[30] The best introduction to Breasted's point of view is through Chapter I and the Epilogue (pp. 387-420) of his *Dawn of Conscience*, New York, 1933. On his approach see also my remarks below, Chapter 9.

which revolutionizes our understanding of the relation between the Bible and the world in which it came into being. This new knowledge yields insights of extraordinary significance for a truer understanding of the relation between higher culture, religion, and history.

ARCHAEOLOGICAL PROGRESS IN THE NINETEENTH AND TWENTIETH CENTURIES

In 1940 the writer undertook to give a survey of the present state of our knowledge in different fields of Ancient Oriental archaeology, with particular attention to the development of scientific method in recovering and interpreting the new data. I shall not go over that ground again here, except occasionally to recapitulate for the sake of clarity.[31] Since then, great progress has been made in spite of slowing down as a result of the Second World War and the subsequent cold war. In addition to numerous excavations—chiefly since 1945—many publications of earlier discoveries have appeared and there has been a steadily increasing use of archaeologically obtained data for interpretative studies and syntheses.

Over 140 years have now passed since Champollion first announced the success of his decipherment of Egyptian (1822). Twenty years later began the excavation of Assyrian and Babylonian mounds, followed within a few years by the decipherment of Mesopotamian cuneiform. In 1890 systematic excavation was first undertaken in Palestine; it was followed in 1907 by the opening of work at the ancient Hittite capital (modern Boghazköy) in northern Anatolia. Recovery of the lost Canaanite literature began with the first campaign at Ugarit (Ras Shamra) on the North Syrian coast in 1929 and the ensuing decipherment of the Canaanite cuneiform alphabet. Systematic excavation was not undertaken in South Arabia until 1950, after a century of collecting inscriptions. Meanwhile, the recovery of pre-Hellenic Aegean culture, which com-

[31] For surveys of this field see pp. 105-119, 130-136. More detailed surveys will also be found in my books, *From the Stone Age to Christianity*, 1957 ed., pp. 4-5, 25-81 (1st ed., 1940); *Recent Discoveries in Bible Lands*, 1955 ed.; reprinted from a Supplement to *Young's Analytical Concordance to the Bible*; my two chapters in *The Old Testament and Modern Study*, ed. H. H. Rowley, Oxford, 1951, pp. 1-47; my chapter on "Digging into the Past" in *An Outline of Man's Knowledge of the Modern World*, ed. L. Bryson, 1960, pp. 298-321. In the following survey only areas not touched on elsewhere in the present book will be sketched.

menced with the first campaign at Troy in 1870, was greatly advanced by the discovery of some sixteen hundred inscribed tablets at Knossos in Crete since 1900 and by the finding of over a thousand more in the same script (Linear B) at Pylos and Mycenae in the Peloponnesus (1939, 1952 ——); in 1953 Linear B was successfully deciphered. On the eastern periphery of Bible lands, excavations in Iran and the Indus Valley have yielded other still undeciphered scripts, as well as extensive remains of previously unknown civilizations. Our knowledge of remoter regions in antiquity has increased with comparable speed, though with fewer sensational finds.

Even more important than comparative archaeology as a stabilizing agent amid this welter of discoveries, which cover the habitable regions of the globe with a network of interlocking ancient cultures and assemblages of objects, are new physicochemical methods of dating, especially by means of radiocarbon.[32] Since the discovery of this method was publicly announced in 1948, many thousands of counts have been made and the chronology of archaeological and geological remains of organic origin is being established independently in many different countries. There are now dozens of laboratories where this research is being carried on. It is certain from the work of Kathleen Kenyon at Jericho, Jean Perrot in the northern Jordan Valley, and James Mellaart in southwestern Anatolia (Turkey) that permanent villages were flourishing in the Mesolithic period, during which agriculture came into use in southwestern Asia, not later than the end of the last Ice Age (the last Pluvial of the Mediterranean basin). This date is now fixed by a great many radiocarbon dates at about 9000 B.C. (11,000 B.P.). It is also certain that pre-pottery Neolithic followed it in the same regions, with well-built towns extending from Pakistan to mainland Greece. At Jericho there was a strongly fortified town between ca. 7000 and ca. 5500 B.C.; at Çatal Hüyük in Pisidia (southwestern Turkey) there was an even larger town with elaborate mural paintings.[33]

[32] See esp. W. F. Libby, *Radiocarbon Dating*, 2d ed., 1955, and his *mise au point* in *Science*, April 19, 1963, pp. 278-280, on "Accuracy of Radiocarbon Dates."
[33] Owing to the large number of early sites being excavated and correlations of culture and chronology being set up all over the eastern Mediterranean basin and the lands to the east of it, the bibliography is too scattered to be listed here.

It is now quite certain that V. Gordon Childe and others were right in holding that there was a pronounced lag as sedentary culture moved out in different directions from the Fertile Crescent (Mesopotamia and Syria-Palestine). By the time sparks of civilization reached America (or were kindled there independently) many thousand years had elapsed. It was proved by Paul Mangelsdorf in early 1963 that Indian corn was at the very beginning of its evolution as a domesticated grain about 5000 B.C. By ca. 3000 B.C. agricultural village life had begun in Middle America, but pottery was introduced much later; ceramic culture did not reach Peru until the early first millennium B.C.[34]

WHERE SCIENCE AND HISTORY MEET

We have already stressed the revolutionary effect of the application of nuclear physics to archaeology in radiocarbon counts. The direct impact of natural science on archaeology will undoubtedly lead to results undreamed of a few years ago. For example, geophysicists have discovered that careful measurement of magnetic declination in iron molecules of ancient pottery ovens and baked-clay objects is not only opening up a new method of determining archaeological dates, but may eventually lead to a complete record of variations in magnetic north over the past few thousand years. Soil scientists have found that it is necessary to work in close cooperation with archaeologists in order to determine the precise nature and succession of characteristic features of old and new soils. After some false starts, the cooperation of archaeologists with meteorologists has now been resumed and is already leading to fruitful results. These and many other new forms of close collaboration between natural science and archaeology must be added to the long existing and steadily increasing exchange of data between chemists, technologists, botanists, zoologists, etc., on the one hand, and archaeologists and historians of science, on the other. It is now certain that among the scores of thousands of discoveries, inventions, processes, manipulations, and uses of materials introduced by unknown inventive geniuses before the beginnings of Greek science,

[34] The preceding paragraph summarizes the state of our knowledge in early 1963. Comparison with the sketch given in the Bryson volume (see n. 31), pp. 317-318, illustrates five years of rapid progress. The dates are all fixed by radiocarbon counts.

there are many lost arts. Among these items of forgotten knowledge are the problems of how copper was used to saw through granite blocks (in Egypt) and how copper was smelted in the refineries of the Solomonic age on the Red Sea. Recent chemical research has determined how Attic black- and red-figured glaze were made, and other similar lost ceramic arts are now in process of being recovered. While it is most unlikely that the rediscovery of these lost arts will appreciably affect modern life, the fact that they so tenaciously resist our attempts to recover them is rather humbling to our pride in the achievements of this technological age. After all, we stand on the shoulders of two hundred generations of inventors, enormously aided by scientific and mathematical methods introduced by the Greeks, while the unsung inventors of the ancient world had nothing but their own experience and that of their precursors, as well as simple methods of testing by trial and error!

At the same time that this increasing interaction between archaeologists and natural scientists may actually do more to impress the academic world and the educated public, the most important scientific triumph of archaeology is its autonomous development of scientific method. Here I refer primarily to the formation of two concurrent procedures: the analysis of stratigraphic sequences and the classification in categories of all objects made by the hand of man (artifacts). The two principles of stratigraphy and typology are just as basic to scientific archaeology as they are to geology and paleontology. Through careful excavation of superimposed layers of human occupation it becomes possible to ascertain just what the material cultures of successive strata were and how to relate them in sequence. Absolute dates come later, and are dependent on comparative archaeology, radiocarbon, inscriptions, etc. The typology of human artifacts is just as Aristotelian in principle as is that of genetic variation; we have the same general division into classes, genera, species, etc., though the terms for categories may differ. Imitation produces phenomena which are in some ways analogous to genetically produced structures. The evolution of artifact types is now known to follow—superficially at least—the same course as the development of corresponding phenomena in the biological world.

Not only are there rigorous principles of patterning and classification in archaeology, there are also many procedures which are logically quite comparable to experiment in the natural sciences. It is true that mathematical control remains as a rule elementary and does not give rise to the complex forms of mathematical validation which we find in the physical sciences today. It is also true that we have no sexual reproduction to make genetic experiments possible, as in biology. *Mutatis mutandis*, however, the archaeologist proceeds along just as logical lines. First he observes, classifying types and determining inductive patterns. He then devises hypotheses and tests them by further digging and observing under carefully controlled conditions. For example, if an archaeologist wishes to confirm or disprove a hypothesis he has formed with regard to the chronological relation of two given assemblages of types found in neighboring sites but never previously found in stratigraphic succession at the same site, he will look for a new site of approximately the proper age, examine the surface and surroundings of the site to see whether both assemblages are illustrated by potsherds or other artifacts belonging to them, and then dig carefully, noting particularly whether the stratigraphy is intact or has been upset by any disturbing agency. This case is simple; many procedures are more complex. But they follow the same basic logical method in experimentation that is characteristic of all valid science today.

Nor will we find any less logical rigor if we turn to the best modern work in the fields of linguistics and philology, both so essential to the correct interpretation of ancient inscriptions and written documents, which have been recovered from their long concealment by the hundreds of thousands. Thanks to modern methods of exact photographic and other mechanical reproduction, as well as to the systematic use of induction and classification in creating grammars and dictionaries, Egyptian, Accadian (Assyro-Babylonian), Sumerian, and Hittite, as well as several different Northwest Semitic tongues, can all be read and understood. In the hands of recognized scholars, Egyptian and Accadian texts are almost as clear as Biblical Hebrew.[35] Sumerian and Hittite are not far behind.

The ancient Northwest Semitic languages and dialects have the

[35] This would probably not be true if the Hebrew text were preserved in its original form. As it stands, a substantial part of Biblical Hebrew poetry is either quite unintelligible or is wrongly understood, in spite of the painstaking efforts of later scribes and commentators.

advantage of resembling their sister tongues, Hebrew and Aramaic, but such differences as exist are all the more significant. As a matter of fact, the student of Biblical Hebrew is learning almost as much from texts and documents in Phoenician, South Canaanite, Ugaritic, etc., as the decipherers of the latter learned from Hebrew in the first place.[36] As we shall see, the decipherment of Ugaritic since 1930 has revolutionized our approach to early Hebrew literature. In considering the results of this enormous mass of work, it must again be emphasized that the interpretation of scores of previously unknown scripts and languages, now wholly or partly understood, has been rendered possible only by the use of innumerable working hypotheses, tested and developed by application of the standard principles of induction and classification, deduction and analogy. No work, no matter how clever or even brilliant, which neglects any of these principles, can have better than a mere chance of success (though it may be heuristically useful to subsequent students who do apply them).

REVOLUTION IN HISTORICAL METHOD

Few professional historians have grasped the significance of this revolution in historical method. Every historian will at once admit that it is important to have recovered the pre-Hellenic past—though few have any real idea of the extent, depth, or meaning of this addition to knowledge. And even fewer recognize how fundamental is the revolution thus brought about, for the simple reason that scarcely any nonspecialist has even a superficial knowledge of what has actually been done and how it was accomplished. Since the early nineteenth century there has unquestionably been a great advance in scientific historical method, illustrated and described in the two standard manuals: E. Bernheim's *Lehrbuch der historischen Methode und der Geschichtsphilosophie* (1894), which was philosophically oriented; Ch. V. Langlois and Ch. Seignobos, *Introduction aux études historiques* (1898),[37] which was a practical introduction to the evaluation of sources and the critical writing of history.[38] It is

[36] Mitchell Dahood, S.J., of the Pontifical Biblical Institute in Rome, is particularly successful in recovering new Biblical words and idioms by use of contemporary or earlier texts from Palestine and Syria.

[37] See also the English translation: *Introduction to the Study of History*, 1907.

[38] Books written since then, such as W. Bauer, *Einführung in das Studium der*

significant that neither Eduard Meyer nor A. T. Olmstead (1880-1945),[39] two of the leading ancient historians in the first decades of the twentieth century, diverged from the approach of L. von Ranke and his followers in order to lay more secure epistemological foundations. One reason is obvious: neither scholar was himself able fully to control the basic methodology employed by archaeologists and philologians and thus had to resort to acceptance of data on scholarly authority. The other is less obvious, but is integrally connected with the general application of modern logical analysis to the foundations of knowledge; neither scholar was philosophically minded and both shared a common tendency among historians to evade a thorough analysis of their underlying logical postulates and philosophical principles—their "protophilosophies," to use the terminology of George Boas.[40]

In 1940, following Maurice Mandelbaum, I differentiated between two main types of historical cognition: judgments of fact (i.e., judgments about specific events and data) and judgments of value (whether historical material is important or not, beneficial or not, etc.).[41] His insistence on calling these types of cognition "judgments" rather than "statements" is based on an incisive criticism of the historical relativists, who assume that historical fact depends on its treatment by a given historian, conditioned as he is by environment and predilections. But the facts and data in question have a real existence established by public observation and by masses of

---

Geschichte, Tübingen, 1921, and G. J. Garraghan, S.J., *A Guide to Historical Method*, New York, 1946, continue very definitely in the same tradition; the former is philosophically oriented, the latter is designed for practical use. An extremely valuable addition to our literature in this field is *L'Histoire et ses méthodes: Recherche, conservation, et critique des témoignages* (*Encyclopédie de la Pléiade*, XI, ed. Charles Samaran, Paris, 1961). The volume contains nearly 1,800 pages.

[39] See Olmstead's instructive discussion of historical method as applied to Biblical and related literatures in his "History, Ancient World, and the Bible," *Journal of Near Eastern Studies*, 2, 1943, pp. 1-34.

[40] See his paper, "The Role of Protophilosophies in Intellectual History," *Journal of Philosophy*, 45, 1948, pp. 673-684.

[41] See Mandelbaum, *The Problem of Historical Knowledge*, New York, 1938, and my discussion in *From the Stone Age to Christianity*, 1957 ed., pp. 7, 112-117. Judgments of fact, when sufficiently well attested by independent observers and concurrent evidence, are not subject to modification by the world view or the prejudice of a competent historian.

concurrent material preserved in our archives or excavated by the archaeologist. The "facts" are true (or false if our knowledge of them is in error) regardless of an historian's judgment about them. I then added a third type, already discussed but not utilized by Mandelbaum, "judgments of typical occurrence," to cover judgments involving an indefinite number of individual data which can be established by the same processes of logical induction employed in the natural sciences.[42] For instance, in a given group of strata and deposits belonging to a single period and a single region, the archaeologist invariably finds pottery and other human artifacts belonging to a restricted number of types, which seldom or never appear in any other period or region (except as heirlooms or by diffusion through trade or conquest). The results at any one site can be verified by the examination of other sites (see above, pp. 20 f.). If we rise in the scale of phenomena characteristic of men, we find, for example, that all documents belonging to a given district and period are likely to be written in a given language or dialect; in any case a single language will prevail over competitors. The analysis of a text can similarly be verified by the analysis of other related texts (see above, p. 21). Judgments of this class include everything that can be predicated about a given people at a given period; they can hence be determined by a statistical census of suitable material. Judgments of (about) typical occurrence dominate the fields where history and sociology meet, but they are also of vital significance for the history of science, the history of ideas and religion, economic and political history, etc.

Other classes of historical judgments could be added to the three

[42] Mandelbaum (pp. 3-4) discusses this class of judgments but does not admit it for historians, who are "not interested in the typical, the uniform, the readily repeatable." Facts of this type have been called "general facts" as against "particular facts"; cf. the remarks of Seignobos, *Introduction to the Study of History*, p. 203. This designation obscures their wholly different epistemological basis. It is very significant that no current treatment of historical epistemology bothers with such problems as types of historical judgment; cf. the two recent Oxford studies, W. H. Walsh, *An Introduction to Philosophy of History*, London, 1951, and Patrick Gardiner, *The Nature of Historical Explanation*, London, 1952, as well as the symposium on "What is Philosophy of History?" in *Journal of Philosophy*, 49, 1952, pp. 317-362. Much better than the preceding is E. H. Carr, *What Is History?*, London, 1962, which may be heartily recommended.

just defined. For example, a fourth category is "judgments of (about) cause and effect," which play a considerable role in historical writing, though often controversial.[43] Ever since Werner Heisenberg introduced his principle of indeterminacy in nuclear physics (1927), there has been an increasing tendency to play down the principle of causation in natural and social sciences, and to substitute a looser idea, often verging on contingency. There can be no doubt that it is extremely hazardous for an historian to declare that he has found the cause of the fall of the Roman Empire, or the reason for the development of modern capitalism in Protestant rather than Catholic countries. But, while it is true that emergent historical situations are often too complex to be reduced to simple formulas, simple causes and effects can often be stated with confidence. The Black Death did cause the partial depopulation of Europe in the fourteenth century. The flight of artists and intellectuals from Hitler's Germany did cause a marked upswing in American higher culture. The conquest of the Byzantine Empire by the Turks was largely responsible for the fifteenth-century increase in West European opportunities to learn Greek and read Greek books. Going back to ancient times, we correctly infer that the voluntary and involuntary exile of Israelites in connection with the Assyro-Babylonian destruction of the states of Israel and Judah dispersed them through adjacent lands and was the direct cause of the Jewish Diaspora.[44]

Since multiplication of descriptive categories causes obvious overlapping and frequent confusion, we limit ourselves to a single additional type of historical judgment—but one altogether too often

---

[43] Mandelbaum (pp. 203 ff.) includes this type of judgment under judgments of fact ("concrete facts possess a definite meaning, significance, and order of their own," p. 202). The writer prefers to consider them separately.

[44] A striking example of disregarding sound methodology in dealing with cause and effect is Homer W. Smith's book, *Man and His Gods*, 1952. According to him all intolerance and persecution are the result of religious fanaticism. He traces to this source nearly every historical persecution about which we have any record, often in flagrant violation of elementary principles of historical criticism. Though a very well-known physiologist at New York University, he pays no attention to such a basic logical principle as concomitant variation. Thus he nowhere seems to mention the bloody massacres carried out by antireligious Nazis and Communists, presumably because they do not conform to the neat picture of religion as the *fons et origo malorum* which he has painted.

neglected by historians: judgments of (about) personal reactions. Many historians are exceedingly careless about attributing to their characters all sorts of personal and psychological reasons for acting in situations where there is no evidence to show what motives or emotions may have operated. Where an historical figure describes his own motives, which are then corroborated by more than one friend and accepted by more than one enemy, we may have good reason for taking him at his word, but such agreement is extremely rare in modern times and is virtually unobtainable in dealing with antiquity. When we have a complex personality like that of Cicero, who wished to impress posterity as well as contemporaries, objective judgment is obviously difficult, if not impossible. In dealing with Biblical characters, such judgments ought to be omitted entirely in serious historical writing.

Arranging the types of historical judgment discussed above according to a scale of descending verifiability, we have the following series:[45]

1. Judgments of (about) Typical Occurrence
   The logical basis is inductive and statistical.
2. Judgments of (about) Particular Facts
   Based on public observation and report, subject to repeated testing, or on verifiable evidence of scientific nature—e.g., astronomically fixed dates, medically established cause of death, etc.
3. Judgments of (about) Cause and Effect
   See the discussion above.
4. Judgments of (about) Value
   Subjective ancient or modern, personal or public opinion.
5. Judgments of (about) Personal Reactions
   See the discussion above.

Since the first three are objective in character, even though determination of the truth or falsehood of any given judgment may involve the historian in subjective considerations, I need scarcely point out that data derived from them are not basically different from data employed by the natural scientist, especially in describing

[45] This classification was worked out while I was conducting a seminar on the nature of historical knowledge at Harvard in the summer of 1960. I wish to express my gratitude to the members of the seminar for their cooperation and their suggestions.

and classifying his material. But may we not dismiss the last two types of judgment as unworthy of the historian? Emphatically not, since this would compel the historian to declare war on didactic and paradigmatic use of history, on most good school texts, on the application of history to clarification of contemporary problems, and on most biographies and historical novels of literary merit. Just as all sciences with practical applications, from economics and agriculture to medicine, must use value judgments, so it is with history. The historian must be careful not to abstain from such judgments where they are needed. Rather he should always bear in mind the respective place of objective and subjective judgments. In many such cases he can quote the value judgments of tradition, or refer to respected ancient or modern authorities. Similiar caution should be employed in dealing with judgments of cause and effect, which are listed between the first two and the last two precisely because objective solutions are so often difficult.

Note that only the last two categories are affected directly by existential considerations. Both are almost purely subjective, since they cannot yield any appreciable quantity of historical data and by their very nature can rarely be controlled by experimental psychology—the only kind which possesses any scientific verifiability. The arbitrary introspective principles which guide existentialists are thus doubly hostile to sound historical methodology, first by their very epistemological nature, and second by the inability of existentialists to make their methods operationally useful in the interpretation of history.

The epistemological importance of archaeology and comparable fields ancillary to history, is that they deal almost entirely with judgments of fact and typical occurrence rather than with judgments of cause and effect, value or personal reactions, thus redressing the imbalance which has given rise to exaggerated forms of historical relativism.[46] In these extreme forms of historical interpretation, all past history is treated as relative to the viewpoint of the individual historian who describes it, or even to the temper of the age in which the historian in question lives. There is, of course, a certain amount of truth here, but the damage done to clear thinking

---

[46] See the discussion by Mandelbaum, *op. cit.*, and see my remarks in *From the Stone Age to Christianity*, 1957 ed., pp. 5-8, 82-126.

by this school is much greater than the gain it has brought to our understanding of the past. The relativistic approach is of little use in determining the factual content of history and is absolutely useless in dealing with judgments of typical occurrence. On the other hand, it might be of service in warning students against the abuse of value judgments in historical writing, but for the fact that most relativists have taken advantage of the situation to introduce their own dubious value judgments, on the specious ground that their precursors have done the same; or they have contended that their predecessors' judgments were relative but their own are not.[47]

ARCHAEOLOGICAL DISCOVERY AND LITERARY-HISTORICAL CRITICISM OF THE BIBLE

In view of my central interest in the Bible, as the often-neglected source of inspiration for theistic humanism, I shall briefly survey the bearing of archaeological discovery on our present historical understanding of the Old and New Testaments. I shall limit myself to a few outstanding illustrations of the light thrown by archaeology on the Bible, with special emphasis on the sweep of the new data, which leaves scarcely a corner of the entire Bible unaffected.

The Patriarchal narratives of Genesis and the Mosaic tradition of the following books of the Pentateuch have been discredited by modern higher criticism, culminating in the long regnant school of Julius Wellhausen. The stories of the Patriarchs (Genesis 12-50) have been regarded mainly as reflecting the period of the Divided Monarchy of Judah and Israel, a thousand years later, or as containing myths and legends gathered from different quarters and attached to the eponymous founders of early peoples and tribes. Some more conservative critics treat them as essentially a record of tribal his-

[47] Oddly enough, the Oxford philosopher-archaeologist, R. G. Collingwood, became more of a Neo-Hegelian and historical relativist as he grew older; see his posthumous book, *The Idea of History*, Oxford, 1946, and esp. the illuminating preface of the editor, T. M. Knox, *ibid.*, pp. v-xxiv. To one who reads his archaeological and philosophical works, it is instructive to note the lack of cross-fertilization between them; Collingwood was interested in ideas rather than methods, and his archaeological works concern themselves largely with interpretation. In my opinion Collingwood's dependence on Croce and Dilthey (i.e., Hegel and Schleiermacher) made it impossible for him to contribute to historical methodology through philosophical analysis, since he became interested more and more exclusively in value judgments of various types.

tory, however little factual matter may have survived. The traditional place attributed to Moses as codifier of Israel's laws and organizer of its religious beliefs and practices is rejected by nearly all critics. Some treat Moses as a legendary figure, and even those who grant a certain amount of historicity to the stories deny that he had anything appreciable to do with the foundation of the Israelite commonwealth and the form taken by later Yahwism.[48]

Meanwhile archaeological material has been accumulating at an accelerated pace. We know from discoveries all over the Near East how well the Patriarchal narratives fit into the Middle Bronze Age, between ca. 1900 and ca. 1500 B.C. The excavation of Mari on the Middle Euphrates since 1933 has yielded many thousands of cuneiform tablets belonging to the then recently settled Northwestern Semites of Abraham's time, whose language and customs were very close to those of the early Hebrews. Excavations in Egypt have thrown light on the background of the period of Joseph, on the settlement of the Hebrews in the Delta, and on the life and religion of Egypt in the pre-Mosaic and Mosaic ages. The picture of Hebrew Patriarchal beginnings has been put into an entirely new light by the discovery that the word "Hebrew" originally meant something like "donkey man, donkey driver, caravaneer, huckster" in Sumerian, Accadian, Egyptian, Canaanite, and Hittite texts from the second millennium. The 'Apiru (later *'Abiru*, from which *'Ibrî*, "Hebrew," is derived) were stateless people of heterogeneous origins but prevailingly seminomadic Northwestern Semites like the Biblical Hebrews. After a remarkable expansion of donkey-caravan trade during the twentieth-nineteenth centuries B.C., it began a rapid decline in the eighteenth century, and the Hebrews were forced into other activities in the following centuries. The evidence for this conclusion is very extensive; it explains not only the Biblical traditions about Abraham, but also the religious beginnings of the Hebrew people; e.g., the attachment to a personal high god, the ambivalent tradition about Patriarchal monotheism and polytheism, and the importance of the Covenant principle in Hebrew-Israelite

[48] This point of view is still maintained by such leading German scholars as Martin Noth, *Geschichte Israels*, 2d ed., 1954, pp. 105-130 (rev. Eng. trans., *The History of Israel*, pp. 109-137), and Gerhard von Rad, *Theologie des Alten Testaments*, Vol. I 4th ed., 1962, pp. 17-28, but there is a steadily accumulating mass of evidence against such a negative approach; see below.

history. Since the donkey caravaneers can be shown to have centered in Babylonian Ur and Northwest Mesopotamian Harran, we
understand the persistence of Mesopotamian cosmogonic, historical,
and literary motifs in the Old Testament, as well as the dominance
of Mesopotamian customary law and legal practices in both Patriarchal and Mosaic tradition.[49]

Cuneiform finds have brought to light six law-codes from ca.
2100-1100 B.C.; one of them, the Code of Hammurapi (ca. 1690 B.C.)
is quite complete. In addition, scores of thousands of legal and
economic tablets from Babylonia, Mesopotamia, and Syria provide
an unrivaled body of material for the study of comparative legal
practice in ancient southwestern Asia. There is no longer any reason for dating the substance of the Mosaic laws later than the
thirteenth century B.C. Wellhausen's Hegelian view that Law had to
follow Prophecy becomes wholly untenable. It is equally clear that
the only period in the Ancient Orient suitable for the emergence
of the Mosaic structure of religion and law was precisely where
tradition places Moses—in the last century or two of the Late Bronze
Age, i.e., the fourteenth-thirteenth centuries B.C.[50]

The discovery by G. E. Mendenhall that the oldest Covenant
outline which we possess, Joshua 24, is closely parallel in both order
of elements and legal background to the Syro-Hittite suzerainty
treaties of the second half of the second millennium B.C., is being
followed by a burst of research activity which has drawn both the

---

[49] For the evidence underlying most of the preceding paragraph see my highly
condensed but comprehensive discussion, "Abram the Hebrew: A New Archaeological Interpretation," *Bulletin of the American Schools of Oriental Research*, No. 163, 1961, pp. 36-54, with further analysis *ibid.*, No. 168, 1962, pp.
36-42, and a summary with additional details in my Harper Torchbook, *The
Biblical Period from Abraham to Ezra: An Historical Survey*, 1963, pp. 5-12, 26.
[50] In my forthcoming "History of the Religion of Israel," being prepared for a
series of volumes under the editorship of Louis Finkelstein, I have two long
chapters on Moses in which I present evidence of three principal types: (1)
direct archaeological and documentary proof of the antiquity and relevance of
many details of the extant tradition about Moses and his period; (2) demonstration of the high antiquity of the language and style of such poems as the
Song of Miriam and the Oracles of Balaam, as well as of many poetic quotations embedded in the narratives of Exodus-Numbers (which are earlier in any
case than the eleventh century, as can be shown by stylistic sequence dating);
(3) fixing the approximate relation of Mosaic institutions, law, and ritual to
earlier Bronze Age and later Iron Age data of comparable nature.

Convenants of Sinai and Shechem, on the one hand, and the Cove-nant pattern immediately underlying the work of the Writing Prophets (eighth-sixth centuries B.C.) into the full light of contem-porary Southwest Asiatic documentary sources.[51]

From the twelfth century B.C., when Israel consolidated its oc-cupation of the hill country of Palestine,[52] down to the end of the fifth century B.C., Biblical tradition is increasingly illuminated by archaeological and documentary material of all kinds. Excavations in scores of major and minor Israelite sites, interpreted in the light of steadily improving method and dated by more and more reliable criteria, enable specialists to agree on chronology within narrow limits. We now have Israelite inscriptions from every century of this period, and the total number runs into the hundreds. Contemporary Assyrian records continue to be found, and they are being increas-ingly supplemented by documents from Egypt, Nubia, Anatolia, Palestine, and Syria. The amphictyonic character of the Israelite tribal confederation is now better understood, and the traditional view of Israelite polity turns out to be essentially correct, against the reconstructions of the Wellhausen school and its congeners.[53]

The importance of Samuel's role (latter part of the eleventh century B.C.) in making possible a relatively smooth transition from charismatic leadership to dynastic kingship is now recognized, and his significance as the founder of the Prophetic movement, which was to become the second great contribution of Israel to the world,

[51] See esp. Mendenhall, *Law and Covenant in Israel and the Ancient Near East,* 1955, reprinted from his two papers in *Biblical Archaeologist,* 17, 1954. Based on the same material is Klaus Baltzer, *Das Bundesformular,* 1960. For the development of basic Covenant ideas from the Ancient Orient of the second millennium B.C. to the Deuteronomic-Prophetic literature of Israel, see esp. Julien Harvey, S.J., "Le 'rîb-pattern,' réquisitoire prophétique sur la rupture de l'Alliance," *Biblica,* 43, 1962, pp. 172-196, and W. L. Moran, S.J., "The Ancient Near Eastern Background of the Love of God in Deuteronomy," *Catholic Biblical Quarterly,* 25, 1963, pp. 77-87. Two important monographs should be out soon, also dealing with the influence of Near Eastern treaty forms on Deuteronomy and the Prophets, one by N. Lohfink, S.J., the other by Delbert Hillers.

[52] For my interpretation of this episode in the thirteenth and early twelfth centuries B.C. see *The Biblical Period from Abraham to Ezra,* 1963, pp. 24-36.

[53] This we owe largely to the work of Albrecht Alt and especially of Martin Noth; see the latter's classic monograph, *Das System der zwölf Stämme Israels,* 1930, and John Bright, *A History of Israel,* 1959, pp. 128-160 and *passim.*

has recently been clarified.[54] The partial replacement of an hereditary priestly hierarchy by the charismatic Prophets eventually led to a division of religious authority between the two classes of leaders. As I have recently written,

> The Judeo-Christian religious continuum is historically a synthesis of two main factors. First we have a developing pattern of Covenants between God and early Israel, governing faith, ethics, and cult. Second we see the interaction of two distinct elements in periodic tension: an institutionalized hierarchy of religious functionaries and an upsurge of charismatic spiritual leaders. Because of this ever-renewed tension between hierarchy and charism, the Judeo-Christian continuum has always been capable of periodic self-criticism—a process to which Western conscience owes its persistent revivals of sensitivity.[55]

Of all aberrations of historical criticism, the attempt—beginning in the 1890s—to discredit the traditional picture of the total destruction of Judah by the Babylonians and their allies between 597 and 582 B.C. is one of the most extraordinary. This necessarily involved rejection of the historicity of the Restoration. There would thus be no Captivity and no Return from Exile in any conventional sense. In order to reach such radical conclusions, Chronicles was dated in the third century B.C and its stylistic affinity to the Ezra memoirs in the first person was thought to prove that the latter were spurious.[56] Some scholars went so far as to reject the Chronicler's work, Ezra, Ezekiel, and even Jeremiah. The history of the sixth and fifth centuries B.C. was completely rewritten. Today, thanks to a steady flow of material from archaeological sources, now growing to the dimensions of a flood, we can categorically disprove almost every serious argument for such positions.[57] Of course, some erroneous

---

[54] See my Goldenson Lecture for 1961: *Samuel and the Beginnings of the Prophetic Movement*, Cincinnati, Hebrew Union College Press, 1961, and *The Biblical Period from Abraham to Ezra*, 1963, pp. 42-48.

[55] See *Samuel and the Beginnings of the Prophetic Movement*, p. 19.

[56] See C. C. Torrey's two books, *Composition and Historical Value of Ezra-Nehemiah*, 1896, and *Ezra Studies*, 1910, together with my discussion, *Journal of Biblical Literature*, 40, 1921, pp. 104-124, and *Alexander Marx Jubilee Volume*, 1950, pp. 61-74.

[57] See John Bright, *A History of Israel*, 1959, pp. 356-386, as well as my own latest synthesis, *The Biblical Period from Abraham to Ezra*, 1963, pp. 90-95, 111-114.

older ideas about what may have transpired in Israelite-Jewish circles during the period between 700 and 300 B.C. have had to be corrected.[58]

The Qumran finds (Dead Sea Scrolls) have made it possible to show that many Hebrew books of the Old Testament were already represented by different recensions not later than the fifth-fourth centuries B.C., for we have widely varying text-forms among the thousands of fragments from the third-first centuries B.C. excavated at Qumran. Since the Qumran recensions fit very well into the pattern of the Greek translations (Septuagint) made during the third-second centuries B.C., we can be quite sure that the Hebrew text underlying the latter exhibited the same recensional variations. These discoveries have completely altered our picture of Old Testament textual history, proving that it was much more complex than commonly supposed and that it is impossible to build elaborate hypotheses on the basis of the Massoretic Hebrew text alone.[59] The contents of Genesis-Numbers are in part very ancient, and there is nowhere any evidence for dating the final compilation and edition of these books after the seventh century B.C.[60] The contents of the historical books from Deuteronomy to II Kings are in general much earlier than their final editing in the seventh-sixth centuries B.C.[61]

[58] For instance, we now have a much better understanding of the North Israelite Dispersion after the Assyrian invasions of the late eighth century than we used to have; see my discussion, *Bulletin of the American Schools of Oriental Research*, No. 149, 1958, pp. 33 ff., and *The Biblical Period from Abraham to Ezra*, 1963, pp. 73 f.

[59] See my remarks in *Catholic Biblical Quarterly*, 25, 1963, pp. 1 ff., and in *Journal of Bible and Religion*, 31, 1963, pp. 111 f. (with D. N. Freedman).

[60] See the writer, *Catholic Biblical Quarterly*, 25, 1963, pp. 10 f. My position is quite close in certain respects to that of M. Noth, whose views on the *Grundlage* (G) and the relation of "J" and "E" to it are presented in his book, *Überlieferungsgeschichte des Pentateuch*, 1948, esp. pp. 40 ff. The chief difference between us is in my insistence on the reliability of the original narrative, which was based largely on verse tradition as well as on official tradition in both verse and prose. I also defend somewhat earlier and more precise dates for the written form. My theory of the origin of the J and E nomenclature of God in much earlier religious poetry and ritual is original, though suggested by Robert G. Boling's paper in *Journal of Semitic Studies*, 5, 1960, pp. 221-255.

[61] On this great historical work see M. Noth, *Überlieferungsgeschichtliche Studien*, 1943, pp. 3-110, and my own remarks in *The Biblical Period from Abraham to Ezra*, pp. 82 f. and 109.

(The development of the recensional differences which we have stressed above, is naturally later than the publication of the archetype manuscripts of the historical compilations themselves.)

Critical scholars, following Wellhausen and Duhm, formerly tended to date most Psalms, a large part of the Prophetic books, and virtually the whole Wisdom literature in the Persian and Hellenistic period.[62] There are still many who hold to a Maccabean date for some of the Psalms. Here two series of wholly unexpected finds have brought evidence of the weightiest kind for a return to essentially traditional dates. First came the sensational recovery of a substantial part of the lost early Canaanite literature in Ugaritic recensions dating in their extant form from the early fourteenth century B.C. The original compositions, which had been handed down orally, were, of course, earlier—chiefly from the first half of the second millennium, though part of the Baal Epic may be even earlier. Language, as well as place names, etc., establishes a provenience in Phoenicia and its hinterland, just north of Palestine.[63] In poetic structure and style, archaic grammar and vocabulary, these texts closely resemble the earliest poetry of Israel, among which we may now count the Song of Miriam (Exodus 15) and the Oracles of Balaam (Numbers 23-24), as well as the Song of Deborah (Judges 5). The slightly later Blessings of Jacob (Genesis 49) and Moses (Deuteronomy 33) now prove to be older in both style and content than the Lament of David over Saul and Jonathan (II Samuel 1), while there are Psalms which are stylistically even earlier.[64] Many

[62] The most recent independent treatment by Moses Hadas, *Hellenistic Culture: Fusion and Diffusion*, New York, 1959, takes a strangely anachronistic attitude toward the chronology of the Hebrew Wisdom literature, which he dates mostly in the Hellenistic period; for a concise criticism see my review in *American Historical Review*, April, 1961, pp. 1005 f.

[63] See my remarks in *The Old Testament and Modern Study*, ed. H. H. Rowley, 1951, pp. 31 ff.; *Supplements to Vetus Testamentum*, 3 (Rowley Volume; 1955), pp. 1 ff.

[64] There is already quite an extensive literature, beginning with my paper on the Oracles of Balaam in *Journal of Biblical Literature*, 63, 1944, pp. 207-233. Among important items are the papers by F. M. Cross and D. N. Freedman on the Blessing of Moses in *ibid.*, 67, 1948, pp. 191-210, and on the Song of Miriam in *Journal of Near Eastern Studies*, 14, 1955, pp. 237-250. For a bibliography (to 1958) see D. N. Freedman, *Zeitschrift für die alttestamentliche Wissenschaft*, 72, 1960, p. 101, as well as my more recent survey in *Hebrew and Semitic Studies* (G. R. Driver Volume; Oxford, 1963), pp. 1 ff.

peculiarities of our transmitted Massoretic Hebrew text, both in consonants and vowels, now turn out to reflect archaic usage, with a steadily growing list of previously unknown survivals of early Northwest Semitic grammar and vocabulary. There can be little doubt, in my opinion, that there are scores of Psalms whose composition may best be dated in the tenth century or shortly afterwards, and it becomes hypercritical to reject the tradition of Davidic sponsorship (which was tantamount to authorship at that early period) of a substantial nucleus of the present Book of Psalms.[65] At long last we have a solid linguistic basis for a history of Hebrew literature!

That there are few, if any, surviving intrusions from the Maccabean period in the Psalter or in the corpus of Prophetic writings is evident from the following considerations. The text of many Psalms and poetic sections of the Prophets is very obscure, and was not understood by the Greek translators of the Septuagint in or about the second century B.C. Now we know, thanks to the discovery of the Dead Sea Scrolls (see above), that the consonantal text of the proto-Massoretic recension of the Psalter has been handed down with astonishing fidelity since the last two centuries B.C.,[66] so that we are no longer justified in emending it without the utmost caution. Ugaritic and other Northwest Semitic parallels enable us to explain the consonantal text of hundreds of passages in the Psalter and the Prophets, and sound new interpretations are now accumulating so fast that their number has been multiplied many times over within the past decade. In virtually all these cases the archaic words and expressions were no better understood by

[65] On the date of the Psalter see esp. my papers in *Hebrew Union College Annual*, XXIII, 1, 1950-1951, pp. 1-39, and *Interpretationes* (Mowinckel *Festschrift;* Oslo, 1955), pp. 1-12. The forthcoming treatment of Psalms in the Doubleday-Anchor series of commentaries on the Bible, by Mitchell Dahood, S.J., will advance our understanding of the text enormously, with concomitant clarification of chronology.

[66] See esp. J. A. Sanders on the new Psalms scroll from early Herodian times, *Bulletin of the American Schools of Oriental Research*, No. 165, 1962, pp. 11-15; *Zeitschrift für die alttestamentliche Wissenschaft*, 75, 1963, pp. 73-86. (There are several unrecognized archaisms which suggest a date for Psalm 151 in the seventh-sixth centuries B.C.) Note also that there are not many divergences between the Greek and Massoretic Hebrew texts (except in the superscriptions, which had presumably been transmitted orally).

the Greek translators of the second century B.C. than they were by modern specialists only a few years ago. To attribute such Psalms to the Maccabean period is absurd, and to put them in the earlier Hellenistic period is scarcely more plausible. Furthermore, the Dead Sea Scrolls are now introducing us to many original Hebrew compositions of the Maccabean age; neither in prosody nor in language do they resemble the Psalter or Prophetic writings, except when quoting them directly. In fact, such poems as the Thanksgiving Hymns (from the late second century B.C.) are in large part mosaics of Biblical quotations.

The present state of New Testament criticism confronts us with a rather strange situation. In spite of reluctance to use new evidence on the part of extreme liberals and conservatives alike, the Old Testament is now being fitted without strain into the framework of the ancient Near East; each year there is less room for the sort of criticism which consistently disregards sound archaeological and linguistic evidence. One might think that the New Testament would suffer less, since its background was in many respects well known before the rise of modern archaeological research, owing to the rich material preserved in the Old Testament, intertestamental Jewish literature, Philo, Josephus, rabbinic sources, and the whole wealth of extant Greco-Roman literature. This was actually not the case at all. The very fact that its background was in some ways so well known made lacunae in our information all the more obvious, tempting scholars to try to fill them by analogy or "intuition." When literary criticism of the New Testament was in its cradle, no less a man than the founder of critical historiography, Barthold Niebuhr (1776-1831), was writing to a friend, "I am an historian, for I can make a complete picture from separate fragments, and I know where the parts are missing and how to fill them up."[67] Influenced by the historiographic overconfidence of the Niebuhr school and by the dialectic philosophy of Hegel, F. C. Baur (1792-1860) founded the Tübingen school of New Testament criticism, which was more radical than Wellhausenism.[68] During the *floruit* of the Tübingen school nothing worth mention was yet known about the chronology of Greek pottery or Hellenistic-Roman ar-

[67] Quoted from G. P. Gooch, *History and Historians in the Nineteenth Century* (Beacon Press reprint; 1949), p. 19.
[68] See *From the Stone Age to Christianity*, 1957 ed., pp. 87 f.

chitecture, and papyrology had not even come into existence as a discipline. There was little but "common sense" to check the excesses of the Tübingen or the early Dutch school of Loman and van Manen which followed it along equally radical lines. Almost nothing was then known about the background of rabbinic Judaism, though most of the extant sources had been published. Even more serious was the fact that the language of the New Testament was in large part so different from any other Greek known—despite similarities with the Septuagint, with Josephus and other contemporary writers, and with sub-apostolic Christian writings—as to seem like an undatable foreign body.

Beginning in the 1890s, the discovery of extensive deposits of papyrus remains in the Egyptian Faiyum proved conclusively that New Testament Greek was the non-literary medium of communication (Koine) throughout the eastern Mediterranean basin, at various levels of literary cultivation.[69] At first there was a strong tendency to disregard the fact that the paratactic style and numerous Semitisms found in most of the books set New Testament Greek apart from ordinary Koine. Actually, as C. C. Torrey and others never tired of emphasizing, New Testament Greek is in part a kind of translation Greek, that is, it reflects Semitic syntax and modes of speech.[70] At first this Semitic substratum was supposed by nearly all Semitists to be Aramaic, but recent discoveries at Qumran have demonstrated that Hebrew influence was probably greater in general than Aramaic, since Hebrew was then the prevailing language of Jewish religious composition. From Matthew to Revelation, Hebrew-Aramaic linguistic influence is almost ubiquitous. Even where Greek literary influence is dominant, as in the Epistle to the Hebrews, Hebraisms remain. Luke's Greek is relatively literary, yet Hebrew-Aramaic influence is in some ways clearer in his Gospel than elsewhere.[71]

[69] See esp. the fine treatment of the subject by Hans Lietzmann in Knopf-Lietzmann-Weinel, *Einführung in das Neue Testament*, 5th ed., 1949, pp. 5 ff.
[70] Cf. my discussion in *From the Stone Age to Christianity*, 1957 ed., pp. 382 ff.
[71] See esp. Paul Winter, "The Proto-Source of Luke 1," *Novum Testamentum*, 1, 1956, pp. 184-199, with references to his earlier papers. If there were any doubt as to his thesis it should be removed by study of the religious poetry of Qumran. On the probable Jewish origin of Luke see my statement in the *Trantham Memorial Volume* to be published by Baylor University.

Then came the discovery of the Qumran caves (since 1947), with the now famous Dead Sea Scrolls.[72] Most of the non-Biblical manuscript material is now known to have been written by Essenes between ca. 140 B.C.[73] and the Christian Era, after which there was less and less scribal activity, though study of the transmitted books seems to have continued actively until after the middle of the first century A.D. The Qumran texts provide an increasing body of Jewish sectarian literature from the last century and a half B.C., all in Hebrew or Aramaic, with virtually no scribal errors to confuse the specialist. To appraise its significance we must remember that no rabbinic literature antedates ca. A.D. 135, and that the Mishnah was not codified until the late second century A.D., while the Palestinian Talmud belongs to the late fourth century and the Babylonian Talmud is over a century later still. To be sure, oral transmission of legal and ritual matter was in general reliable, but most of the historical tradition from before the destruction of the Second Temple (A.D. 70) is of very mixed character. The extant non-Biblical Jewish religious literature, which had been composed in Hebrew or Aramaic before A.D. 135, had survived in translation (Greek, Latin, Syriac, Ethiopic, etc.),[74] but much of it could not be correctly dated until the new Qumran evidence became available. It turns out that some of these Apocryphal and Pseudepigraphical

[72] Because of the welter of inferior, or not really comprehensive, books on this subject, it may be well to recommend the following four books as best calculated to furnish an adequate idea of the history and contents of the find: Millar Burrows, *The Dead Sea Scrolls*, 1955, and *More Light on the Dead Sea Scrolls*, 1958; J. T. Milik, *Ten Years of Discovery in the Wilderness of Judaea*, 1959; Frank M. Cross, Jr., *The Ancient Library of Qumran and Modern Biblical Studies*, 1958. The last-mentioned still remains the most reliable up-to-date account, though there are other good surveys.

[73] See esp. Cross, *op. cit.*, pp. 104 ff., for this date. Incidentally, it agrees well with my own view, held for many years, that there was an important Babylonian Jewish element in early Essenism, presumably brought to Palestine by refugees fleeing from Babylonia during the troubled years which followed the Parthian irruption ca. 141 B.C.

[74] The Hebrew Ben Sira (Ecclesiasticus) is only an apparent exception, since it is now commonly agreed that the manuscripts found by S. Schechter in the *geniza* of the medieval Ezra Synagogue in Old Cairo (1896-1897) go back to a copy found in a cave in the Jericho region not too long before. Fragments of it from Qumran Cave Two have now been published (*Discoveries in the Judaean Desert of Jordan*, III, 1962, pp. 75 ff., by M. Baillet).

writings antedate the Greek period, a few items probably going back as far as the sixth century B.C. Many of them are earlier than the rise of the Essene movement.

Today it can be said with confidence that the Qumran material has very great relevance for the New Testament. Thanks to the Essene writings themselves, together with non-Essene books which can now be more correctly dated and interpreted (e.g., Jubilees, Enoch, Testaments of the Twelve Patriarchs), we can now set the books of the New Testament against the actual Jewish background of the Herodian age. There are three dominant sources of Jewish influence on the writers of the New Testament, who were probably all of Jewish origin themselves:[75] (1) the Hebrew Bible, understood in the light of the prevailing schools of interpretation which then existed; (2) the orthodox oral tradition as handed down by the Pharisees and like-minded Jews; (3) the writings, teaching, and practice of the Essenes and their congeners, as well as the derived school of John the Baptist. The first two were fairly well known before the Qumran discoveries, but virtually nothing was understood about the third.[76]

About the same time as the initial group of Qumran manuscripts was found, the first of some thirteen codices from Nag Hammadi (Chenoboskion) in Upper Egypt, containing about forty-nine treatises in Coptic, forty-four of which were previously unknown, came to the attention of Togo Mina and Jean Doresse. Several of these codices have now been published, and thanks to the latter's initiative the contents of most of them are fairly well known.[77] Doresse is doubtless correct in identifying the Gnostics of Chenoboskion in general with the Sethians of the Christian heresiographers, but it is quite impossible as yet to attribute the origin of

[75] See above, n. 71, on the probable Jewish origin of Luke.
[76] See esp. W. H. Brownlee, "John the Baptist in the Light of Ancient Scrolls," in *The Scrolls and the New Testament*, 1957, ed. K. Stendahl, pp. 33-53, and Jean Daniélou, *The Dead Sea Scrolls and Primitive Christianity*, 1958, pp. 15-24. For the state of research in this field just before the Qumran Scrolls began to revolutionize it, see the then excellent book of Carl H. Kraeling, *John the Baptist*, 1951. Needless to say, the level of our knowledge today is considerably higher than it was when any of these surveys was written.
[77] See esp. Doresse, *The Secret Books of the Egyptian Gnostics*, 1960, which contains important revisions of his *Les livres secrets des Gnostiques de l'Égypte*, Vols. I-II, 1958-1959.

most of the books to any particular sect. Only one treatise is clearly Valentinian in origin; the other Gnostic treatises belong to early pre-philosophical Gnostics of Simonian and Nicolaitan type, who are variously called Barbelo-Gnostics, Sethians, Ophites, etc.[78] The earliest Gnostics came from Greater Syria; Simon Magus and his disciple, Menander, were Samaritans, while Deacon Nicolas was a proselyte of Antioch (i.e., a pagan convert to Judaism who had become a Christian; Acts 6:5).[79] From Justin Martyr and the Pseudo-Clementines (both well back in the second century A.D.) on through Irenaeus and Hippolytus in the late second and early third centuries, Simon was reputed to come from Samaria and to be the founder of Simonian Gnosticism. Scholars who multiply "Simons" should remember Occam's razor (*entia non sunt multiplicanda praeter necessitatem*)![80] While it is certainly not always possible to distinguish the teachings of Simon and Nicolas from later Gnostic accretions and new doctrines, there is no reason to doubt the essential correctness of the tradition of Irenaeus and Hippolytus, especially since pre-Chenoboskion denials of their reliability in other respects have been roundly disproved by the new codices themselves. Moreover, it can now be shown that it is precisely in the systems credited to the Nicolaitans and their offshoots that we find the most Jewish material as well as Syro-Phoenician myths and names of divinities: e.g., Barbelo, Ialdabaoth, Achamoth, etc.[81] The Simonian system is

[78] There is still much reluctance on the part of some scholars to date any of the known Gnostic sects before the second century A.D. This is an attitude which was quite natural before the discovery of the Chenoboskion codices, when eminent authorities were still able to date the mythopoeic Gnostics after the "philosophical" Valentinians. Now it is impossible. For one thing, the Hermetic treatises of Chenoboskion contain more archaic Egyptian mythology than anything preserved in the previously known Hermetic literature, and the same thing is proving to be the case with the new Gnostic treatises, some of which preserve more archaic Syro-Phoenician mythology than anything previously known in Gnostic writings.

[79] On the Syrian origin of these systems see already H. C. Puech, *Revue de l'Université de Bruxelles*, 1934-5, pp. 137 ff., and Doresse, *op. cit.*, pp. 12 ff.

[80] A refusal to recognize more than one Simon "Magus" does not mean that "Simon" was not one of the commonest Jewish names of the first century A.D.; see J. A. Fitzmyer's refutation of Cecil Roth's attempt to deny the name currency in this period (*Harvard Theological Review*, 54, 1961, pp. 91 ff.; 56, 1963, pp. 1 ff.).

[81] On these Syrian names and myths in early Gnosticism see my forthcoming treatment in Vol. II of this series.

also characterized—in some ways even more strikingly—by a mixture of Jewish and pagan Syrian material. Doresse seems to have identified original Simonian teaching in one of the new treatises.[82]

It follows that the Gnostic systems of pre-Valentinian times (i.e., from before Valentine's *floruit* in the middle of the second century A.D.) did indeed arise in Palestine and Syria, as held by such authorities as Puech and Doresse. They probably started as reactions against the Christian kerygma on the part of disillusioned converts who looked for an easier escape from the burden of remorseless destiny (*heimarmenē*) than was offered by the Christian Gospel.[83] These systems, with their cosmic Iranian dualism, their rejection of the created kosmos, which they considered the work of the evil god of the Old Testament and his hordes of archons and demonic angels, their fallen Wisdom, who descended from the God of light into the world of matter and sin to be ultimately rescued by the descent of the Savior, their belief in salvation from the power of archontic determinism[84] through knowledge (gnosis) of all cosmic mysteries, stand in direct opposition to the Gospel. No wonder that the orthodox, whether New Testament writers or Church Fathers, reacted violently against the radical ideas of the Gnostics, who tended to express themselves either in extreme asceticism and rejection of the world or in equally excessive libertinism.

The discovery and partial publication of the codices of Chenoboskion, when combined with the even more significant Dead Sea Scrolls, make it absolutely clear that the New Testament is to be placed historically between the end of the creative period of Essenism and a time not long after the beginnings of Gnosticism. We shall see that most of the books of the New Testament, including the latest, show strong Essene influence in language, imagery, concepts, turns of phrase, and teachings. This is especially true of the Gospel of John and the Pauline corpus, and parallels with other

---

[82] Doresse, *op. cit.*, pp. 329 ff.

[83] Robert M. Grant's thesis (*Gnosticism and Early Christianity*, 1959), that Gnosticism arose because of disappointment at the apparent failure of eschatological expectations, is probably true in part, but the lack of polemic against eschatology in early Gnostic literature does not favor a primary role for the failure in question.

[84] It must be remembered that the most widespread form of religious faith in this general period was astral determinism under Stoic auspices. This has been proved by Cumont, Gressmann, and many others.

New Testament books are numerous throughout. However, there are scarcely any new parallels with sub-apostolic literature except in the Book of Two Ways imbedded in the Didache and the Epistle of Barnabas.[85] Combined with what we already knew about the archaeological accuracy of the references to names and sites in John and the Hebrew-Aramaic background of its language, this new material is a powerful argument for an earlier date.[86] The new parallels in concept and phrasing are closer than anything in the Philonic, rabbinic, Hermetic, Mandaean, or other literatures with which it has been compared. The persistent attempt to prove that the Fourth Gospel utilized Gnostic materials must be completely discarded, since there are no "Gnostic" features in the Johannine literature which cannot be explained much better as heirlooms from the Essenes and the followers of John the Baptist. In particular there is not the slightest evidence for either the supposed Gnostic original form or the later ecclesiastical redaction posited by Bultmann.[87]

The light thrown by Qumran literature on the Pauline Epistles is in some ways no less significant than the illumination of Johannine writings. It is true that Paul was trained as a Pharisee in the school of Gamaliel and that both his theology and his hermeneutics are

[85] On this see Jean-Paul Audet, *Revue Biblique*, 59, 1952, pp. 220 ff., and his book *La Didaché: Instructions des apôtres*, 1958, pp. 122 ff. Audet's date for the Didache (ca. 50-70 A.D., p. 219) seems a little early, but I am inclined to think that this impression is merely due to habitual dating at a later period. He has made a strong case—in my opinion—for a date ca. 60-80, i.e., shortly before or after the end of the apostolic period in Palestine.

[86] See my study, "Recent Discoveries in Palestine and the Gospel of St. John," in *The Background of the New Testament and Its Eschatology* (C. H. Dodd *Festschrift*, 1956), pp. 153-171. (Incidentally, Dodd subsequently withdrew his objections to the use of Qumran material for Johannine studies. Following other scholars he had not even mentioned Qumran in previous studies on John.) The best study of the relation between Qumran and the Johannine corpus is that of Raymond E. Brown, "The Qumran Scrolls and the Johannine Gospel and Epistles," in *The Scrolls and the New Testament*, ed. K. Stendahl, 1957, pp. 183-207, 282-291.

[87] No synopsis of his analysis seems ever to have been published by Bultmann, but this has been admirably done by Burton Scott Easton, *Journal of Biblical Literature*, 65, 1946, pp. 73 ff., 143 ff. The contrast between the spiritual dualism in John and the cosmic dualism of the Gnostics could scarcely be brought out more strongly than by printing the words of Bultmann's RQ source (i.e., the discourses of Christ). As for the SQ source (narratives of miracles), the alleged difference in original language (RQ Aramaic or Syriac, SQ Greek) is

more Pharisaic than Essene in type.[88] Yet penetrating study by such men as K. G. Kuhn, Johannes Munck, David Flusser, and others has greatly clarified extensive areas of Pauline thought.[89] One of the most important contributions has been made by Raymond E. Brown, S.S., who has demonstrated conclusively that the Pauline *mysterion* had nothing to do with the Greek mysteries, but is used in a way almost wholly concordant with Essene practice.[90] It is significant that it is precisely the Book of Ephesians, rejected by many critics, which exhibits the largest proportion of Essene reminiscences, as shown by K. G. Kuhn.[91] Even the Pastoral Epistles can no longer be denied to Paul, since the only serious argument against Pauline authorship, the well-developed system of overseers (*episkopoi*), supposedly late, has close parallels in the Scroll of Discipline and the Damascus Document.[92] The argument from style and vocabulary is very weak, since Paul (though doubtless a fluent speaker of Koine) had almost certainly never had any but elementary Greek education. (He admits repeatedly that his hand was very poor.) His letters were dictated, and his Greek was naturally corrected and often rewritten by his amanuenses. Accordingly, no verbal statistics, even with the aid of a computing machine, can tell

---

baseless. Both the "sources" are equally Semitic in substratum, and the redactional matter is not only in the same language but it has the same proportion of Qumran reminiscences. On Bultmann's 1962 claim that the Qumran sectarians were also Gnostics see below, p. 277.

[88] On rabbinic (i.e., Pharisaic) elements in Paul's teaching see esp. the excellent book by W. D. Davies, *Paul and Rabbinic Judaism*, 1948; 2d ed., 1955, first published just before the first Qumran scrolls became known. As is well known, instruction in a rabbinic academy had to begin in a boy's early teens, so there was no time for advanced Greek education of any kind. The difference in the nature of exegesis between the Qumran commentaries and Paul is easy to explain: roughly half a century before the latter studied under Gamaliel, Hillel the Elder had introduced the Aristotelian hermeneutics of Alexandria into rabbinic instruction (on this see below, n. 115). The earlier Jewish type, found at Qumran, survived in the tradition compiled by Matthew; see esp. Krister Stendahl, *The School of St. Matthew*, Uppsala, 1954, pp. 183 ff.

[89] As parade examples note Kuhn, *Zeitschrift für Theologie und Kirche*, 49, 1952, pp. 201 ff.; Flusser, *Scripta Hierosolymitana*, IV, 1958, pp. 215 ff. Munck's position is very important, since he has become a leader in research on the relation between the New Testament and the Qumran scrolls, following the publication of his masterly study, *Paulus und die Heilsgeschichte*, 1954 (Eng. trans., *Paul and the Salvation of Mankind*, 1959), which did not yet utilize the

us anything important about the author—though such methods will certainly throw light on the number and education of Paul's secretaries. The Synoptic Gospels show a great many points of contact with Jewish sectarian literature, especially Essene.[93] The Epistle to the Hebrews turns out to be directed to the Essenes (or the closely-related followers of John the Baptist).[94] The Catholic Epistles, including the homogeneous Johannine corpus, all contain many Essene reminiscences; this includes especially II Peter, often dated late in the second century. The Book of Revelation is so saturated with earlier Hebrew and Aramaic apocalyptic elements that R. H. Charles and C. C. Torrey are being largely vindicated in their defense of a Hebrew (Charles) or Aramaic (Torrey) proto-type. That Torrey was substantially correct in dating the book about 68 A.D. is highly probable.[95]

In the light of both finds, Qumran and Chenoboskion, it is per-fectly clear that the New Testament stands squarely between them; it cannot be earlier than the decline of the Essene movement or later than the spread of Gnosticism after the middle decades of the first century A.D. But we must emphasize that, in spite of all the back-ground material in Jewish religious literature of the last three

---

Scroll material but moves in the same direction as his subsequent Qumran re-search.

[90] See his monograph on "The Semitic Background of the New Testament Mysterion" which appeared in three parts: *Catholic Biblical Quarterly*, 20, 1958, pp. 417-443; *Biblica*, 39, 1958, pp. 426-448; 40, 1959, pp. 70-87. A similar point of view had been firmly maintained by Arthur Darby Nock since pre-Qumran times (see *Mnemosyne*, S. iv/5, 1952, pp. 177-213, for his fullest statement), but continues to be rejected by Bultmann and his disciples, who still derive it from the Greek mysteries.

[91] Kuhn, *New Testament Studies*, 7, 1961, pp. 334-346.

[92] Joachim Jeremias already saw this thirty years ago, on the basis of the account of the "overseers" (*mebaqqerîm*) in the Damascus Document, known since 1910. Now that fragments of it have been found in the Qumran caves, its Essene origin is certain. The account given of the *mebaqqerîm* in the Scroll of Discipline is so similar that there can no longer be any doubt that the institu-tion of the *episkopoi* was at least influenced by Essene practice (see also my discussion in the Trantham Memorial Volume to be published by Baylor Uni-versity).

[93] See esp. Kurt Schubert, *The Dead Sea Community and the New Testament*, 1959. Study of the Synoptics in the light of the Qumran scrolls will mark time until more unpublished material has become available. Since it is quite generally

centuries B.C. and the elements common to Essenism and the New Testament, there is a spiritual gulf between the Essenes and the Gospel of Christ which involves the very heart of the Christian message. Among the Essenes there was no Messiah dying on the cross in order to atone for the sins of mankind, and their rigid predestinarianism and separation of the elect from the world was directly contrary to Christ's offer of salvation to all. Yet the Essenes were the immediate precursors of John the Baptist, himself the forerunner of Christ. The following table[96] lists (with simplifications) some of the essential differences between the religious teaching of the Essenes and the New Testament:

1. Role of Messiah (Christ). The Messiah appeared on earth to suffer and die as a vicarious sacrifice for man, not to reign over His followers in earthly splendor.
2. Soteriology. The Messiah came to save sinners, both Jews and Gentiles, not merely the elect.
3. Ministry of Healing. The Messiah came to heal the physically and spiritually sick, not (merely) to sanctify His followers.
4. God of Love. The Messiah taught the Gospel of love, not merely the Gospel of righteousness.

---

agreed that the Synoptics reflect a more orthodox (i.e., Pharisee) Judaism than the Gospel of John, it is not surprising that their data are more limited.

[94] See Yigael Yadin, *Scripta Hierosolymitana*, IV, 1958, pp. 36-55, and H. Kosmala, *Hebräer-Essener-Christen*, 1959.

[95] Note in this connection Delbert R. Hillers' observation (*Bulletin of the American Schools of Oriental Research*, No. 170, 1963, p. 65) that the attribution of the famous "number of the beast" in Rev. 13:18 to Nero (often doubted because the normal spelling of the name in rabbinic sources, NRWN QYSR, is not numerically equivalent in Hebrew script to 666) is confirmed by an Aramaic document of the year 56, found at Murabba'at (*Discoveries in the Judaean Desert*, II, 1961, pp. 100 ff.), in which the name is written NRWN QSR (=666). Torrey's date about A.D. 68, the year of Nero's death, is thus substantially confirmed. For the latest treatment of Qumran reminiscences in Revelation see Lucetta Mowry, *The Dead Sea Scrolls and the Early Church*, 1962, pp. 25 ff. Further illustrations have turned up in the Aramaic fragments of the description of the New Jerusalem published by M. Baillet in *Discoveries in the Judaean Desert*, III, 1962, pp. 84 ff. (note the twelve city gates as in Rev. 12:12, 21), and more will doubtless be found in the remains of a scroll on the same theme discovered in Cave Eleven (to be published soon).

[96] This is a slight expansion of the table in the C. H. Dodd *Festschrift* (see above, n. 86), p. 170.

This bald catalogue of differences shows how immeasurably superior Christianity was to Essenism in its spiritual possibilities. It also suggests the immense superiority of orthodox Christianity to Gnosticism, whose founders tried, like many modern theologians, to discard the rich experience of God's historical relation to His people which makes the Old Testament indispensable as a basis of Christian belief, and to replace it with some kind of metaphysical speculation. Just as so often today, the Christian message was replaced by the popular science and wisdom of that day. Trying to escape from the tyranny of astral determinism, Gnostic leaders claimed to know the secrets of the universe, very much like modern leaders of religious thought who try to escape from the tyranny of mechanistic science and its robot creations by elaborate existential and other structures lacking Biblical, historical, or scientific validation.

Religion in history

RELIGION AND CIVILIZATION

Thanks to the archaeological discoveries of recent decades, we can no longer remain in doubt about two very important points which are almost invariably neglected by neutral or anti-Christian historians and are seldom, if ever, taken into full account by Christians. In the first place, there is no known past culture of any kind without religion, and no experienced archaeologist expects to find one, since all known "primitive" or retarded cultures of today have their own religions. In the second place, archaeologists have now proved the historical as well as the contemporary primacy of Western civilization. To state this archaeological fact, now demonstrated by radiocarbon, should not carry with it any implication of inevitable superiority. It would be very strange if we could not learn from the ancient and modern cultures of the Orient, even in spiritual things. But such humility is a far cry from the superstitious belief in some profound "mystical" wisdom, somehow transmitted from antiquity among certain elusive groups of Asia. Such humility is just as lacking in the facile internationalism, so fashionable in contemporary circles, which assumes that Christianity, Islam, Buddhism, Hinduism, Jainism, and even Taoism, somehow meet on a common level and that a future world religion may adopt beliefs and practices from all.

Archaeologists and historians cannot help agreeing that religion is the nucleus of all cultures of the past. It is true that philosophical idealists tend to agree with positivists and naturalists that religion will no longer be necessary when a "rational" culture can be developed to replace it. Yet the history of all such movements as ethical culture, anthroposophy, and "religious culture"—to name only a few—belies this expectation, since their supporters have never been numerous and every such movement has in the past quickly died out or lost all vitality. The two totalitarian antireligious movements which have been propagated by dictators in our own day, Nazism and Communism, have actually had to introduce emotional and ceremonial practices in imitation of older religions, particularly Germanic paganism and Eastern Christianity. The Nazis, with their cult of *Blut und Boden,* with their emphasis on *die heilige Urquell deutscher Macht,* and their paganizing festivals, went back over a thousand years to recapture an imaginary spiritual vitality supposed to have launched the Germanic hordes on their waves of conquest. The Communists, with their cult of such allegedly unique leaders as Lenin, Stalin, and Mao, and with their Marxist salvation through class warfare and the triumph of the proletariat as a substitute for Christian salvation through the grace of God and the cross of Christ, very definitely imitate Christianity, even though awkwardly and perhaps without deliberate intent. Marx himself, as is now generally recognized, was strongly influenced by Judeo-Christian ideas.

Must we, then, go farther and agree with the anthropological functionalists that every primitive religion is such an integral part of that culture that it cannot be suppressed or replaced without inflicting a mortal wound on it? The coryphaeus of current functionalism, the late Bronislaw Malinowski (1884-1942), maintained that missionary work is peculiarly lethal in its effect on primitive cultures; and some of his followers are even more radical in their antimissionary propaganda. I believe that functionalism goes much too far, and that the truth respecting outside interference with cultural patterns lies roughly in the middle between the instrumentalist and functionalist points of view.[97] Followers of the experimentalist tendency best represented by the late John Dewey (on whose sympathies see above) treat social forces and institutions as essentially independent of one another and as therefore subject to quasi-scientific experimentation. The model for such experimentation

[97] See above, pp. 8-9, and below, pp. 178-180.

comes chiefly from the biological sciences, where, for the purpose of simplifying complex problems, parts of an organism must be treated as though they were independent of other parts. The success of such biological experimentation depends on the experimenter's ability to isolate phenomena for the purpose of his experiment. Against hasty utilization of results thus obtained for medicine and psychiatry, protests are being made increasingly from the standpoint of synergism and psychosomatic medicine.

Functionalists, on the other hand, treat associated aspects of a given homogeneous (or superficially homogeneous) culture as interdependent and as functionally interrelated. Omitting such obviously secondary features as the technology of native cultures, they insist on the integration of all or most other characteristic elements. According to their theory, interference with such elements will destroy any simple culture. In fact, the typical applied anthropologist in contemporary America insists that functional interdependence is characteristic even of complex modern societies.[98] Theoretically there should be no agreement between functionalists and instrumentalists. I once heard the late Edward Sapir (1884-1939), one of America's most brilliant anthropologists, state the fundamental opposition between them with characteristic incisiveness. In practice, few American social scientists clearly realize how basically contradictory the two tendencies are, largely because of the common dislike for Christianity and history which marks both of the otherwise antipathetic groups. (It is, of course, always easy for nominal functionalists and instrumentalists to declare that features selected for experiment are not of functional significance!)

[98] I was severely criticized by certain functional anthropologists at the 1945 meeting of the Conference on Science, Philosophy, and Religion in New York for objecting to the assertion made by one of them that trying to export our own concepts of democracy to modern Greece would be a serious mistake, since the Greek conception of democracy is quite different and should not be displaced by ours. Actually, of course, there is no homogeneous modern Greek concept of democracy; it includes a heterogeneous variety of ideas, derived partly from ancient Athens, but mainly from Republican France in the nineteenth century, America in the late nineteenth and twentieth, and Russia since 1917. Incidentally, I challenged my most outspoken critic, who went so far as to deny, in the course of a prolonged discussion, that he was a functionalist, to state some basic difference between his views and those of Malinowski and Radcliffe-Brown. In spite of the fact that the anthropologist is question began his career as a professional philosopher, he could not find a word to say.

Since there is no known culture, past or present (with the possible exception of the still young Communist "culture"), which lacks a religion, functionalists might properly be expected to treat religion as the most vital manifestation of any culture. Without exception—so far as I have been able to gather from many discussions—functionalists do take this attitude with respect to contemporary non-Christian religions, and a few are willing to admit for the sake of argument that it may apply also to Christianity. In practice, however, not a single leading functionalist who has stated his views publicly treats Christianity with respect, and efforts on the part of defenders of Christianity to employ the historical approach are countered either with hostility or with disgusted resignation.

The historian of older cultures cannot fail to recognize that exceedingly vigorous new cultures have frequently arisen as the result of the collision of different civilizations, and that the spread of religions often brings new life to apparently moribund cultures. The history of Christian missions since the first century A.D. is the most conclusive demonstration of the fact that cultures can change their religions without national suicide. In fact, historical experience shows clearly that viable cultures are the product of a series of geographical collocations and reciprocal adaptations. Some such a term as "empirico-adaptive" would thus be far preferable to "functional."[99]

In spite of the anti-historical bias of anthropologists of the functional school and their congeners, there are some historians and archaeologists who have become enamored with the idea of functionalism in culture. Among them we may mention the great Assyriologist, Benno Landsberger, who has introduced the German term *Eigenbegrifflichkeit* to describe the functional interrelationship of elements of Sumero-Accadian culture in Mesopotamia.[100] A similar point of view was formerly stated by John A. Wilson, who emphasized the self-sufficiency of Egyptian civilization and the intrinsic improbability of any important cross-fertilization between Egypt and surrounding peoples.[101] While applauding the desire to

[99] See *From the Stone Age to Christianity*, 1957 ed., p. 104.

[100] See his essay in *Islamica*, 2, 1926-1927, pp. 355-372. Landsberger's point of view at that time seems to stem rather from the idealist tradition than from modern functionalism.

[101] See *The Burden of Egypt*, Chicago, 1951, *passim*, but esp. pp. 309-318; a more general functional position is stated in Wilson's presidential address in

look for interlocking relationships between different phases of a given culture before looking for parallels outside that culture, one must protest against much resulting blindness to the spread of ideas as well as of technological devices. The lands of the Ancient Orient were in some ways as interdependent as medieval Europe or Islam, or as the countries of the modern Western world, and there have been few periods in history during which the lands of the eastern Mediterranean basin and the regions directly east of them were not interchanging elements of higher culture as well as tools, weapons, and materials. Furthermore, very often a weakness in some area of a given culture is compensated in another area. For instance, in the early Roman principate, philosophy was a Greek specialty whereas law was Roman; in the Middle Ages, Western Christianity was Aristotelian in its theological structure while the East tended strongly toward a Platonizing mysticism. Because of religious limitations, ancient Israel seems to have been far behind in representational art but exceptionally well developed in music.[102]

No one who devotes himself honestly to studying the role of religion in Western literatures, can fail to see how vital it was. Nearly all the now-known literature of ancient Egypt and Mesopotamia is religious in character. This is also true of Canaanites and Phoenicians, as well as of the Israelites. Most pagan Greek literature comes from the centuries after the rise of skeptical philosophies in the sixth century B.C.; yet it is also to a great extent religious in content or spirit, from Homer and Hesiod down through the tragedians to Plato and the Stoics. Almost all literature that has survived to us from the Jewish world of the Hellenistic and Roman periods is religious: Apocryphal and Pseudepigraphical writings, Dead Sea Scrolls, Mishnah, Gemara, and contemporary rabbinic books. The same is true of early Christian and sectarian writings from the first century A.D. on. It is in ancient religious

---

Journal of the American Oriental Society, 72, 1952, pp. 49 ff. Wilson thinks that "physical forms and manual and mechanical means are transmitted from one culture to another" (p. 50b), but that "the essential expressions of mind and spirit . . . are not inherited by one culture from another." This is typical functionalism. However, with the candor characteristic of him, he admitted that this principle should not be carried too far. In 1958 he assured me that he no longer held the functionalist point of view.

[102] See *Archaeology and the Religion of Israel*, 1956 ed., pp. 15 f., 125 ff.

literatures that we find the profoundest statements of human aspirations and the most poignant expressions of human needs. These literatures are of more interest to the student of psychology than anything else handed down from antiquity; in this respect we may agree with C. G. Jung, even though we may differ radically with him on interpretation. Yet, as we shall see, the psychological value of ancient religious literature is incomparably less to the Christian who surveys them *sub specie aeternitatis* than their historical significance as preparation for Christianity.[103]

HIGHER CULTURE PREPARES FOR CHRISTIANITY

In the earliest religious literature which has come down to us from the ancient Near East of the third and second millennia B.C., we find many ideas and points of view which sound strange to us. Egyptian and Sumerian art is also strange when judged by classical standards. If we compare the higher culture of these early civilized peoples with corresponding features of the higher culture of modern primitive tribes, we find a great deal in common: similar mythologies and cultic practices; absence of definition, classification, or other logical procedures; vagueness of conceptual outlines; art with canons that violate our most elementary notions of representation and perspective. A generation ago Lucien Lévy-Bruhl labeled primitive thinking as "prelogical," pointing out that it disregarded our logical categories, including the principles of identity and contradiction, rational causation, etc. In 1940 I used this term, but pointed out that Lévy-Bruhl had failed to recognize the logical stage which I labeled "empirico-logical," covering the logic born of experience which dominates the Old Testament and much of the ancient Near East.[104] Under no conditions can the thinking of Old Testament writers be termed prelogical, though they certainly knew nothing of Aristotelian categories. Meanwhile Lévy-Bruhl himself had been rethinking his position in reaction to severe criticisms launched against his ideas by field anthropologists. Extracts from his notebooks of 1938 were published posthumously in 1947; in them he abandoned his earlier position, acknowledging that there was no real prelogical

---

[103] This was, of course, one of the principal themes of Eusebius' *Praeparatio Evangelica*, and has recently been taken up again in *From the Stone Age to Christianity*.

[104] See esp. my *Archaeology and the Religion of Israel*, pp. 26-33.

stage. "In all that has to do with everyday human experience," he wrote, "in business dealings of every kind, in public life, in domestic economy, in counting, etc. . . . primitives behave in a way that implies the same use of their faculties that we make of ours."[105] If he had limited his prelogical stage to the higher culture of early and primitive man, little retraction would have been necessary.

Since 1949 I have, therefore, substituted the term "proto-logical" for Lévy-Bruhl's prelogical, which I had previously used for this stage of thinking. Not only has the term prelogical been compromised by unwarranted extension of its use, but it is basically unsatisfactory. The processes of thought which we find reflected by early Egyptian and Sumerian literature may not seem logical in our sense, but they had their own inner coherence and they were strongly influenced by empirical thinking. Symbolism ran wild, and names of things were as real to the Egyptian mythopoeists as were natural phenomena or human actions. If two names of objects sounded alike, the objects themselves were often identified. A god might be at one and the same time identified with half a dozen mutually exclusive phenomena. In a single line of Canaanite mythological poetry a vessel might be of gold or of silver; it might be held in the right hand or in both hands; a goddess rides on the back of a young male donkey or of a she-ass.[106] Art was similarly indefinite: many different interpretations are possible for some Egyptian representations of groups of dancers; it is often impossible to determine whether a given scene pictures events as happening together or successively. H. A. Groenewegen-Frankfort has shown that there was no clear distinction between representations of space and time in certain types of representational art.[107]

This proto-logical stage of thinking was not only necessary, it was by no means without permanent value, and under closely related forms it continues to exist today. As Heinrich Schaefer pointed out effectively, Egyptian line-drawing is no more "primitive" in many respects than most "modern" art, which specializes in disregarding

---

[105] See *Revue Philosophique*, 1947, pp. 265 f., and my remarks in *From the Stone Age to Christianity*, 1957 ed., pp. 7 f.

[106] Exactly the same thing appears in the Song of Deborah (Judg. 5:26, R.S.V.) where tent peg and mallet are interchangeable.

[107] See her important book, *Arrest and Movement*, Chicago, 1951.

Greek canons of representation and perspective.[108] Primitive paintings of today strikingly resemble certain forms of pre-Greek art;
this is also true of the spontaneous drawing of children or the art
of primitive peoples. In the same way much modern poetry delights
in throwing overboard all the traditional ballast of form and logic,
and in substituting successive dream states or random associations in
the stream of consciousness for ordered thought or narration. Mysticism always tends to revive primitive modes of "corporative participation," to use one of Lévy-Bruhl's terms. In short, we can never
escape the immediate association between thinking and affective
reaction which characterizes the earliest stages of all higher culture,
before man learned how to use his inborn mental tools. And if we
were to lose our capacity to think on occasion in proto-logical terms,
it would be calamitous—we should cease to be human beings and
become thinking machines.

While the polytheistic peoples of the ancient Near East kept their
essentially proto-logical higher cultures with little change as late as
Greek times, official Israelite religion rejected mythology as well as
the pseudo-sciences of magic and divination, which were shot
through and through with proto-logic. In place of a kaleido-
scopically shifting pantheon and a bewilderingly variegated mythology, the orthodox faith of Israel had only one god, lord of the
entire universe, and no mythology at all. Magic and divination were
sternly prohibited. Higher culture became in some respects almost
as rigorously consistent in early Israel as it was in rabbinic Judaism,
where the canons of reasoning were Hellenistic. The logic born of
experience, which had won great triumphs in the practical world of
the Ancient Orient, became dominant in all Old Testament thinking.[109] No matter where we turn in the extant literature of Israel,
we find sobriety and consistency beyond anything known in the
older cultures. Israel discarded almost all proto-logical thinking; for
instance, Hebrew poetry is almost totally devoid of the extravagant
figures of speech which characterize earlier verse, and it shows an
almost classical Hellenic restraint.[110]

Yet we must not jump to the conclusion that Hebrew thinking
can be judged by Hellenic categories of logic. In the Hebrew

[108] See his *Von ägyptischer Kunst*, 3d ed.; Leipzig, 1930.
[109] See below, pp. 92-100.
[110] See my discussion, *Archaeology and the Religion of Israel*, pp. 15 f.

Bible we find monotheism taken for granted and illustrated in many ways, but we nowhere find it defined, much less delimited in categorical terms. We know what the Prophets believed it to be important as a basis for action, but they left no creeds and no theological abstractions. In fact, our oldest Jewish theological credo —still very far from a formal creed—is probably in the recently discovered Essene Scroll of Discipline, composed in the late second century B.C.[111] The Israelites were quite as able as their neighbors to generalize abstract qualities, but they did not have the intellectual tools to give abstract names to social institutions or systems of belief. We are quite justified in using our own terms, such as monotheism, or *charisma*, since the Israelites believed in the concepts underlying these words, though they never thought of classifying or defining the phenomena.

On the other hand, the logic of the Old Testament, even though empirical in its agreement with later formal categories, has a strength and soundness which can never be found in any philosophical structure, no matter how logically it may be constructed. The reason is simple: all such philosophical structures start with more or less elaborate sets of assumptions and presuppositions, which often rise to the proportions of protophilosophies,[112] but their basic postulates are seldom carefully analyzed, and the superimposed edifice lacks solid foundations. It may even be said with some justification that the correctness of their results is often in inverse proportion to the soundness of the logic employed in deriving them, since good logic carries unsound premises to conclusions which are often exceedingly dangerous. The writings of the Old Testament employ a direct approach from tacit assumptions which Jews and Christians regard as indisputable, and their thinking is rooted throughout in sound experience of life. In other words, their empirical logic was more secure within its range than the proudest constructions of modern philosophers.

Formal logic probably dawned with Thales of Miletus at the

[111] See, for example, the translations by Millar Burrows, *The Dead Sea Scrolls*, 1955, pp. 374-376; Géza Vermès, *Discovery in the Judaean Desert*, 1956, pp. 137 ff.; A. Dupont-Sommer, *Les écrits ésseniens découverts près de la Mer Morte*, 1959, pp. 94 ff.

[112] See George Boas, "The Role of Protophilosophies in Intellectual History," *Journal of Philosophy*, 45, 1948, pp. 673-684.

beginning of the sixth century B.C. Reputed to be of Phoenician extraction, he had learned a good deal of Egyptian mathematics and Babylonian astronomy, presumably through Phoenician channels.[113] He was the first, so far as we know, to introduce geometrical propositions. The Egyptians had certainly employed cases of these propositions, but they had never stated them as such; they were simply taken for granted in working out practical problems by unformulated analogies. In other words, pre-Milesian mathematics was empirico-logical and its discoveries were implicitly assumed to be true. There is not the slightest indication that Thales had any idea of demonstrating the truth of his propositions by use of any formal method of reasoning. But the mere fact that he was able to abstract such constituent elements as lines and angles from geometrical figures, and such a basic element as water from the complex world of nature, shows that he had gone a long way toward the logical formulation of propositions.

Subsequent Ionian metaphysicians carried speculation in natural philosophy much farther than Thales, but it is a question whether they contributed anything appreciable to the development of logic *stricto sensu.* This seems to have been largely a result of the systematic encouragement of forensic debate in the courts and assemblies of democratic Athens. The Sophists, who educated the youth of Athens in the arts of rhetoric and debate, made the analytical inquiries of Socrates possible, and he was followed by the vast intellectual syntheses of Plato and Aristotle. Aristotelian logic and Euclidean mathematics crowned the noble structure of Greek reasoning with fully-developed concepts of postulation, of syllogistic deduction, of definition and classification, used in ways that were, for practical purposes, little inferior to the best modern use of the same tools—and certainly far superior to our average![114]

With the introduction and dissemination of abstract categories and formal logic, the way was paved for the emergence of Hellenistic Jewish thought. The empirical logic of the Old Testament was combined with the formal logic of the Hellenes. Greek logical methods were introduced into Jewish legal practice in the time of

[113] See the treatment of the background of Thales' innovations in Vol. II of this series.

[114] See Thomas Greenwood's lucid paper, "Euclid and Aristotle," *The Thomist,* 15, 1952, pp. 374-403.

Hillel the Elder during the last generation B.C.[115] Abstract categories and Platonic distinctions between matter and spirit had appeared in the Book of Wisdom somewhat earlier in the same century. It thus became possible for the Jews to understand the teaching of Christ, who replaced Mosaic law by a spiritual Gospel and sacrificial ritual by spiritual analogies. In the same way it was possible a generation later for both Hellenized Jews and Greeks to understand the close reasoning and abstract theology of Paul. Nascent Christianity is not historically intelligible outside the Judeo-Greek milieu in which it arose. Both Jews and Greeks understood the apostolic kerygma, even though the Jews generally rejected it for theological reasons, while most Greeks opposed it on philosophical grounds (see I Corinthians 1:22-24).

THE BIBLICAL DRAMA OF SALVATION

In the light of our foregoing presentation of the development of higher culture, it becomes possible to gain new insights into the historical development of Biblical religion. We have already seen that archaeological evidence throws its weight squarely against the aberrations of evolutionary historicism as found in most modern literary and historical criticism of the Old and New Testaments.[116] Yet such critical analyses and even critical excesses have been useful in drawing attention to historical details or phases of development which might otherwise have remained undetected. After the criticism of the last century we can no longer treat Biblical history as naïvely as was once possible, though we now recognize the substantial historicity of the entire Scriptural tradition from the Patriarchs to the end of the New Testament period.

Again we see the record of revelation as a series of terrible crises. Here there is no continuous organic development without serious interruption. Abraham's migration from Mesopotamia, the sojourn of the Hebrews in Egypt, the extraordinary events of the Exodus, the

---

[115] See already my discussion in *From the Stone Age to Christianity*, 1957 ed., pp. 356 f., and the detailed treatment in David Daube, "Rabbinic Methods of Interpretation and Hellenistic Rhetoric," *Hebrew Union College Annual*, XXII, 1949. The whole question has been cleared up by S. Lieberman's *Hellenism in Jewish Palestine*, 1950.

[116] See my comments, *From the Stone Age to Christianity*, 1957 ed., pp. 88 f., and my Society of Biblical Literature presidential address, below, Chapter 5.

successive destruction of both the Northern and Southern Kingdoms, the Babylonian Captivity, the revolt of the Maccabees, the Crucifixion, the destruction of Jewish and Christian communal life in Palestine between A.D. 66 and 70[117]—these were no ordinary crises, and the religion which could sustain even an extraordinary people through these catastrophic events was no ordinary religion.

The religion of Israel did not change in essentials from Moses to Hillel (who flourished during the last decades before the birth of Christ).[118] There is good reason to suppose that Moses was just as monotheistic as Hillel, though he could certainly not have employed the logical reasoning in support of his beliefs that was possible for the latter. Elsewhere I have emphasized the fact that the emergence of Mosaic monotheism on the world scene can be best understood in the light of cultural and religious conditions in the fourteenth and thirteenth centuries B.C.[119] Fundamental in early Israelite faith was the concept of Yahweh as Israel's God and Israel as Yahweh's people, the people and its God being bound together by a solemn Covenant (*berît*). According to the terms of this solemn pact, probably recited at religious festivals year after year,[120] God swears (by His own name) to protect and favor His Chosen People, while Israel swears that it will obey the commands of God and worship according to the Tabernacle liturgy. Both were bound reciprocally to show one

[117] The basic importance of this last crisis is seldom realized—and almost never entirely appreciated; see provisionally my discussion in *Archaeology of Palestine*, pp. 240 ff., and the somewhat distorted but useful treatment of the subject by S. G. F. Brandon, *The Fall of Jerusalem and the Christian Church*, London, 1951.

[118] When I made a similar statement in 1940 (*From the Stone Age to Christianity*, 1st ed., p. 309), there was some severe criticism; I stand by it without retreat.

[119] *From the Stone Age to Christianity*, 1957 ed., pp. 11-17, 209-272, which may now be supplemented by my discussion in *The Biblical Period From Abraham to Ezra*, 1963, pp. 10-23, 98-100.

[120] On the Covenant between Yahweh and Israel see G. E. Mendenhall, *Law and Covenant in Israel and the Ancient Near East*, 1955, where the parallel between the construction of Syro-Anatolian suzerainty treaties and the Covenant described in Joshua 24 is convincing, but where the theological inferences seem overstated to me. On the Covenant in general see the English translation of W. Eichrodt's great German work, *Theology of the Old Testament*, Vol. I, 1961, and the still classic statement by A. Alt in his *Ursprünge des israelitischen Rechts*, reprinted in *Kleine Schriften zur Geschichte des Volkes Israel*, I, 1953, pp. 328 ff.

another *ḥesed*, the special loyalty which cemented the Covenant relationship. With God it was mercy over and above the require-ments of justice and with Israel it was piety beyond the strict letter of the law.

After several centuries there arose an extraordinary class of men—preachers and reformers who began as ecstatics and ended as preach-ing Prophets. The Prophets saw the wickedness of their time as direct violation of the terms of the age-old compact between God and His people. Their conviction of the nearness of impending judgment was reinforced by the continuous threat of destruction by the Assyrians, renewed almost yearly after 742 B.C., as Tiglath-pileser III and his successors conquered state after state in Syria and Palestine. There was an ancient pattern, found already in Egyptian literary texts of about 2000 B.C., according to which evil times were to be followed by renewed prosperity. Among the Israelite Prophets this pattern was powerfully fortified by conviction of the *ḥesed* of God, who would not cast off His people forever, but would restore them after a period of punishment.[121] Again and again in earlier Israelite history the Chosen People had suffered and had been re-stored to an even more prosperous state than before. Under such conditions it is absurd to label the prophecies of Isaiah and others in pre-Exilic times as *vaticinia ex eventu*; the only possible explanation of the facts is to consider them as exactly what they purport to be—prophecies of impending doom and future restoration.

We have seen already that the Biblical tradition of complete devastation of Judah in the early sixth century, of a prolonged period of abandonment of the land, followed by Restoration in the late sixth century, is in complete accord with archaeological facts. But how could the Jews have been so filled with the conviction that Israel would indeed be restored, even after complete destruction, unless there were prophecies of Restoration to believe? The rational-istic attempt to do away with prophecy raises new problems which

---

[121] I insist on the complementary nature of the term *ḥesed* in early Hebrew which, as first emphasized by Nelson Glueck, refers to loyalty to a Covenant on both sides, regardless of their relative status. It is no accident that the Psalter refers so often to the loyalty of God to His people. Furthermore, this loyalty is not merely legal; it is over and above the strict terms of the Cove-nant, which helps to explain why the Prophets were so sure that God would restore His people, in spite of the latter's failure to keep its side of the bargain.

are much more difficult to solve than acceptance of the uniform early tradition presented by our Biblical sources. So far as we know, no people except Israel has ever been restored to its native land after such a clean break. If there were any remaining doubt, surely it would be removed by the close analogy which we now have in the second restoration of Israel, after twenty-five more centuries! No one can dispute the fact that it was the firmly held rabbinic belief in their ultimate return as a nation to Palestine that brought the Jews back to their ancient home in recent generations. Even secular Zionism merely substituted nationalistic motivation for earlier belief in the literal fulfillment of the prophecies, and the majority of the Jews of Israel now belong to orthodox religious groups which accept the prophecies literally.

But Restoration not only brought fulfillment of dreams; it also involved disillusionment. The restored nation was by no means the ideal theocratic state demanded by Ezekiel and foreseen in the visions of Isaiah. The Persian suzerain was arbitrary and often tyrannical. The priests were not necessarily pious men, and within a generation of Nehemiah and Ezra a high priest had murdered his brother in the Temple. Moreover, the majority of the Jewish people were scattered through the Persian Empire from Upper Egypt to Susiana, and from Lydia to Media. Conditions of life in the Diaspora were often bitterly difficult, and the Book of Esther recounts details of what may have been a recurrent situation in Achaemenian times. The somewhat earlier Book of Job vividly illustrates how an unknown Jew treated the now acute problem of the righteous sufferer, and Qoheleth (Ecclesiastes) represents the skepticism into which a fourth-century Jew might be led.[122]

In general, the conquest of the Persian Empire by Alexander brought little change in the status of the Jews, either in Judea or in the Diaspora. But Hellenistic culture was a far more immediate challenge to Judaism than the relatively undeveloped higher culture of the Iranians had been, since it introduced men of intelligence to a whole new world of rational thinking and practical application. The reaction against Hellenism led to the revolt of the Maccabees and the establishment of a politically independent Jewish state. At last, it seemed, the ancient prophecies were to be literally fulfilled and

[122] See my treatment of these questions in Vol. II in this series.

Israel would again become a nation—this time forever! Scarcely had political independence been assured by the heroic struggles of successive Maccabee brothers than corruption began to set in. The union of high priesthood with royalty weakened both the political and the religious sides of the kingdom. Pious Jews broke away from normative Judaism in increasing numbers and sectarian groups were founded, some deviating from tradition in one direction, some in another. In their efforts to ensure the holy life which was so constantly flouted by the behavior of their rulers, they resorted to extreme measures. On the one hand the Pharisees heaped up rules and regulations in their effort to protect all Biblical ritual and moral laws by surrounding them with warning zones, thus "building a fence around the Torah." On the other hand the Essenes retired into quasi-monastic communities, now being brought vividly to life again by the extraordinary discoveries in the region south of Jericho. Here those who were predestined to salvation might save themselves by the most rigorous observance of the Law and by an elaborate system of simple living and community thought-control. But both the Pharisees and Essenes clung to belief in the coming of the Messiah as earthly king, reigning in splendor in the City of David.

Thus the stage was set for the final act of the Biblical drama of salvation. Instead of appearing in state as a worldly monarch, the Messiah came in the guise of a suffering servant, as foreseen centuries before by one of Israel's greatest Prophets, who was not understood for centuries by those who assiduously studied his words.[123] Instead of celebrating a holocaust of unbelievers and drenching His followers in the blood of the wicked, the Messiah was Himself crucified, thus suffering the most miserable of deaths. Instead of setting up the Torah as binding on all mankind, the Messiah freed even the Jews from its rigor. In place of the tyranny of regulations, the Messiah brought freedom of the spirit, giving men liberty based

---

[123] In *Bulletin of the American Schools of Oriental Research*, No. 132, 1953, pp. 8-15, and No. 135, 1954, pp. 33-38, W. H. Brownlee tried to show that the Essenes had some sort of teaching that the Messiah was expected to undergo a fiery purge before reigning on earth. Against this interpretation see F.M. Cross, Jr., *The Ancient Library of Qumran and Modern Biblical Studies*, 1958, p. 167, n. 52. While Brownlee's view would certainly make the Messianic consciousness of Jesus appear in a vivid new light, and would support the traditional view against most modern critics, it is, at least for the present, better to await clarification.

on faith in spiritual salvation and on acceptance of Him as savior and model. Through the Messiah of the New Testament the humble is exalted and the unheroic becomes heroic. From being an object of apprehension to cringing humanity, suffering becomes victory through the imitation of Christ. This Christian drama of salvation can never be displaced nor can it be antiquated, for it represents the ultimate reality of life. To demonstrate it should be the profoundest aim of Christian humanism.

Chapter 2

The human mind in action:
magic, science, and religion[1]

Frazer on magic, religion, and science

One of the most important books dealing with religion is Sir James George Frazer's *The Golden Bough*, the first edition of which appeared in 1890, and which was enormously expanded in subsequent editions.[2] Frazer's work exerted very great influence in Anglo-American—and later in French—circles; he contributed notably to the growth of interest in comparative religion during the past half century. The origin of Frazer's evolutionary scheme—magic, religion, and science (in that order!)—is to be found in Auguste Comte's positivistic system, developed in the early nineteenth cen-

[1] This chapter is a completely revised form of a lecture given at the School of Religion of the University of Iowa, in the annual "Science and Religion Series," March 3, 1960. I wish to thank the administrative director of the School, Dr. Robert Michaelsen, for permission to publish the lecture here, and also for innumerable courtesies during my stay there at the time as well as during my term of teaching in the spring of 1962. None of this lecture has been published elsewhere. It should be noted that the title has been taken in part from Bronislaw Malinowski's famous monograph, "Magic, Science and Religion," which was first published as a chapter in *Science, Religion and Reality*, ed. Joseph Needham, London, 1925. It was reprinted without change in *Magic, Science and Religion, and Other Essays*, ed. Robert Redfield, 1948, now available in a paperback edition. Malinowski was not yet the extreme functionalist of his later years.

[2] Frazer, *The Golden Bough*, Vols. I-II, London, 1890; 2d ed., Vols. I-III, Lon-

tury. According to Comte, there was a threefold development: fetishism, religion, and science. Frazer describes religion as "the melancholy record of human error and folly,"[3] a typically positivistic verdict on religion. Though, from my point of view, Frazer's description of religion was fundamentally wrong—in spite of folly and error in the religious record—there were some sound emphases in his words. For example, he was the first clearly to emphasize the fact that science is to some extent rooted in magic. There is a certain continuity of development between magic and science. This should not appear strange when we recall that astronomy was in large part an outgrowth of astrology, and that chemistry was chiefly a development from alchemy.[4]

Today we may look at Frazer again and try to place magic, science, and religion in their proper relationship to one another.[5] To do this, one must analyze the components of these areas of human psychic activity and the ways of thinking which are involved. One cannot simply take phenomena in their fully-developed forms and compare them. One must study their history and analyze their epistemology; that is, the types of cognitive judgment and modes of thought which are involved.

What are magic, science, and religion?

First and foremost let me define what I mean by the terms magic, science, and religion. What is magic? No definition is really adequate to include everything considered important about the subject which one is trying to define. Magic may be succinctly described as the effort of man to control his environment and his destiny by proto-logical patterns of analogical thinking.[6]

The principal type of magic is sympathetic or dynamistic, and is sometimes called white magic; it deals with matters such as en-

---

don, 1900; 3d ed., Vols. I-XII, London, 1907-1915. See also T. H. Gaster's condensed and annotated edition, *The New Golden Bough*, 1959, reviewed by Arnold Toynbee and the writer in *The Griffin*, July, 1959.

[3] See Frazer, "Farewell to Nemi," *The Golden Bough*, Vol. XI, 1913, p. 304; see also p. 308.

[4] See, for example, the account of these two areas by Mark Graubard, *Astrology and Alchemy: Two Fossil Sciences*, New York, 1953.

[5] Frazer's succession appears most explicitly in his words: "The movement of

suring or increasing fertility by various rites which have some analogy with happenings in nature: for example, making rain by sprinkling water or producing fertility in nature by ritual cohabitation. Another type is sorcery or black magic, familiar to us from such West Indian practices as sticking a pin in a figurine or statuette of a person whose death is desired. Such magic survived until recent times among Pennsylvania German "witch doctors," who practiced "hexing"—condemnation of a person to illness or death by sympathetic rituals. These practices are officially forbidden in almost all cultures, but they still survive in most of the world. In some regions they may even be more popular today than in the recent past.

The arts of divination gained ground rather steadily in antiquity, and in Mesopotamia they developed into a whole series of "protosciences." Astrology was most successful in maintaining its existence, thanks chiefly to its quasi-scientific astronomical basis (developed by the "Chaldeans" in the Hellenistic period), but long previously the Etruscans had imitated the Babylonians successfully, and had influenced early Roman religion through their *disciplina Etrusca*. (See below on modern developments.)

A definition of science is probably superfluous. Let us describe it as the systematic effort of man to control or at least to understand his environment by increasing his knowledge of it. Historically speaking, science has progressed from primitive empirical data and empirico-logical analogies to experimental and mathematical methods following established principles of inductive and deductive logic. Ancient science also had to begin with simple observations which were repeated again and again, often unconsciously, until men finally learned their broader meaning. Some early analogies seem

---

. . . higher thought . . . has on the whole been from magic through religion to science" (*loc. cit.*). The order followed in my title was employed by Malinowski in his monograph cited in n. 1 above.

[6] In Malinowski's essay (see n. 1 above) he holds that magic and religion belong together in the sacred sphere, whereas science lies in the profane sphere; he also rejects Frazer's derivation of science from magic, holding that science is born from experience, while magic is traditional. Science is guided by reason, corrected by observation; magic is impervious to both (in other words it is proto-logical—though Malinowski takes sharp issue with Lévy-Bruhl on pp. 8 ff. of the 1948 edition).

absurd to us, and they belong rather to the domain of magic than to that of science, yet they ultimately gave rise to scientific hypotheses.

And now we must ask the question: What is religion? This is by far the most difficult of the three to define, and definitions vary widely.[7] I shall not attempt any general description but will offer definitions at two levels of religion. At one level, I should describe religion as the effort of man to enlist the favor of superior powers and to regulate his life with their aid. All primitive—ancient and modern—religions emphasize, as one of the most essential purposes of religious rites and observances, the maintenance of traditional standards of behavior, both in society and in cult or worship. On a much higher level, religion may be described as the effort of man to learn the will of God and to regulate his conduct accordingly. As man's understanding of God increases, his ethical motivations are heightened.

Let me analyze briefly some dominant aspects or tendencies of higher religious thought. In the first place, most higher religions of today emphasize mystical communion with God. This is particularly true of monotheistic faiths. In the religion of Israel there is no mystical *union* with God, but only mystical *communion* with God. In most orthodox Christianity and Judaism the same thing is true.[8] There is also a mystical union with God which is characteristic of most pantheistic religions, for instance in Hinduism and in certain dervish sects of Islam. Medieval Christian as well as

[7] One of the best discussions by an anthropologist of what constitutes religion— on a primitive level—is that of William Howells, *The Heathens: Primitive Man and His Religions,* New York, 1962, pp. 18-23. To him religion "may be said to complement science." He would prefer to use the term "religious behavior" instead of religion, and to describe it as adopted "by a group of people" who act "under an unconscious compulsion in order to tidy up their distraught relationships with one another and with the universe as they perceive it." He apologizes for the inadequacy of this definition. If we go back to the ancient Near and Middle East we find that the earliest recorded religions, with which are bound up nearly all the oldest known literatures, are a great deal more than mere "religious behavior," and include the most elaborately organized complexes of higher culture. For my own point of view in succinct form see my article, "Religion," in *American Peoples Encyclopedia,* 1959 ed.

[8] See J. Lindblom, *Zeitschrift für die alttestamentliche Wissenschaft,* 58, 1940, pp. 65-74; my remarks in *From the Stone Age to Christianity,* 1957 ed., p. 308, n. 44, and esp. A. J. Heschel, *The Prophets,* 1962, pp. 355-366.

medieval Jewish mysticism also tended toward pantheism, not distinguishing clearly between God and His creation.

Love of humanity—altruism in its highest sense—tends to weaken in proportion to the degree of separation, conscious or unconscious, of the individual from God. This principle is easy to document, since the vitality of Christian churches is closely correlated with the charity and generosity of its members. One need only contrast the feeble altruism of professedly nonreligious organizations from Communism to ethical culture. Communists consider altruism as bourgeois weakness, while atheistic humanists devote their energies to opposing religion.

The three principal stages in the development of human thinking

In order to lay a foundation for my analysis of the types of thinking we find in magic, science, and religion, I will describe briefly the three principal stages in the development of human "rational" thinking, which begins quite irrationally. These three stages were first presented in my book, *From the Stone Age to Christianity* (1940).[9] They are partly based on the work of Lucien Lévy-Bruhl, the French philosopher, psychologist, and anthropologist of the first half of this century, but with a vital modification. Lévy-Bruhl distinguished between two types of thinking: one was prelogical mentality (*mentalité prélogique*) and the other was logical mentality (*mentalité logique*). He saw that most religious ideas of primitives and much of their magical beliefs and practices are based on a failure to understand such logical principles as the principle of identity and the principle of contradiction. In other words, among primitives a thing may perfectly well be two entirely different things simultaneously. This is also characteristic of the thinking of children. And, as we shall see, it emerges again and again in the highest forms of current cultural life and thinking.

In 1939, Lévy-Bruhl became skeptical about his classification and

[9] See the 1957 ed., pp. 168-169, greatly expanded in *Archaeology and the Religion of Israel*, pp. 26-35. In the French edition of the former work, *De l'Age de Pierre à la Chrétienté*, 1951, pp. 86-87, the writer called attention to Lévy-Bruhl's recantation, and modified his own original statement in certain respects (changing the designation "prelogical" to "proto-logical").

wrote in his notebooks, partly published in 1947,[10] a complete retraction of his views on prelogical thinking. But his reason for retracting his ideas on prelogical thinking was precisely the reason which made me, in the same year (1939), propose an intermediary stage, namely the stage of empirical logic or empirico-logical thinking. Lévy-Bruhl recognized that, in most respects, primitives reason quite as logically as ordinary Westerners, and are much more practical about the affairs of their daily life than the average Westerner is when he comes to live among them; they know the habits of useful animals, as well as the habits of animals which are dangerous. They know the effects of plants, deleterious or beneficial, whether one can eat given plants or animals safely; they know the best ways to hunt and fish; they know about the seasons; they know how to utilize natural resources with such tools and devices as they possess. In all these respects, they are incomparably superior to civilized foreigners who try to live with them as they live. Accordingly, Lévy-Bruhl realized that it is quite wrong to attribute "prelogical" mentality to primitives. But he retracted too much, in that all the reasons why he originally proposed to distinguish this stage of thinking (for which I prefer the term proto-logical) are true of higher culture, including religion, magic, primitive art, primitive literature, and so on. In lower culture and social relations, where primitive man was—and is—able to learn by the experience of daily living, he learned to live quite logically. But in his higher culture, where he was unable to check his acts by their effects (history being virtually nonexistent), he was unable to make any marked progress. Therefore, we must distinguish between proto-logical thinking, where experience is nearly useless, and empirico-logical thinking—the logic born of experience.

It would be a serious error to look down on proto-logical thinking from our modern point of view and think that we have left it behind. Actually, proto-logical thinking has been making a most extraordinary recovery during the past two generations. Of course there will be a reaction; various reactions have set in already. I particularly have in mind modern painting and sculpture, literature, and music. I do not need to explain that the Museum of Modern Art in New York and many other comparable museums throughout

---

[10] A selection appeared in *Revue Philosophique*, 137, 1947, pp. 257-281; for the most complete publication see *Les carnets de Lucien Lévy-Bruhl*, Paris, 1949.

the West (modern art is not well received by the Communists) contain much material which is very similar to native African, Polynesian, Mayan, early Egyptian, Anatolian, Hittite, and Mesopotamian art. Modern art has gone on to new levels of abstraction (or expressionism) and has returned in some cases to infantile or even to subhuman levels. Much modern sculpture is also geometric, especially in such extreme cases as wire sculptures. In the work of even our greatest modern sculptors, such as Sir Jacob Epstein, there is a deliberate imitation of primitive art. African art from the past few centuries has exerted disproportionate influence on various aspects of modern sculpture. Similarly, literature, especially since James Joyce, has emphasized the "stream of consciousness." This literature deliberately ignores inner logic and symmetry; it turns to emotional reactions and "empathy"; it tries to express underlying subconscious "symbolism," usually in the service of some contemporary psychological school (especially Freudianism or Jungianism). Poetry, similarly, has become extremely proto-logical. Much of the religious poetry of the third millennium B.C., as we know it from Egyptian and Sumerian literature, was strongly proto-logical in that a single god is described in a dozen different poems not as similar to various entirely separate phenomena but as identical with them. The sun-god is a ship sailing across heaven; the sun-god is also a scarab (dung) beetle, or a falcon winging its way across heaven—all in the same context. Similarly, gods and goddesses change sex with the most disconcerting ease. In other words, a single figure may be a god at one time and a goddess at another. No attempt was made, so far as we know, to make such myths "hang together" or agree logically, because there was little idea of logic in the realm of higher culture. That was to develop later. Empirical logic is quite rare and seldom recognizable as such; there is no trace of formal logic.[11]

[11] In 1947-1948, the brilliant algebraic geometrician and historian of science, B. L. van der Waerden, a Dutch scholar who was for many years at Leipzig and is now at Zürich, spent a year at Johns Hopkins, where I made his acquaintance. When we began to discuss the forms of ancient thinking, he was very much opposed to my ideas. So he read over all the translations of Ancient Oriental documents, including the Bible, which he could locate. He found no evidence anywhere of formal logic. He expected at least traces—but there were none. Of course there are approaches; there are adumbrations and promises; but there is no formal logic, no syllogistic reasoning, no systematic classification or definition in any of these sources prior to sixth-century Greece.

It is true that science has made tremendous strides and that the popular mind generally accepts the results or the application of science. Yet it is not so long ago that I remember hearing from different American sources such statements as the following: "For practical scientists such as Edison and Burbank we have nothing but the profoundest respect. But all these so-called pure scientists are worthless, we can dispense with them." "The Republic has no need of men of science," was said by a French revolutionary leader when Lavoisier, founder of modern chemistry, was executed. Today we are witnessing a return of innumerable forms of ancient divination such as astrology, which is almost purely Babylonian in origin and the sources of which we can now trace clearly almost throughout. Astrology is spreading with unexampled rapidity. The best-known adept of recent times is Hitler, who is said to have made no important decision without an astrologer's advice. In America, astrology has recently made tremendous gains, not only on the Pacific coast but throughout the country. According to a recent survey[12] there are now five thousand professional practitioners of astrology, not counting scores of thousands of amateurs and perhaps ten million people who are ardent devotees of the "science" of astrology. These numbers obviously greatly exceed the numbers of professional astronomers and amateur enthusiasts.

If we turn to theosophy, parapsychology, spiritism, and other related fields, one can see how widespread modern divination has become. It was not so long ago that the state geologist of British Columbia was a dowser (rhabdomancer).[13] Her first action reputedly was to spread geological maps of the province on the floor and tables of her office and to move a willow rod over them, dispensing with the services of field geologists. All she had to do was to think gold, water, or oil, and move the willow wand systematically over the maps until it dipped automatically, indicating the places where the minerals were.[14] In Europe between the wars, the enthusiasm for dowsing (rhabdomancy) became so great that almost every city or town of any size had enthusiastic societies of

[12] Henry B. Darrach, Jr., "Up Horoscope!" *Life*, Feb. 22, 1960, pp. 96-106.
[13] See Samuel Iwry, "New Evidence for Belomancy in Ancient Palestine and Phoenicia," *Journal of the American Oriental Society*, 81, 1961, pp. 27-34. Belomancy is closely related in origin to rhabdomancy.
[14] This I was told by the president of the British Society of Dowsers, who called on me in Jerusalem during the early 1930s.

dowsers.[15] One of the most famous American novelists made himself notorious a few years ago by writing a book in support of dowsing.[16]

Empirical logic, the logic born of experience, is as old as animals. A dog will soon learn to run across a square instead of going around the corner, and we all know what white rats can do with a little practice. Dolphins are proving to be extraordinarily quick learners. This is empirical logic on a very low level, but it is logic born of experience all the same. Nearly all ancient crafts were dominated by it, yet the ancients were no mean inventors. There were inventors in those days who proceeded by essentially the same methods as Thomas A. Edison, although they were, to be sure, more primitive and without benefit of the scientific discoveries on which Edison drew. But they used the same trial and error, through systematic application of which nearly all of Edison's inventions were made. (In order to invent the tungsten filament, according to report, he tried over a thousand materials in succession.) The ancients made thousands of discoveries empirically. For example, a very extensive pharmacopoeia consisting of medicinal plants, drugs, and other materials, was developed by the ancient Egyptians, taken over in general by the Greeks, and handed down through them to modern times. The early Aztecs and early Chinese also had elaborate pharmacopoeias. In fact, some of the most important drugs used in modern medicine were taken over from folk medicine, for instance quinine from the American Indians and ephedrine from Eastern Asia.

By the fourth millennium B.C., ancient Near Eastern man had scores of thousands of devices and gadgets, uses of material, adaptations of one material to another purpose, etc., which were used in many scores of arts and crafts. Some of these arts were lost in antiquity. Some have been recovered in recent years. For example, two American archaeological chemists have discovered how to make Attic red-figured glazes, which have baffled the efforts of hundreds of previous workers—chemists, specialists in ceramics, archaeologists, and others. The art of black-figured glaze had been

---

[15] A very considerable literature on the subject sprang up, and numerous underground *Etzelgräber* (alleged tombs of Attila) were located and even planned with willow wands; needless to say, no excavations confirmed the alleged finds!

[16] The late Kenneth Roberts, *Henry Gross and his Dowsing Rod*, 1951.

recovered by a German chemist in the early 1940s.[17] There are still many lost arts of antiquity. Ancient man was indeed inventive. Even primitives, ancient and modern, have been and still are inventive. The late Lord Raglan used to emphasize the inventiveness of primitives in favorable environments, which are not necessarily environments where everything is easy; they are more likely to be environments where life becomes hard for them.[18]

It is interesting to note that, if we contrast the second millennium B.C. with the third millennium, there is tremendous progress in empirical logic. It is visible in the great advances in science, based on observation and on putting data together in a prescientific but, nonetheless, more systematic way than had been known before. For example, among the Babylonians of the first centuries of the second millennium there were such inventions and discoveries as Diophantine algebra, named for a Greek mathematician of the Roman period who probably flourished in the third century A.D., and geometry, including individual cases of the famous Pythagorean theorem named for the Greek philosopher and mathematician of the sixth century B.C. The Egyptians had developed remarkable skill in surgery, anatomy, mensuration, and other fields. The Babylonians, having two languages which were totally different in structure, made remarkable progress in analyzing the structure of languages. The Egyptians did not even begin to develop philology because they had only one language. A greater triumph, however, was the remarkable development of ancient Near Eastern law, particularly in the Law of Moses in Exodus, which follows identically the same formulation and patterning as Ancient Oriental law-codes of the second millennium, but is distinctly advanced in detail. The greatest triumph of empirical logic was Israelite monotheism. As we shall see in Chapter Three, the Hebrew Bible is by far the most impressive monument of empirical logic in existence.

In the Old Testament there is no formal logic because virtually all of it, and certainly all its source materials, goes back to pre-philosophical times before the Greek awakening. There is no trace of anything like philosophical thinking either in the Ancient Orient

---

[17] See Farnsworth and Wisely, *American Journal of Arch.*, 62, 1958, pp. 165-173.
[18] One of the most useful results of Toynbee's labors is to have demonstrated the truth of this once recognized and more recently doubted principle, with a wealth of examples; see *A Study of History*, Vol. II, 1934, pp. 1-73.

or in Greece before Thales of Ionian Miletus in the early sixth century B.C. Thales was perhaps the most universal genius before Plato and Aristotle; he was a famous lawyer as well as an engineer, astronomer, mathematician, and speculative thinker. Presumably following current tendencies in law, he systematized the older practical learning by formulating it in propositions and analyzing causes and origins.[19] Thales and his pupil Anaximander, apparently no less gifted in a speculative way than Thales was in more practical matters, taught the Greeks how to connect things in causal relationships. They worked out non-mythological cosmologies and cosmogonies, which began to be scientific, although in part adapted from earlier mythological sources. In their way they demythologized as successfully as the earlier Israelites had done. It was, however, the law courts of Athens which gave rise to dialectic logic, since Athenian law banned the pleading of cases by professional lawyers, thus encouraging the rise of a professional class of teachers of forensics, the famous Sophists.[20] There would have been no Plato or Aristotle if there had no Socrates; but there would have been no Socrates without the Sophists, who were the intellectual leaders of Athens in its democratic heyday during the sixth and fifth centuries B.C. In the agora of Athens men learned to debate and to reason. Subsequently, Aristotle systematized the reasoning which men had learned by practical experience and which Socrates had developed by his never-surpassed dialectic method.[21]

Today, in spite of important advances beyond Aristotelian logic, all scientific progress and technological achievement, including all now-accepted nuclear physics, are based on a logic which is wholly Aristotelian. Much mathematics may be non-Euclidean, but it is still Aristotelian. There can be little doubt that non-Aristotelian logic will celebrate its own triumphs in the future,[22] but so far all

[19] For further details on the share of Thales in transforming empirical case knowledge into generalized propositional knowledge, see Volume II in the present series.

[20] For this situation, the comprehension of which is a prerequisite to any adequate view of the origin of formal logic, see Bonner and Smith, *The Administration of Justice from Homer to Aristotle*, Vol. II, 1938, pp. 7-38.

[21] Without a grasp of the *Sitz im Leben* of the Sophists (see above), it is quite impossible to assess the role of Socrates; most attempts are futile. A great man's significance is in no way diminished by analyzing the sources of his greatness.

[22] It is only recently that Robert S. Ledley announced (*Proceedings of the*

our mathematics of any significant bearing on physical science and technology is logically Aristotelian.[23] Aristotle's contributions to logic are still basic, even though his views are far behind the times in scientific details.

The use of analogy in magic, science, and religion

The use of analogy, i.e., the resemblance of individual things, words, patterns, and principles, is very ancient. So far as we know, it was first isolated with more or less clarity by Plato, who employed it to a very great extent in his philosophical thinking.[24] Some phases of it were worked out in detail by the scholastic philosophers of the Middle Ages. The Schoolmen concentrated on verbal and ontological analogy, i.e., analogy of being (*analogia entis*), which was the highest form of analogy to them. They tried to prove the existence of God by abstracting being from its concrete manifestations. The latest grand attempt to combine science and religion into a synthesis on the basis of analogy was made by Bishop Butler in his famous work, *The Analogy of Natural and Revealed Religion* (1736), which was still a standard textbook in the late nineteenth century in many theological seminaries and philosophical faculties in America. However, the principle of analogy was so overworked and so often misused by Hegel and other idealistic philosophers of the eighteenth and nineteenth centuries, that analogy has become a term of disapprobation, like "teleology" (the assumption that there must be some goal or aim in existence) or "homeopathy" (a very antiquated medical theory which now serves mainly to conceal dubious activities on the part of "naturopaths" and others).[25] But I wish to concentrate here on the history

---

National Academy of Sciences, 41, 1955, pp. 498-511) the first successful effort at practical application of the results of non-Aristotelian logic.

[23] I must thank my son Hugh (Brother E. Alban, F.S.C.) for many interesting discussions of the foundations of modern mathematics, in which this subject was often examined.

[24] See Grenet, *Les origines de l'analogie philosophique dans les dialogues de Platon*, 1949.

[25] Kant and his followers (including the Neo-Kantians) were very chary about using the principle of analogy, which was being so misused by their philosophical contemporaries.

of the use of analogy, not on applying analogy to systematic think-ing. To begin with, analogy is an essential part of proto-logical religion and magic. For example, in sympathetic magic analogy plays a tremendous role. If rain is needed, water is sprinkled—a very primitive analogy indeed. If one wishes to ensure fertility of crops, then one carries out some fertility rite, preferably on the plowed field. If one wishes to harm or kill somebody, one pro-nounces incantations, sticks pins into a clay or wax figurine of the person in mind, etc. It is the same with divination. Astrology is largely built up on a supposed analogy between what is believed to happen among the stars and what actually happens on earth. The same is true of a host of mythological patterns.

In empirical logic we find a more sober use of analogy; flights of fancy do not belong in this domain. For instance, one of the most remarkable generalizations in Old Testament law, compared to slightly earlier Ancient Oriental law, is the use of the principle known as *lex talionis*—"an eye for an eye, a life for a life." This principle may seem and is often said to be extraordinarily primitive. But it is actually not in the least primitive. Whereas the beginnings of *lex talionis* are found before Israel, this principle was now ex-tended by analogy until it dominated all punishment of injuries or homicides.[26] In ordinary Ancient Oriental jurisprudence, men who belonged to the higher social categories or who were wealthy sim-ply paid fines, otherwise escaping punishment. In primitive law the idea of revenge is dominant. For example, the penalty for killing a member of a clan was often destruction of the murderer's clan.

Even in our own time we have not really outgrown either the principle that wealth and position bring a certain measure of im-munity or the idea that one must avenge all injuries as strongly as possible. So the *lex talionis*, far from being something which is completely outworn today, is something which we have not begun to attain—the principle of equal justice for all!

Analogy also was an important element in Greco-Roman science and philosophy. For example, the Pythagoreans of the sixth century B.C. and later, as well as the Neo-Pythagoreans of the last centuries B.C. and the first centuries A.D., applied principles of arithmetical number and geometric form to everything in nature. The Pythago-

[26] For other examples of the growing soberness of Biblical analogy, see below, Chapter 3.

reans introduced the pentatonic music of the spheres—five planets, five different musical notes in the scale (instead of our eight celestial spheres, a musical octave). They felt that just as when someone takes an object of the right shape and twirls it faster and faster until it sings, i.e., makes high musical sounds, likewise the rapid whirling of celestial spheres, the planets, around the earth necessarily brought with it musical sound—a music of the spheres. Another case is that of Platonic ideal forms, the analogical basis of which has been worked out by a number of scholars, including, most recently, the brilliant Rumanian historian of religion, Mircea Eliade.[27] Similarly, Stoic philosophy adopted Babylonian astrology as its dominant feature, which meant that the learned and even the popular religion of much of the world in the centuries immediately preceding and following Christianity was astrology in terms of Stoic philosophy. The analogy was simple. The Stoics believed in destiny, *heimarmenē*, and this ineluctable, inescapable destiny was essentially identical with the "fate" of the Babylonian astrologers, which could be learned through the movements, configurations, and constellations of the planets and stars.

Even today there is a revival of metaphysical "science" based almost entirely on systematic application of improved analogies. Collingwood, the brilliant philosopher of Oxford, used to emphasize the fact that psychoanalysis and analytic psychology hold roughly the same place today as astrology and alchemy did in medieval science. Fortunately a strong reaction on the part of experimental psychologists and neurologists is setting in today against the arbitrary structures of Freud, Jung, Adler, and others, which are based on tremendous sweeps of analogy which can never be proved experimentally.

Communist science is in an even worse predicament. One of the most curious developments has been the growth of a new phase of science devoted to "mitogenetic radiation," which was developed by A. Gurwitsch and others in Russia in the late twenties and

---

[27] See the English translation of his book, *Le mythe de l'éternel retour: archétypes et répétition*, 1949, published as *Cosmos and History: The Myth of the Eternal Return*, 1959 ed., *passim*. In the Forword to this edition Eliade points out that he does not use the ambiguous word "archetype" as "a structure of the collective unconscious," with Jung, but rather as a synonym for "exemplary model, paradigm."

thirties of our century.[28] There was an international congress on mitogenetic radiation held at Bologna in 1935. At all events, the principle was pure analogy, and a very dubious analogy at that. It was by then well known that atoms have nuclei and that nuclear fission produces radiation. So the advocates of mitogenetic radiation inferred analogically that living cells, when their nuclei divide in mitosis, must also produce radiation. Another example is the supposed principle of inheritance of acquired characteristics, first proposed in systematic form by Lamarck in 1815 and then developed by Michurin in Russia; under Stalin, Michurinism became the only permitted genetics. Its chief contemporary advocate, Lysenko, who suffered a short eclipse under Krushchev, returned to favor in 1959. Communist Russia has never rejected the genetics of Michurin, which is based on supposed analogy between individuals and species which are biologically adapted to their environment.[29]

Different stages of thinking in religion

All these dominant types of thinking—proto-logical thinking, empirico-logical thinking, formal logic, and analogy—are found in religion. Religion was never a simple phenomenon. I fully agree with Mircea Eliade, who has emphasized the antiquity of religion and its complexity as far back as we can go. The latest prehistoric finds and radiocarbon counts are confirming Eliade's insistence on the antiquity of religious phenomena. They are as old, so far as we can tell today, as man as a toolmaker and man as a speaker of languages, which probably means at least 200,000 years.[30] All simple evolutionary formulas for the development of religion are out of date.

In all pre-Hebrew religion, whether in Mediterranean or Indic polytheism (without the metaphysical and philosophical overtones

[28] On this subject see Alexander Hollaender, *The Problem of Mitogenetic Rays*, New York, 1936, and *An Experimental Study of the Problem of Mitogenetic Radiation* (with W. D. Claus), which appeared as *Bulletin of the National Research Council*, No. 100, 1937.

[29] See below, p. 290.

[30] Contrast the six million years of Ernst Benz, *The History of Religions: Essays in Methodology*, ed. Mircea Eliade and J. M. Kitagawa, 1959, pp. 130-131, which is possibly his own exaggeration of the 600,000 years often stated to be the length of the Ice Age.

of later Hinduism), we have classic examples of proto-logical thinking. Consider the figure of the goddess Kali or Durga, the bloody
goddess, who is strikingly similar in many respects to the Canaanite
goddess Anath, as shown by Marvin Pope. Israelite monotheism
and Chinese Confucianism stand almost alone as examples of empirical logic applied to religion. In both we have social and individual morality wedded to cosmic unity. In both there is a basic
divine revelation which has been demythologized. However, we
must emphasize the fact that Confucianism has proved sterile from
the standpoint of further religious development, whereas the religion
of Israel gave birth to the entire Judeo-Christian complex, including Islam. And the extraordinary vitality of Christianity and Judaism
today is a continuing effect of the tremendous momentum built
up by ancient Israel in its religious thinking. An acid test of the
empirico-logical character of Judeo-Christian tradition is found in
the attitude of the Hebrew Bible, intertestamental literature (Apoc-
rypha and Pseudepigrapha), the New Testament, rabbinic literature, most medieval Jewish and Christian philosophers, and orthodox
Jewish and Christian thinkers generally toward astrology. Astrology
is denounced in the Old Testament; it is denounced in the intertestamental literature; it is denounced by most of the rabbis and
most of the Church Fathers; it is denounced by most of the Schoolmen and by most orthodox Christian and Jewish thinkers in more
recent times.

I should also stress the importance of the conflict between
Aristotelianism and Neo-Platonism in European scientific and religious thinking from the twelfth to the seventeenth century. Alex-
andre Koyré of Paris and Princeton has been insisting for years
that seventeenth-century science was in large part a reaction under
Neo-Platonic auspices against Aristotelian science. It was not a
reaction by defenders of inductive logic and experimental science
against Aristotelian logic, which is mainly deductive, but rather
a reaction against monolithic Aristotelian physical science along
Neo-Platonic lines, beginning with Marsilio Ficino in the fifteenth
century, going on down to the great astronomers of the late sixteenth and seventeenth centuries, Tycho Brahe and Johannes Kepler,
who had a strong Neo-Platonic and Neo-Pythagorean bent. Today,
in the light of our present knowledge, we look back and are shocked
by most of the Neo-Platonic speculations. Yet both these great

astronomers earned their living, as did many other astronomers of that period, as professional astrologers. And so, as professional astrologers, they could not accept Aristotelian ways of thinking which rejected astrology. They had to become anti-Aristotelian in self-defense, as is being recognized more and more by historians of science.

Recently there has been a revival of quasi-religious or quasi-scientific speculation based on misuse of the principle of analogy.[31] One example is the philosophy of Paul Tillich, well known to many as the principal theoretician of current liberal Protestantism.[32] Tillich lays great stress on the principle of correlation. This is nothing else but the principle of analogy used in its loosest sense, a confrontation and comparison of patterns in philosophy and theology. His particular philosophical patterns are drawn from different kinds of philosophy and psychology, from Friedrich Schelling to Freud and Jung, on which existentialist ideas of various origins are superimposed. He then correlates miscellaneous philosophical and psychological ideas with different eclectically chosen theological ideas, all of which he has reworked. For example, Tillich says that there are three stages of being. But he offers what is essentially a Neo-Platonic type of idealistic philosophy which goes back to Schelling. These three states of being are (1) pure being (*Sein*), (2) structured being, and (3) existence (*Dasein*). (*Dasein* and existence do not always mean the same thing, though they have much in common.) But these three states—pure being, which is God; structured being; and existence, which is created being—are only a more abstract statement of the three stages which we find in all of Platonic and post-Platonic thinking, namely the planner, the plan, and the execution of the plan.[33]

---

[31] Study of the use of the principle of analogy has been neglected recently. For example, the great German philosopher, Ernst Cassirer, in his *Die Philosophie der symbolischen Formen*, 3 vols.; Berlin, 1923-1929 (Eng. trans., 3 vols.; New Haven, 1953-1957) does not have a single reference to the principle of analogy. He might have used it to advantage in working out the underlying principles of thinking which determined the activities of ancient, medieval, and modern societies; he has neglected it entirely, with a resulting atomizing of his symbolic thinking. His omission of analogy is naturally due to his Neo-Kantian training.

[32] See above, pp. 14-15.

[33] This sequence of creation and history was already well known to the Babylonians; see my discussion in *Journal of Biblical Literature*, 39, 1920, pp.

A second example is Pierre Teilhard de Chardin's book, *The Phenomenon of Man*.[34] This is full of the most amazing examples of loose analogical thinking, and *metabaseis eis to allo genos* based on loose applications of patterns which somewhat resemble one another, usually quite superficially. I will give one illustration. Father Teilhard lays great stress on the "within" (*dedans*) and the "without" (*dehors*). He thinks that the "within" is conscious. In other words, he thinks that all existence has an external phase and an internal phase, which is consciousness. It is a kind of panpsychism, but since this book was written in China toward the end of the 1930s under very unfavorable conditions with respect to library facilities (Teilhard headed the national Geological Survey), he is probably not directly indebted to the panpsychism of Fechner, despite striking similarities. He distinguishes energy as the tangential aspect of any system and consciousness as the radial aspect. By this he means, though usually misunderstood, that in the space-time continuum, treated mathematically as a fourth dimension, the tangential aspect is external and the radial aspect is internal.[35] He is here dealing with two vague analogies. One is the quasi-pantheism—here panpsychism—of the mystic, and the other is a sublimated Christian dualism in which the evolutionary process results in ultimate convergence of man and God at the "omega" point, which is the terminal of a rising evolutionary curve of human progress. Ernst Benz hails this idea, recognizing it correctly as another form of the expectation of superman. Man becomes superman in Christ.[36]

143-151, which, though antiquated in detail, has never been properly followed up and remained unknown to J. Bidez in his *Eos ou Platon et l'Orient*, 1945, as well as to Eliade, *Cosmos and History* (though the latter's general treatment of the question is admirable).

[34] P. Teilhard de Chardin, *Le phénomène humain*, Paris, 1955; Eng. trans. Bernard Wall, New York, 1959.

[35] This understanding I owe to my son Hugh (Brother E. Alban, F.S.C.), who is a trained mathematician.

[36] This bald statement may sound strange, but it does reflect Teilhard's lack of interest in human beings as such or in their history; cf. his extraordinary notion that the masses of China were still neolithic "well into the nineteenth century" (*op. cit.*, p. 209). In conversation with Catholic missionaries in China who knew him, I have received a strong impression of his fundamental fastidiousness verging on snobbery—an impression confirmed by my own conversations with him. This aspect of Teilhards thought has been rightly emphasized by E.

After this travesty of New Testament eschatology, it is refreshing to read two eminent anthropologists, whose pessimism stands in stark, but healing, contrast to the rosy illusions of a dreamer. One is Raymond Dart, the agnostic physical anthropologist of South Africa, whose tireless efforts yielded most of what is known today about the Australopithecine relatives of our missing direct ancestors. Knowing the bloody history of South Africa, which he vividly describes in a chapter entitled "From Vortrekkers to Man-Apes," he writes a chapter on "The Antiquity of Murder," in which he tells of the carnage wrought by the Australopithecines in their sub-human simplicity.[37] Again and again Dart repeats the phrase "mark of Cain." Man came into the world with all the potential guilt of his future already weighing him down. Dart was a much more productive scientist than Teilhard, and he saw much more clearly into the heart of man. Another eminent anthropologist resumes the story in his eloquent Sigma Xi-Phi Beta Kappa address delivered before the December 1962 meeting of the National Association for the Advancement of Science. Loren C. Eiseley entitled his address, "Man: The Lethal Factor,"[38] pointing out that man's present capability of self-destruction provides an obvious answer to the question of his ultimate end on earth, an end he may reasonably be expected to share with all other species of the animal kingdom, fossil and still existing. But this agnostic scientist also points out that the indestructible symbol of Christ on the cross gives us the answer. Eiseley's interpretation of the symbol may not be quite that of the Christian believer, but it is immensely more credible than the smug self-confidence of the ultraconservative who is likely to hold that

Benz (who seems to agree with it in principle); see his articles "Teilhard de Chardin" and "Teilhard de Chardin und die Zukunft des Menschen," *Zeitschrift für Religions- und Geistesgeschichte,* 14, 1962, pp. 229-246 and 316-333. It is instructive to note that the first article in Benz's 1962 trilogy is entitled, "Der Übermensch: Grundprobleme des heutigen Menschenbildes." In Teilhard's other posthumous book, *The Divine Milieu,* 1960, the way of the cross "is the way of universal progress" (pp. 76 ff.). In my opinion, G. Hauptmann's *Der Narr in Christo* is essentially closer in some respects to the heart of the Christian message than the measureless confidence in man's terrestrial future shown by Père Teilhard.

[37] See Raymond Dart and Dennis Craig, *Adventures with the Missing Link,* 1959, pp. 84 ff., 106 ff.

[38] See *The Key Reporter,* XXVIII/3, 1963, pp. 2-4.

he is somehow immune to sin and suffering, or the equally complacent professional religious liberal, who often seems to feel that, having saved himself from the imputation of sin, he is free to behave as he pleases—provided he does not get caught!

The function of religion

Religion has always been the heart, or the soul—using a well-known metaphor with some justification—of every known culture of the past.[39] It is not necessary to agree with the functionalists or with any of the various related schools of anthropology which claim that the religion of any primitive or isolated culture is an inseparable part of it. I do not accept functionalism as a system, but there is some truth in it. Certainly Western European culture cannot be imagined without its Judeo-Christian and, more specifically, its Christian background. Personally, I do not believe that Western culture can exist without a Christian background, or at least a sympathetic Jewish background. (But Christianity has existed in many places without Western culture.)

Another point we must recognize is that both the Judeo-Christian tradition and science have one thing in common: they must wage perpetual war against all forms of magic and quasi-magical science or religion, in the future as in the past. Religion is not magic; science is not magic, although both occasionally act as though they were. Men of faith and men of science have a great deal more in common than they sometimes realize. Science cannot set up value judgments without betraying the basic function of science, which is to discover truth and then to apply it regardless of the values which may emerge. The maintenance of moral and altruistic ideals remains the function and duty of religion.

Philosophical analysis remains essential, but all philosophical systems are Hellenic or post-Hellenic in conception; they are, therefore, based on either explicitly stated or presupposed postulates or assumptions. Since the ultimate postulates are not themselves subject to proof, philosophers have to reason logically from what George Boas calls their protophilosophy, seldom explicitly developed. The more rigorous the internal logic of any system, the more uncertain

[39] See above, pp. 46-51.

are its conclusions, given the fact that one cannot rigorously prove any of the basic presuppositions of a philosophical system. And the more closed any system is, the more impossible it is to predict the future by extrapolating its regularities.

The roots of religion strike so deep as to be more basic and incapable of logical derivation than the bases of our physical and biological existence. If one recognizes that the foundations of our physical and biological existence cannot be demonstrated—they can only be probed—one must also recognize the basic character of religion. One cannot prove it by scientific methods but one cannot do without it. Religion is still the hope of the world, as in the past. Religion alone unites the intellectual and aesthetic in man with the affective and altruistic. If man's biological and psychological evolution have required the synergistic collaboration of his genetic structure and environmental background, surely we cannot reject the religious feelings and aspirations of man as irrelevant to the evolution of the human spirit. Man needs religious values today more than ever before, as he sees his environment transformed into irrecognizable shapes of an unknown future.

Chapter 3

The place of the Old Testament in the history of thought[1]

Introductory remarks

No one is more ready than I to admit that the Bible can be understood by the humblest and often by the most primitive of men. But in order to grasp its religious profundity and its extraordinary meaning for history, we require aid from all pertinent disciplines, including archaeology, philology, and other ancillary branches of history, as well as from such other fields as comparative religion, anthropology, and psychology. Archaeology has been placed first, since through it we are opening up the previously unknown world in which the Old Testament came into existence.

Three widely diverse attitudes toward the Old Testament are familiar in our day; the first and third apply equally well to the New Testament:

1. Ancient Hebrew thought is too primitive to have relevance for modern man.

2. The Old Testament is Oriental and exotic, with a radically different outlook and with a different logical syntax, which create a gulf between the Hebrews and ourselves.

[1] This lecture was delivered as the first Harry D. Koblitz Lecture, at the Reformed Jewish Temple in Cleveland, February 5, 1961. It has been rewritten and considerably expanded, and notes have been added. I wish to thank Rabbi Abba Hillel Silver and his son and successor, Rabbi Daniel Jeremy Silver, for permission to include the lecture in this volume. It is my first publication on this theme—aside from scattered remarks.

3. It contains much philosophical content, part of which is almost Greek in its attitude toward the problems of human existence.

My own point of view is radically different from all three approaches. I place the Old Testament, from the standpoint of the history of ways of thinking, between the proto-logical thought of the pagan world (which includes non-metaphysical Greco-Roman and Indic polytheism) and Greek systematic reasoning. Biblical Hebrew thought lacks Greek logical method; it has no systematic analysis of propositions, no hierarchic classification of phenomena, no formal postulates, no deductive syllogisms, no definition of abstract terms, and hence nothing which can be called a creed. At the same time, it gains certain advantages from the very absence of these elements, precisely because it also lacks the structural weaknesses built into any philosophical system based on premises or postulates from which elaborate ideologies are deduced, with more or less rigor. For these ideologies are no stronger than their foundations, and since the foundations are never quite solid, the structures built on them are weak. The Hebrew Bible, i.e., the Christian Old Testament, is almost entirely free from this type of weakness, since it is, as we shall see, based chiefly on experience and history —which is the experience of mankind. It is admittedly basic to the thought of Judaism, Christianity, and Islam; it is therefore basic to the whole of Western higher culture, now sweeping the world. The Old Testament, accordingly, will live forever in the intellectual as well as the spiritual history of mankind.

Three views of the nature and relevance of Old Testament thought

One often hears in both academic and popular circles that Hebrew thought is primitive and therefore irrelevant to modern man. Here we are faced with a serious fallacy. The point of view behind it is very simple: because things are earlier, therefore they are more primitive or, conversely, because things seem to be more primitive they must therefore be earlier. Here we must first clarify our literary chronology on the basis of our present archaeological knowledge, especially in regard to dating the poetry and prose of the Hebrew Bible. Old Testament poetry was handed down much better than prose since it is fixed by form (*gebundene Rede*) and can be remembered by its rhythm, its assonance, and also, in Hebrew, by the *parallelismus membrorum* of each line, the first half of which usually expresses the same meaning as the second, but in different words. It is also fixed by music, because all poetry was sung or chanted in antiquity. There was no such thing in antiquity as poetry recited as we do it today. Poetry was orally transmitted, it was remembered, sometimes for many centuries, before it was put into writing. In all other known poetry and literary prose of ancient and modern nations, poetry preceded literary prose. This fact was understood by J. G. Herder in the late eighteenth century and by H. G. A. Ewald in the early nineteenth, but was forgotten by nearly all modern Biblical scholars. We are only just realizing that if the usual scholarly datings were correct, Hebrew literature would be an exception to all other known national literatures.[2] We can now say with confidence that Biblical Hebrew literature—both poetry and prose—dates almost entirely, in substantially its trans-mitted form, between the thirteenth and the fourth centuries B.C., i.e., during the millennium between the Mosaic age and the end of the Persian period. There are passages which are earlier and some which are later,[3] but in general I think this dating may be accepted as definitive. Thanks especially to the new knowledge obtained from the recovery of steadily increasing masses of Northwest Semitic pre-Biblical literature, found by C. F. A. Schaeffer at Ras Shamra on the Syrian coast, and to the discovery of the Dead Sea Scrolls, we have ample evidence today for dating.[4] The religious literature of Israel is therefore mostly later in date than the now known canonical religious literature of Egypt, Babylonia, Assyria, the Hit-tites, Canaanites, etc.[5] Nearly all these literatures reflect mythologi-

---

[2] See below, pp. 267-269, and my discussion in my Goldenson Lecture for 1961: *Samuel and the Beginnings of the Prophetic Movement*, Cincinnati, Hebrew Union College Press, 1961, pp. 21 ff.

[3] Now that fragments of the Daniel cycle of the Persian period have been recovered from Qumran, it is clear that part of Daniel is older. Esther and Canticles probably date from the fourth century B.C.

[4] See above, pp. 34-36, and below, p. 133.

[5] Nearly all known Egyptian religious literature antedates the eleventh century B.C., and what we have from the Ethiopian, Saite, and later periods represents late copies or collections of much older material. Nearly all known Assyro-Babylonian religious literature dates from before the tenth century B.C. Hittite and Canaanite religious texts all antedate ca. 1200 B.C.

cal, i.e., proto-logical ways of thinking.[6] This has been called by Voegelin "cosmological" religion, but it may be better termed "physiocentric," since it is focused on nature.[7] It is not cosmological in the sense that today's scientific thinking is beginning to be cosmologically oriented, and some religious thinkers (e.g., Bultmann, Karl Heim, Julian Hartt) try to build new theologies on new cosmologies, forgetting that human ideas of cosmology always change, whereas human nature does not.

On the other hand, the literature of the Bible is earlier than any clear evidence of specific Greek literary or philosophical influence. There is no historical writing in the Old Testament which is later in date than the earliest possible time at which the Greek historians of the fifth century B.C. could have influenced it. The poetry of Israel is in part contemporary with Greek poetry, but there is no extant Greek prose literature before the sixth century B.C., except for fragments of laws. The oldest Greek literary prose dates from the sixth and fifth centuries; it is only a little earlier than the latest parts of I and II Chronicles as well as Ezra and Nehemiah (from about the last third of the fifth century B.C.). The Old Testament, for all practical purposes, belongs chronologically between the Ancient Orient and the Greek intellectual age which began in the sixth century. Plato and Aristotle both wrote in the fourth century, a time probably after the date of the latest of the Old Testament writings except Daniel, possibly also Ecclesiastes, and some other short compositions.

In the Hebrew Bible we have, accordingly, something quite different from what preceded or followed it. The Old Testament exhibits very little proto-logical thinking, which was characteristic of early Oriental religious literature and which was carried on into Greek times, subsequent to the end of the Old Testament, by means of commentaries and new compositions which imitated older literature. Except for collections of proverbs and didactic writings there is no religious literature from the Ancient Orient, whether in hieroglyphs, cuneiform texts, or alphabetic script, earlier than or contemporary with the Old Testament, which resembles the kind of thinking we find in the latter. On the other hand, the Old Testa-

[6] See Chapter 2, above.
[7] See below, pp. 264-265.

ment precedes the logical and philosophical reasoning of the classical Greeks, subsequently inherited by Western Christians and Moslems.

The second attitude is also unfavorable; it, too, represents Old Testament thought in a way tending to make it irrelevant to Westerners of today. According to many scholars the Hebrew Bible is Oriental, it is exotic, it cannot be explained in terms of Western philosophical and logical thinking, therefore it is more or less irrelevant to us. Or if it is relevant, it only becomes so with the aid of drastic assumptions, which really assume its basic irrelevance. There are a number of recent approaches which I shall discuss here. For instance, there is a widespread notion, which in my opinion is entirely baseless, that radically different linguistic structures involve different logical "syntax." This has been maintained by Count Alfred Korzybski,[8] a Pole who settled in Chicago and founded the school of "General Semantics"; it has been popularized by such writers as Thurman Arnold,[9] a well-known attorney, and S. Hayakawa, a Canadian-born professor of English who has written a best-seller on the subject,[10] and then, from a more scholarly point of view, by Benjamin Lee Whorf, a graduate engineer, later an insurance agent, who nevertheless seriously pursued linguistics (especially American).[11] Whorf was extremely original and his views are still held by many philosophers and anthropologists.[12] However, I shall limit myself to a few observations in opposition to these views. But first and foremost a concession. Of course there are differences in the meanings of words in different languages. For example, in French the word *conscience* means not only "conscience," but also and more commonly "consciousness." *Conscience*

[8] See A. Korzybski, *Science and Sanity; An Introduction to non-Aristotelian Systems and General Semantics*, Lancaster and New York, 1933; 2d ed., 1941.
[9] See his *The Symbols of Government*, 1935, and *The Folklore of Capitalism*, 1937.
[10] S. I. Hayakawa, *Language in Action*, 1941, a Book-of-the-Month Club selection, followed by a number of other publications.
[11] See his posthumous volumes, *Four Articles on Metalinguistics*, Washington: Foreign Service Institute, Department of State, 1952, and *Language, Thought and Reality*, ed. J. B. Carroll, New York, 1956.
[12] See the published symposium on Whorf's views, in Harry Hoijer, ed., *Language in Culture*, Chicago, 1954 (also published as *Memoir* No. 79 of the American Anthropological Association, 1954).

(French) is often translated into English as "conscience," whereas what is really meant is "consciousness." The confusion which results may be illustrated by the work of a distinguished Dutch scholar who, throughout an English monograph on the fundamental concepts of the early Christian Gnostic, Valentinus, rendered Greek *nous* as "conscience." On the basis of French *conscience* he unwittingly introduced "conscience" (English) into a Gnostic system which had nothing to do with it.[13] German philosophical thought has often been distorted in translation because of words with German fields of meaning different from any corresponding English words. What has happened in the case of *Geist* is almost incredible. Since this German word has many meanings which are not found in English "spirit," when it is translated literally as "spirit" and *geistig* as "spiritual," hopeless confusion results. Differences between such fields of meaning are indeed significant.

But this phenomenon has little or nothing to do with the structure of languages, as may be illustrated by the fact that there was one and the same intellectual culture in the formerly bilingual country of Austria-Hungary (Magyar and German). Literate Hungarians were virtually always bilingual, and always if they wrote much or were leaders in thought. Swedish Finns were nearly always bilingual and are still bilingual, using both Swedish and Finnish. These two languages, as in the case of Hungarian and German, are totally different in structure. In antiquity the same was true of the Babylonian culture shared by the Sumerians and Accadians for at least a thousand years (from ca. 2700—or earlier—to ca. 1700 B.C.). It has proved quite impossible to distinguish Semitic from non-Semitic components—except, of course, in language. And yet the two languages were even further apart in structure than Ugro-Finnic and Germanic. The very fact that the early Babylonians were bilingual gave them an insight into the phenomena of language and a freedom from the "tyranny of words" which the Egyptians never acquired.

The same judgment applies to the recent work by a Norwegian scholar, Thorlief Boman, now in a second German edition (1954) and a first English edition (1960). In this book, *Das hebräische Denken im Vergleich mit dem griechischen* (English title: *Hebrew Thought Compared With Greek*), Boman maintains that Greeks and

[13] A study by Gilles Quispel, one of the foremost authorities in the field, in *Vigiliae Christianae*, I, 1947, pp. 43-73.

Hebrews thought differently. He says that whereas Hebrew thought is dynamic, Greek thought is static. Hebrew thought is temporal—in terms of time; Greek thought is spatial—in terms of space. This is comparable to a popular conception, which I have heard even from distinguished Old Testament scholars, that the Greeks were eye-minded, whereas the Hebrews were ear-minded; they listened to the word of God while the Greeks saw nature around them. Actually there is no difference known to comparative psychologists between the relative proportion of auditory versus visual memory and imagination among different linguistic or racial groups. Boman's approach is completely wrong. For example, he stresses the fact that the Hebrew word *hayah* means properly "he came to be, he became," whereas the Greek *einai* means "to be." The difficulty is that in the many pages which he devotes to the difference between Greek "I am, he is, to be" and Hebrew "to be" in the sense of "coming to be" (*hayoh*), he forgets that there is another Greek word which means "to become" in the same sense as Hebrew *hayah*, viz. *gignomai*, and that there is an everyday Hebrew expression which is formed with the personal pronoun "he" and expresses the copula, "I am, he is, etc." Boman just took a concept, "to be," which is somewhat differently expressed in Hebrew and Greek, and arbitrarily assumed that the differences were characteristic of different ways of thinking. If he had looked through his dictionaries carefully, he would have found that exactly the same ideas can be expressed, though in somewhat different ways. The hypothesis of different forms of logic and different mentalities based on difference of languages is erroneous.[14]

It is a pity that the late Frank Ringgold Blake[15] was never able (for lack of funds) to publish his labors of many years on descriptive grammar. Since he was particularly interested in a semantic approach to the way in which all possible actions, states, and relations are expressed in different languages, he was able to show

[14] A thorough critique of Boman's views, as well as of analogous misinterpretations of languages and linguistic structures, can be found in James Barr, *The Semantics of Biblical Language*, Oxford, 1961.

[15] Dr. F. R. Blake (1875-1962) was my teacher and colleague (1913-1919, 1929-1955); he was one of the greatest Semitic linguists of modern times, though his innate modesty and his perfectionism prevented him from becoming as well known as should have been his due.

that all languages are quite able to express anything which can be expressed in any one of them, as long as they reflect approximately the same level of culture. (This has nothing to do with linguistic descriptions of technological or philosophical complexities.) Blake completed his great work at a time when structural linguists had pre-empted the use of the term "descriptive," and before they had become interested in semantic problems, so it proved quite impossible to obtain aid for publication. About the same time, moreover, Whorf (see above) was winning posthumous plaudits for his alleged dem-onstration that languages of different structure are logically different. The evidence for this was incredibly flimsy; it consisted essentially of an attempt to fix the meaning of formative elements (morphemes) by analyzing their "etymologies," thus arriving at what he called the basic meaning of syntactic complexes. The inferences he drew were, of course, no stronger than the putative etymologies, just as the personality acculturation studies of social anthropologists about the same time were no stronger than the Freudian psychiatrists' analyses of the Rorschach (ink blot) tests on which they depended for interpretation of personality! That Greek was better able to distinguish philosophical nuances than Hebrew, *once philosophy had developed into a formal discipline*, we grant, just as German is better able to distinguish metaphysical subtleties than English or French. But this has nothing to do with the approach of Boman and Whorf. We must remember that Aristotle came back to Europe via Arabic and Hebrew, not through direct Latin transmission.

Even in our own time an opposite point of view has been stated by would-be defenders of the Old Testament, who contend that Hebrew thinking was essentially philosophical in the Greek sense. Admittedly, the thought of the great medieval Jewish scholastic, Maimonides, is indeed philosophically Greek in substance and methods. There is nothing more Greek than the logic of Maimon-ides, and, of course, there is nothing more completely Jewish in origin than Maimonides' religious tradition. But we are not dealing with Maimonides, we are dealing with the Old Testament. It is quite true that Philo of Alexandria, in the first century A.D., produced a complete fusion between Greek and Hebrew ways of thinking. Philo, however, was taken up by the Christians, who preserved him for posterity. Philo's interpretation of the Torah in the light of Greek philosophy was rightly rejected by orthodox Jewry in the rabbinic period. In fact, it was not until the seventeenth century

(Spinoza) that Philonic thought was rediscovered by Jews.[16] But it was taken seriously by Christians from the second century A.D. on and, as has been shown by Harry Austryn Wolfson, Philo underlies much patristic Christian theology.[17] Philo, though an orthodox Jew in his fundamental belief and practice, was nonetheless one of the great precursors of standard Christian theology.

In recent years we have heard much of the "Hebrew philosophical genius," to quote a distinguished Islamic scholar, Duncan Macdonald, a Scotsman who taught for decades at the Hartford Seminary Foundation. In these words, which formed the title of one of Macdonald's best-known books, he maintained that the writers of the Old Testament thought philosophically, and that their writings expound philosophical teaching. My colleague, George Boas (who has one of the keenest analytic minds in America), in a review of Macdonald's book, *The Hebrew Philosophical Genius* (Princeton, 1936),[18] pointed out that Macdonald was confusing implicitly held beliefs with logical analysis of them, probing with demonstration, and questions with propositions. In fact, if we examine the Wisdom literature of the Bible carefully we will see in it a very important pre-philosophical stage of thought, as we will show in Volume II of the present series. Yet none of the characteristics of Greek philosophy is found in the Hebrew Bible. There is no logical reasoning; there is no abstract generalization of the type familiar from Plato and subsequent Greek philosophers; there is no systematic classification; there are no creeds. Formal creeds were impossible before classification, generalization, and syllogistic formulas were invented by the Greeks, between the time of Thales of Ionia in the early sixth century and that of Aristotle in the fourth century. The Old Testament is not philosophical, but no subsequent philosophies are as interested in the basic problems of humanity. Nor could the Hebrews develop any postulational reasoning from undemonstrable premises, arriving at conclusions which may or may not be correct. Because of our propensity to assume that correct conclusions imply sound demonstrations, we sometimes arrive at these conclusions as a result of unsound reasoning from faulty premises—and never know the difference! It

[16] See Harry A. Wolfson, *The Philosophy of Spinoza*, 1934.
[17] See H. A. Wolfson, *Philo: Foundations of Religious Philosophy in Judaism, Christianity, and Islam*, 2 vols., 1947, and *The Philosophy of the Church Fathers*, Vol. I, 1958.
[18] See his review in *Journal of Biblical Literature*, 56, 1937, pp. 133-137.

is precisely because the Old Testament depends so largely on the logic born of experience, with no errors based on the innumerable weaknesses of deductive reasoning, that it remains the great behavioral and moral classic of all time.

In order not to appear to neglect the important religious literature of India, the following remarks are pertinent here; I have developed them elsewhere in this volume.[19] At a recent conference in Cincinnati (January, 1961), some fifty specialists in the fields of philosophy, ethics, religious culture, and modern literatures came together to study the relation between religion and the humanities today. It was pointed out by Brand Blanshard, the distinguished analytical philosopher of Yale University, that during a recent visit to India as exchange professor he discovered that Indian students could seldom understand our inherited Greek forms of philosophy. They thought metaphysically along the lines of the Upanishads and subsequent Hindu thought; they could not think in terms of Greek logical categories. He pointed out that a tremendous gap separates Hindu philosophical thinking, still largely couched in the language of ancient metaphysics and its medieval and modern sequels, from the thinking of the West. He thought that the gap between the philosophical systems of East and West was greater than that between their religions. This is a very interesting observation, confirmed when one reads many (not, of course, all) modern Hindu philosophical writers and notes that they are still thinking in relatively primitive metaphysical terms, disregarding Greek patterns of logic. It must be emphasized that there is nothing unsophisticated about native Indic metaphysics and that it has simply bypassed the empirical logic of Israel and Confucian China, as well as Greek forms of logical reasoning. It has its own logic, which is refractory to Western methods of analysis. But the West has already learned much and will doubtless learn more from Indian religious tradition.[20]

The Old Testament as a masterpiece of empirical logic

The Old Testament exhibits everywhere the logic born of experience, empirical logic. As we have seen, it is just as "logical" as any formal logic of the Greeks and their successors, but this logic is

[19] See pp. 145-146.
[20] See below, p. 214, on the influence of Gandhi.

implicit; it emerges from experience and is not expressed in formal categories. To illustrate, let us first turn to the early chapters of Genesis, where, if anywhere, one should find proto-logical reasoning. These chapters are full of poetic quotations and reminiscences. Their prose is obviously derived from an older poetic form.[21] The poetry of the first chapter of Genesis is especially transparent, although it is no longer couched in verse forms. It embeds within itself verse quotations, poetic forms of phraseology, and reminiscences from originally poetic sources.[22] However, the first chapters of Genesis are always monotheistic. At most one can see what may be traces of forgotten polytheistic gods. It is important to note that in Hebrew the word for God is usually in the plural, *elohim*, which means properly "gods," and various forms of *adonim*, "lords" (*adonai* properly means "my lords"), which long before the time of Moses had come to mean the totality of all manifestations of god, the totality of lords, so that the plural of "god" and the plural of "lord" could be used for a single great god or for a great king. This is familiar to us from the pre-Mosaic Amarna tablets, Northwest Semitic texts of various kinds from Ugarit, Phoenicia, etc.[23]

The late Umberto Cassuto of Rome and Jerusalem pointed out years ago that the statement that God created the "great sea monsters," the *tanninim* (Genesis 1:21), refers to the primordial dragons of Northwest Semitic mythology; these *tanninim* were not uncreated monsters of chaos, as believed in pre-Mosaic times, but were created by God.[24] In virtually all ancient Near Eastern cosmogonies we find a god or gods who destroy a monster or monsters of chaos at the beginning of creation. Only then can the gods begin to create.

[21] See Umberto Cassuto, *A Commentary on the Book of Genesis, Part 1: From Adam to Noah (Genesis I-VI, 8)*, trans. I. Abrahams, Jerusalem, 1961, pp. 8 ff.; Hebrew ed., 1944, pp. 2 ff.

[22] See esp. my paper, "The Refrain 'And God Saw *ki tob*' in Genesis," *Mélanges bibliques rédigés en l'honneur de André Robert*, Paris, 1957, pp. 22-26; and J. B. Bauer, "Die literarische Form des Heptaemeron," *Biblische Zeitschrift*, nf 2, 1957, pp. 273-277.

[23] See the selected Amarna tablets translated by the writer in *Ancient Near Eastern Texts*, ed. J. B. Pritchard, Princeton, 1950, pp. 483-490, several of which are addressed "To the king, my lord, my pantheon, my Sun-god" (*ana šarri bēliya ilāniya šamšiya*). See also *From the Stone Age to Christianity*, 1957 ed., pp. 213-214; and Marvin Pope, *El in the Ugaritic Texts*, "Supplements to *Vetus Testamentum*," 2; Leiden, 1955, pp. 20-21.

[24] See Cassuto, *op. cit.*, pp. 49-51, Hebrew ed., pp. 25 f.

The monsters were uncreated; they were older than the gods who destroyed them. Not so in Israel. Throughout the first chapters of Genesis one finds the process which has been named demythologizing. To a large extent the old words are kept, but they have a new meaning, divested of all clear mythological connotations.

The present Hebrew text of Genesis 1 opens:

> "When God began to create heaven and earth—
>   the earth being chaotic and void,
>   with darkness over the Nether Sea (*tehom*),
>   and the spirit of God soaring
>   over the face of the water—
>   Then God said, 'Let there be light . . .' "

Since Tehom elsewhere in the Bible refers also to the dragon of primordial chaos, we may safely suppose that this was once true here as well. Somewhere between the end of verse 1 and the beginning of verse 3 there was presumably an allusion to the defeat and destruction of the dragon of chaos, later deleted. Here again we have a clear instance of demythologizing, probably in the early seventh century B.C., since we have an allusion to the primeval dragon, Tehom, slain by Yahweh, in Amos 7:4.[25]

If there were no traces of mythology left in Biblical poetry, how immeasurably poorer would be its phraseology, imagery, and style! John Milton, in order to enrich his poetic imagery, drew heavily on Greek mythology, and he was certainly no pagan, but a very conservative Puritan. Even Milton found it necessary to bring in a host of mythological reminiscences for the sake of enhancing his picture of Creation.

I have many reservations in regard to Rudolf Bultmann's *Entmythologisierung*, the "demythologizing" of the Bible, especially the New Testament. I think that his whole approach is unfortunate;[26] but there is much to be said for the word in question, if properly used. Certainly later editors of the first chapters of Genesis saw to it that the hallowed traditions of their forefathers about the creation of the world and of mankind were demythologized wherever possi-

[25] This passage will soon be discussed by Delbert Hillers, who presented a paper on it at the meeting of the Society of Biblical Literature in December, 1962 (to appear in *Catholic Biblical Quarterly*).
[26] See below, Chapter 13.

ble. We must remember that these traditions, transmitted orally from the remotest past, were not only sacred, but carried on historical memories.[27]

If we examine Old Testament poetry and compare it with the verse of pre-Israelite Canaan, written in a dialect (Ugaritic) closely related to Biblical Hebrew but going back to the period from about 2000 B.C. to the fourteenth century B.C., well before Moses, we find much self-contradictory description. In fact, frequently in the same line one half-line contradicts the other. For instance, the first half-line says that a god "drank wine from a cup of gold," the next half-line that he "drank it from a flagon of silver." A variation on this theme is that a god is given "a cup in one hand, two flagons in both hands." Obviously, he could not have held both simultaneously. Evidently these poets, following ancient stylistic tradition, were unconsciously trying to create a vague, changing outline in order to make the picture shimmer, so to speak, in the mind of the listener. Whether this stylistic device made the resulting text sound more sacred, or simply more poetic, we cannot say because we cannot fully penetrate this mentality. We have similar phenomena in a few of the earliest poems of the Bible, such as the Song of Deborah (see below), but nowhere in later times, at least not obviously.

In a few cases we are able to check the meaning of an early Hebrew poetic text by the accompanying prose interpretation or tradition. The most striking case is Judges 5:26, where we have a poetic device almost identical in character with the Ugaritic examples given above:

> Her hand she put out to the tent-peg,
> And her right hand to the workman's mallet;
> She hammered Sisera, crushing his head,
> She smote him, shattering his temple.

[27] One such case is the Flood Story, which is closely related to the Sumerian and Accadian accounts, but almost certainly reflects a stage of Mesopotamian transmission not later than about 2000 B.C. It is being connected more and more with the floods which devastated southwestern Asia at the end of the last Glacial Age, about 9000 B.C. (radiocarbon dating). Another is the Biblical account of the creation of man in Gen. 2:7, 21 ff., which may reflect religious customs of the pre-pottery Neolithic, before 6000 B.C.; see Ruth Amiran, *Bulletin of the American Schools of Oriental Research*, No. 167, 1962, pp. 23-25.

In the light of Ugarit the meaning is very clear; it had already been recognized by some scholars. There was no time to risk being discovered, so Jael grabbed whatever came to hand—tent-pin or mallet —and struck Sisera over the head with all her force. The empirico-logical tradition of later centuries completely misunderstood this Bronze Age stylistic device (Judges 4:21) and made Jael drive a tent-peg through Sisera's skull with a mallet! A closely similar case is found in the Poem of the Conquest quoted in Joshua 10:12-13:

> O Sun, be still at Gibeon,
> O Moon, in the valley of Aijalon—
> And the sun was still, the moon stood
> While the folk was being saved[28] from its foes.

The supposed astronomical miracle is the result of empirico-logical interpretation of a Bronze Age stylistic device!

Naturally, one can always assert that words of similar meaning in parallelism conflict with one another, but since the meanings of most words are not very precise, even in contemporary philosophical writing, it is impossible to expect complete logical consistency in poetry. In fact, today we have returned in poetry (see above) to a proto-logical stage in which the words of a poet defy any attempt to construe them logically. We are being introduced again into vague horizons which, in their indefiniteness and inconsistency, exceed anything known in the proto-logical poetry of the Ancient Orient. Yet modern verse has probably added to our range of poetic appreciation, even though it has not increased our clarity of thought.

In the famous narrative of the succession to the throne of David (II Samuel 9-20; I Kings 1-2) we have the most remarkable historical monument of the ancient world before Herodotus, five centuries later. In some respects it is better than Herodotus in its precision, its vividness of outline, and its deep sense of the drama of unfolding events. In all early Hebrew historical narrative, including especially the J-E complex in the Pentateuch,[29] parts of Joshua-Judges and

[28] Hebrew *NQM* seldom means "avenge" but rather "save," as I saw first in *naqāmu* (not *ekēmu*) of the Amarna tablets and G. Dossin saw first in the still earlier Mari texts. G. E. Mendenhall's study of *NQM*, which he has felicitously combined with Latin *vindex* and *vindicare*, is still to be published; it should revolutionize our knowledge of whole areas of Israelite religious terminology.

[29] On the literary character of J-E see my observations in *Catholic Biblical*

Samuel, we have a clarity, a simplicity and objectivity completely lacking in earlier historical writing from the Ancient Orient.[30] If we turn to law, the story is somewhat different. Whereas in science—for instance in mathematics—the Ancient Orientals never stated general theorems or propositions, but only listed individual cases in the form of specific problems, in law the Babylonians early reached the point where they could begin to generalize. Casuistic law of Mesopotamian inspiration is now illustrated by six non-Israelite codes and collections of laws, ranging in date from the reign of Ur-Nammu, founder of Ur III (ca. 2050 B.C.), to the twelfth century B.C. Some of the laws in question were actually copied some time after their original compilation, so these dates are probably too late in several instances. These codes would then all be pre-Mosaic.

Nowhere in pre-Israelite laws can one find the degree of generalization that there is, for example, in the Ten Commandments. In the so-called apodictic law of Israel, i.e., in the moral and religious law which commands peremptorily without basing itself on court cases, one finds generalization far beyond anything known in the Ancient Orient: "Thou shalt not kill." (This does not mean "thou shalt not kill" in the modern English sense but in the Elizabethan meaning of "kill": *lo tirṣaḥ* means "thou shalt not commit murder." We do not have *lo taháróg*, "thou shalt not slay," i.e., "thou shalt not kill" in present-day English, nor *lo tiṭbaḥ*, "thou shalt not slaughter [an animal].")

It is important to bear in mind when dealing with this early codified law that the seeds of formal syllogistic reasoning are already there, merely waiting for a favorable climate in order to sprout. To illustrate, let us take one of the simplest Babylonian case laws (from Eshnunna, ca. 1800 B.C.): "If a man cuts off a man's finger, he shall pay two-thirds of a silver mina" (§ 43). This may be put into syllogistic terms as follows:

A man who cuts off another man's finger shall pay two-thirds of a silver mina;

Quarterly, 25, 1963, pp. 1-11; and Martin Noth, *Überlieferungsgeschichte des Pentateuch*, 1948, pp. 20-44.
[30] Note the words of Eduard Meyer, *Geschichte des Altertums*, I, 1, 3d ed.; 1910, pp. 227-230. Contrast R. G. Collingwood, *The Idea of History*, Oxford, 1946, pp. 16-17, who dismisses the Old Testament as "theocratic history."

This man has cut off another man's finger;
Therefore he shall pay two-thirds of a mina of silver.

If an early Babylonian had been presented with such a cumbersome way of formulating a simple law, he would doubtless have considered it an insult to his intelligence just as, when I was a boy of ten plunged into the midst of a third-form class in Euclid, I became exasperated listening to a classmate explain how to locate the center of a circle according to Euclid—I wanted to bypass the demonstration and locate the center with a compass. Yet Aristotle was to revolutionize thinking with the syllogism!

Essentially the same fallacy in reverse appears in E. Adamson Hoebel's analysis of modern primitive customary law, in which he finds whole series of postulates and corollaries.[31] One after another, he analyzes the laws (never codified by the natives, of course) of the Eskimo, the Ifugao (Philippines), the Plains Indians, the Trobriand Islanders (east of New Guinea), and the Ashanti (Africa), reducing them all to terms of formal logic. Of course this can be done, since of all human institutions law is perhaps most affected by experience. But it is the modern investigator who does this, not the more or less primitive tribesman; it is thus characteristic of modern analysis of all pre-Greek cultural elements of empirical origin. Hoebel's mistake is that he fails to draw this distinction and so has been quoted as attributing logical reasoning to primitives (cf. above on Macdonald).

Proportionately, the generalizations in Biblical law far exceed the legal generalizations of the Ancient Orient. For example, the principle "an eye for an eye, a life for a life," etc., the so-called *lex talionis*, is often supposed to be very primitive. Not at all! It is nowhere found in the Ancient Orient except in late Phoenician texts, where it appears in a religious context.[32] (In the Code of Hammurapi, ca. 1690 B.C., it is presupposed as a practice within social classes, but even then it is implicit, not explicit.) I do not deny that it may go back to pre-Israelite times, but we actually find it first in the Old Testament. For the first time in any legislation the prin-

[31] See Hoebel, *The Law of Primitive Man: A Study in Comparative Legal Dynamics*, 1954, pp. 67 ff., 100 ff., 127 ff., 177 ff., 211 ff.
[32] See Albrecht Alt, "Zur Talionsformel," in *Kleine Schriften zur Geschichte des Volkes Israel*, Vol. I, 1953, pp. 341-344.

ciple of equal justice for all, regardless of class or wealth, is enunciated. That alone was a tremendous advance. Furthermore, in the Hebrew Bible we never find use of the common Babylonian and Hittite assumption that a man can escape a severe penalty if he is rich or well-born, a penalty which would fall without mitigation on the poor man or the slave. Equal justice for all is at the heart of Mosaic jurisprudence. No rabbinic or Christian refinement can abolish this uniqueness of Mosaic legal tradition.[33]

And lastly the religion of Israel—only one God. This is the view of the entire Old Testament—only one God who reigns over all that exists. In the ancient Orient there were many gods, and there was constant conflict of interest, conflict of sex, conflict of function, conflict of territorial claims, and even conflict of name. The gods shade into one another and change form constantly. There is utter confusion, a confusion affecting gods by the scores and hundreds. The Canaanites assumed that they had seventy gods, seventy sons of the great god El and his consort, Asherah. The Babylonians listed thousands of divine names and appellations. Hundreds of them are mentioned in the earliest lists from before 2500 b.c. But in the Old Testament there is no conflict between the functions of God. He is one God who is over all, one God of morality and human relations,[34] one God of all nations, one God over all nature. There is one God who is in supreme control of destiny, one God who creates man with free will—man who may rebel if he wishes and whose rebellion becomes the archetypic sin. The Old Testament thus marks an epoch in human thinking—a transformation which was to revolutionize man's relation to man. This change was largely due to the intuitive[35] discovery that the incongruities of polytheism flouted the

[33] Note also that there is a wealth of data illustrating the empirical origin of *kóšer* and *ṭerēfah*, and of a host of other practices and regulations in the cultic law of the Pentateuch, with which I expect to deal in my "History of the Religion of Israel" (already in its first manuscript draft).

[34] The Wisdom literature of Israel is another rich source of empirically derived material, with which I expect to deal in Volume II of the present series.

[35] By "intuition, intuitive" I mean subconscious interpretation of empirical information received and registered by the human brain. All ordinary intuition is of this kind, but as a theist I gladly accept the role of divine Providence in the process. Since we shall never be able to explain in full how our minds operate, there is not the slightest chance for our experience of the normal regularities of mental action to be upset except in the case of true miracles.

empirically recognized unity of nature. Without for a moment denying the intuitive nature of revelation or its source in Almighty God, we can, as human beings, speaking in the light of personal and historical experience, see how the thought of the Old Testament fits into wider patterns and configurations, attaining—within its own limits—universal cogency. In this thought there are no arbitrary postulates; all assumptions are implicit in experience (though the experience may have to be corrected in the light of new situations, as in Hebrew theodicy). From the empirico-logical thought of the Old Testament one simply cannot deduce ideological conclusions suitable to the purposes of demagogues. Neither Fascism nor Communism is imaginable in the thought-world of ancient Israel.

PART TWO

SURVEYS OF SPECIAL AREAS

Chapter 4

How well can we know
the ancient Near East?[1]

The study of the ancient Near East stands on the frontier of humanistic research, since it is perhaps the most difficult branch of learning to justify on obvious utilitarian grounds. Not only does it belong to a remote and now relatively unimportant part of the earth, but it appertains to a time which has been called "the past past" in the jargon of a certain group of thinkers. It is not strange that students of the Ancient Orient must often be asked to give reason for their faith in the value of their chosen field of investigation. Nor is it remarkable that attacks on this field become more frequent as its absolute importance grows. In some places the unprecedented expansion of Ancient Oriental studies since 1885 has led to their being given a somewhat factitious academic place, as in Germany before 1933, with the natural result that the representatives of other disciplines rebel against the apparent lack of proportion.

The brilliant career of the late James Henry Breasted has made America the focus of interest in the recovery of the Ancient Orient. With the rapid decline of attention to our studies in the German

[1] Presidential address, delivered at the annual meeting of the American Oriental Society in New Haven, April 15, 1936, and published in the James Henry Breasted Memorial issue of the *Journal of the American Oriental Society*, 56, 1936, pp. 121-144. There have been numerous minor stylistic changes and some deletions in the text; over a score of notes have been added (in brackets) to bring the story up to date, contrasting the state of knowledge in 1935 with what we know in 1963.

universities since 1933, America is in process of becoming the academic center of research in this field. Our leading universities have recognized its importance by establishing departments in which it receives attention. Our museums are fast leaving the universities behind, with the notable exception of the University of Chicago. However, all this interest is somewhat artificial, since it rests too exclusively on the organizing ability of a very few enthusiastic scholars, and not on a spontaneous academic demand. It behooves us, accordingly, to inspect our defenses, in order that we may not be caught napping by an onslaught from an unexpected direction. We are always surrounded by real or potential foes who think that they can use our modest income to balance some tiny deficit in their budgets.

A determined onslaught on our position has been made by the German classical historian of the University of Leipzig, Helmuth Berve, known for two large works in the field of Greek and Hellenistic history.[2] His attack, which is only a symptom of a widespread attitude in Germany, appeared in Walter Goetz's *Archiv für Kulturgeschichte*. In this paper, entitled "Zur Kulturgeschichte des alten Orients," Berve describes the state of this research, as illustrated by the work of Kees, Goetze, and Christensen, praises the brilliant synthesis produced by these scholars, and maintains that with the appearance of their publications the field has been exhausted, so far as its utility for the general historian is concerned. "The *Kulturgeschichte des alten Orients* is by no means superfluous or without significance. On the contrary, it is epochal in its importance, precisely because it stands at the end of the positivistic age, whose tremendous work it synthetizes in splendid fashion. . . . It stands at the boundary (of the two ages) as a proud monument of German scholarly investigation. . . ."[3]

Why has Berve declared that the field now ceases to have any value as a subject of academic research? He writes: "The science of the Ancient Orient is condemned to inactivity at the moment when the formulation of intellectual problems passes beyond the domain in which facts may be established by reason, in so far as it is concerned with peoples of another race, of another nature, which are,

[2] *Das Alexanderreich auf prosopographischer Grundlage*, 2 vols., 1926; *Griechische Geschichte*, 2 vols., 1931-1933.
[3] *Archiv für Kulturgeschichte*, 25, 1934, p. 230 (article pp. 216-230).

therefore, incomprehensible (to us) in the depths of their individuality. This science thus fails to measure up to the requirements of the new standard of values, and consequently loses its right to exist. For the requirements of the new standard of values have become inexorably real for the historical sciences, at least within the realm of German intellectual spirit."[4] Again he says: "Without a definite, universally binding evaluation, it is impossible to carry on productive investigation. This is not only an irresistible deduction from our present cultural or political situation, which denies the right of existence to a science without (our) standard of values, but it is also an inner necessity of science itself, which is beginning to find its way back to the instinctive judgment expressed by Treitschke in the beautiful words, 'Man can only understand what he loves.' "[5] Berve then proceeds to assert that one cannot understand the exotic, uncanny life of the Ancient Orient, and that accordingly one cannot love it. Q. E. D.

It is not necessary for us to dwell at length on the further discussion of the subject by Berve. As might be expected, it pivots on the dogma of the *Rassengedanke*, and the author quotes with approval the views of Ludwig Ferdinand Clauss, *Die nordische Seele*. For Anglo-Saxons, whose sober realism revolts against the metaphysical subtleties of racist psychology, and above all, for Americans, proud of the many racial and national strains which have gone into the formation of our synthetic people, it is impossible to love these romantic unrealities, though we may claim to understand them, just as we may try to comprehend quantum physics. But Berve has made it necessary for the Orientalist who would be an impartial thinker to take stock and to justify his labor to himself, as well as to others.

First we shall make a rapid survey of the progress achieved hitherto in the recovery of the Ancient Orient, in all spheres of investigation. Then we shall compare the methods employed in our field with those used in other comparable fields. Thirdly, we shall frankly ask ourselves, What is the utility of our studies? Finally, we shall contrast the nihilism of a Berve with the buoyant optimism of a Breasted.

In 1835 almost nothing was known about the Ancient Orient, outside of the information to be secured from the Bible and from a few fragmentary Greek sources. Champollion's posthumous grammar of

[4] *Ibid.*, p. 229, below.
[5] *Ibid.*, p. 227.

Egyptian was just beginning to appear in print, thus closing the period of stagnation that set in after the great decipherer's death. Wilkinson was about to publish the first serious attempt to gather the rich pictorial material from Egyptian tombs and temple walls together in a description of ancient Egyptian life. Hincks and Lepsius were just beginning the researches which later transformed Egyptology into a respectable young science. Cuneiform studies were still in their swaddling clothes; Grotefend's first essays at the decipherment of Persian had been finally published, but were still regarded with skepticism by the few who knew of them; Burnouf's important treatise, in which sound philological method was first employed, was just about to appear. Nothing whatever was yet known about Assyrian; Gesenius and Rödiger had not yet published the results of their studies in the Phoenician and South Arabian inscriptions; hardly any other of the many scripts and languages now known had even been discovered. The state of field and comparative archaeology was worse, since no one had even made a beginning in these disciplines, now of so great importance.

During the half century from 1835 to 1885, the foundations of our knowledge of the Ancient Orient were solidly laid. Egyptology was developed by a remarkable little group of men, led by scholars of the caliber of Lepsius and Brugsch, Birch and Goodwin, de Rougé and Chabas. Lepsius' colossal publication, *Denkmäler aus Aegypten und Nubien* (1849-1856) provided a mass of reliable monumental material for study, and Brugsch's *Hieroglyphisch-demotisches Wörterbuch* (1867-1868, 1880-1882) gave an elaborate collection of words and meanings, which was not to be superseded for over half a century. But at the end of the period in question there was still no clear idea of the grammatical structure of Egyptian, and the only grammar with any claim to scientific method was Erman's *Neuägyptische Grammatik* (1880). In 1850 Mariette began his long career as excavator, but his undertakings were nearly always conducted in his absence by natives, and never rose beyond the category of archaeological treasure hunts, however great their value as pioneer work under difficult conditions may have been. It was not until the end of 1884 that Flinders Petrie began excavating at Naucratis, where he laid the foundations of a new excavating technique.

In the field of Assyriology even more spectacular successes were achieved. The decipherment of Old Persian was completed with the publication of Rawlinson's edition of the great Behistun inscription in 1846. The Assyrian enigma proved harder to unravel, but yielded to the onslaughts of Hincks, Rawlinson, and others, between 1846 and 1855. By the latter year general agreement was reached among cuneiformists, but it was over twenty years before all competent Semitists were convinced that cuneiform had been successfully deciphered. This failure to be convinced was naturally due to the lack of strict philological method on the part of cuneiform scholars like George Smith and Jules Oppert. It was not until the German school of Assyriology was founded by Schrader in 1872, and developed by Friedrich Delitzsch (1874 ――) and his pupils, especially Haupt (1879 ――), Zimmern (1885 ――), and Jensen (1885 ――), that rigid linguistic and philological methods were employed. But at the end of our period there was still no proper grammar or dictionary of Assyrian. Mesopotamian excavation, thanks to the devoted efforts of men like Botta, Layard, Place, and de Sarzec, was definitely on a plane above that of Egyptian excavation, though still primitive when measured by present-day methods. The interpretation of West Semitic inscriptions, brilliantly inaugurated at the opening of our period by Gesenius, reached a high-water level with Schröder's *Die phönizische Sprache* (1869), and continued to develop, thanks to the work of Renan, Clermont-Ganneau, and others. The state of archaeological research remained exceedingly low in Syria and Palestine, however, though Clermont-Ganneau and de Vogüé laid solid foundations, and though an invaluable archaeological survey was undertaken by the English Palestine Exploration Fund. In Asia Minor the Hittite inscriptions had been identified and partly collected (Sayce, 1877 ――); Schliemann (1870 ――) had begun stratigraphical excavation with his work at Troy. But neither scientific philology nor scientific archaeology, as we understand these disciplines today, had come into the scene yet, though both had already appeared on the horizon.

The years from 1885 to 1935 have been a period of increasingly intensive research, and of the most extraordinary expansion in our knowledge of the Ancient Orient, in every possible direction. Let us first consider the advance made in the field of linguistics and philology, and then we may turn to examine the state of the added disciplines, systematic excavating technique and comparative archaeology.

It was at the very outset of the latest period that a solid foundation for the knowledge of Egyptian and Accadian (of which Assyrian is only a dialect) was laid by Erman, Sethe, Steindorff, and Delitzsch. In the Egyptian field three grammatical works of the highest importance were published: Erman's *Sprache des Papyrus Westcar* (1889), *Aegyptische Grammatik* (1894), and Sethe's great work, *Das Aegyptische Verbum* (1899-1902). Together with Steindorff's work on the laws of Coptic vocalization, these volumes transformed the vague conception of Egyptian grammar which had been cherished by all scholars into a well-knit structure. Egyptologists like Naville, Renouf, and even Maspero rejected most of the "Berlin grammar" to the end of their life; now, of course, there is not a single competent Egyptologist left who does not accept it fully. In 1897 Erman began to collect material for a complete Egyptian dictionary, which began publication in 1925; by 1931 all words and meanings were available in five large volumes.[6] Gunn (*Studies in Egyptian Syntax*, 1923) and Gardiner (*Egyptian Grammar*, 1927) progressed notably beyond the stage reached by Erman and Sethe, while Erman himself, in his *Neuägyptische Grammatik* (second edition, entirely rewritten, 1933) brought the important language of the New Empire into linguistic shelter.[7] Even the problem of vocalization, particularly difficult in a script where only consonants are written as a rule, is being solved (Sethe, Albright, 1923 ——).[8] We are now ready for a period of fruitful activity in the field of comparative Hamito-Semitic research, which will undoubtedly contribute much to our understanding of the evolution of the Egyptian language, as well as of the relations between Egypt and Asia.

[6] [In 1935-1963 appeared the five volumes of *Belegsstellen*, without which the *Wörterbuch* has only limited effectiveness. H. Ranke's magnificent two-volume collection of Egyptian personal names (*Die ägyptischen Personennamen*) was completed in 1952.]

[7] [We now have excellent additional aids, such as the third edition of Gardiner's *Egyptian Grammar*, 1957, and Elmar Edel's *Altägyptische Grammatik*, I, 1955.]

[8] [In 1934 appeared my monograph, *The Vocalization of the Egyptian Syllabic Orthography*, which remained without impact—except for various studies by myself and T. O. Lambdin—until it was accepted in full by W. Helck in his monumental work, *Die Beziehungen Aegyptens zu Vorderasien im 3. und 2. Jahrtausend v. Chr.*, 1962. (Such thirty-year lags are common enough in science and scholarship, especially in border fields.) The reconstruction of the vocalization in general, begun independently by Sethe and myself (first publication in 1923), is now being carried forward energetically by such able men as J. Vergote and G. Fecht.]

In the cuneiform field we can chronicle equal progress. Delitzsch's three books, *Assyrisches Wörterbuch* (1887 ——), *Assyrische Grammatik* (1889), and *Assyrisches Handwörterbuch* (1897), based mainly on his own and Haupt's work, have proved to be an even more solid foundation for Accadian than Erman's were for Egyptian, owing again to the disadvantage at which the latter was placed by the absence of vocalization in Egyptian. The field has grown more and more complex, because of the constantly increasing mass of published cuneiform inscriptions from every historical period and from every country in Western Asia. Thanks especially to the efforts of Zimmern, Meissner, Ungnad, and Landsberger, our knowledge of Accadian is remarkably exact, and a relatively complete historical grammar can be written in which the phonetic, morphological, and syntactic peculiarities of Babylonian and Assyrian can be traced for about 2500 and 1200 years, respectively, while much can be said about local dialects.[9] Owing to the progress of comparative Semitic grammar in the hands of Barth, Brockelmann, and many others, it is possible to trace the evolution of Accadian through a period of over three millennia. The lexicographical studies of Meissner, Landsberger, Bezold, and others have vastly enriched Accadian lexicography, while work on the Chicago Assyrian Dictionary will before long provide an invaluable tool for research in this field.[10] It is surprising how few passages in Accadian literature still defy interpretation. Owing to the wealth of material available, the prospect of rapid progress in clearing away the remaining obscurities and uncertainties is much brighter in Accadian than in Egyptian.[11]

When we turn to the remaining scripts and languages of the ancient Near East, it is impossible not to be surprised by the uninterrupted discovery of new scripts as well as new languages. The

[9] [See esp. W. von Soden, *Grundriss der akkadischen Grammatik*, 1952, and I. Gelb, *Old Akkadian Writing and Grammar*, 2d ed., 1961, and *Glossary of Old Akkadian*, 1957, which contains much grammatical material.]

[10] [The *Chicago Assyrian Dictionary* began finally to appear under the editorship of A. L. Oppenheim in 1956; seven volumes have subsequently appeared. Also in progress is another important dictionary, W. von Soden's *Akkadisches Handwörterbuch*.]

[11] [This is even truer in 1963 than in 1935, since the gap between the total amount of published Egyptian and cuneiform written material is widening all the time in favor of the latter. After all, clay tablets are much more enduring than papyrus!]

day of diminishing returns has not dawned; every year or two seems to yield at least one new script, and the number of new languages and dialects increases by geometric progression.[12] Hittite cuneiform has been deciphered, and Hittite may now be read better than Accadian was in 1885. Thanks to Hrozný (1915 ——), Forrer, Friedrich, Goetze, Sommer, Sturtevant, and others, our knowledge of Hittite grammar and lexicography is as solidly established as that of Accadian then was, though perhaps not so complete.[13] But with the publication of the Boghazköy texts, numerous other tongues have become accessible to the investigator, including Hurrian and Luwian. The former has become particularly important, owing to the decipherment of the Ugaritic alphabet, in which a number of Hurrian texts are found, and to the publication of the tablets from the Kirkûk region, which are full of Hurrian names and words. The Hurrian field is being opened up rapidly, owing to the work of Messerschmidt, Bork, Ungnad, Thureau-Dangin, Friedrich, and Speiser, to mention the men who have worked most effectively here.[14] Its potential importance is very great. Closely related to Hittite and Luwian is the tongue of the Hittite hieroglyphic texts, which long defied decipherment, but has been attacked with marked success by Meriggi (1928 ——), Forrer, Gelb, Bossert, and Hrozný.[15] We have no room here to speak of the progress made in the study of Lycian, Lydian, Vannic, etc., in which domains Friedrich and Meriggi are easily the ablest of the men now at work. Nor can we speak of Elamite in detail, but it must be observed that the recovery from Persepolis of thousands of documents written in Neo-Susian provides a mine of material for future investigators.[16]

---

[12] [This optimistic statement was still true in 1935, but the rate of decipherment has since outstripped that of discovery of new scripts.]

[13] [We now have two admirable works by J. Friedrich, *Hethitisches Elementarbuch, I: Grammatik*, 2d ed., 1960, *II: Lesestücke*, 1946, and *Hethitisches Wörterbuch*, 1952-1961. Among the most active scholars in this field today are H. G. Güterbock, H. Otten, and A. Kammenhuber.]

[14] [E. A. Speiser's *Introduction to Hurrian*, 1941, placed the study of this language on a solid footing.]

[15] [In 1946 H. Th. Bossert discovered and subsequently published the Karatepe bilingual inscriptions in Hittite hieroglyphs and Phoenician. The decipherment of this script is virtually completed by the work of E. Laroche, *Les hiéroglyphes hittites*, 1960, and P. Meriggi, *Hieroglyphisch-Hethitisches Glossar*, 2d ed., 1962.]

[16] [This work has been carried on especially by G. G. Cameron, H. Paper, R. T. Hallock, and W. Hinz.]

The most interesting and difficult of all the languages written in cuneiform is undoubtedly Sumerian, a tongue which was already dead before 1500 B.C., though it was cultivated in Babylonian priestly circles even beyond the Christian Era. For decades there were able scholars who denied its existence as a real speech, maintaining that it was an artificial creation of the priests. Since 1900 no competent student has held this view, which seems absurd in the light of our present knowledge. Thanks especially to the work of Thureau-Dangin, Langdon, Delitzsch, Deimel, and Poebel, whose *Sumerische Grammatik* (1923) was epoch-making, we possess a very good knowledge of Sumerian. In Delitzsch's *Sumerisches Glossar* and Deimel's *Sumerisches Lexikon* we possess useful dictionaries, though the number of workers in this field is too small for rapid progress. However, the importance of Sumerian is undoubtedly growing steadily, and new workers are certain to be attracted to so interesting and productive a field.[17]

If we turn to the Semitic alphabetic scripts and the inscriptions written in them, we shall also note unprecedented progress. First came the discoveries of very early Canaanite (Hebrew) and Aramaic inscriptions at Sham'al (Zinjirli) in northern Syria (1888 ——). In 1923 the discovery of the sarcophagus of Aḥîrâm, king of Byblus, carried the antiquity of the Phoenician alphabet back several centuries, and nearly every year since then has witnessed the finding of additional evidence for the antiquity of the alphabet. Gardiner's partial decipherment (1915) of the Proto-Sinaitic inscriptions, found first by Petrie in 1905, was followed by the discovery of more inscriptions and by numerous attempts at decipherment (Cowley, Eisler, Grimme, Sprengling, Butin, Albright, etc.), none of which is convincing.[18] Meanwhile several finds have almost closed the gap

[17] [S. N. Kramer began his already long and brilliant career as a Sumerologist in 1936, as a pupil of A. Poebel. Since then he has accomplished miracles in gathering and publishing the vast collections of Sumerian tablets and fragments in the museums of the world. Some idea of his astonishing achievements may be obtained from his latest book, *The Sumerians: Their History, Culture, and Character*, 1963. While he has been busy with publication, A. Falkenstein (e.g., *Grammatik der Sprache Gudeas von Lagaš*, 1949-1950) and Th. Jacobsen have greatly advanced our knowledge of Sumerian philology.]

[18] [My 1935 attempt at decipherment was not as bad as I thought. In 1948 (*Bulletin of the American Schools of Oriental Research*, No. 110) I was able to make a decisive advance, after the Sinai expedition of 1947-1948, and I am now about to publish the results of my continued work on these and related

between these texts and the oldest ones of Phoenicia.[19] The Phoenician alphabet is thus carried back a thousand years before the date of the Mesha Stone. However, the most recent discoveries have complicated the problem of scripts in Syria-Palestine by disclosing the existence of at least four other systems of writing: the cuneiform alphabet of Ugarit, the syllabic script of Byblus,[20] a new alphabetiform script from the same place,[21] and a linear script from Moab.[22]

The decipherment of the cuneiform alphabetic texts merits a special paragraph, because of its exceptional importance. Discovered almost entirely at Ugarit (Ras Shamra and Mînet el-Beiḍā) on the coast of northern Syria by Schaeffer and Chenet since 1929, they were deciphered by H. Bauer and E. Dhorme, and have been published by Virolleaud. The most important work in the interpretation of these documents has been accomplished by the above-mentioned scholars and Friedrich, Ginsberg, Montgomery, and others.[23] Since they prove to be in a northern dialect of Canaanite, and to be closely related to the Phoenician mythological literature described by Philo Byblius, there can be no reasonable doubt that we have

---

inscriptions since 1957. My 1948 results have been confirmed in general and corrected or extended in detail; the inscriptions date between ca. 1550 and 1450 B.C. and are written in good South Canaanite, with close Ugaritic and Hebrew affinities.]

[19] [On the latter see esp. Albright, *Journal of the American Oriental Society*, 67, 1947, pp. 153 ff.; F. M. Cross, Jr., *Bulletin of the American Schools of Oriental Research*, No. 134, 1954, pp. 15-24; No. 160, 1960, pp. 21-26 (with T. O. Lambdin); No. 168, 1962, pp. 12-18.]

[20] [For the official publication of these syllabic inscriptions see M. Dunand, *Byblia Grammata*, 1945. A number of attempts to decipher them have been made but the results, as far as published, do not inspire confidence. Consonants and vowels, morphology and syntax, personal and divine names must be correct; so far they are incredible. That the script is to be dated between ca. 2300 and 1800 B.C., in accord with Dunand's original views, and that it reflects early Northwest Semitic, seem likely presuppositions.]

[21] [In the autumn of 1936 I proposed that it be read, following a suggestion of H. Grimme, as early Phoenician (*Bulletin of the American Schools of Oriental Research*, No. 63, pp. 10-11), and in 1949 (*ibid.*, No. 116, pp. 12-14), in collaboration with D. N. Freedman, I proposed some modifications of my decipherment. If my views are correct they suggest a date about the twelfth century B.C.]

[22] See Horsfield and Vincent, *Revue Biblique*, 41, 1932, p. 425 and pl. XI. The

here part of the long-lost Phoenician literature of the second millennium B.C. [24]

Between 1885 and 1935 very great progress was also made in collecting and interpreting the South Arabian inscriptions, as well as the inscriptions and graffiti in derived alphabets found in North Arabia, and generally called Lihyanic, Thamudic, and Safaitic. At the beginning of the period the number of available texts was greatly increased by the explorations of Glaser, and lately there has been a new influx of material, together with the first excavations. To list all the scholars who have contributed materially to the interpretation of these inscriptions would be tedious; we may single out Rhodokanakis as by far the most important recent investigator in this field.[25]

Modern archaeological technique is almost entirely the product of the half century between 1885 and 1935, and the rapidly developing field of comparative archaeology is still in its infancy. The pioneer work between 1842 and 1880 consisted almost exclusively of unsupervised digging by natives, whose work was occasionally visited by the archaeologist in charge. Perhaps the worst sinners in this respect were Mariette Pasha in Egypt and Hormuzd Rassam in Mesopotamia; the work of Botta and Layard, but especially

---

writer believes that the inscription is much older than the relief, perhaps belonging to the latter part of the third millennium. In favor of this rather revolutionary dating are the following facts. First, the inscription is carved more lightly, and has been weathered far more than the relief. Second, the relief is in a rectangular space which was lowered considerably in order to receive it, the raised figures being still materially lower than the original flat surface of the stone. Third, the horizontal line below the fourth line of text, originally separating it from a no longer existing fifth line, stands in no recognizable relationship to the upper edge of the depressed space employed for the relief. Fourth, the form of the stele resembles that of the Narâm-Sin steles from the middle of the third millennium much more closely than it does any stele of the second millennium yet known. Fifth, the script itself is not at all like any known later script, but may easily be a variant of the syllabic script of Byblus. Sixth, Balûʻah, like many other large sites in this region, was occupied in the last third of the third millennium; cf. Glueck, *Annual of the American Schools of Oriental Research*, XIV, 1934, p. 55. [See my *Archaeology and the Religion of Israel*, p. 189, n. 53; *The Archaeology of Palestine*, pp. 186f.]

[23] [Research in the field of Ugaritic received a powerful stimulus from C. H. Gordon's *Ugaritic Grammar*, 1940, which followed the unpublished system of H. L. Ginsberg, and was further encouraged by his *Ugaritic Handbook*, 1947,

of Place, was on a somewhat higher level. Best of the undertakings in this field at that time were the little-known excavations (1849 ——) of the English geologist, Loftus, who excelled in accuracy, in understanding of the possibilities of stratigraphy, and in attention to unexciting detail.

In 1870 a new era dawned in field archaeology—strangely enough as the result of the work of a dilettante banker, Heinrich Schliemann, at Hissarlik, generally believed to be the site of Homeric Troy. Here for the first time it was recognized that a town site might contain the accumulation of many successive periods of occupation, separated by more or less complete destructions. This discovery, which seems so obvious today, was long opposed by archaeologists of standing. However, Schliemann's method remained primitive and rather ruthless until Dörpfeld joined his staff in 1882 and created the technique of digging mounds. Dörpfeld's outstanding achievement lay in the emphasis he placed on accurate planning and leveling of constructional remains, with careful analysis of details.

The next major contribution was made by Flinders Petrie in Egypt (1880 ——). Possessed of uncommon originality and independence of approach, he soon discovered that such unimportant

---

and *Ugaritic Manual*, 1955, both of which represented revisions and expansions of the 1940 work. New Ugaritic texts continue to be published by Ch. Virolleaud, and the contents of the 1960 archive promise to rival the original finds in importance. The latest dictionary of Ugaritic is J. Aistleitner's *Wörterbuch der ugaritischen Sprache*, edited by O. Eissfeldt, 1963. My own active publication in the Ugaritic field began in April, 1932, and continued until 1944; since then my unpublished studies have continued to accumulate, and I hope to resume publication very shortly.]

[24] [See the detailed treatment in Vol. II of the present series.]

[25] [Scientific excavation began in 1937-1938 (Gertrude Caton Thompson at Ḥureiḍa in Ḥaḍramaut), and was resumed in 1950 by the American Foundation for the Study of Man; for details as to the work accomplished since then see G. W. Van Beek, "South Arabian History and Archaeology," in *The Bible and the Ancient Near East*, 1961, pp. 229-248. There is an excellent grammar by the leading member of the Rhodokanakis school, Maria Höfner's *Altsüdarabische Grammatik*, 1943, and an admirable handbook of South Arabian studies by Adolf Grohmann: *Arabien* (*Handbuch der Altertumswissenschaft*, III.1.3.3.4, 1963). The foremost students of the inscriptions today are G. Ryckmans and his pupil, A. Jamme; the latter's volume, *Sabaean Inscriptions from Maḥram Bilqîs* (*Mârib*), published in 1962, marks an era.]

remains as broken pottery might be used to advantage for chronological purposes. The turning point came at Naucratis in 1885, where Greek painted pottery provided the point of departure. At Tell el-Ḥesī in Palestine, five years later, he excavated stratigraphically in the second mound to be attacked in this fashion, Troy being the first; in his publication the following year he included numerous plates made up exclusively of drawings of potsherds. Contemporary archaeologists jeered, but Petrie was absolutely right, and no archaeologist who is worthy of the name today fails to devote careful attention to broken fragments of unpainted pottery, which have become the type fossils of the excavator. In 1901 Petrie capped his previous ceramic research by publishing in *Diospolis Parva* his brilliant discovery of sequence-dating.

The method of excavating, analyzing, and recording stratified constructional remains and fortifications, first introduced by Dörpfeld, was applied by his contemporary, Koldewey, who began digging at Assos in the same year that the former began at Troy, then continued at Zinjirli in Syria, and finally undertook his lifework at Babylon (1899 ——). Koldewey and his able pupils, Andrae, Jordan, Nöldeke, and others, have established the highest standards yet attained for architects' excavations in stratified sites; Koldewey himself was inclined to neglect artifacts, but his pupils have utilized them fully, as may be seen from the reports on the excavations of Assur and Warka (Erech). The architectural publications of the Koldewey school are by far the best which have yet appeared. The methods of Dörpfeld and Koldewey were brilliantly applied in Egypt by Borchardt and Hölscher.

In 1900 Reisner began his excavations in Egypt, and soon developed a new technique, which gradually superseded all earlier ones. Reisner was strongly influenced both by Borchardt and by Petrie, from whose respective schools he drew the best that they could supply. With characteristic thoroughness, he introduced American filing and recording methods, with a vastly increased use of photography. No excavator anywhere in the world has equaled the care in digging and the completeness in recording exhibited by Reisner in his best work, as in the tomb of Queen Ḥetep-ḥeres. In his archaeological work it may be said that no phase was neglected, whether the technique of field work, the recording of details, or the treatment of surveying, architecture, photography, and drawing.

Of course, all this vastly increased the cost of excavation, especially in dealing with major sites. Followed closely by his pupils, Fisher, Winlock, and others, Reisner has created the most important recent school of excavators. His methods have been copied by British archaeologists, notably by Woolley, Frankfort (whose training was almost wholly English), Garstang, Guy, Rowe, and Starkey, and have powerfully influenced German and French excavators.[26]

A high-water mark in field archaeology during the decade 1925-1935 was attained by the expeditions of the Oriental Institute, which drew the best available talent from every source. In the excavation of mounds Fisher, Frankfort, and their pupils have shown how much historical material may be recovered by digging relatively wide areas, recording everything, and interpreting the results by the most up-to-date methods of comparative archaeology. In recording inscriptions and reliefs Nelson and his assistants have raised a new standard of mechanical accuracy, artistic excellence, and sound interpretation. Hölscher's architectural work represents the culmination of the progress so far achieved by the German school. We may rest assured that, in coming years, archaeological method will become more and more refined, so that the amount excavated with a given sum of money will progressively dwindle, and the relative importance of the results obtained in a given area or volume will steadily increase. The importance of chemical, geological, and biological methods, such as pollen analysis and dendrochronology, is certain to become greater as time goes on.[27]

[26] [Since the above was written, the technique of archaeology has been greatly advanced by the work of Kathleen Kenyon, building on the foundations laid by Sir Mortimer Wheeler, her teacher in archaeology. Her excavation of Jericho (1952-1958) was in every sense an epoch-making undertaking; see esp. her *Beginning in Archaeology*, 1952, *Digging up Jericho*, 1957 and *Archaeology in the Holy Land*, 1960. See also R. E. M. Wheeler, *Archaeology from the Earth*, 1954. The importance of the new technique has been obscured by the misleading presentation of the Reisner-Fisher method and the violent attacks on its exponents by H. J. Franken in numerous reviews and other publications —somewhat toned down in his 1963 book, *A Primer of Old Testament Archaeology* (with C. A. Franken-Battershill).]

[27] [Such scientific tools are being used more and more, notably by Robert J. Braidwood and his students; for a parade example see Braidwood and Howe, *Prehistoric Excavations in Iraqi Kurdistan*, 1960. In 1948-1949 the technique of dating organic remains by radiocarbon was introduced by W. F. Libby; it has completely revolutionized all early chronology.]

Comparative archaeology is a relatively new discipline, which arose first in the study of prehistoric European materials, during the second half of the nineteenth century, as well as more or less contemporaneously in the study of painted Greek vases. It was not until the last decade of the century that the comparative study of pottery reached a level, thanks to the work of men like Furtwängler and Pottier, where it could claim independent historical value. With the general acceptance of Petrie's new point of view, this discipline has continued to develop until it is now a most effective instrument in the hands of a Frankfort. The comparative treatment of architecture in the Ancient Orient has also reached a very high standard in the work of Andrae, Watzinger, and Engelbach. Since 1919 the study of ancient art has been revolutionized by the brilliant book of H. Schäfer, *Von der ägyptischen Kunst;* the best work in the field of comparative Oriental art is being done by scholars like Moortgat. Most investigation in this field is still of unequal value, and the methodology is decidedly heterogeneous. So long as men of the caliber of Herzfeld and Moortgat (with whom the writer agrees) differ by over a millennium and a half with regard to the date of the Tell Ḥalâf orthostates, it is obvious that we are in some respects still in the kindergarten.[28] However, material improvement here can be expected only from additional stratigraphic evidence; in other words, the future development of comparative archaeology is contingent on the further extension of the methods employed by contemporary schools of field archaeology.

That we have now reached a point in our knowledge of the Ancient Orient where successful handbooks and syntheses may be

[28] [While we have advanced considerably beyond the kindergarten stage since 1936, there are still extraordinary differences of opinion. In 1936 I was still under an archaeological cloud because of my supposed major error in dating the Ghassulian culture of Palestine in the middle of the fourth millennium instead of in the late third and early second millennia B.C. Soon afterward my view was shown to be correct; it is now taken for granted. I was under another cloud for many years because of my refusal to accept H. Frankfort's view that there was no architecture or art worthy of the name in Syria, Palestine, Anatolia, and neighboring regions between ca. 1200 and ca. 850 B.C. This extraordinary position on the part of a very able archaeologist is now giving ground to a more reasonable point of view; against it see my papers (forming a trilogy) in *The Aegean and the Near East: Studies Presented to Hetty Goldman,* 1956, pp. 144-164; *Anatolian Studies,* 6, Garstang Number, 1956, pp. 75-85; *Eretz-Israel,* 5, Mazar Volume, 1958, pp. 1*-9*.]

written, has been emphasized by Berve, though we do not agree that this point marks the end of productive investigation—quite the contrary! Egyptian culture has been adequately and authoritatively portrayed by Erman, Ranke, and Kees; Mesopotamian civilization received the same treatment in Meissner's remarkably complete work; Asia Minor has been given similar consideration by Goetze; Watzinger and Nielsen have prepared handbooks of Palestinian and Arabian culture. The *Reallexikon der Vorgeschichte* and the *Reallexikon der Assyriologie* are examples of efforts to fill the increasing need for cyclopedic treatment of the Ancient Oriental data, a need well provided for in the classical field by Pauly-Wissowa, Daremberg-Saglio, etc.

Comparisons are often invidious, but they are always instructive if accurately and clearly made. The student of the Ancient Orient may properly ask whether he is abreast of investigators in other similar fields of research, comparing each separate phase with analogous phases elsewhere. We may safely expect that the general result of such comparisons will be satisfactory, but that there will be departments of investigation in which the Orientalist has either not caught up with scholars in other fields, or has fallen behind them. When we take the relative paucity of workers in our field into account, this expectation seems only reasonable.

In the department of linguistic study a comparison will yield very unequal results. The Orientalist is undoubtedly more at home in the technique of decipherment, and is, therefore, more likely to be successful in problems of this nature. The methods used by grammarians and lexicographers are the same, and considering the relative difficulty of our material, our results are as good. In fact, the classical scholar is perhaps more likely to accept meanings and methods on authority. On the other hand, the temptation to be cavalier in the treatment of grammatical obscurities is undoubtedly greater in the interpretation of imperfectly understood texts, and is characteristic of many contemporary students in our field. Comparative linguistic science has been more honored in the breach than in the observance, as pointed out in 1935 by Roland G. Kent, but it must be emphasized that the situation in the Semitic field was not nearly as serious as he indicated, since his illustrations were drawn from the work of scholars recognized as linguistically incompetent in nearly all Orientalistic circles.[29] While it is quite true that analytical and interpretative philological research of the kind now familiar in the classical, modern European, and Biblical fields has only been begun by Egyptologists and Assyriologists, it is also true that the gain from this negative orientation of research has been much greater than the loss: first, because its necessarily subjective character would injure the reputation of our studies; secondly, because our field would be cluttered with unfounded hypotheses before it was completely ready for cultivation. However, Grapow and Pieper have begun to study Egyptian stylistic and literary phenomena, while Schott has commenced the historical arrangement of Accadian literary texts by statistical observation of their stylistic usages.[30]

It is not necessary to repeat what we have said about the historical relation between archaeological research in northern Mediterranean regions and in the Near East. From its very nature, archaeological technique is not bound by sharp limits, and technique may be transferred from one region to another with relative ease. On the whole, European archaeology owes more to Near Eastern studies than the reverse. The precise and painstaking attention to detail that characterizes the best Scandinavian archaeology, for example, is no greater than what was shown by Reisner and Woolley in digging royal tombs. Of course, the best North European and American archaeological work can hold up a standard of meticulous care in dealing with unexciting houses and areas which Orientalists have seldom reached. Climatic and other causes also make it difficult for the members of a staff to do much of the actual digging themselves. It is instructive to note that Kjaer's efforts to transplant Danish methods to Palestine in 1926, 1929, and 1931 did not produce the expected results; his work was very good, but did not yield any new technical method. In comparative archaeology we are witnessing a remarkable fusion of fields, especially in the hands of Childe, Frankfort, V. Müller, Matz, and others, following in the footsteps of Poulsen.

We have passed rapidly over the principal fields of Ancient

[29] [See his paper in *Journal of the American Oriental Society*, 55, 1935, pp. 121-137.]

[30] [In this field B. Landsberger and W. von Soden have been leaders; W. G. Lambert also is now doing brilliant work (see his *Babylonian Wisdom Literature*, 1960).]

Oriental research, and have appraised their present state in the light of their history and of conditions in parallel fields. Shall we set ourselves the task of estimating the extent to which we can penetrate into the heart of the Ancient Orient and can understand it as we would understand a more modern civilization? Berve's use of such terms as "exotic" and "strange" at once removes us from the domain of solid anthropological investigation to that of romanticism. His comparison of the relation between ancient Egyptian culture and modern European with the contrast between the Egyptian landscape and the European (German?) is singularly illogical. To Americans, whose country includes geographical regions as diverse from one another as the forests of Maine, the prairies of Nebraska, the jungles of central Florida, and the torrid deserts of Arizona, such a comparison belongs in the realm of the unreal. The writer, who up to 1935 had lived for twelve years of his life in Chile, for sixteen consecutive years in different parts of the United States, and for sixteen years mostly in Palestine, finds the Nile Valley, with which he is familiar, far more homelike than Prussia, where he has spent three days.

Since there is no direct, objective criterion by which we may measure the extent of our penetration into the ultimate nature (whatever that obscure term may mean) of any psychological organism, whether individual or social, we must find indirect means of estimating our knowledge. A brief consideration of the possibilities and limitations with which we are faced in dealing with any cultural phenomena of psychological nature, may be of decisive importance to us at this stage of our inquiry. The intelligent biographer has long since recognized that he cannot pierce the veil of personality, with its infinite complexity and the intricate play of combinatory factors under the visible surface. It is a commonplace that a man's wife or intimate friends often understand him much better than he does himself; yet close friends will differ radically in their estimate of a man's personality, and the gulf between Plato's and Xenophon's description of Socrates may be paralleled innumerable times in later literature. The biographical school represented by Strachey, Maurois, Nicolson, and Ludwig has tried to solve the enigma of personality by psychological methods, but this simply introduces a new group of unknown factors into an already complex situation, since the measure of correctness found in the widely diverging systems of Freud, Adler, Jung, Wertheimer, etc., cannot be objectively calculated. Maurois frankly admits that the role of the biographer is like that of the portrait painter, to reproduce the subject as he sees it, with accurate delineation of facts, with such psychological insight as he can obtain by analysis aided by flashes of intuition, and with constant attention to artistic completeness of the resulting picture.

Nor are we situated much more favorably when we deal with cultural or social groups, since the difficulty of estimating concealed psychological factors in the individual is replaced by the equal one of combining the innumerable elements and tendencies of any culture into a picture which is fair to most of the data. The same is true when we try to evaluate historical movements and to control the hidden causes of cultural mutations. Robinson's "new history" of a few decades back was really the same type of critical historiography that his predecessors had developed in the nineteenth century, colored by a new dogmatism, born of a melioristic enthusiasm. Modern historical methods have revolutionized the writing of history, because they have given us new ways in which to gather, sift, and interpret facts, and because they have placed constant emphasis on the importance of accuracy, impartiality, and caution, but they have scarcely advanced our objective grasp of causes at all. The importance of the philosophy of history is very great—never perhaps greater—but its value consists in widening our horizon and in giving us a clearer understanding of epistemological questions, not in enlarging our store of factual data. The same is true, *mutatis mutandis*, of the philosophy of science, in which interest has grown so steadily of late.

It is, therefore, true that we cannot fully understand any culture or any historical field. The more we love it, in fact, the more prejudiced we become and the less able to see it in proper perspective. Even facts are distorted when we see them through a diffracting medium. Treitschke's dictum, cited above, is thus in part directly opposed to the facts. It is not an accident that the two most remarkable pictures of American culture, from different aspects, which we possess, come from the British statesman Bryce, and the French journalist Siegfried. Both saw America with interested, but critical eyes. All that prevented Eduard Meyer's wartime description of America from being equally good is probably the hostile, and consequently unfavorably prejudiced, attitude which war psychology imposed upon his otherwise remarkably fair judgment. In other words, the soundest judgments come, not from the blind lover of country and culture, but from the sympathetic, yet dispassionate, foreign observer. An Erman or a Breasted could understand ancient Egypt better in some ways than a pharaoh or a learned scribe, even though the modern interpreter may lack many details needed to present a complete picture. The main difference between our comprehension of ancient and of modern culture is that our knowledge of the former is more fragmentary than our knowledge of the latter. In all fundamental respects there is little difference.

The doubter may ask with Berve: But what of the strange Ancient Oriental world or worlds of ideas and religion? Our reply will be identical: There is no fundamental psychological difference. The religions of Egyptians, Mesopotamians, pre-philosophical or illiterate Greeks, and of pagan Germans were closely parallel in their conceptual imagery and in the tendencies which they exhibited. The far-reaching studies of Bertholet on *Dynamismus*, on *Götterspaltung und Göttervereinigung* apply with equal cogency to all. As we shall see below, there is no road from primitive and savage thought to Europe which does not pass directly through the Ancient Orient. It is likely that we have a clearer idea of the *ku3* ("ka") than the ancient Egyptian possessed, and that the term *ikkibu* means as much to us, in every conceptually significant sense, as it did to the Babylonian; if this is not quite true, it is simply because our material is not yet as complete as it will become. Of course, these terms connoted many more concrete associations to the men of the Ancient Orient, but the genetic and comparative data which clarify our understanding of them were denied to the latter.

There is another, highly important, side to the question of the extent of our knowledge, a side which Berve has correctly emphasized, the *Wertforderung*. Knowledge is not only useless, we can not even obtain full possession of it unless it can somehow be made serviceable, unless it proves fruitful. This certainly does not mean that knowledge must be exposed for sale in the market place at the earliest opportunity; it does not mean that Egyptian medicine may supplant modern practices, nor that knowledge of Sumerian may mysteriously bring its possessor nearer to the fountainhead of theosophic wisdom. In other words, it does not mean that knowledge should be utilitarian in the shortsighted meaning which this term generally has. But racist romanticism and rational empiricism agree that knowledge must somehow be made useful if it is worth cultivation, and even if it merits the designation "knowledge." Our final task will thus be to point out some ways in which our knowledge of the Ancient Orient can be useful.

Our knowledge of the Ancient Orient is so many-sided that one is at a loss which elements to stress. Its most obvious importance lies in the field of history. Every archaeological and philological discovery made in the Ancient Orient has contributed something to show the continuity and essential solidarity of Western culture, beginning in the eastern Mediterranean basin, including Mesopotamia, and shifting to Europe. The recovery of the Ancient Orient has doubled the span of human history as recorded in contemporary written documents; it has nearly trebled the duration of archaeologically recorded sedentary society. In thus extending the chronological scope of Western, European history, it has given us a vastly enlarged perspective in studying all phases of history, from material culture to the history of religion. The light cast by this new knowledge on the development of the religious institutions which preceded and partly inspired our own, is alone worth all the effort put into the Ancient Oriental field. Some idea of the increasing influence exerted by the latter on philosophers of history may be obtained from a survey of the widespread repercussions of Petrie's theory of cycles of civilization, as recently sketched by O. G. S. Crawford. Spengler's grandiose but oracular synthesis will be followed by many others.[31]

It would be easy to give innumerable illustrations of specific gains in various branches of the disciplines which deal with man. The futility of attempting to separate man's past from his present seldom needs to be emphasized in the Old World, all too conscious of the impracticability of escaping from the past, but in the New World it has not been clearly recognized except by a limited number of scholars and thinkers. In fact, there is a certain school of thought, once centered in Chicago, which speaks of the "past past"—as though there were any fundamental difference between a past that is partly accessible through direct oral testimony, and a past that is

[31] [See esp. my discussion, *From the Stone Age to Christianity*, 1957 ed., pp. 5-8, 82-126, (Chapter II), and see also on Toynbee, below, Chapter 11.]

accessible chiefly through the written record of oral witnesses! We need not follow Jung and believe that man's subconscious mind transmits countless impulses inherited from the past and translatable into symbolic form, but the fact remains that our modern culture may be traced back to an even greater number of sources, partly in barbarian Eurasia, but at least as often in the Ancient Orient. Since our thinking remains conditioned by cultural forms, we are just as much children of the past as though we actually inherited ancestral motifs and symbols of thought.

Contemporary scientific thought is coming more and more to see the importance of studying any organism which is the result of an evolutionary process in the light of that process—in other words, genetically or historically. This is true of biological organisms, it is true of any system of thought, and it is just as true of any science. Modern sociology is unintelligible to the philosopher without a rather intimate knowledge of its history—a much longer one than many contemporary sociologists believe. In the history of a given type of social organization, or a given system of law or religion, it will be impossible in the future to overlook the wealth of data available as the result of our work. The history of law, economics, and political science has a vast mine of material in the legal codes, business documents, contracts, and treaties which have been deciphered and interpreted by Assyriologists and jurists. We venture to predict that the observations of Koschaker with regard to the relation between ancient customary law and legal formulation, or of Alt with reference to the distinction between casuistic and apodictic law, will before long be recognized as fundamental by all historians and philosophers of jurisprudence, just as the observations of Schäfer have revolutionized our understanding of the nature and development of art.

The value of the Ancient Orient for the student of cultural anthropology has not yet been adequately recognized, either by anthropologists or by specialists in the Ancient Orient. In a sense our branch of investigation is really a part of cultural anthropology, since the Ancient Orientals were in many respects in the same intellectual stage of evolution as the more advanced peoples with which the anthropologist has been concerned, e.g., the Mayas. The anthropologist is faced with many problems of a general type which he cannot solve with the data now at his disposal, as, for example, the question of the relative or absolute age of the belief in a supreme god of abstract nature, the age and source of certain myths, or of specific cultural elements. The old question of diffusion versus the principle of *Völkergedanken*, the problem of the primary or secondary character of "totemistic" phenomena, and many similar ones, demand solution. Since our written sources for primitive cultures rarely antedate the seventeenth century, and seldom, in fact, precede the nineteenth, it is obviously of the very greatest importance to have authentic material of the same kind going back five thousand years. Further discoveries and fresh decipherment will never yield any remotely comparable material in India, China, and Central America, where the texts are either recent, as in Middle America (since the Christian Era), or brief and formulaic, as in all three regions, whose earliest epigraphic records are tantalizingly terse.

In one little-appreciated respect, our new knowledge of the Ancient Orient will perhaps be of fundamental significance in the future, and here it may even help to save our seriously threatened scientific civilization. We have no historical justification for considering our boasted scientific progress as permanent; it stagnated and finally became completely inert less than two thousand years ago—why not again? Unhappily, it seems impossible for man to advance steadily in any direction for more than a relatively short time. During the past three centuries the unprecedented development of science has actually been a surface phenomenon; the hosts of magic and Neo-Gnosticism have been far more numerous, and have repeatedly gained the upper hand. So far from the situation being more favorable today [1935], precisely the opposite is true. Even in Germany, the intellectual leader of the world for a century, the movement toward irrationalism had been gaining momentum for two decades before Hitler's triumph. In 1925 the Astrologische Gesellschaft was larger than any half-dozen scientific societies together and its list of publications was more impressive than theirs. In Erman's instructive autobiography he spoke with feeling of the growth of irrational ideologies and the unmistakable eclipse of inductive science after the end of the First World War. The speed with which such forms of Ancient Oriental magic, thinly disguised, as spiritism, clairvoyance, and rhabdomancy (dowsing) were sweeping over the world in 1935 is absolutely terrifying. Dowsing was being used all over Europe (there was a flourishing British Society of Dowsers) for detecting sources of water and minerals of all kinds, as well as for plotting archaeological remains! At the Sorbonne and in British Columbia there was official recognition of the principle of dowsing over large-scale maps, instead of passing the willow wand over the actual terrain. By 1935 it had become increasingly hard to find people who did not believe in some form of spiritism, clairvoyance, astrology, or rhabdomancy. When an Assyriologist like Alfred Jeremias (d. 1935) became an admirer of Hermann Wirth, and when other forms of theosophy and of anthroposophy were accepted by numerous scholars and scientists, science was clearly in serious danger. And most of these pseudo-sciences and pseudo-disciplines have their root in the Ancient Orient; some of them, such as astrology, can be traced directly back to Babylonian sources, and the successive stages of their evolution and transmission can be mapped with considerable detail. It would be strange if the Assyriologist were yet to come to the defense of the serious astronomer!

In comparison with the value of Ancient Oriental studies for the anthropological, sociological, and historical sciences, their importance for the natural sciences and technology is insignificant. And yet it is greater than we may think. We shall not speak of accidental finds, such as Glueck's discovery of iron in the Arabah of Palestine, or of the numerous by-products of an archaeologist's activity, since they do not spring from the science of the Ancient Orient. It is, however, quite germane to speak of the increasing cooperation between archaeologists and philologists, on the one hand, and geologists, geographers, botanists, zoologists, climatologists, etc., on the other. The dating of recent geological and geographical movements or events is often in the hand of the archaeologist. The Ancient Orientalist has thrown light on the date of many geophysical processes such as the movement of the north shore of the Persian Gulf or the date at which the Euphrates and Tigris changed their courses. The difficult problem of climatic cycles is almost entirely dependent on archaeological and documentary data, as was well illustrated by all Ellsworth Huntington's earliest work. Since the latter's conclusions were adopted in handbooks of meteorology, one of which devotes a special chapter to his work, the verdict of the competent archaeologist and historian is naturally important. The writer, in common with Olmstead and Edward

Meyer, maintains that Huntington was entirely wrong, and that all his archaeological and documentary data have been misinterpreted. Many problems of irrigation, forest ecology, and soil conservation are bound up with archaeological evidence to a much greater extent than we may realize. The flourishing young field of dendrochronology is inseparable from archaeology, and we may have to wait for generalization of its assumptions until it is successfully applied to Ancient Oriental material. Such physical sciences as mineralogy, chemistry, and physics may be most useful to the archaeologist, but the reverse will probably be rarely the case, if ever.[32] Even in mineralogy, however, we owe the discovery of the importance of the copper deposits of 'Omân partly to the work of a committee of the British Association for the Advancement of Science which was entrusted with the task of finding the source of Sumerian copper![33] Some very interesting chemical discoveries have arisen from the study of problems set by archaeologists. Wood's brilliant solution of the elusive problem of Tutankhamun's purple gold[34] not only yielded new scientific results, but it also brought about the rediscovery of a most interesting lost technical process— not the only one, we may safely suppose. The biologist may also gain much by cooperation, as shown by the remarkable additions to our knowledge of the history of Holocene fauna and of animal domestication by Hilzheimer, or by the instructive researches of Keimer on Egyptian flora. In fact the Ancient Orient provides a surprisingly large amount of the data employed by biologists who are interested in the evolution and migration of domesticated animals and plants.

We have spoken little of the contribution of the Ancient Orient to the humanities, as distinct from historical research. The discovery of new literary masterpieces, of new forms of written activity, of artistic *chefs d'oeuvre*, and of novel types of aesthetic expression have probably been justification enough in themselves.

---

[32] [This is no longer true. The correctness of Libby's radiocarbon technique for dating was first established by archaeological cross-dating, though its value for archaeology is now much greater than the converse. Similarly in several other fields, such as soil history and past climate, archaeological evidence often proves decisive.]

[33] Peake, *Antiquity*, 1928, pp. 452-457.

[34] See *Journal of Egyptian Archaeology*, 20, 1934, pp. 62 ff.

But the greatest justification of all from this point of view is perhaps the career of the late James Henry Breasted, whose memory this Society must ever cherish as one of its greatest assets. What he accomplished for the humanities and for humanistic research in this country cannot easily be measured, since it is so far-reaching and so many-sided. A few words with regard to it will, therefore, be decidedly germane to our theme.

In recent decades there has been no lack of provision in the United States for the natural sciences. Academic departments, industrial laboratories, and government bureaus have competed with one another in supporting teachers and investigators, while wealth has been poured into them with the hope of far-reaching technical returns. More recently there has been increasing interest in the social sciences, which have been liberally supported both by the state and by private foundations. The humanities, however, have not fared so well, for reasons which lie on the surface, but are not always realized.[35]

In part this latent hostility to the humanities is the outcome of a feeling that research in fields relating to the past history and achievements of man is useless, especially in a new land with its history before it. It arises partly also from the shortsighted conviction that only research which yields immediate results in the form of mechanical inventions and technical processes is worth while. Since most men of science are idealistic in their aims and willing to be convinced, while some are amateurs of literature and the arts, there must be another reason for this opposition to humanistic research on their part. In 1835 the study of Latin and Greek was intrenched in all American institutions of higher learning, and

[35] [Though this was written in 1936 it is even truer today. Now, however, able Orientalists can nearly always get academic posts, even though on occasion in other fields. Financing research in the humanities has become so difficult that the attention of academic circles is being directed increasingly toward the solution of the problem. When I first became a member of the Committee on Research of the American Philosophical Society in April, 1936 (just after presenting the material in this paper before the American Oriental Society), most of our grants were disbursed in aid of projects in the natural sciences. Now, after my twenty-seven years as a member of this committee, there are virtually no applications from the natural sciences, since the sums involved are too large for our resources; nearly all applications for grants come from the social sciences and especially from the humanities.]

little or no place was allowed for instruction, much less investigation, in the fields of natural science. In earlier centuries Latin and Greek had been essential elements in any adequate professional training, while experience had shown their merit as vehicles of general literary, historical, and philosophical culture. But by the middle of the nineteenth century the direct practical value of Latin and Greek in America became more and more questionable, especially since few students acquired anything but a useless smattering of them. The movement to abandon them and to substitute modern languages and science was led by the natural scientists, who fought a bitter and often discouraging battle against conservatism. This battle has long since been won, but the natural scientists have inherited from their predecessors a hostility to the very word "humanities" which by 1920 had brought humanistic research to a singularly low level in American intellectual life. That the situation is now incomparably more encouraging we owe mainly to the vision of one man, James Henry Breasted.

It is not our place here to sketch the career of our late colleague; his achievements are so well known to the members of this Society that the effort would seem rather feeble.[36] We wish, however, to stress one fact, recognized over fifteen years before this lecture by his prophetic vision: the recovery of the Ancient Orient is giving so great a spur to historical studies in general that it can only be compared with the effect upon scientific research in general of the revival of learning. In the fourteenth century few would have ventured to predict that the rediscovery of Greek literature would result in unexampled progress in the natural sciences—yet the connection is admitted by all historians. Few historians of the nineteenth century would probably have believed that the rediscovery of the Ancient Orient would revolutionize historical investigation—yet the philosopher of the twenty-first century may well regard this as self-evident.

---

[36] See now the writer's sketch, "James Henry Breasted, Humanist," below, Chapter 9.

Chapter 5

The ancient Near East and the religion of Israel[1]

Before we can advantageously compare the religion of Israel with the religions of the ancient Near East, we must appraise the state of our knowledge in both fields. Moreover, we must ask ourselves whether our interpretation of the data is affected by extrinsic considerations, such as preconceived theories of the evolution of religion. Each field has its own pitfalls. In dealing with the ancient Near East we must carefully estimate the degree of assurance with which we can translate our documents and interpret our archaeological materials. In approaching the Old Testament we must reckon not only with textual corruption but also with the elusive problem of dating. All our efforts to reconstruct the chronological order of events and documents, and to infer a satisfactory scheme of historical evolution from them, are inevitably influenced more or less strongly by our philosophical conceptions, as will be pointed out briefly below.

There are four main groups of religious literature from the ancient Near East which are of particular importance for the light

[1] The Presidential address delivered at the meeting of the Society of Biblical Literature and Exegesis on Dec. 27, 1939, at Union Theological Seminary, New York City, and published in expanded form in *Journal of Biblical Literature*, 59, 1940, pp. 85-112. The present form represents a revision to date, with changes in the text whenever necessary for clarity or accuracy. New paragraphs and notes are enclosed in brackets.

they throw on the origin and background of Hebrew religion: Egyptian, Mesopotamian (Sumero-Accadian), West Semitic (Canaanite, Aramean, South Arabian), and Hurro-Hittite. In every case it is much more important to know whether a translation is philologically reliable than whether the translator is a specialist in the history of religions. Comparative treatment is relatively futile until the texts on which it is based have been correctly explained as linguistic documents. It is quite true that a trained student of religions may divine the true meaning of a text before philological confirmation is available. In such instances comparative religion has a definite heuristic value. An excellent illustration is furnished by Julian Morgenstern's happy interpretation of a passage in the Gilgamesh Epic (XI, 289) as somehow connected with widely diffused stories of the theft of the divine gift of immortality from man by a serpent.[2] However, this remained only a plausible hypothesis until the present writer corrected the reading *qulultum*, supposed to mean "curse," to *quluptum* (*quliptum*), "slough of a serpent."[3] The writer would not have stumbled upon this correction, now accepted by all Assyriologists, without having read Morgenstern's paper.

For convenience we may distinguish three main periods in the history of the interpretation of ancient Near Eastern documentary sources: 1. decipherment and rough translation; 2. the development of grammatical and lexicographical study, accompanied and followed by much greater accuracy in interpretation; 3. detailed dialectal and syntactic research, accompanied by monographic studies of selected classes of documents.[4] In Egyptology the first phase may be said to have begun with Champollion's famous *Lettre à M. Dacier* (1822) and to have come to an end with the appearance of Erman's *Neuägyptische Grammatik* (1st ed., 1880). The second phase includes the principal grammatical and lexicographical work of Erman and Sethe and was brought to a close by the publication of the grammatical studies of Gunn and Gardiner (1923-1927) and

[2] *Zeitschrift für Assyriologie*, 29, 1915, pp. 284-301.
[3] *Revue d'Assyriologie*, 16, 1919, pp. 189 f.; *American Journal of Semitic Languages*, 36, 1919-1920, pp. 278 ff.
[4] See the general discussion of the progress and present state of Near Eastern studies above, Chapter 4. [See also *From the Stone Age to Christianity*, 1957 ed., pp. 4-5, 32-41; *Archaeology and the Religion of Israel*, 1956 ed., pp. 36-59; and *Recent Discoveries in Bible Lands*, 1955 ed., pp. 1-60.]

of the main part of the great Egyptian dictionary of the Berlin Academy (1925-1931). The third phase began in the middle 1920s and is still in progress; notable illustrations of its achievements are the publication of detailed documentation for the words listed in Erman's *Wörterbuch* (since 1935), the publication of Sethe's translation and commentary to his edition of the Pyramid Texts (since 1935), the Egyptological publications of the Oriental Institute of the University of Chicago (since 1930), Gardiner's publication of the Chester Beatty papyri (since 1931), the appearance of the *Bibliotheca Aegyptiaca* of Brussels (since 1932), etc.[5]

Assyriology has passed through a similar cycle.[6] The first phase may be said to have begun about 1845 and to have closed with the establishment of the Delitzsch school of trained philological exegesis about 1880. The second phase saw the solid foundation of Assyrian philology through the work of Delitzsch, Haupt, Zimmern, Jensen, Meissner, and Ungnad, and of Sumerian through the work of Delitzsch and Thureau-Dangin. With the emergence of the Assyriological school of Landsberger in the 1920s and the appearance of Poebel's *Sumerische Grammatik* (1923) the third and current phase began. This phase is characterized by intense activity in detailed grammar and lexicography, especially among the members of the now scattered Landsberger school and at the Oriental Institute, where it centers about the great Assyrian dictionary project. It is also marked by monographic activity in all important fields of Assyriology, continuing and supplementing the work of the second phase, which was synthesized by Meissner in the two volumes of his *Babylonien und Assyrien* (1920-1925).

[The third of the main groups of documentary material to which we have referred above is West Semitic. By this term we mean inscriptions in both Northwest Semitic (Canaanite, Ugaritic, Aramaic, etc.) and South Arabic (Sabaean and Minean, etc.), as well as the rapidly increasing number of graffiti and formal inscriptions in early North Arabic (Thamudic, Lihyanite, Safaitic, etc.). We shall not attempt to retell the story of their discovery, decipherment, and interpretation here.[7] It is enough to say that inscriptions in Canaanite proper (including Phoenician) are now known to go

[5] [See also above, pp. 106-108.]
[6] [For further details see above, pp. 106-109, and the references in n. 4 above.]
[7] [See above, pp. 111-114.]

back at least to the seventeenth century B.C. and probably several centuries earlier (though these last are not yet known to have been deciphered).[8] The Proto-Sinaitic and related texts, from between ca. 1700 and 1400 B.C., now number several score, most of which can be read.[9] There are quite a number of inscriptions from the fourteenth-eleventh centuries B.C., as well as, of course, an abundance of Phoenician, Hebrew, and early Aramaic inscriptions from the eleventh-sixth centuries B.C. Aramaic inscriptions on papyrus, stone and pottery, etc., from the Persian Empire (fifth and fourth centuries B.C.) are known in vast numbers; the great majority of the texts in Imperial Aramaic have to do, directly and indirectly, with the Jews.]

[Since 1929 there has been a swelling tide of new Northwest Semitic written material from Ugarit, all apparently from the fourteenth-thirteenth centuries B.C. Several archives and remains of libraries have been found (most recently in 1960), and it can now be said that these documents will be of inestimable value for our understanding of Biblical Hebrew and the history of the religions of Canaan and Israel. What has already been published is relatively limited in scope, but it has revolutionized our approach to every aspect of Old Testament study.[10] The language of these texts belongs to several phases or dialects of North Canaanite: the mythological epics are written in archaic Ugaritic, with a generalized dialectal form which reminds one strongly of the generalized archaic "dialect" of Old Accadian religious poetry and the similar "dialect" of Homer; the prose texts are in a different speech form which is closer to Hebrew prose (though not identical with it).[11]]

[8] [See above, p. 112, n. 20.]

[9] [The writer expects to publish his revised decipherment in the near future.]

[10] [In general see now the excellent survey by M. Dahood, S.J., "Ugaritic Studies and the Bible," *Gregorianum*, 43, 1962, pp. 55-79; see also the material collected by J. Gray, *The Legacy of Canaan* ("Supplements to *Vetus Testamentum*," 5; Leiden, 1957), esp. the last chapter. On the linguistic importance of Ugaritic see W. L. Moran, S.J., in *The Bible and the Ancient Near East*, Albright Volume, 1961, pp. 54-72. The most recent survey of Ugaritic mythology is by Marvin Pope, in *Wörterbuch der Mythologie, I: Die alten Kulturvölker, Vorderer Orient*, ed. H. W. Haussig (ca. 1962), pp. 217-312, *passim*.]

[11] [See my remarks in *Bulletin of the American Schools of Oriental Research*, No. 150, 1958, pp. 36-38.]

[The story of the recovery of the Hurro-Hittite languages and literatures is much more complex; we refer to other treatments of it, in order not to burst all our limitations of space.[12] Most important, of course, is Hittite, both cuneiform and hieroglyphic; between them they span Anatolian and Syrian history from the eighteenth to the seventh century B.C. It is now known that both these two dialects, as well as Luwian and Palaic in the second millennium, and Lydian, Lycian, and Carian in the first millennium B.C., are Indo-Hittite—that is, they form a separate group of Indo-European languages which can be traced so much further back in time than any other known group that they may have separated from the ancestral stock much earlier. Then comes Hurrian, also in many dialects and phases, which may be traced for nearly two thousand years (ca. 2400-600 B.C.); its direct and indirect influence on Canaan and Israel is now known to have been considerable. There are many other languages and literatures of ancient southwestern Asia which are beginning to become known, but this is not the place to describe them.]

In this connection we may briefly refer to the tremendous advance in our knowledge of Anatolian and Aegean religion which may be confidently expected [1939] from the impending decipherment of Mycenaean and Minoan script. The 1,600 tablets from Cnossus in the cursive script known as Linear B, excavated by Sir Arthur Evans forty years ago, would probably have been deciphered already if any appreciable part of them had been published. Blegen's sensational discovery of 600 more tablets in this same script in Messenian Pylus (spring of 1939) renders decipherment merely a question of time and effort, since these documents are almost certainly in archaic Greek and many phonetic values are probably deducible from the Cypriote script. Once the phonetic values of the syllabic characters of Linear B have been obtained in this way, it will only be a matter of time and availability of material until the Cnossian tablets are also deciphered. To judge from the evidence of place names, their language may be only dialectally different from cuneiform Hittite, Luvian, and Proto-Lycian. In short, many prob-

[12] [See O. R. Gurney, *The Hittites*, 1952, esp. pp. 1-14; A. Goetze, *Kleinasien* ("Handbuch der Altertumswissenschaft," III.1.3.3.1; 2d ed., 1957), *passim*; and H. Güterbock's chapter in *Mythologies of the Ancient World*, ed. S. N. Kramer, 1961, pp. 139-179.]

lems connected with the relation between Mycenaean and later Greek religion may soon find their solution, at least in part. Since the Cnossian tablets date from about 1400 b.c. and the Pylian ones apparently from the thirteenth century, their decipherment will cast direct light on the sources of Homer, thus perhaps enabling us to decide the question of the extent to which the Iliad and Odyssey reflect the Late Bronze Age.[13]

Progress in the field of Old Testament criticism, whether textual, literary, or historical, has been incomparably less marked during this period.[14] Moreover, practically all important forward steps in the historical criticism of the Old Testament since 1840 fall in the generation from 1850 to 1880, that is, at a time when the interpretation of Egyptian, Mesopotamian, and South Arabian documents was still in its first stage, and before there was either sufficient material or philological foundation strong enough to bear a reliable synthesis of any kind. The greatest Semitic philologian of modern times, Theodor Nöldeke, stubbornly disregarded the young field of Assyriology, though after he had passed his sixtieth year he expressed regret that he had not mastered it. For all his profound control of Arabic, Ethiopic, Hebrew, and the Aramaic dialects, he

[13] [In order to illustrate the nature of scholarly forecasting, I have not changed a single word in the foregoing paragraph as written in 1940. Only one mistake was made in the forecast—the tablets in Linear B from Cnossus are in the same Greek dialect as those from Pylus. It is, however, probable that Linear A, belonging to the centuries immediately prior to Linear B, was used for a language closely related to Luvian, etc. Since Linear B was deciphered by Ventris, aided by Chadwick, in 1953, great progress has been made in the interpretation of these texts. It is easy to see in retrospect (see also below) that the dialect of Pylus and Cnossus could not have been the generalized poetic "dialect" of Homer in any case, since it appears to have been an Achean koine, while the present text of Homer reflects a mixture of dialects—an Aeolic base on which Ionic and Attic elements have been superimposed. This happens to be precisely the situation of the comparable epic dialect of Ugarit, which is not the same as the prose dialect of Ugarit in the thirteenth century b.c. but approaches South Canaanite and Proto-Hebrew. We have a close analogy in the relation between the pantheon of Homer and that of Pylus or Cnossus, on the one hand, and the relation between the pantheon of the Ugaritic epics and that of the city-state of Ugarit, on the other. In both cases the epic pantheons are generalized, while the local pantheons differ in many respects from one another. This observation does not favor the attempt made by some to date Homer much later because of its generalized pantheon. Just as at Ugarit, the

was helpless, as he candidly confessed, in the terrain of Assyrian, Egyptian, and Sabaean.[15] What was true of Nöldeke was true *a fortiori* of the great founders of modern Old Testament science: Wellhausen, Kuenen, Robertson Smith, Budde, Driver, etc. No less a man than Wellhausen, great Semitist though he was, neglected the new material from the Ancient Orient with a disdain as arrogant as it was complete. In his invaluable work, *Reste arabischen Heidentums* (second edition, 1897) he does not even apologize for his total disregard of the newly revealed South Arabic sources. Nöldeke at least had the grace to apologize. Of course, one cannot help sympathizing with the suspicion which the greatest Semitists showed toward the new disciplines of the Ancient Orient when one thinks of their parlous state at that time. Nor can one fail to recognize that the adventurous expeditions of a Winckler or of a Hommel into the terra incognita of historical synthesis were not calculated to win the approval of masters of exact method in the older disciplines. At the same time, there can no longer be the slightest doubt that neglect of the Ancient Orient, whether justified at that time or not, could result only in failure to understand the background of Israel's literature and in consequent inability to place the religion of Israel in its proper evolutionary setting.

No great historian or philologian is likely to construct his system in a vacuum; there must be some body of external data or some exterior plane of reference by the aid of which he can redeem his system from pure subjectivity. Since no body of external data was recognized as being applicable, men like Wellhausen and Robertson

---

opposite inference is more likely. In passing, it may be observed that my views on Homer (*American Journal of Archaeology*, 54, 1950, pp. 162-176), which have been accepted by several leading classical scholars, have been strikingly confirmed in a number of respects by the decipherment of Linear B—e.g., my observation that Mycenaean Greek had at least one velar consonant.]

[14] [For surveys of Old Testament scholarship during this period see H. F. Hahn, *Old Testament in Modern Research*, Philadelphia, 1954, and H.-J. Kraus, *Geschichte der historisch-kritischen Erforschung des Alten Testaments von der Reformation bis zur Gegenwart*, Neukirchen Kreis Moers, 1956. On the important recent progress in textual criticism due to the Dead Sea Scrolls see F. M. Cross, Jr., *The Ancient Library of Qumran and Modern Biblical Studies*, 1958, pp. 124-145.]

[15] See Nöldeke, *Beiträge zur semitischen Sprachwissenschaft*, I, 1904, p. v, II, 1912 p. v.

Smith were forced to resort to the second alternative: the arrangement of Israelite data with reference to the evolutionary historical philosophies of Hegel (so Wellhausen) or of the English positivists (so essentially Robertson Smith). Graf, Kuenen, and Wellhausen, the joint creators of the so-called Wellhausen system, were all Hegelians and Wellhausen, who was the greatest thinker of the three, avowed his allegiance in unmistakable terms when in the introduction to his famous *Prolegomena* (1878) he wrote (Eng. trans., p. 13): "My inquiry . . . comes nearer to that of Vatke, from whom indeed I gratefully acknowledge myself to have learnt best and most." Now Vatke was, we must remember, an ardent disciple of Hegel, who was one of the first and certainly the most successful exponent of Hegelianism among German Protestant theologians; his most important work appeared in 1835. This Hegelianism, more implicit than explicit with Wellhausen, became even clearer with his followers, especially in the books of Marti, whose influence was much greater than his scholarly merit would seem to warrant. Old Testament literature was now divided into three phases: early poetry and saga, Prophetic writings, and legal codes. The religion of Israel exhibited three stages: polydemonism, henotheism, monotheism. To Wellhausen the fully-developed religion of Israel was latent in its earlier stages, spirit and law replacing nature and primitive freedom from fixed norms, all this development following strictly Hegelian dialectic: thesis (the pre-prophetic stage), antithesis (the prophetic reaction), synthesis (the nomistic stage).

Robertson Smith was no less a positivist because he nowhere described his theory of the evolution of Israel in formal positivistic terms than Wellhausen was a Hegelian because he failed to reduce his system to explicitly Hegelian language. The historical chain of students of comparative religion formed by Tylor, Robertson Smith, and Frazer was largely dependent on the philosophical temper of the age in England, a temper which was powerfully influenced by the work of John Stuart Mill and Herbert Spencer, through whom the positivism of Comte passed into the history of religion and related fields. It is quite impossible to understand the development of Robertson Smith's thought without understanding the nature of English positivistic philosophy. English Old Testament scholarship subsequently fell even more completely under the domination of the positivist tradition, as is particularly evident in the writings of

S. R. Driver, to name only its most prominent representative since Smith's death. In France the positivist tradition has also been dominant, except in Catholic circles, as is clear from the work of such Protestant scholars as Lods and Causse.[16] With the latter we move into a new stage, which has been deeply influenced by the sociological schools of Durkheim and Lévy-Bruhl. It is historically important to stress the fact that, in spite of the far-reaching resemblances between the conclusions of the German and of the Anglo-French schools, they go back to essentially different philosophical horizons. Accidentally, however, it happens that there is a striking superficial resemblance between the evolutionary religious schemes of Hegel and of Comte, since the latter also thought in triads as illustrated by his progressive sequence: fetishism, polytheism, monotheism. On the other hand, Comte's triple hierarchy of modes of thought (theological, metaphysical, and positivistic or scientific), which was in some respects diametrically opposed to Hegelian doctrines, led Anglo-French and subsequently American Biblical scholarship into more and more drastic evolutionary materialism. Under the influence of current instrumentalist philosophy, American Biblical scholarship tends to construct unilateral schemes of evolution, oriented either toward some form of socialism or toward ethical humanism. In these systems mechanical progressivism competes with a remorseless meliorism to produce increasingly artificial results. Whenever doubts arise they are quickly suppressed by appeal to the authority of Biblical criticism, which by establishing the chronological sequence, early poems and sagas, Prophetic writings, legal codes, appears *superficially* to confirm the evolutionary schemes in question.

The reaction against these suspiciously aprioristic constructions came first in Germany, where they originated. The first competent scholar to give formal utterance to the new attitude was none other than Rudolf Kittel, in his historic address, "Die Zukunft der

[16] I take this opportunity to correct the erroneous emphasis I placed on the Hegelian atmosphere of Causse's work in my review (*Journal of Biblical Literature*, 57, 1938, p. 200), where I wrote: "The sociological determinism of the author is thus essentially Hegelian." In a letter to me, Professor Causse protests against this statement, insisting that he is actually opposed to Hegelianism. The "rigid Wellhausenism" for which I tax him later does, in fact, give his picture of Israelite evolution a Hegelian appearance. However, direct influence on his work is mostly of neo-positivistic character (Frazer, Durkheim, Lévy-Bruhl).

Alttestamentlichen Wissenschaft," delivered at the first German Orientalistentag in Leipzig, September 29, 1921: "Es fehlte dem Gebäude [d.h., der Schule Wellhausens] das Fundament, und es fehlten den Baumeistern die Massstäbe."[17] In his address he stressed, as we have, the fact that the founders of modern Old Testament science had no idea of the great world of the Ancient Orient, which was just then opening up, and that their successors also failed to reckon with it, in spite of the vast increase in our knowledge. There were two weaknesses in Kittel's presentation. In the first place, he was premature. Since 1921 our knowledge of the ancient Near East has been enormously extended and deepened; real syntheses were still absolutely impossible when Kittel spoke. Even in 1932, when I wrote my first partial synthesis of the results of Palestinian archaeology for Biblical scholarship,[18] the time was not ripe for a successful effort to reinterpret the history of Israel's religion in the light of archaeological discoveries.[19] Kittel's second weakness was that he lacked the perspective from which to judge the philosophical tendencies inherent in the development of Biblical research, especially in Germany. It is all very well to declare that the historico-religious edifice of Wellhausen lacked a solid foundation and to point out his ignorance of the historical and cultural background of Israel, but demonstration is not possible without explaining the intrinsic reasons for the artificiality of this edifice and without substituting a better structure, founded on solid historical material.[20]

Since 1921 there have been increasingly frequent attempts to shake off the yoke of a rigid Wellhausenism, but it cannot be said that any has succeeded, though there have been numerous partial successes and many correct observations. However, voices are more and more often heard decrying the artificiality of most modern

---

[17] *Zeitschrift für die alttestamentliche Wissenschaft*, 39, 1921, p. 86.
[18] *The Archaeology of Palestine and the Bible*, New York, 1932; 2d ed., 1935. For an accurate foreshadowing of my present attitude see "Archaeology Confronts Biblical Criticism," *The American Scholar*, 1938, pp. 176-188, with W. C. Graham's reply, "Higher Criticism Survives Archaeology," *ibid.*, pp. 409-427.
[19] [The writer offered such a reinterpretation in his volumes *From the Stone Age to Christianity*, 1940; last partial revision, 1957, written in the summers of 1939 and 1940 (the present paper was first written in early 1940), and *Archaeology and the Religion of Israel*, 1942; last partial revision, 1956.]
[20] [See esp. the chapter by G. E. Mendenhall in *The Bible and the Ancient Near East*, 1961, pp. 32-53.]

theories of the religious evolution of Israel. The important and influential school of Albrecht Alt has performed exceedingly valuable services for Israelite history as a whole, but it is clear that it is weak in the sphere of religious history.[21] The crisis of religious faith in Central Europe which heralded the victory of National Socialism in Germany, brought with it a violent reaction against historicism (*Historismus*) in all its manifestations, a reaction almost as pronounced among foes of the movement as among its friends. The Swiss scholar, Walter Eichrodt, expresses my own conviction in emphatic words: "It is high time that the tyranny of historicism in Old Testament studies was broken and the proper approach to our task rediscovered. This is no new problem, certainly, but it is one that needs to be solved anew in every epoch of knowledge—the problem of how to understand the realm of Old Testament belief in its structural unity."[22]

This is hardly the place in which to present my philosophical credo, but a few observations are in order, since one's philosophical position is inseparably bound up with one's efforts at synthesis—perhaps more in the field of this paper than in most essays at historical interpretation.[23] In the first place, I am a resolute "positivist" —but *only in so far as positivism is the expression of the modern rational-scientific approach to physical and historical reality.* I would not call myself a positivist at all if it were not for the insistence with which National-Socialist theorists have rejected the rational-empirical approach to reality, calling it "positivism." I am even in a sense an instrumentalist, but only to the extent that I acknowledge the truth of an instrumentalism *sub specie aeternitatis*, in complete opposition to the metaphysical system of the Dewey school. Men can judge the value of a movement or of a method only by inadequate criteria, and to set up such criteria as absolute guides

---

[21] [See my remarks on Alt in *Journal of Biblical Literature*, 75, 1956, pp. 169-173. More recently, the publications of G. von Rad have extended the work of the Alt school into the area of religious history. On the important work of the Scandinavian school see the surveys by C. R. North and G. W. Anderson in *The Old Testament and Modern Study*, ed. H. H. Rowley, 1951, pp. 48-83, 283-310.]

[22] W. Eichrodt, *Theology of the Old Testament*, Vol. I, trans. J. Baker, 1961, p. 31 (first published in 1933), with underlining omitted.

[23] [See also *From the Stone Age to Christianity*, 1957 ed., pp. 5-8, 82-126.]

is the most dangerous possible procedure, both in science and in life. I am an evolutionist, but only in an organismic, not in a mechanical or a melioristic sense. All such aprioristic evolutionary systems as those of Hegel and Comte are so artificial and so divorced from physical or historical reality that they cannot be safely used as frames of reference, though they have undoubtedly possessed real heuristic value—a partially erroneous classification is generally better than no classification at all. Subsequent evolutionary philosophies are so unilaterally determined that they can at best reflect only one facet of a polyhedron. Favorite forms of determinism in our day are socio-economic, ranging all the way from the brilliant and often correct work of Max Weber[24] to the doctrinaire reconstructions of orthodox Marxists.

The most reasonable philosophy of history, in my judgment, is evolutionary and organismic. Evolution is not unilateral progress, it is more than a series of abrupt mutations; yet, like organic development, it falls into more or less definite forms, patterns, and configurations, each with its own complex body of characteristics. The past generation has made us familiar with "Gestalt" in psychology, with "patterns" in the history of religions and sociology, with "cultures" in archaeology and ethnography. A comparison of successive organismic phenomena discloses definite structural relationships, which cannot possibly be accidental and which require some causal or purposive explanation, whether it be some latent or potential entelechy or whether it be interpreted teleologically. But the task of the historian, as distinguished from the philosopher or the theologian, is to study the phenomena as objectively as possible, employing inductive methods wherever possible. My task is restricted as far as possible to historical description and interpretation, leaving the higher but less rigorous forms of interpretation to others. Though I am, as will be clear from the above sketch, essentially an historicist, my point of view remains very different from that of the older representatives of *Historismus*, whose interpretation was distorted by erroneous postulates and false frames of reference, and who sinned grievously in subordinating structural and organismic considerations to sequential (diachronic) relationships.

[24] I do not wish to give the impression that all Weber's work was characterized by socio-economic determinism. Far from it. I wish here only to emphasize the relative soundness of this phase of his work.

Broad classifications of historical phenomena are inevitably inadequate, yet if they are planned with sufficient care they can be illuminating. I have found the following classification of mental operations very useful in the study of the history of religions. The late L. Lévy-Bruhl[25] introduced the term "prelogical" thought in order to describe primitive mentality, which ignores the logical principles of identity and contradiction. However, since so-called primitive peoples are often quite logical in practical matters, Lévy-Bruhl later abandoned his category. His initial distinction is nevertheless instructive, although it is necessary to add the category of empirical logic to describe the implicit logic characteristic of ordinary human activity of material or social nature. In other words, ancient man and modern primitives share a type of thinking which never rises to the logical level, but always remains more or less fluid and impersonal, not distinguishing between causal relationship and coincidences or purely superficial similarities, unable to make precise definitions and utterly unconscious of their necessity. Most ancient mythology goes back to this stage of thinking, which I term "proto-logical." Next above this stage is what I should term "empirico-logical" thought, in which sound, though unconscious, observation and simple deduction from experience, subconscious as a rule, play an important part. This stage, in which most of the fundamental discoveries and inventions of primitive man were made, was to a large extent contemporary with the proto-logical stage, but it assumed the dominant role during the third millennium B.C. and continued until the dawn of logical reasoning in sixth-century Greece. Empirical logic became self-conscious in the systematic "science" of the Babylonians and Egyptians, at least as early as 2100 B.C.; it is best illustrated by the elaborate systems of magic and divination developed in Babylonia during the following centuries, where we find a "proto-inductive" method of gathering data and methodical deduction from these "inductions" as well as from empirically developed or mythologically conditioned postulates. Empirical logic survived long after the discovery of logical reasoning by the Greeks, even in some dominant intellectual circles. It goes without saying that proto-logical thinking has never become extinct among primitives and children, and that a disconcerting proportion of contemporary adult

[25] See esp. Lévy-Bruhl, *La mentalité primitive*, 1922. [See above, pp. 66-73.]

thinking is essentially proto-logical, especially among uneducated people, in the most civilized lands. Empirico-logical thinking is still commoner. However, since we must classify modes of thought according to their best examples and since chronological progress in dominant types of thinking is certain, our classification is just as instructive, *mutatis mutandis*, as the archaeologically useful (but culturally somewhat misleading) series, stone–bronze–iron.

In the light of the foregoing observations, let us turn to a comparison and contrast between the ideas of the peoples of the ancient Near East between ca. 2000 and 1000 B.C. and those prevailing in Israel between 1200 and 800 B.C. with regard to the nature of deity. Since the national and cultural evolution of Israel shows an inevitable lag (which must not be exaggerated!) when compared to that of the surrounding peoples, this apparent chronological disparity is quite justified. When we remember that Israel was situated in the middle of the ancient Near East and that all streams of influence from the richer and older centers of culture percolated into Palestine, when we recall that Israelite tradition itself derived both its ancestors and its civilization from Babylonia, Egypt, and Canaan (Phoenicia), then our chronological postulate is not only justified but becomes inevitable. Incidentally, it has the practical advantage of scrupulous fairness, since we are not retrojecting ideas which are expressed in documents of—say—the seventh century B.C. into the middle of the second millennium, following the example of many members of the *Religionsgeschichtliche Schule*, who did not hesitate to relate the Gospels and the Pauline Epistles to the Mandaean liturgies and the Corpus Hermeticum, though the latter cannot antedate the third century A.D., and the former can scarcely be earlier than the sixth century A.D. Slight chronological uncertainties must remain: it is by no means always certain that a given religious text from the Ancient Orient (including the Bible) actually reflects the period when it was ostensibly compiled; it may belong to a considerably earlier period, being handed down orally or in writing and then adapted to a special purpose, with no change in its religious atmosphere. Moreover, in dealing with Biblical literature unusual care must be exercised in dating and interpreting our material, both because of its complicated transmission and because of frequent textual and lexical uncertainty.

Among the most serious methodological fallacies of most current Old Testament scholarship is the tendency to telescope an evolution that actually took many thousands of years into the space of a few centuries.[26] This is a direct result of adherence to a unilateral evolutionary scheme which requires a definite succession from simpler and cruder to more complex and more refined forms, and which tries to eliminate the latter from early stages and the former from later stages of a given development. Actually, of course, the order of evolution is, in the main, correct, but we must go back several thousand years to find proto-logical thinking dominant in the most advanced circles. The religious literature of the Ancient Orient is mainly empirico-logical and there is little evidence of true proto-logical thought except in such bodies of material as the Pyramid Texts, unilingual Sumerian religious compositions of the third millennium, Ugaritic mythological epics, and other documents transmitted to later times but redolent of their primitive origins. Even in magic and divination after the beginning of the second millennium, there was increasing tendency to restrict the proto-logical to inherited elements (very numerous, of course) and to employ empirico-logical methods to innovate and develop. The mythological substratum of fertility cults and ritual retains its proto-logical character longest, but after 2000 B.C. there is an increasing tendency to explain away inconsistencies and to turn the originally impersonal, dynamistic figures of the "drama" into definite forms with tangible personalities, fitted into a special niche in an organized pantheon. On the other hand, of course, empirico-logical thinking generalizes by intuitive "induction," and reasons by intuitive analogy, so we cannot be surprised to find that the highest religious thought of the late third and the second millennia B.C. modified the fluid dynamism of early religious expression in two directions: pantheism and monotheism. Both in Egypt and in Babylonia pantheistic tendencies appear clearly but remained in general abortive. After the middle of the second millennium B.C. monotheistic tendencies also appear in our sources, but were also repressed by the standard pluralistic polytheism of the age—except in Israel, where

[26] This tendency is by no means the exclusive property of Old Testament scholars. An example of it, though much less drastic, is Breasted's book, *The Dawn of Conscience*, 1933, in which he dates the effective emergence of social conscience in Egypt in the Old Empire.

monotheism flowered.[27] In India, on the other hand, primitive dynamistic ideas persisted and were transformed into pantheistic conceptions by the partly empirico-logical thought of the Upanishads.[28]
In this paper we are not so much interested in sporadic evidences
of pantheism or of monotheism in the ancient Near East as we are
in the nature of the organized polytheism of the Assyro-Babylonians,
Canaanites, Hurrians, Hittites, Acheans, Egyptians, in the second
millennium B.C. All of these peoples possessed a definite pantheon,
which naturally varied from district to district and from period to
period, but which was surprisingly stable. In the time of Hammurapi
of Babylon, about 1700 B.C., the Babylonian pantheon was organized
on the basis which it occupied for a millennium and a half, with
little further change.[29] Head of the pantheon was Marduk of Babylon, henceforth identified with the chief god of the Sumerian pantheon, Enlil or Ellil, "lord of the storm." As head of the pantheon
Marduk was commonly called *bêlu*, "lord," and the appellation *Bêl*
soon replaced his personal name for ordinary purposes. In Assyria
Marduk's place was naturally held by Asshur, chief deity of the city
Asshur, who was also identified with the old Sumerian god Ellil.
Under the head of the pantheon were many hundreds of other

[27] [See also *From the Stone Age to Christianity*, 1957 ed., pp. 213 ff.]
[28] [The Upanishads (between ca. 800 and 600 B.C.) are not empirico-logical
in the sense that the Old Testament (see above, Chapter 3) and the wisdom
of Confucius are, but there can be so doubt that we have in them a clear
development in the direction of pre-Platonic Greek thought. The outstanding
impression made by Indian metaphysical philosophy is that, after a remarkable
start in the Upanishads, it continued to be dynamistic in fundamental respects
until the middle centuries of the first millennium A.D., when various forms
of systematic logic came into use (on this see the brilliant classification by
Karl H. Potter, *Journal of Asian Studies*, 21, 1961, pp. 25-32, and the discussion
by Heinrich Zimmer, *Philosophies of India*, 1950). Indian formal logic was
never organized along rigorous mathematical-postulational lines, and today (as
I know from several distinguished American specialists in philosophy and history of science who have been recently in India, see above, Chapter 3, p. 92)
the ordinary Indian university professor and student cannot understand Western philosophical reasoning (except, of course, where it has itself been strongly
influenced by Indian thought, as in the case of some Western idealistic systems). On the other hand, empirical reasoning continued after the Upanishads
until it attained the high level (unreached anywhere else in antiquity) of
Pāṇini's classification of grammatical phenomena in Vedic Sanskrit (undatable,
but somewhere between ca. 500 and 100 B.C.). Influence from Greek thinking
on Pāṇini is unlikely, especially since O. Neugebauer has proved that Indian

deities, ranging from the great gods to minor divinities, often of only local significance. The boundary line between gods and demons was none too clear and fluctuated constantly. For our present purposes it is important to stress the fact that most of the gods were cosmic in character and that the multiplication of names was due largely to the differentiation of originally identical divinities, whose appellations became attached to different local cults,[30] as well as to the introduction of many foreign deities. Only a small part of these figures may be said to have developed clear-cut personalities, as was undoubtedly true of Ea, Nabu, Shamash, Ishtar, etc. Almost any important deity was at the same time connected with numerous different localities and temples; he was charged with some cosmic function which required his presence in many different places and under many different conditions; he was considered to have his own residence in heaven or the underworld, or both. Nowhere except in astrological speculation of relatively late date is a great god assigned exclusive dominion over a given district or country. Marduk is called "king of (foreign) lands" (*lugal kurkurra*) by Kurigalzu III (fourteenth century). In the Prologue of the Code of Hammurapi (ca. 1690 B.C.) we are told that Anu and Enlil had destined Marduk to be lord of all peoples. In a list of gods composed in the Late Bronze Age, we find numerous identifications of Sumero-Accadian deities with Hurrian and Northwest Semitic ones; e.g., Ishtar is identified with Hurrian Shaushka and Canaanite Ashtartu, Adad is identified with Ba'al or Dad(d)a and with Teshub. Nothing can be clearer than the universal cosmic significance of the great gods, es-

---

astronomy was influenced more from Babylonia than from Greece; cf. his discussions in *The Exact Sciences in Antiquity*, 2d ed., 1957, *passim* (for references see his index, s.v. "Hindu astronomy"), as well as the excellent survey by David Pingree, *Isis*, 54, 1963, pp. 229-246. In general, for a remarkably percipient treatment of underlying differences between Greek and Indian thinking, see Zimmer, *op. cit.*, pp. 1-47. See further the admirable volume by Karl H. Potter, *Presuppositions of India's Philosophies*, 1963.]

[29] [Marduk was already prominent at this time; see below with reference to the Code of Hammurapi. W. G. Lambert (and others, e.g., Ravn and Schmökel) dates the rise of Marduk later. He favors the Second Dynasty of Isin (ca. 1100 B.C.); see his forthcoming paper in the Meek volume ("The Reign of Nebuchadnezzar I: A Turning Point in the History of Ancient Mesopotamian Religion").]

[30] See, e.g., Bertholet's instructive study, *Götterspaltung und Göttervereinigung*.

pecially of Marduk in the Creation Epic, which dates in its present form from about the twelfth century B.C.[31] In the considerably earlier Gilgamesh Epic we are told that Gilgamesh journeyed a prodigious distance westward in search of his ancestor, the Flood-hero Ut-Napishtim. In order to reach the Source of the Rivers[32] he traversed the western desert; he reached the mythical mountains of Mashu; he traveled in darkness for twenty-four hours, with gigantic strides; he emerged into the beautiful garden of Siduri, the goddess of life;[33] he crossed the redoubtable waters of death, shunning no toil in order to attain his goal. But no matter how far Gilgamesh traveled he could not escape Shamash, who traveled around the earth in a single day. Even at the Source of the Rivers the gods are all-powerful, for they placed Ut-Napishtim there after the Flood, following the command of Ellil.

Whenever the Mesopotamians came into sufficiently close and lasting contact with a foreign cult to become acutely conscious of the existence of its deity, they adopted him into their own pantheon, either identifying him directly with one of the native deities, or assigning him some special place or function in their pantheon. Theological disputes must constantly have arisen over details. One school, for example, regarded Ishtar as daughter of the old god of heaven, Anu (Sumerian *An*, "Heaven"), while another considered her as daughter of the moon-god, Sin. Similarly, one group regarded Ninurta as the greatest and most powerful of the gods, while another group insisted that this honor belonged exclusively to Marduk.

The recognition that many deities were simply manifestations of a single divinity and that the domain of a god with cosmic functions was universal, inevitably led to some form of practical monotheism or pantheism. To the second half of the second millennium belong, on clear intrinsic evidence, two illustrations, one monotheistic and the other pantheistic in tendency. The first is the well-known tablet in which Marduk is successively identified with a whole list of deities, each of whom is called by his name; e.g., Sin is Marduk as

---

[31] [For this date see Lambert, as quoted by L. Matouš, *Archiv Orientální*, 29, 1961, p. 33, n. 9 (twelfth-eleventh centuries B.C.).]

[32] See *American Journal of Semitic Languages*, 35, 1919, pp. 161-195.

[33] See *American Journal of Semitic Languages*, 36, 1920, pp. 258 ff.

illuminer of the night.[34] The second is a document which lists all important deities, male and female, as parts of the cosmic body of Ninurta; e.g., Ellil and Ninlil are his two eyes, Marduk is his neck.[35]

Among the Hurrians and Hittites the process of syncretism was carried so far that it becomes almost impossible to guess the origin of a god's name by the place of his residence, or rather, by the places where he is specially worshiped. The extraordinary fusion of Sumero-Accadian and Hurrian pantheons is illustrated by documents from Nuzi in northeastern Mesopotamia, from Mitanni proper, from Mari, and from Ugarit, but nowhere so clearly as in the rich material from the Hittite capital (Boghazköy). One Hurrian myth describes the primordial theomachy, in which the father of the gods, Kumarbi, is presumably defeated by the storm-god, Teshub, with whom are allied an impressive list of Hurrian and Accadian deities.[36] Three Sumero-Accadian goddesses ranged particularly far to the west: Nikkal, whose cult is attested from different parts of Syria and Cappadocia in the second millennium; Kubaba, who apparently started as the Sumero-Accadian *Kú-Baba* (the holy Baba)[37] and became increasingly popular, especially in Asia Minor, where she was finally borrowed by the Greeks as Cybebe, indentified with Cybele; Ishtar of Nineveh, a long list of whose cult-centers in different countries is found in a Hittite document from about the thirteenth century.[38] To the Hittites all storm-gods were Teshub, all mother-goddesses Hebat; in Hittite literature there is no

---

[34] [For this text see Ebeling's translation in *Altorientalische Texte*, ed. H. Gressmann, 2d ed., 1926, pp. 329-330. See also *From the Stone Age to Christianity*, 1957 ed., p. 217. Note also the texts edited by Lambert in his article cited above, n. 29.]

[35] [See Ebeling's translation, *op. cit.*, pp. 250-251; see also W. von Soden and A. Falkenstein, *Sumerische und akkadische Hymnen und Gebete*, 1953, pp. 258-259, 385 (trans. von Soden).]

[36] [For a translation of this text see A. Goetze in *Ancient Near Eastern Texts*, pp. 121-125; see also H. Güterbock, *Journal of Cuneiform Studies*, 5, 1951, pp. 135-161; 6, 1952, pp. 8-42.]

[37] [See *Bulletin of the American Schools of Oriental Research*, No. 78, 1940, pp. 26 f., n. 21, and *From the Stone Age to Christianity*, 1957 ed., pp. 234 f., n. 46.]

[38] See J. Friedrich, *Der Alte Orient*, XXV, 2, 1925, pp. 20-22. The Ninevite goddess is summoned to come to the Hittite capital from Ugarit, Alalakh, and other places as far south as Sidon in Syria, from parts of northern Mesopotamia as far south as Asshur, from Cyprus, and from southern Asia Minor as far west

such thing as henotheism. The religious catholicity of the Hittites is shown not only by their wholesale adoption of Accadian and Hurrian deities, but also by their use of ritual formulas and incantations in several different tongues, including Babylonian.

It is increasingly evident that in many respects there was close similarity between the Anatolian (Hurro-Hittite) religion of the late second millennium B.C. and the Aegean, both as we see it in Minoan and Mycenaean monuments and as we find it vividly portrayed in the Iliad and the Odyssey. While it is, of course, true that the Homeric epics in substantially their present form belong to the beginning of the first millennium, it is now recognized by virtually all scholars that they reflect the culture and the conceptual world of sub-Mycenaean times, i.e., of the last two centuries of the second millennium—in certain respects even of Late Mycenaean (fourteenth-thirteenth centuries). In the Iliad and the Odyssey there is no suggestion that any of the great gods were restricted by nationality in their sphere of action, though they often play favorites. Zeus, Hera, and Apollo are worshiped by both Acheans and Anatolians; Odysseus encounters Poseidon and is aided by Athene wherever he wanders. From Zeus, who still bears the Indo-European appellation "father of men and gods,"[39] to Helius, whose favorite abode is in the land of the Ethiopians in the far south, the great gods are cosmic in function and unlimited in their power of movement.

Turning to Canaanite religion, we find ourselves in an entirely different situation from our predecessors, thanks especially to the religious literature of the fourteenth century B.C. from Ugarit, but also to archaeological discoveries at Ugarit, Byblus, Beth-shan, Megiddo, Lachish, and Hazor. It is now certain that the religion of Canaan was of the same general type as that of Mesopotamia, Asia Minor, and the Aegean in the second millennium. Organized cult in temples played the chief role, and sacred rocks, trees, and springs were much less significant than has been supposed. Moreover, the religion of Canaan was true polytheism, not polydemonism. Thanks to the documents from Ugarit we now know that the account of

---

as Masa and Karkaya (probably the Achemenian Karkâ and therefore Caria). [For the invocation of gods from a comparable area see the text translated by A. Goetze in *Ancient Near Eastern Texts*, pp. 351-353 ("Evocatio").]
[39] See Nilsson, *Archiv für Religionswissenschaft*, 35, 1938, pp. 156-171.

Phoenician mythology preserved by Sanchuniathon of Berytus (about 500 B.C.)[40] and condensed by Philo Byblius (first century A.D.) into the form in which we have it, reflects, with substantial accuracy, the mythology of the Canaanites in the middle of the second millennium. A mass of fragmentary data from Canaanite, Egyptian, and Greek sources helps to round out and complete the picture. The titular head of the pantheon was the high god, El, who no longer took too active a part in the affairs of men, and who lived in Phoenicia "at the source(s) of the (two) rivers, in the midst of the fountains of the two deeps."[41] At the same time, El's cosmic home, as in the case of other gods, was far removed, requiring a journey through "a thousand plains, ten thousand fields." El and his consort Asherah were the progenitors of gods and of men. Next to him was the head of the pantheon *de facto*, the storm-god Hadad, the lord (*Ba'lu*, *Ba'al*) *par excellence*. That *Ba'al* early became his personal name as well as his appellation, just as was later true of *Adonî* (Adonis), of Aramean *Bêl* and *Bêltî*, etc., is certain from the fact that it was borrowed by the Egyptians in this sense as early as the fifteenth century and that it was listed as such in a Babylonian list of gods (see above). Baal was the lord of heaven, the giver of all life, the ruler of gods and of men, to whom it is said: *tíqqaḫu múlka 'ôlámika dárkata dâta dardârika*, "thou shalt take thy eternal kingdom, thy dominion for ever and ever."[42] The throne of Baal is on a lofty mythical mountain in the far north, certainly to be compared with the Mesopotamian mountain of the gods, Arallu, also in the far north and also the mountain of gold.[43]

[40] [For this date see Volume II in the present series.] An earlier date is defended by Eissfeldt, *Ras Shamra und Sanchunjaton*, 1939, pp. 67 ff. [see also *Sanchunjaton von Berut und Ilumilku von Ugarit*, 1952], against onomastic and historical probability.

[41] [For this translation see *Archaeology and the Religion of Israel*, 1956 ed., p. 194, n. 7, following J. A. Montgomery. The residence can now be located at Afqā-Yammûneh in Lebanon; see M. Pope, *El in the Ugaritic Texts* ("Supplements to *Vetus Testamentum*," 2, Leiden, 1955, pp. 61-82.) Note however the ambivalence: El was located in the remote distance as well as at Afqā, just as the home of Baal was both in heaven and on Mt. Casius.]

[42] [For the text see Gordon, *Ugaritic Manual*, Rome, 1955, text 68.10. See also the translation by Ginsberg, *Ancient Near Eastern Texts*, p. 131a.]

[43] [For the text see Gordon, *op. cit.*, '*nt* iv.44 f., translated by Ginsberg, *Ancient Near Eastern Texts*, p. 137a.] For the imagery and the cosmological ideas in-

The extent to which Canaanite gods were fused with Egyptian has become very clear as a result of Montet's excavation in the ruins of Tanis, which was the capital of the Ramessides in the thirteenth century B.C. The native god of Tanis, Sûtaḫ (later Seth), who became the patron deity of the dynasty, was identified with Baal, and his consort Nephthys became Anath. Canaanite Haurôn was identified with Horus, Astarte with Isis. The Ugaritic texts show that the artificer of the gods, Kôthar (later Kûshôr), was identified with Egyptian Ptaḥ, as had long ago been correctly guessed by G. Hoffmann,[44] and a hieroglyphic inscription from Megiddo now proves that there was a temple of Ptaḥ at Ascalon.[45] Much older, of course, is the identification of the West Semitic Baʿlatu, "the Lady," with Egyptian Hathor, both at Byblus and in Sinai and Egypt itself. To the Canaanites there was no limit to the power of their deities; of Ptaḥ-Kôthar it is said, "for his is Crete, the throne on which he sits, Egypt, the land of his inheritance."[46] Similarly, Canaanite, Amorite, and Accadian deities were exchanged and identified to a disconcerting degree. Gods like Hadad and Dagan, Ashirat (Asherah) and Astarte (Ishtar) were worshiped in the second millennium from the Delta of Egypt to the mountains of Iran. In the cuneiform tablets found in Syria from the period 1500-1200 B.C., we find Sumero-Accadian names and ideograms used so widely for native deities that we are often quite unable to say what their

---

volved see esp. Delitzsch, *Wo lag das Paradies?* pp. 117 ff.; Jensen, *Die Kosmologie der Babylonier*, pp. 203 ff. (to be rectified in the direction of Delitzsch's position); Jeremias, *Das Alte Testament im Lichte des alten Orients*, 2d ed., p. 568; Albright, *Journal of Biblical Literature*, 39, 1920, pp. 137 ff. [and *Festschrift Alfred Bertholet*, 1950, esp. pp. 3 ff.]

[44] *Zeitschrift für Assyriologie*, 11, 1896, p. 254, independently discovered by H. L. Ginsberg through his study of the Ugaritic material; see *Orientalia*, 9, 1940, pp. 39-44. [See also my remarks below, pp. 170-172.]

[45] [See Wilson in *Ancient Near Eastern Texts*, p. 263b. Ptaḥ had earlier been identified with El.]

[46] [For the text see Gordon, *op. cit.*, *ʿnt* vi.13-16, trans. Ginsberg, *Ancient Near Eastern Texts*, p. 138a.] My translation differs slightly from Ginsberg's, since I translate the word *klḥ* (*kî-laḥu*) "for to him (is)." The second passage [2 *Aqht* vi.20 f., 30f., trans. by Ginsberg, *Ancient Near Eastern Texts*, p. 151a], which threw Ginsberg off the track, is characteristically abbreviated by haplography (*homoioarkton*) and should be read: *bʿl ḥkpt ʾel. klḥ* (*Kptr ksʾu. ṯbṯh. Ḥkpt ʾarṣ. nḥlth*), "lord of Egypt-of-God, for to him (i.e., to Kôthar) belongs (Crete, the throne on which he sits, etc.)."

native names may have been. Such cases as Bêlit-ekalli of Qaṭna, Damu of Byblus, Ninurta of a town in the territory of Jerusalem, are the rule, not the exception. Some of these deities became permanently domiciled in the West.

In Egypt also we find a similar situation, though its advanced civilization and its natural conservatism combined to produce a remarkable polarity, in which pantheistic and rarefied monotheistic conceptions are found side by side with extremely primitive myths and beliefs. The god Amûn-Rê', who was not only the sun-god but was also creator and lord of the universe, is praised in the following terms in the great hymn to Amûn (from the fifteenth century B.C., but unquestionably older in conception):

> Thou far traveler, thou prince of Upper Egypt, lord of the land of the Matoi (Eastern Desert of Nubia) and ruler of Punt (East Africa),
>   Thou greatest of heaven, thou oldest of the earth, lord of what exists . . .
>   Whose sweet odor the gods love, as he comes from Punt, rich in fragrance as he comes from the land of the Matoi, with fair countenance as he comes from "God's Land" (Asia) . . .
>   "Hail to thee!" says every foreign land, as high as heaven is and as wide as earth is and as deep as the sea is . . .[47]

The archaism of the language and of the geographical terminology should not prevent us from recognizing the fact that this text forms a perfect conceptual bridge between the ideas of the third millennium, as illustrated by the hymns to Rê' in the Pyramid Texts, and the great Hymn to the Aten, which dates from the fourteenth century.[48] Even after the reaction had set in strongly against monotheism in the late fourteenth century, we find that Wen-Amûn can say to the prince of Byblus in the early eleventh century: "There is no ship on the waters that does not belong to Amûn, for his is the sea and his is Lebanon, of which thou sayest, 'It is mine.' "[49] It is interesting to note that the Canaanite prince is represented as admitting freely that Amûn is supreme and as add-

[47] For good translations see Scharff, *Aegyptische Sonnenlieder*, 1921, pp. 47 ff., and Erman, *Die Literatur der Aegypter*, 1923, pp. 350 ff. [See also Wilson's translation in *Ancient Near Eastern Texts*, pp. 365-367.]
[48] [For translation see Wilson, in *Ancient Near Eastern Texts*, pp. 369-371.]
[49] [For translation see *ibid.*, pp. 25-29.]

ing that Amûn taught and equipped Egypt first, so that Egypt was able to instruct the Canaanites in the art of civilization. It may be observed that this idea agrees with the conceptions of the Ugaritic texts of the fourteenth century regarding Ptaḥ-Kôthar, as well as with the Biblical view that Canaan was son of Ham and brother of Mizraim; so there is no reason whatever for suspecting its essential authenticity.

The general character of the Aten religion is so well-known that there is no occasion for us to dwell on it here at length. In spite of occasional denials by scholars, there can be no doubt that it was a true monotheism, though specifically solar in type and consequently far below the lofty spiritual monotheism of a Second Isaiah. This is proved not only by many statements in the Hymn to the Aten which sound monotheistic but also by the wave of erasing names of other gods from public monuments which then swept over the country. It is also confirmed by other points, such as the absence of shrines of other gods or of their representations in contemporary remains at Tell el-'Amârna. The solar disk is addressed as "the only god, beside whom there is no other," as creator and sustainer of Syria and Nubia as well as of Egypt, as creator and lord of all, including the most distant lands.

After the Aten cult had been, at least officially, stamped out, the priests of Amûn had a brief period of glory. Not, however, for long. The north reacted a second time against the religious tyranny of the south, and Sûtaḥ of Tanis was made patron of the Ramesside kings of the Nineteenth Dynasty. Above we have sketched the remarkable fusion of the Egyptian and Canaanite pantheons which took place at Tanis. So complete was the fusion that it is difficult to determine the origin of any given image of Sûtaḥ-Baal from iconography alone without clear stylistic indices; from Nubia to Ugarit we find substantially the same iconographic type. The extent of this amalgamation of cults may be illustrated in many ways. The phenomena are absolutely certain and it is, therefore, quite clear that nothing remotely like the "henotheism" of Biblical scholars is reflected by our Egyptian sources during the period from 1500 to 1000 B.C.

In spite of the inadequacy of our treatment, which could easily be extended and amplified in many directions, the picture of ancient Near Eastern polytheism in the second half of the second millennium is entirely clear. It was this world into which Israel was born and in which it took up its inheritance. It is scarcely necessary to observe that this is not the world pictured by Wellhausen and his followers.

It is quite impossible to develop my conception of early Israelite religious history here in detail. Though accepting many results of modern Biblical criticism, I fail absolutely to see that they carry the implications for the religious evolution of Israel with which they are generally credited. The very fact that J, E, D, and P often reflect different streams of tradition gives us reasonable confidence that the outstanding facts and circumstances on which they agree are historical.[50] Moreover, thanks to recent archaeological discoveries and to the research of the Scandinavian scholars, we are now coming to have a much higher respect for the historical value of oral tradition than we had a few decades ago. If we eliminate the Book of Genesis because it reflects many pre-Israelite traditions, whose originally polytheistic character is sometimes transparent, and if we eliminate all the rhapsodist Prophets of the eighth century and later, together with the Hagiographa as a whole, D and P, the latter part of the Book of Kings, and clear Deuteronomic and Priestly elements in the earlier books, we still have a very considerable body of material to illuminate the period from 1200 to 800 B.C.[51] Only the most extreme criticism can see any appreciable difference between the God of Moses in JE and the God of Jeremiah, or between the God of Elijah and the God of Deutero-Isaiah. The rebellion against historicism of which I spoke above is justified, yet it should not be a revolt against sound historical method but rather against the unilateral theory of historical evolution which makes such an unjustified cleft between the official religion of earlier and of later Israel. A balanced organismic position may consistently hold that the religion of Moses and of Elijah, of David and of the Psalmists was the same in all essentials, just as the religion of Jesus was subtantially identical with that of St. Francis and the faith of Paul was also the faith of Augustine. (This does not mean that all their *theological* concepts were

---

[50] [See my discussion in *Catholic Biblical Quarterly*, 25, 1963, pp. 1-11, and Martin Noth, *Überlieferungsgeschichte des Pentateuch*, 1948.]

[51] [See my discussion in *Catholic Biblical Quarterly*, 7, 1945, pp. 5-31. On the historical books see now M. Noth *Überlieferungsgeschichtliche Studien*, 1943.]

the same.) In other words it is not history that is at fault, but rather the philosophy of history which is too often associated with it.

I am, of course, fully aware of all the conventional arguments brought by scholars against early Israelite monotheism, but I consider virtually all of them as invalid and some of them as quite absurd. This is, however, not the place to refute them in detail. I wish only to point out that the literature of early Israel all comes from an empirico-logical age, in which there were no such concepts as philosophical interpretation or logical definition.[52] Wisdom was gnomic or graphic; long inherited expressions were used without thought of their being treated as material for analytical hermeneutics or for philosophical deduction. The sixth century B.C., with Thales and Pythagoras, with Deutero-Isaiah and Job, had not yet come. No one could have predicted that the First Commandment would be explained in the nineteenth century as henotheistic; no one could have imagined that the words of Jephthah or of Elijah, written down in their present form about the seventh century, but presumably following old tradition, would have been interpreted otherwise than as simple statements of what everybody knew to be the Ammonite or Tyrian point of view. As a matter of fact there is nothing in the earlier sources which sounds any more polytheistic than the words attributed to Solomon by the Chronicler about 400 B.C.—"for great is our God above all gods" (I Chronicles 2:5). Nor is any allusion to the "sons of God," to the angels, or to the possible existence of other deities in some form or other (invariably very vague) any more henotheistic than the views of Philo, of Justin Martyr, or of the Talmud with regard to pagan deities. As should be clear without explanation, much of the onslaught on early Israelite monotheism comes from scholars who represent certain theological points of view with reference to monotheism, i.e., who deny that orthodox trinitarian Christianity, whether Protestant or Catholic, is monotheistic, or that orthodox Judaism and orthodox Islam are monotheistic. I do not need to stress the fact that neither of the last two religions can be called "monotheistic" by a theologian who insists that this term applies only to Unitarian Christianity or liberal Judaism. But no "dictionary" definition of monotheism was ever intended to exclude orthodox Christianity.

[52] [See above, Chapter 3.]

If monotheism connotes the existence of one God only, the Creator of everything, the source of justice and mercy, who can travel at will to any part of His universe, who is without sexual relations and consequently without mythology, who is human in form but cannot be seen by human eye or represented in any form—then the official religion of early Israel was certainly monotheistic. The henotheistic form constructed by scholars sinks below the level attained in the surrounding Ancient Orient, where the only alternatives were polytheism or practical monotheism, henotheism in the sense used by most modern Biblical scholars being apparently unknown. There is nothing to show that the early Israelites were either ethically or religiously below their contemporaries. The highest manifestations of spiritual life among surrounding peoples cannot be raised to the level of corresponding forms among the precursors of Amos, Hosea, and Isaiah. Moses and Elijah still stand high above the religious leaders of neighboring peoples and the God of Israel remains alone on Sinai.

Who is like unto Thee, O Lord, among the gods?

Chapter 6

Islam and the religions
of the ancient Orient[1]

The myth of the unchanging East shows surprising tenacity. Though serious historians have long since challenged its validity, it emerges again and again, among scholars as well as among journalists. Even the obvious fact that the life of the East is changing with vertiginous speed before our very eyes does not discourage this romantic attitude; it only compels a shift of emphasis from external things to the inner world of mental habits and ideas. The psychology of Islamic countries and peoples remains unchanged, we are told, and its manifestations remain essentially the same: *plus ça change plus c'est la même chose!*

To a certain extent one can scarcely quarrel with this impression. The physical environment *has* remained much the same, aside from far-reaching transformations in the agricultural and animal background which have been made necessary by constant shifting in flora, fauna, and human culture. In passing, it may be emphasized that the prevailing forms of domesticated plants and animals have shifted to a quite extraordinary extent, if we compare different historical

[1] This paper was presented in shorter form at the March 1940 meeting of the American Oriental Society, as part of a symposium dealing with Oriental religions; it was printed the same year (*Journal of the American Oriental Society,* 60, pp. 283-301). Text and notes have been brought up to date throughout, but there is scarcely any new material, and stylistic alterations are very few. I wish to thank Dr. Ray L. Cleveland for some observations.

ages in the same Near Eastern lands.[2] Moreover, not a little of what is often considered as specifically "Oriental" is really universally human, or at least generally characteristic of domesticated mankind. This is particularly true of the famous "Oriental" imagery, which would no longer appear so exotic if we compared it systematically with corresponding early European poetic imagery, instead of comparing it sporadically with jejune products of a later stage of literary development.[3]

Both the historian of civilization and the historian of ideas must, however, emphatically reject the conception of an "unchanging East," a conception which has no support in the facts of history. If we take the past five thousand years, from the beginning of the Bronze Age and the stabilization of the art of writing to the present day, we can distinguish three different phases of civilized life in the Near East: the Ancient Orient, the Hellenistic-Roman Orient, and the Islamic Orient. We are now entering a fourth phase, whose precise nature we cannot safely predict. The affinity between the Ancient Orient and the Hellenistic world is, moreover, materially less than between the Hellenistic-Roman culture and the Islamic. As the late Carl Heinrich Becker stressed on many occasions,[4] Islamic civilization is essentially an outgrowth of Hellenism, just as Islam itself is an offshoot of Judeo-Christian religion. Not to recognize this fact and its implications is to misinterpret the course of history and to misunderstand Near Eastern life and thought.

[2] The parade example is certainly the transformation in dominant forms of transportation. From the dawn of history to the second millennium B.C., the ass ruled the field almost undisputed. Then came the camel, which must have been domesticated in the course of this millennium but which does not appear in any dated inscription or graphic representation yet published until the eleventh century B.C., or even later. Since no camel bones prior to the Iron Age have turned up in excavations, so far as I am informed, it is very improbable that the camel was extensively domesticated until late in the second millennium. A few very early figurines from Egypt clearly represent wild camels. The irruption of the camel-riding Midianites into Palestine must probably be dated in the early eleventh century. In our own time the camel is being replaced by the motor car with disconcerting rapidity. [See further my remarks in *Archaeology and the Religion of Israel*, pp. 96-97, 227, n. *31; *Bulletin of the American Schools of Oriental Research*, No. 163, 1961, p. 38, and n. 9.]

[3] Cf. my remarks above, pp. 84-90.

[4] See *Islam-Studien*, I, *passim*, and *Zeitschrift der Deutschen Morgenländischen Gesellschaft*, 77, 1923, pp. 261 ff.

Since the end of the nineteenth century there have been two significant efforts to connect Islam and Arab culture closely with the pre-Hellenistic Near East: the Pan-Babylonian movement and the proto-Semitic interpretation of modern Arabic folk religion. The former school was created by Hugo Winckler, whose *Arabisch-Semitisch-Orientalisch* (1901)[5] served as its program. To Winckler, the literature and folklore of late pre-Islamic and early Islamic Arabia were saturated with reflections of his Ancient Oriental world view. Since he had to resort to far-fetched interpretations and combinations in order to obtain his results, it is scarcely surprising that no first-class Islamic scholar joined the Pan-Babylonian school and that his best-known follower among Arabists was the incurable romanticist, Count Carlo Landberg.[6] The increasing rejection of Pan-Babylonian doctrines by the world of scholarship has precluded any serious influence from this school on Islamic studies generally. On the other hand, Winckler's extraordinary insight into basic historical problems and his recognition of the organismic character of cultural phenomena have been very fruitful.[7] Becker, in eloquent sentences, has emphasized his great debt to Winckler for his conception of history—though Becker opposed Winckler's romantic pseudo-mysticism with energy.[8]

Far less ambitious or sensational, but more influential, has been the scholarly movement initiated and indoctrinated by the American Biblical scholar, Samuel Ives Curtiss of Chicago (1844-1904). Curtiss was fifty-four when he began to investigate the popular religion of the Moslem Arabs of Palestine and Syria, and he devoted most of the last six years of his life to this study. In the field of Arabic popular religion he may be regarded as almost as much of a pioneer as his great fellow countryman, Edward Robinson, was sixty years before in historical geography. Like Robinson, Curtiss was trained in Germany; like Robinson, he was accompanied by a missionary (Rev. J. S. Crawford, whose Arabic was superior to Eli Smith's); and as in the case of Robinson, his book (*Primitive Semitic Religion Today*) appeared in German as well as in English. It is significant

---

[5] *Mitteilungen der Vorderasiatischen Gesellschaft*, VI, 4/5.
[6] Cf. *Daṯînah*, II, 1909, pp. 387 ff.
[7] Cf. my remarks, *Journal of the Palestine Oriental Society*, 1, 1921, pp. 51-52; *From the Stone Age to Christianity*, 1957 ed., pp. 68-70.
[8] *Islam-Studien*, II, pp. 463 ff.

that no less an authority than Count Baudissin wrote the preface to the German edition, which appeared in 1903 under the striking title *Ursemitische Religion im Volksleben des heutigen Orients*. The influence of Curtiss' work on European and American thought has been very great indeed; it may even be compared, in its repercussion on Biblical scholarship and the history of Semitic religion, to the influence of the studies of the Grimm brothers on Germanic and comparative religious studies generally. There can be no doubt that the great increase in attention to modern Arabic folklore during the past generation is directly traceable to the influence of Curtiss.

When I began research in Palestine (1920), I was strongly affected by the views of Curtiss, though never an adherent of his school. Fifteen years of personal research, as well as of constant collaboration with native Arab folklorists,[9] convinced me, however, that his main conclusions with regard to the historical significance of his results were entirely erroneous. So far from reflecting primitive Semitic religion, the *welī* cult of Palestine and Syria is merely a phase of the saint cult of the Mediterranean region and differs only in detail from the saint cults of the lower classes in other Mediterranean lands. Moreover, this saint cult goes back to the Christian saint cult of the Eastern Roman Empire in early Byzantine centuries and is Hellenistic-Roman, not Semitic, in origin. If one studies the standard treatises of Goldziher,[10] Doutté,[11] and Canaan (see below) on the cult of the *auliyā* (welis) and then examines Père Delehaye's standard Catholic treatise *Sanctus* (1927) and P. Saintyves' monograph, *Les saints successeurs des dieux* (1907), written from the standpoint of an historian of religion with anticlerical bias, one cannot doubt the formal parallelism between the two classes of phenomena. To be sure, this formal similarity between Christian and Moslem saint cults decreases rapidly as one goes up the scale of literacy and intelligence in both spheres, and in more cultivated and more spiritual circles there is undoubtedly wide difference in atti-

[9] Their contributions, in so far as they have been published, have nearly all appeared in the *Journal of the Palestine Oriental Society*, 1921-1941.
[10] *Muhammedanische Studien*, I, pp. 275-378.
[11] *Magie et religion dans l'Afrique du nord*, Algiers, 1909. For a survey of the literature see McCown, *Annual of the American Schools of Oriental Research*, II-III, p. 49, n. 6. McCown's paper (*ibid.*, pp. 49-79) contains some valuable material not found elsewhere, though it is too much influenced by Curtiss.

tude and approach to saints. *Ṣûfî* conceptions have also influenced the *welî* cult strongly in the doctrine of a hierarchy of saints containing seven stages, and in attributing powers of levitation, etc., to welis.

The rich collections of Palestinian material in Canaan's *Mohammedan Saints and Sanctuaries in Palestine* (1927)[12] offer a solid foundation for a classification of the principal types of *welî*, with reference to their historical position and origin. Most of the Moslem saints of Palestine are of two classes: Jewish, Christian, Quranic, and early Moslem saints; saints of recent origin, either ancestors of modern families or clans, or dervishes. In addition to these two chief groups, there is a class of eponymous saints, some of whom may go back to Jewish ancestors of clans or to pagan deities, though most seem to belong to Delehaye's class of "les saints qui n'ont jamais existé!"[13] The most interesting group is an extremely small class of figures which certainly or probably reflect pagan deities—mostly of Greco-Roman type, as we shall see below.

I shall illustrate with some examples of Islamic figures, beliefs, and practices which are of much more recent origin than often supposed and which in no case go back directly to the ancient Near East. I shall then give a few cases which do go back to pre-Hellenistic times, though even here sometimes through Greco-Roman transmission. These cases have been selected either because of their intrinsic interest or because I have new data or suggestions bearing on them.

The Qur'ân itself contains a number of references to extra-Biblical figures of Arab tradition, figures which have frequently been traced back to hoary antiquity. It has been supposed that the legendary city of Íram dât al-'Imâd reflects extremely ancient tradition. The discoveries of Horsfield and Savignac have demonstrated that Iram is the ruined Nabatean sanctuary and settlement at Jebel Ram (Ramm) in southern Transjordan, which was built about the end of the first century A.D. and was still standing in the third, possibly in the fourth century.[14] The tribe of Thamûd, to which

[12] First published in *Journal of the Palestine Oriental Society*, 4, 1924, pp. 1-84; 5, 1925, pp. 163-203; 6, 1926, pp. 1-69, 117-158; 7, 1927, pp. 1-88.
[13] Delehaye, *op. cit.*, pp. 208-232.
[14] See *Revue Biblique*, 44, 1935, pp. 245 ff., and Glidden, *Bulletin of the American Schools of Oriental Research*, No. 73, 1939, pp. 13-15. See now also Diana Kirkbride, *Revue Biblique*, 67, 1960, pp. 65-92.

Ṣâliḥ was sent as prophet, had already existed, it is true, in the eighth century B.C., but it did not disappear until about the same time, since it was still mentioned by the Greco-Roman geographers of the first two centuries A.D.[15] As for Ṣâliḥ, it is remarkable that his name, which means simply "sound, sincere, virtuous" in Arabic, has not been shown to occur in pre-Islamic inscriptions or in authentic literature from the Jâhilîyah, so one may suspect that he also is a reflection of some Biblical character like Idrîs (Enoch),[16] Shu'eib (Jethro), etc. One may recall that Job, whose purported home was in North Arabia, was also a "virtuous man" (*iš tām*). Moreover, it is increasingly unlikely that the tribe of 'Âd and its prophet Hûd come from genuine Arabic tradition, since neither name has any parallel in native pre-Islamic nomenclature. The name Hûd is suspiciously like Yahûd or Hûd (an abbreviated form found already in the Qur'ân), "Jews," and one may suspect that it owes its origin, as in the case of some more recent Arab saints (e.g., Nebī Nûn worshiped at Yânûn) to a popular etymology of Yahûd, explaining it as *yâ Hûd*, "O Hûd." The tribe of 'Âd may perhaps go back ultimately to a misunderstood Hebrew *minnî 'ad*, "from of old."[17] Whatever the explanation of these names may be, it is evidently not safe to regard them as reflecting genuine native tradition. There are prob-

[15] Pliny and Ptolemy. The Thamûd seem to have replaced the Nabateans in the region of Midian before the end of the third century A.D.; see Savignac, *op. cit.*, pp. 251-252. If the late Thamudic inscriptions really belong to them and not to another group, the Thamûd continued to exist as a tribe until the fourth century A.D. (F. V. Winnett, *A Study of the Lihyanite and Thamudic Inscriptions*, Toronto, 1937). A. van den Branden, *Histoire de Thamoud*, Beyrouth, 1960, pp. 28-30, is cautious, leaving a date in the fourth or fifth century open.

[16] The best treatment of the problem of Idrîs remains A. J. Wensinck's article in *Encyclopedia of Islam*, II, pp. 449 f. I see no reason, however, to give up my own view, that Idrîs reflects Greek Poimandrēs (a pagan Gnostic form of Hermes which became very popular in the third-fifth centuries A.D.); cf. my provisional observations in *Journal of the Palestine Oriental Society*, 2, 1922, pp. 197-198. Arabic authors expressly identify Idrîs with Enoch and with Hermes Trismegistus (=Poimandrēs). Moreover, the abbreviation of the name has numerous good parallels; e.g., Greek *diabolos* became *Iblîs* in Arabic (no doubt through Aramaic intermediation). It is hardly necessary to observe that Greek *ēta* was pronounced *i* in Roman times and later.

[17] On 'Âd see the sober sketch by F. Buhl, *Encyclopedia of Islam*, I, p. 121 (new ed., I, p. 169). Wellhausen deduced from the form of the name (which he

ably few today who would follow Dérenbourg and Eduard Meyer[18] in identifying Quranic Luqmân with Biblical Balaam, even as a retrojection of the latter. Disregarding the speculations of medieval Arab scholars and their modern successors, who thought that Luqmân was a translation of the name of Balaam (erroneously derived from Hebrew *blʿ*, "to swallow"),[19] we may safely suppose that Luqmân was a native sage.

Among figures of later Islamic hagiography none is more prominent or more intriguing than el-Khiḍr (properly Khaḍir, "the one who becomes green, the green one"). After the elaborate discussions and collections of data already on the part of such scholars as Clermont-Ganneau, Lidzbarski, Dyroff, Vollers, I. Friedländer, R. Hartmann, and A. J. Wensinck[20] one can scarcely add anything of consequence to the subject. I formerly held the view first advanced by Guyard and still assumed in many quarters, that el-Khiḍr reflects the Mesopotamian figure of Atrakhasis, "the very wise one" (Old Accadian Watram-ḫasis or Watar-ḫasisam),[21] then supposed to appear also in the transposed form Ḥasisatra, whence Greek Xisuthros was falsely derived.[22] However, no such transposed form is demonstrable or even plausible, and the Greek is unquestionably derived from Sumerian Ziusudra, name of the Flood-hero, translated into Accadian as Ut-Napishtim (*rûqu*).[23] There are indeed points of

---

compared with Hebrew *ʿôd*) and from the pre-Islamic phrase *min al-ʿÂd* that it was an appellation and not a proper name, referring primarily to an "ancient" people; *Göttingische Gelehrte Anzeigen*, 1902, p. 596.

[18] *Die Israeliten und ihre Nachbarstämme*, 1906, pp. 378-379. The best treatment of the figure of Luqmân is by B. Heller, *Encyclopedia of Islam*, III, pp. 35 ff.

[19] For the correct etymology see *American Journal of Semitic Languages*, 40, 1923-1924, p. 32; *Journal of Biblical Literature*, 46, 1927, pp. 161 ff.; 54, 1935, p. 174, n. 3; 57, 1938, p. 228.

[20] See esp. the article of A. J. Wensinck in *Encyclopedia of Islam*, II, pp. 861 ff., in which most of the pertinent literature of significance is cited. Wensinck did not mention the important discussion by R. Hartmann, *Zeitschrift der Deutschen Morgenländischen Gesellschaft*, 67, 1913, pp. 739-751.

[21] For the alternative forms of the name see *Journal of Biblical Literature*, 54, 1935, p. 201.

[22] For the Sumerian derivation of this name see my discussion, *Journal of the American Oriental Society*, 38, 1918, pp. 60-61; 43, 1925, p. 32 (*Ziusuddu*), and esp. Jacobsen, *The Sumerian King List*, Chicago, 1939, p. 76, n. 34 (*Ziusudra*); both forms may have been used.

[23] *Journal of the American Oriental Society*, 38, 1918, pp. 60-61.

contact between the Mesopotamian figure of Atrakhasis and the Islamic el-Khiḍr, but they are all of so general or indirect a type[24] that they must have been transmitted through such channels as the Alexander Romance or the post-Biblical Jewish Elijah cycle. The suggestion of Clermont-Ganneau and Dyroff that el-Khiḍr reflects Greek Glaukos, whose name also means "the green one," and who attained immortality like the former, becoming like him a patron of fishermen and mariners, is almost certainly correct, as recognized by Friedländer.[25] The principal objection to this view has been that no adequate syncretistic milieu was known for the prerequisite fusion of Greek popular religion with Aramean paganism in the centuries immediately preceding Islam. This objection no longer holds. The remarkable archaeological discoveries at Dura and Palmyra between the world wars, supplemented by the excavation of Syrian and Nabatean temples and by a great increase in the number of Greek inscriptions from pagan Syria, have shown that there actually was such a full-bodied syncretism of Greek and Aramean religion in Syria between 300 B.C. and 500 A.D., a syncretism which reached its height in the third century A.D. In the Dionysiaca of Nonnus, written in the fifth century A.D., we have the best literary reflection of this mixed Greco-Syrian culture;[26] it is characteristic

[24] The so-called Atrakhasis Epic, known from Old Babylonian and Neo-Assyrian tablets, represents its hero as saving mankind successively from famine, pestilence, and deluge, though details are still obscure because of the fragmentary condition of the text; see Speiser's translation in *Ancient Near Eastern Texts*, pp. 104-106. This figure of the recurrent savior of mankind bears unmistakable similarity to the later Elijah cycle and through it may have influenced Islamic el-Khiḍr.

[25] *Die Chadhirlegende und der Alexanderroman*, pp. 113 ff. The variations of the Glaukos myth (best listed in the article in Roscher) show its antiquity and popularity. E.g., Glaukos was a fisherman who tasted a miraculous life-giving plant, leaped into the sea, and became a sea-god and patron of fishermen, enjoying great popularity in the eastern Mediterranean. There was also a Glaukos who was son of Minos and who was restored to life by a miraculous plant which Asklepios (or another) had seen used by a serpent to revive a comrade. This Glaukos is somewhat parallel to Iolaos the charioteer of Herakles, who brought the latter to life according to late Phoenician mythology by making him smell a partridge (apparently sacred to Eshmun-Asklepios).

[26] See the treatment of the material of Eissfeldt. *Ras Schamra und Sanchunjaton*, Halle, 1939, pp. 128-151; also Faris and Glidden, *Journal of the Palestine Oriental Society*, 19, 1939, pp. 5 ff., on the general situation (Nonnus is mentioned on p. 11).

that our Glaukos figures rather prominently in this epic. Of course, the all-pervading figure of el-Khiḍr cannot be understood solely as derived from Glaukos, whether we consider either or both of the beings which bear this name in Greek mythology. El-Khiḍr is also Elias and St. George, and his composite personality contains elements which doubtless reflect various important pagan deities, both Semitic and Greco-Roman.

A far less significant but equally curious figure of contemporary Arab religious folklore is Umm el-Gheith, "Mother of Rain," to whom the common folk address their petitions in time of drought.[27] The term is specifically applied to a rude doll-like figure of a woman, dressed up and carried in procession, with appropriate songs. It is significant that the Christians of Kerak in Transjordan, who preserve archaic practices, used to dress a hay-fork in women's clothes and call it *'arûs ilâh,*[28] "bride of God." Since this appellation can refer only to the Virgin Mary, we may safely infer that the Moslem Umm el-Gheith is a surrogate for the older Christian *el-'Adhrâ'*, the Virgin, to whom Christians still pray in time of drought.[29] The expression Umm el-Gheith should perhaps be compared with various appellations of the Virgin in Christian litanies, such as *stella maris, fons signatus,* and with such imagery as that of

[27] There is already a considerable body of literature which deals with this subject; the latest important treatment is by Canaan, *Mohammedan Saints and Sanctuaries in Palestine,* pp. 219 ff. For a valuable discussion see Jaussen, *Coutumes des Arabes au pays de Moab,* pp. 323 ff.

[28] Or *'arûs Allâh.* For this idea see the discussion by Curtiss, *Ursemitische Religion,* p. 119. Jaussen's skepticism (*op. cit.,* p. 328) is probably due to the natural unwillingness of his Christian interlocutors in Transjordan to admit the existence of this popular belief.

[29] Cf. Dalman, *Palästinischer Diwan,* pp. 56 f., for prayers to the Virgin for rain. Canaan is also of the opinion that Umm el-Gheith originally referred to the Virgin Mary (*op. cit.,* p. 220), though he does not give any special reason for his view. Nor can it be an accident that the female saint es-Sitt el-Bedrîyeh, whose shrine is at the village of Sherāfât near Jerusalem, is regarded as one of the most potent givers of rain (Canaan, p. 227). While it is true that her name and legends connect her with an historical saint, Bedr (see Canaan, pp. 305-308), it is certain that she does not figure in the literary account of the Bedr family from the fifteenth century (Mudjîr ed-Dîn, *Uns al-Djalîl*) and that she accordingly belongs to the category of "Les saints qui n'ont jamais existé." In other words, Bedrîyeh is again a surrogate for the Virgin, once worshiped at Sherāfât, which was a Christian village down to the late Middle Ages.

Gideon's fleece, which was wet when the ground around it was dry and thus became the symbol of the Virgin Mary. While we may safely suppose that the last pagans prayed for rain to Atargatis, later replaced by the Virgin, Umm el-Gheith would thus be directly attached to the cult of the latter.

As is well known, thanks particularly to the researches of Dr. T. Canaan, the peasants of Palestine and neighboring lands believe that many springs, especially those that flow intermittently or are peculiar in some way, are inhabited by good or evil spirits, either saints, male or female demons, or animals, especially chickens, camels, and sheep. The animal demons are considered to be *jinn*. Nearly half of the female demons are designated as *'arûs*, "bride," or are described as beautiful young women. There can, of course, be no doubt, despite the absence of scholarly recognition of the fact, that the term *'arûs* is derived directly from the Syro-Hellenistic conception of the nymph which guards the spring, since Greek *nymphē* means precisely "bride." This Greek mythological idea has survived in Greek lands as well as in the Near East proper. The jinn which inhabit springs are similarly offshoots of minor Greco-Syrian divinities and spirits. As might be inferred from the fact that the domestic fowl was not introduced into common use in the Near East until the Persian age (though known a little earlier), cases where springs are supposed to be haunted by cocks, hens, and chickens, though relatively common, cannot be very ancient. One, at least, is traceable to a popular etymology: 'Ain Dûq near Jericho, which receives its name from the fortress Dôq, the Dokos of Josephus, is now called 'Ain ed-Dyûk, "Spring of the Cocks," and the natives believe that it is haunted by several cocks! It must be strongly emphasized that these ideas cannot be traced back to the pre-Hellenistic Near East, contrary to the opinion of some modern scholars, who have insisted without the slightest proof that animal names applied to springs in the Bible reflect similar ideas.[30]

[30] For animal names of springs in the Bible cf. L. B. Paton, *Annual of the American Schools of Oriental Research*, I, p. 52, with which cf., e.g., Canaan, *Journal of the Palestine Oriental Society*, 1, 1921, p. 160, n. 1. These Biblical designations (En-eglaim, "spring of the two calves"; En-gedi, "spring of the kid"; En-hakkore, "spring of the partridge"; En-hattannin, "spring of the dragon") are, however, ordinary place names and require no explanation except in the first and last cases. The first name belongs with the parallel Beth-eglaim,

The jinn themselves were probably introduced into Arabic folklore in the late pre-Islamic period. I have pointed out elsewhere,[31] utilizing suggestions of Nöldeke and Lidzbarski, that the word is neither Arabic nor Ethiopic, but a slight modification of Aramaic *gᵉnê*, "hidden," plural *gᵉnên*, "hidden things," and emphatic plural *gᵉnayyâ*, which appears as the name of a class of deities in inscriptions from the first three centuries A.D. at Dura, Palmyra, and in the Jebel esh-Shâ'r, northwest of Palmyra (written *gny'*).[32] On Aramaic incantation bowls of about the sixth or seventh century A.D. from Babylonia we find the word appearing in the sense of "(evil) spirit."[33] In Syriac the derived substantive *genyâṯâ* (emphatic feminine plural) means "pagan shrines" and "female divinities"; in the Peshîttâ it stands for Hebrew *'Aštārôṯ* while Ephrem Syrus (fourth century) and Jacob of Serûg (fifth century) use it as a synonym of *gaddâ*, "(good) fortune" and "pagan divinity, demon."[34] The passage from an Aramaic **ganyâ* or **genyâ*, feminine **gᵉnîtâ*, "demon," to Arabic *jinnîy(un)*, *jinnîyat(un)*, offers no difficulty whatever when one remembers that the Aramaic verb *gᵉnâ* and Arabic *janna* are synonyms and that a slight morphological adaptation would therefore be normal. The occult figures of depotentized pagan deities with which the imagination of the Christian Arameans peopled the underworld, the darkness of night, ruined temples, and sacred fountains, were organized by Arab imagination into the jinn of the Arabian Nights, creatures of smoke, intermediate between the fiery devils of hell and the angels of light.

---

name of an ancient town near Gaza (cf. my remarks in *American Journal of Semitic Languages*, 55, 1938, p. 337, n. 1); the last name is presumably on a par with such German place names as *Drachenfels*, and does not indicate any permanent sojourn on the part of a dragon.

[31] *Journal of the American Oriental Society*, 57, 1937, pp. 319 f.

[32] See now H. Seyrig and J. Starcky, "Genneas," *Syria*, 26, 1949, pp. 230-257, for a first-century stele from Jubb el-Jarrah; for the designation of deity in the monuments from Jebel esh-Shâ'r see Ingholt and Starcky, *La Palmyrène du nord-ouest*, Paris, 1951, pp. 135-137, 186 (index).

[33] Cf. Montgomery, *Aramaic Incantation Texts from Nippur*, p. 80, and Gordon, *Archiv Orientální*, 6, 1934, p. 334, as well as my observations, *Journal of the American Oriental Society*, 57, 1937, p. 320. It is possible that the form *gyn'* is a loan word from Arabic, but the reverse is probably true, since there are no other certain indications of Arabic influence in these texts.

[34] See the references given by Payne Smith, *Thesaurus Syriacus*, I, p. 476b.

A peculiar custom of the modern Arabs, which may be traced back with virtual certainty to Christian Aramaic practices, is that of making a paste of powdered henna and water or melted butter which is then smeared on the walls of a *welī*, especially around the prayer-niche or *miḥrâb*.[35] When the natives are asked what the purpose of this rite is, they invariably respond that it is performed in payment of a vow or as a sign that a vow has been duly fulfilled. Struck by the fact that I had found similar ancient daubs on the walls of a recently opened Byzantine tomb near Beit Jibrîn, I was led, nearly forty years ago, to compare this custom with the Syriac practice of making a paste of dust and oil, which was then smeared on a sick person, or on an object, or was dissolved in water and drunk.[36] The Syriac word for this *Heiligendreck*, as German Orientalists call it, is *ḥᵉnânâ*, "(act of) mercy, grace," and it is obvious that the Arab use of henna (*ḥinnâ'*) as the principal ingredient of the paste is due, in part at least, to some popular etymology or association of words. Originally, we may safely derive the Syriac practice from New Testament tradition: Jesus mixed dust and spittle, smearing the resulting paste on the diseased part of a patient. There was naturally a conceptual background for the idea in Ancient Oriental magic and medicine. The *tertium comparationis* between Syriac and modern Arabic practices may be the connection of the paste with sanctuaries; the Nestorians collected the dust from holy places and the Arabs smear the paste on the walls of holy places.

A great deal of confusion has been introduced into our field by the naïve assumption of many modern scholars and students that folk beliefs and practices of the modern peasants and nomads of the Arab world go back to pre-Arab times, whether to recent or to remote ages, without essential modification. We have seen that this assumption is quite wrong in certain selected cases; moreover, this assumption was a priori improbable and ought never to have been advanced even as a working hypothesis. Certainly students of Doutté, Canaan, and other authorities on magical beliefs and customs, can scarcely help but realize that popular astrology, popular magic, popular divination, etc., are almost throughout derived from literary sources. The astrology comes straight from the Arab

---

[35] Cf. Canaan, *op. cit.,* p. 14.
[36] See the references in Payne Smith, s.v. *ḥᵉnânâ*. In 1928 I called the late Hans Bauer's attention to this parallel, with which he was much struck.

systematists of the classical age, such as Abū Ma'shar in the ninth century. Even oneiromancy, or the prediction of the future from dreams, goes back through the latest and most popular authority, 'Abd al-Ghānī of Nâblus in Palestine (late seventeenth century) to Artemidorus.[37] The frequency with which Canaan, for example, resorts to 'Abd al-Ghānī for an explanation of popular belief illustrates the derivation of the latter from learned tradition. It may confidently be said that the form and content of Arabic amulets have changed but little for many centuries; the tradition regarding them is a learned and not a popular one, using "popular" in the usual sense of "folkloristic."

As for the stories and songs which circulate among the people, nearly all of the former are derived with comparatively slight modification from such repertoires as the Arabian Nights and the Sîrat 'Antar, which took their form in the late Middle Ages. Juḥā and Qaraqôz are, as is well known, of Turkish (i.e., Byzantine) origin. The songs are generally of comparatively recent date, going back either to café songs composed for the cafés of Cairo, Beirût, Damascus, and other urban centers,[38] or to local poets such as Nimr ibn-'Adwân, who flourished in Transjordan in the first years of the nineteenth century.[39] W. Norman Brown pointed out long ago that the folk tales of India are mostly derived from the great literary repertoires, such as the Panchatantra, which themselves, of course, come from still older oral sources.[40] No student of folklore can afford to neglect this cyclic aspect of his material, which seldom goes back directly to any considerable antiquity in any given land or group.

It would, of course, be absurd to deny that there are any direct reflections of the Ancient Orient in Islamic literature and folklore. By direct reflections we mean cases where passing through Hellen-

---

[37] Cf. the remarks of A. Fischer, *Zeitschrift der Deutschen Morgenländischen Gesellschaft*, 68, 1914, pp. 305 f.

[38] Cf. Stephan, "Modern Parallels to the Song of Songs," *Journal of the Palestine Oriental Society*, 2, 1922, pp. 199 ff., esp. pp. 223 ff.

[39] He died in A.H. 1238 (A.D. 1821-1822) and his poems first became known in the West through an article of Wallin in 1852; see H. H. Spoer, *Journal of the American Oriental Society*, 43, 1923, pp. 177 ff.; *Zeitschrift für Semitistik*, 7, 1929, pp. 29 ff., 274 ff.; 9, 1931, pp. 93 ff.

[40] *Journal of the American Oriental Society*, 39, 1919, pp. 3 ff.

istic-Roman channels has not appreciably altered the resulting picture, or where practices and figures escaped Greek influence entirely. Since Aramaic survived through the millennium of Hellenism, and since Aramean and Arabic paganism sometimes persisted into the Islamic Age, as at Ḥarrân, the existence of such direct reflections is not surprising; it is only remarkable that there are relatively few of them. The following illustrations will clarify the situation as we see it.

Some expressions, like *qaus quzaḥ*, "rainbow," literally "bow of (the North Arabian storm-god) Quzaḥ,"[41] and *zauw al-manîyah*, literally "the scissors of fate,"[42] belong to the domain of linguistic fossils and are not properly to be considered as illustrations of religious survival. Such expressions belong to the same class as the Lithuanian expletive *Perkunas*, really the name of the pagan Lithuanian storm-god, but explained to me once by an illiterate Lithuanian immigrant as meaning "son (of) a bitch." To this category belongs the Quranic *hapax legomenon*, *kautar* (Sûrah 108). The sûrah runs as follows:

"Behold we have given thee *kautar*—
And pray to thy Lord and offer sacrifices—
Behold he that hateth thee is childless!"

[41] The best treatment of this deity still remains that of Tuch more than a century ago; see *Zeitschrift der Deutschen Morgenländischen Gesellschaft*, 3, 1849, pp. 208 f. However, there can be little doubt that Josephus, who calls the chief Idumaean god Koze (i.e., Quzaḥ), confused the Edomite deity Qôs (*Kôs*) with the similar Arab divinity Quzaḥ. The god Qôs is now well known from a score of personal names scattered through Greek, Aramaic, Hebrew, Old North Arabic, and cuneiform inscriptions (a partial list is given by Glueck in *Bulletin of the American Schools of Oriental Research*, No. 72, 1938, pp. 11-12) and the original form is known to have been Qaus (*qws*, Assyrian cuneiform Qauš, Babylonian Qus). Wellhausen's idea that Edomite Qaus is Arabic Qais (*Reste arabischen Heidentums*, 2d ed., 1897, p. 67) is scarcely tenable; on the other hand, I see no reason not to identify the Edomite name of the storm-god with Arabic *qaus*, "bow," which is then to be separated etymologically from Hebrew *qešet*, "bow," and its cognates.

[42] This convincing explanation of the enigmatic Arabic phrase was first proposed by Wellhausen (*Zeitschrift der Deutschen Morgenländischen Gesellschaft*, 66, 1912, pp. 697 f.), on the basis of the passages where the expression occurs and the fact that *zawwâ* actually has the meaning "shears" in Aramaic. Wellhausen's suggestion was favorably received by no less a scholar than A. Fischer; see *Zeitschrift der Deutschen Morgenländischen Gesellschaft*, 67, 1913, pp. 113-122.

The word *kauṯar* is explained by some native commentators as meaning "abundance (of good, of wisdom, of prophecy)," from the stem *k-ṯ-r*, "to be abundant." That this etymological explanation is too simple is indicated by the variant interpretation according to which *kauṯar* is the name of a river of Paradise which is specially connected with the Prophet. While we cannot be sure of the idea actually present in Mohammed's mind when he used this word, we can scarcely be far wrong in combining it with the old Northwest Semitic figure of Kauthar, which is known from Ugaritic, Phoenician, Biblical, and Aramaic sources. Kauthar (whence Ugaritic Kôṯar, Phoenician Kûšōr)[43] was the name of the Phoenician Hephaestus, the skilled craftsmen and artificer *par excellence*, and the inventor of musical instruments and of the art of music generally. As G. Hoffmann[44] and H. L. Ginsberg[45] have shown, Kauthar was identified with Egyptian Ptaḥ. Kauthar (Kautar) is also said to have been the father of Tammuz in Aramean mythology,[46] a fact which shows that he is concealed under the name of Kinyras, the eponym of players on the lyre and harp, who was the father of Paphian Adonis in Cyprian Greek mythology.[47] Both in Ugaritic and in the Bible the word *kôṯar-kôšār* is also a word for "musician," properly, "the very skillful, the highly skilled."[48] As a personal name the word may be traced from the twentieth century B.C. to about the third century A.D.[49]

[43] Cf. Phoenician *'ûlōm*, "eternity," for Herbrew *'ôlām*, originally **'aulam* (the Aramaic and Arabic forms are loan words from Hebrew), according to the phonetic principles discussed by Harris, *A Grammar of the Phoenician Language*, pp. 34, 37.

[44] *Zeitschrift für Assyriologie*, 11, 1896, pp. 253 ff.

[45] *Orientalia*, 9, 1940, pp. 39 ff. Ginsberg's main contention is strikingly confirmed by an Egyptian inscription from Megiddo, which proves that there was a temple of Ptaḥ at Ascalon in the thirteenth century B.C.; see Wilson in *Ancient Near Eastern Texts*, p. 263b.

[46] Mentioned by Pseudo-Melito; cf. Hoffmann, *loc. cit.*; Baudissin, *Adonis und Esmun*, p. 74.

[47] The ancient derivation of the name from Greek *kinyra*, "lyre," itself a loan from Phoenician *kinnûr* (Hebrew *kinnôr*, Late-Egyptian *kennûra*), "lyre, harp," may now be regarded as certain. *Knr* (Kinnâr) is now known to have been a minor deity at Ras Shamra; see *Archiv für Orientforschung*, 18, 1957, p. 170.

[48] See Ginsberg, *Bulletin of the American Schools of Oriental Research*, No. 72, 1938, p. 13.

[49] The earliest occurrence is in the hieratic execration texts which were published by Sethe. Here it appears as *Kwšr*, name of a chief of *Šwtw* (in Trans-

The Bible calls Heman and his musical colleagues "sages" on one occasion and "seers" on others, illustrating the extraordinary interpenetration of these ideas.[50] If we suppose that the word *kauthar* meant to Mohammed something like "supernatural gift of poetic inspiration and of clairvoyant or prophetic power," we are perhaps not far from the truth.

A very curious rapprochement, almost certainly correct, was made by P. de Lagarde when he derived the Greek word "anemone" from the Semitic precursor of literary Arabic *šaqâ'iq an-Nuʿmân,* "the anemone."[51] Since Greek *anemōnē* can at a pinch be derived from *anemos* "wind," as the "wind-flower," and since an-Nuʿmân was a famous king of al-Ḥîrah in the late sixth century A.D., it is not surprising that sober scholars like Wellhausen rejected the idea.[52] However, the equation is really very plausible indeed. In the first place it is quite certain that Adonis was sometimes called Nuʿmân or Ne(a)ʿmôn in Phoenician, as we know from a number of occurrences of *Nʿmn* as a divine appellation in the Keret and Danʾel epics of Ugarit,[53] from the term *niṭʿê naʿᵃmānîm,* "Adonic gardens," found in Isaiah, from the fact that the native name of the river Belus in the Plain of Acre is preserved in Arabic as the Nahr Nuʿmein (properly a diminutive of Naʿmân, a common place name in Syria and Arabia), and from the fact that the word *naʿem* is found in Canaanite and Aramean inscriptions as an appellation of deity both in the singular and the plural.[54] Moreover, just as we

---

jordan; see *Bulletin of the American Schools of Oriental Research,* No. 163, 1961, p. 42, and n. 32), along with a Job and a Zebulun (cf. *Journal of the Palestine Oriental Society,* 8, 1928, p. 239); in these names original *ṯ* appears as *š*. The latest occurrence is in a Greek inscription of about the third century A.D. from Syria, where the name is spelled *Chauthar* (see *American Journal of Archaeology,* 42, 1938, p. 593a), a perfect transcription of Aramaic *kwtr.*

[50] See provisionally my remarks in *Archaeology and the Religion of Israel,* pp. 126-128.

[51] *Semitica,* I, 1878, pp. 31 f., and *Uebersicht über die im Aramäischen, Arabischen und Hebräischen übliche Bildung der Nomina,* 1889, p. 205, note; cf. Löw, *Aramaeische Pflanzennamen,* pp. 200-201, 411, and Baudissin, *Adonis und Esmun,* p. 88.

[52] *Reste des arabischen Heidentums,* 2d ed., p. 10, n. 2.

[53] His two most striking appellations are "page of El" (*ǵlm ʾel*) and "strongest of men" (*ʿmq nšm*).

[54] Cf. Baudissin, *op. cit.,* pp. 86 ff. See Harris' glossary, Gesenius-Buhl, *ad. voc.,*

have the parallel forms *šulmân* and *šalmôn*, *Yordân* and *Yardôn*,[55] where the first of each pair is the primary form and the other a secondary dissimilation from it, characteristic of Phoenician proper, so we may be reasonably sure that the Phoenician form of the name, about 1000 B.C., was **Ne'môn* (form like *'Eprôn* from **'Uprân*). The initial *alpha* in the Greek form of the name would then be due to congeneric assimilation of **nemōnē* (like Greek *argemōnē*, "poppy," from Phoenician **argamôn*, Hebrew *argāmān*) to *anemos*, "wind," a process for which innumerable parallels exist.[56] Unfortunately, we do not know what Arabic *šaqâ'iq*, or its singular *šaqîqah*, means in this connection; the usual explanation that it means "wounds," being thus a reflection of the Greek myth, where the anemone sprang from the blood of the dying Adonis, is lexicographically hazardous. Perhaps the native lexicographers are correct in explaining it as "lightning flashes of Nu'mân."[57] That Nu'mân of al-Ḥîrah should replace Adonis is on a par with Queen Stratonike's replacement of Astarte in the Kombabos myth.[58]

In modern Syria and Palestine there are a very few direct reflections of paganism in the names and legends of modern welis. The most remarkable is the female saint remembered until recently by the common people as Seiyidet ez-Zahrah (= ez-Zuharah) or

---

and cf. Ugaritic *'lm n'mm*, "the gracious gods," and the later feminine Na'mat, which seems to be the name of a goddess (Baethgen, *Beiträge zur semitischen Religionsgeschichte*, p. 150).

[55] For the morphological principle involved see my provisional observations in *Journal of the Palestine Oriental Society*, 8, 1928, p. 238, n. 2; 14, 1934, p. 133, n. 172a; *Archiv für Orientforschung*, 7, 1931-1932, p. 168; *The Vocalization of the Egyptian Syllabic Orthography*, 1934, p. 36, IV.6; *Bulletin of the American Schools of Oriental Research*, No. 63, 1936, p. 28, n. 22. For Amorite Rušpân see J. Lewy, *Mélanges syriens offerts à M. René Dussaud*, I, 1939, pp. 274-275 (*Ra-sa-ap*, with Amorite *s*, is the normal Mari form). It may be added that the vocalization Rašap for the form of the *name* without an ending ("Resheph"), now established by the Mari texts (Lewy, *loc. cit.*), has been employed by the present writer since 1930; see *Journal of the American Oriental Society*, 50, 1930, p. 339; *Archiv für Orientforschung*, 7, 1931-1932, p. 167, n. 20.

[56] For the linguistic process which Maurice Bloomfield named "congeneric assimilation" (German "Mischbildung" and "Reimwortbildung") see F. R. Blake (*Studies in Honor of Maurice Bloomfield*, New Haven, 1920, pp. 35-48) and C. Brockelmann (*Zeitschrift für Semitistik*, 5, 1927, pp. 6-38), both writing from a Semitistic point of view. The treatment of the etymology of the word *anemōnē* by E. Boisacq, *Dictionnaire étymologique de la langue grecque*, p. 61,

Seiyidet Afqā, "the lady Venus" or "the lady of Aphaca," whose husband was slain while hunting.[59] As is well known, the greatest shrine of Aphrodite and Adonis in Greco-Roman Syria was at Aphaca, at the source of the river Adonis. The "Green Lady" (el-Khaḍrā) at Ascalon can hardly be anything but a reflection of Derceto,[60] once goddess of the city. The saint called "Father of the Two Eyes" (Abū 'l-'ainein) near Rāmallāh, from whose two eyes sprang a tree,[61] can hardly be separated from a precursor of the Adonis type. A class of curious eponymous figures, such as Sheikh Riḥâb near Beisân, Nebī 'Ajlân near Gaza, Nebī Ṣeidûn in Sidon, whose names carry us back to pre-Israelite times, may possibly echo their remote pagan precursors.[62] On the other hand,

---

is inadequate and he does not even try to explain the origin of the anomalous suffix which he appears to assume.

[57] For convenient orientation see the data given by Lane, *An Arabic-English Lexicon*, I, p. 1578c. There is no indication anywhere that there ever was an Arabic word *šaqîqah*, "wound," as often assumed without proof. Since the Arabic expression can hardly antedate the sixth century A.D. and may be still more recent, it is imprudent to set up an unattested word. On the other hand, the Arab lexicographers illustrate the meaning "lightning" in many ways. The verbal froms *šaqqa*, *tašaqqaqa*, and *inšaqqa* are all used of lightning which "splits" the sky; *šaqîqatu 'l-barqi* is "a flash of lightning which splits the clouds" (syn. *'aqîqah*). The *Lisân al-'Arab* (XII, p. 48 below) elucidates the meaning of *šaqqa* as follows: *hua 'l-barqu 'lladî tarâhu yalma'u mustaṭîlan ilâ wasṭi 's-samâ'* "that is the lightning which you see prolonging itself to the midst of the sky as it flashes." Of the anemone the Lisân says (XII, p. 49 above): *summiyat bi-ḍâlika li-ḥumratiha 'alâ 't-tašbîhi bi-šaqîqati 'l-barq*, "It has been called by this (name) for its redness for the sake of comparing it to a flash of lightning." It must be remembered that Adonis was often identified with the storm-god Baal and that it is at best very hard to distinguish between the functions and myths of the dying god and of the storm-god. At Ugarit Baal (Hadad) appears as the dying god; we also find later that Hadad was the dying god in different local cults. Moreover, expressions of this type were known in Canaanite: cf. *benê* *Rašap* as "vultures" (*Haupt Anniversary Volume*, pp. 149 f.) and the name of the town Benê *bârâq (Massoretic *beraq*, cuneiform *barqa*, modern Arabic *ibrâq*), literally, "Children of Lightning." The original myth may have traced the creation of the anemone to a blow on the ground from the thunderbolt-spear of Baal (see the Ugaritic stele found by Schaeffer, illustrated in *The Ancient Near East in Pictures*, ed. J. B. Pritchard, Princeton, 1954, p. 168, no. 490), just as Greek mythology traced the origin of the olive tree to a similar act of the storm-god Poseidon.

[58] Cf. also my remarks in *Bulletin of the American Schools of Oriental Research*, No. 78, 1940, p. 27, n. 21.

they may be quite recent saints, whose personal names have been replaced by the names of the towns or villages where they resided. In conclusion, we wish to assure our readers that our sampling has not been unfairly weighted on either side. There is a mass of evidence in favor of the relatively recent date of most concrete elements in Islamic religion and culture. Becker was right in insisting on the thoroughgoing dependence of Islamic culture on Hellenistic. The gap which separates Greco-Roman civilization from Ancient Oriental is much greater than that which divides Islam from Hellenism. Religiously, Islam is an integral part of the Judeo-Christian tradition and owes very little directly to the religions of the Ancient Orient.[63]

---

[59] Curtiss, *op. cit.*, pp. 173 f.; Paton, *Annual of the American Schools of Oriental Research*, I, pp. 55 f. (the spelling "Ṣaʿîdat Afḳā" is naturally wrong).

[60] On this name cf. my remarks, *Journal of the Palestine Oriental Society*, 14, 1934, pp. 130, 153, where I propose a derivation from Ugaritic *darkatu*, "dominion." It is most improbable that the name has anything to do with that of Atargatis. [See Schaeffer, *Archiv für Orientforschung*, 20, 1963, p. 214, on *bʿlt drkt*, "Mistress of Dominion," as a title of Anath.]

[61] This saint has a shrine near Rāmallāh in Palestine. The Moslems believe that the sheikh is buried under a tree which sprang from his two eyes. With this motif compare the myths of Bitis, from two drops of whose blood sprang two persea trees, and of Agdistis, from whose testicles grew an almond or pomegranate tree (see *Journal of Biblical Literature*, 37, 1918, p. 126).

[62] Cf. Canaan, *Mohammedan Saints and Sanctuaries*, pp. 286 ff. Nearly forty years ago I was present at a most interesting informal discussion between a teacher and a peasant at Beit Jibrîn, in which the latter maintained that the saint locally called Nebî Jibrîn was a true prophet (*nebî*) while the Hebronite teacher insisted that he was only a holy man (*welî*). The people of Beit Jibrîn believe that this "prophet" was their ancestor. Since the Israelites and Arameans shared a belief that the second element in a place name formed with the element *bêt* (house) was the name of an ancestor of the people who lived there, this idea may go back to the Aramean town of Bêt-gabrâ (Talmudic *Bêt-gubrîn*), regardless of the original meaning of the name. However, it is hard to separate the designation *nebî* from the fact that the second element, Jibrîl= Jibrîn, was explained in the Middle Ages as *Jibrāʾîl*, the angel Gabriel.

[63] In the discussion of this paper when it was presented at New York (in 1940), a number of points were brought out. Professor Calverley called attention to rites and practices taken over by Mohammed or his followers from pre-Islamic times, such as the procession around the Kaʿbah and the rite of circumcision. There can be no doubt that he is right, and I have not intended to exclude such survivals from the picture. Above I expressly stress the fact that there are many exceptions, though the sum of the exceptions is still far inferior to the total of

later borrowings. In my report on the excavation of the earliest high place at Petra, *Bulletin of the American Schools of Oriental Research*, No. 57, 1935, pp. 29 ff., I have stressed the great antiquity of the *ṭawâf*; see also R. L. Cleveland, in *Annual of the American Schools of Oriental Research*, XXXV, 1960, pp. 76-77. Professor Jeffery called attention to certain survivals from ancient Egypt in the folk beliefs and practices of modern times. He is unquestionably correct, but the relative proportion of survivals remains insignificant. Professor Ogden pointed out that there are also Iranian, Zoroastrian elements in Islam. He is undoubtedly right, and some of these elements (Hârût and Mârût, etc.) go back to the time of Mohammed. Yet the relative importance of the Iranian factor in Islam is very much smaller than is that of the Hellenistic-Roman factor, and some phenomena which are credited to the Iranians were really borrowed by the latter from the West.

Chapter 7

Historical adjustments of political authority in the Near East[1]

Introductory remarks

In analyzing historical concepts, one must beware of distortions arising from the historian's own approach to his data. To have clearly indicated this danger is a major contribution of the historical relativists to our thinking. Unfortunately, they have been so carried away by their controlling idea that they have tended to lump all historical judgments together indiscriminately, regardless of their basic nature. To one who recognizes the fundamental distinction between historical judgments of fact, of typical occurrence, and of value, this confusion seems to be a serious hindrance to the successful analysis of underlying factors in history. In our sketch below we shall deal principally with the second of these classes of judgment, typical occurrence, since our data for social forms and concepts are nearly all derived from the agreement of many independent data. Where we proceed to interpret, judg-

---

[1] This article was originally published as Chapter I in *Approaches to World Peace* (Fourth Symposium of the Conference on Science, Philosophy, and Religion in Their Relation to the Democratic Way of Life; New York, 1944), pp. 1-16, under the imposed title "Historical Adjustments in the Concept of Sovereignty in the Near East." The title has been changed in order to fit the content, and the text has been revised in order to bring it up to date. The notes are all new. I wish to thank Mr. Melvin Arnold of Harper & Brothers (now Harper & Row) for securing permission to reprint the chapter here.

ments of value are in place; but we shall try to label them as such and to justify them by logical considerations.[2]

Two divergent tendencies stand out today among thinkers who investigate human group phenomena. The first and more common tendency consists in treating social concepts and forces as independent of one another, often without even considering the possibility of their organic interrelation. This tendency is probably still exemplified by most social theorists, according to whom drastic experimental modification of social structure and its conceptual field is not only justified but is the duty of the sociologist and social reformer. Recently there has been intense agitation on the part of social theorists for a concerted drive to raise mankind somehow to a level comparable to its present technical mastery of environmental conditions. Each such experimental modification must, according to them, be subject to concrete verification of its success. The instrumental theory of validating social experiments is inevitably most hospitable to nonfunctional doctrines of social organization. We need scarcely add that it is found in some form wherever the influence of John Dewey has penetrated, though it is too symptomatic of the age to be entirely attributable to him.[3]

The second tendency to which we have referred, consists in treating associated social phenomena as functionally interrelated, as dependent in large degree upon one another. To theorists of this school, all essential aspects of an integrated culture are bound closely together. If one element is dislocated, the entire structure may be in imminent danger of collapse. Necessarily, the viability, or capacity for continued life, of a culture depends largely on the elasticity of its structure. Tinkering with any persistent element of any culture is considered by functionalists as intrinsically dangerous. They are also apt to regard any apparently declining culture as standing in need of sympathetic isolation, with as little interference as possible on the part of would-be reformers. This tendency is best illustrated by contemporary American cultural anthropologists, most of whom are functionalists of one kind or another. Their philosophical approach may be just as positivistic as that of the instrumentalists, but is generally organic, not experimental, in orientation.

[2] See above, pp. 26-27.
[3] See above, pp. 8-9, 47-48.

Since it is quite possible to combine certain forms of instrumentalism with certain types of functionalism, it is doubtful whether many contemporary students are fully aware of the real gulf which exists between typical exponents of the two positions. My own position is intermediate: all social structures are organismic rather than organic in nature, with their own distinctive characteristics and their own definite life cycle. Such structures appear at every level of history and exhibit great variability in extent and pattern, as well as in viability. Often they overlap in time, space, and function. They are usually bound together into larger and less stable organisms, both in space and time.[4] Because of this organismic character of a culture, which presupposes some bond between its constituent elements, it is intrinsically dangerous to meddle with any element which seems to be characteristic of it. Attempts to interfere with its normal functioning may result in irreparable injury, sometimes in complete extinction. Experiments on any society are perilous, but not impossible; they cannot, however, be safely validated by the instrumental method, since it may take generations to show clearly whether there is net gain or loss in any given case. For instance, national prohibition of beverage alcohol seems to have proved a rather complete failure (though competent opinion differs widely), but it may take decades of statistical analysis before reliable judgment can be passed. Birth control has been advocated vigorously by most social theorists, and its effects have been widely alleged to be beneficial; but now that our nuclear Anglo-Saxon stock appears to be declining relatively to other groups, the instrumental point of view may perhaps be shortsighted. Instrumentalism, in brief, can be tested only over quite a long period, as a result of which its practical application is more often likely to be discredited than otherwise. When we come to the most fundamental and yet the most intangible aspect of any cultural unit—its religion or ideology—instrumentalism breaks down completely as a practical philosophy, since there is no acceptable method of measuring results of change, except perhaps over a long period of time. Centuries may elapse before the effect of a given concept on any social entity becomes evident.

On the other hand, rigid functionalism is not only arbitrary in

[4] See my discussion in *From the Stone Age to Christianity*, 1957 ed., pp. 120-126.

itself, since it cannot be demonstrated by observation, but is also highly improbable from the historian's point of view. Too many mixed cultures have been successful, and there is too much demonstrable diffusion of higher culture. It is, accordingly, not accidental that the strict functionalist shares a pronounced aversion to history with his instrumentalist colleague. Again and again viable new cultures or other social organisms have arisen as a result of the collision of quite heterogeneous bodies. A single innovator has often fashioned powerful new social or cultural structures from miscellaneous materials at his disposal, choosing his building elements more or less eclectically. A single new element injected into a stagnating social structure has often given it new and vigorous life. In fact, it seems clear that social organisms represent the product of a series of empirical collocations and mutual adaptations. Hence I prefer some such term as "empirico-adaptive" to "functional," without for a moment denying that there are many functionally interdependent elements in any organismic unit of social character. Adaptation may lead to a functional relationship, even between structures of entirely distinct phenomenal character. So, for instance, in the case of religion and sex relationships, whether among Australian primitives or Europeans. Interference with group life must follow accredited patterns to be safest, for which reason we must resort increasingly to historical patterns as our guides. The systematic following of historical models has enabled much Christian missionary activity to be successful in improving conditions of primitive life, though it must be remembered that this activity has also been partly responsible for the extinction of whole groups, because of its drastic methods or its external associations. Similarly, modern ethnologists have performed some extremely valuable work by way of saving various primitive peoples from extinction. On the other hand, this has sometimes been accomplished by the establishment of a controlled reservation closely resembling a concentration camp.

Historical patterns of political authority

In the Near East—that is, the basin of the eastern Mediterranean and the lands contiguous to this region on the east—the historian possesses a unique demonstration laboratory. Chronologically,

Near Eastern history covers some ten thousand or more years of sedentary human life, half of which is well documented by written records. At least three-fourths of our present knowledge of the history of the Near East is the result of devoted research by over a century of Western Oriental and archaeological scholarship. Geographically, the Near East is both the center of civilization during most of world history and the route by which divergent civilizations met and exchanged elements of culture. Until less than five hundred years ago there was no practical way in which men could pass from Asia to Africa and Europe, or in the opposite direction, without crossing the Near East. Culturally, the Near East is the cradle of all European and most Asiatic civilization; to its twin foci, Egypt and Mesopotamia, the Hellenic world owed its initial cultural momentum. Here the three great ethical monotheisms which sprang from the Mosaic stem—Judaism, Christianity, and Islam—were born. The Near East thus possesses perennial significance for the historian of ideas and institutions.[5]

For convenience we shall divide our survey into the following periods: the Bronze Age, from about 3000 to about 1200 B.C.; the Iron Age, from about 1200 to about 300 B.C.; Hellenistic-Roman culture, from about 300 B.C. to about 600 A.D.; Islamic culture, from about 600 A.D. to the present. Only a few pages can be given to each period.

At the beginning of the third millennium B.C. we find a complex bureaucratic state emerging in Egypt. At its head stands the king, possessed of absolute power. This system followed an only vaguely known period in which the country was split up into many local districts, which seem to have been loosely confederated into larger states. The old local nobility may have been exterminated by the pharaohs of the Pyramid age; at all events there is no trace in

[5] A good treatment of the field will be found in J. A. Wilson, E. A. Speiser, H. G. Güterbock, and others, *Authority and Law in the Ancient Orient* (Supplement to the *Journal of the American Oriental Society*, No. 17; 1954). H. Frankfort's *Kingship and the Gods*, Chicago, 1948, is virtually without value for our purpose here; see the excellent review by Moses I. Finley, an able student of ancient law and society, in *Political Science Quarterly*, 63, 1948, pp. 275-281. Finley points out in detail how Frankfort's "phenomenological" approach (really an eclectic selection of idealistic motifs going back ultimately to Hegel and Schleiermacher) distorts his avowed effort to be guided by the data themselves.

our written records that it still existed. The king was believed to be the incarnation of the sun-god, who was the chief deity of the land. The king was thus a god in his own right, conceived by the sun-god, reigning as a god over his human subjects and ascending after death to unite with his father in reigning over the gods. The gigantic funeral monuments of the Memphite kings, known to all the world as the pyramids, constituted by far the greatest single achievements of the mightiest princes of the age. The extraordinary concentration of human energy represented by the pyramids of the Fourth Dynasty is an outstanding example of the power exerted by the Egyptian concept that political authority resided in earth-bound deity. This tension may well have played an important part in unifying the Egyptian state, by harnessing its heterogeneous energies and directing them along ways of peace.[6]

The Pyramid age ended in a period of feudalism, in which the appointed officers of the crown were able to hand their functions down to their sons, thus creating local dynasties of feudal princes. Thanks to the research of Jacques Pirenne, son of the great Belgian historian, it has become known that some of the Delta cities reacted against the anarchic conditions which followed the breakdown of the central power in Egypt by organizing themselves into quasi-democratic, properly gerontocratic, communities.[7] We shall see that similar constitutions prevailed in western Asiatic towns at the same time and shortly afterwards. This phase was followed by a reorganized absolute monarchy under the Theban kings of the Twelfth Dynasty, about 2000 B.C. However, the feudal nobles were not crushed but were subjected to direct royal control, and they continued to exercise some check on the

[6] For the material included in this paragraph see such surveys as John A. Wilson, *The Burden of Egypt*, Chicago, 1951, and Rudolf Anthes, "Aegypten," in *Historia Mundi*, Vol. II, 1953, pp. 130 ff. Jacques Pirenne's *Histoire des Institutions et du Droit privé de l'Ancienne Égypte*, 3 vols., Brussels, 1932-1935, is brilliant in places but tends to soar off into space without empirical preparation. His multi-volume world history, *Les grands courants de l'histoire universelle* (rev. ed. since 1959) is so far removed from empirical data that it cannot be used by students.

[7] See J. Pirenne, *Journal des Savants*, 1937, pp. 12 ff., and *Revue d'Égyptologie*, 3, 1938, pp. 1-16. The Asiatic evidence has been gradually accumulating, and I hope to present it before long in the *History of Ancient Palestine and Syria* which I am preparing.

latter. During the ensuing Hyksos age the old nobility was practically wiped out by internecine strife and foreign invasion. As a result of its drastic decimation, the New Empire, established in the sixteenth century B.C., was able to return in principle to the absolutism of the Old Empire. The restored power of the pharaoh was used mainly for foreign conquest and temple construction. In practice, however, royal absolutism was checked by the increasing power of the priests, as well as by the existence of a much larger middle class than ever before, composed of functionaries and professional men. The abortive monotheistic revolution of Akhenaten, in the fourteenth century B.C., was also an attempt to crush the rapidly growing power of the priests and other vested interests by suppressing all older cults and eliminating the old literary and artistic conventions, thus throwing the professions open to new, untrained men. During the reign of Akhenaten, sole responsibility for the functioning of the state, including priestly powers, was attributed to the king. Characteristically enough, almost the only old religious tenet that was kept was the divinity of the king, which was actually reinforced by daring new theological speculations. It is scarcely surprising that the movement in question was swept out of power by a violent revulsion of feeling soon after the death of the heretic king.

Turning to Mesopotamia, we can clearly see that the power of the king was later in developing and that there was much greater variation in forms of sovereignty than in Egypt. Thorkild Jacobsen has demonstrated by comprehensive research that the Sumerians and Accadians of the third millennium still possessed definite vestiges of gerontocratic organization.[8] It is true, of course, that we cannot be sure whether this organization was originally Sumerian or Accadian, or both; the question is not very important, since race seems almost always to be subordinate to culture in the history of the Near

---

[8] This term is preferable to the "primitive democracy" of Jacobsen, since the Sumerian *abba* (Accadian *šibûtum*), "elder(s)," corresponds closely to similar expressions in the Assyro-Babylonian texts, the Amarna tablets, the Old Testament, Phoenician, Carthaginian, Greek, and Roman sources from the second and first millennia B.C. Of course, not every "senator" was necessarily a "senior citizen"; nor do I deny that there was a tendency to "democracy" in primitive times as well as later; see Jacobsen, "Primitive Democracy in Ancient Mesopotamia," *Journal of Near Eastern Studies*, 2, 1943, pp. 159-172, and in *Zeitschrift für Assyriologie*, 52/nf 18, 1957, pp. 91-140.

East. The early Babylonian local town assembly may be properly compared with the Germanic *folkmoot* or the Homeric Greek assembly of warriors and elders. All such institutions among peoples in a relatively early stage of social development may be termed quasi-democratic, but they invariably proved impracticable agencies of government as society became more complex; similarly in recent times the town meeting has been progressively discarded in favor of a representative system. Among the Sumerians and Accadians of early Babylonia we see a steady growth of the power of the king, reaching a climax in the Third Dynasty of Ur, toward the end of the third millennium. In early Sumerian literature the king was a "great man," appointed to his exalted office by the gods, whose authoritative spokesman he thenceforth became. In his hands were all governmental functions—legislative, judiciary, and executive. Many monarchs were believed to be descended from deities, especially at the beginning of a dynasty, when "the kingship descended from heaven." The Accadian kings of the Dynasty of Accad were the first to be deified during their lifetime, so far as we know, presumably on account of the unprecedented military exploits by which they built up the largest empire yet known to have existed in the Bronze Age. After this beginning, king-worship continued with occasional interruptions for some five centuries. That it then disappeared seems to be a result of the irruption of semi-nomadic Western Semitic tribes, which conquered all Mesopotamia in the first quarter of the second millennium B.C. How completely even the memory of king-worship was suppressed may be illustrated by the fact that not a single one of the numerous poetic compositions in honor of the deified king is known to have been copied after the middle of the second millennium B.C. It was completely expunged from Late Mesopotamian theology, according to which the king was always human, never divine; though sycophantic courtiers might *compare* him to deity, they never went so far in our recorded sources as to *identify* him with deity.[9]

Among the Semitic tribes who occupied Mesopotamia in the early second millennium, gerontocratic local government was in full vigor. Our best examples come from the Assyrian trading colonies of the nineteenth century B.C., in Cappadocia; good paral-

[9] See H. Frankfort, *op. cit.*, pp. 295-312 and 405-408; C. J. Gadd, *Ideas of Divine Rule in the Ancient East*, London, 1948.

lels occur in contemporary Babylonia.[10] There is also evidence for parallel developments about the same time or a little earlier in northern Egypt and the coast of Syria.[11] These quasi-democratic communities conducted their own affairs through the "assembly" or "the town and the elders." Their political power was restricted by their allegiance to the remote "prince" of Assyria, as well as to the native rulers of Asia Minor. Gerontocracy appears sporadically in subsequent centuries, but we may safely say that Mesopotamia has never before or since come so close to democracy as at that time. It goes without saying that this atmosphere was singularly unfavorable to deification of reigning kings.

The southward and westward migration of Indo-Aryans and other non-Semitic peoples employing fast horse-drawn chariots led to the rise of a new feudal system in the seventeenth century B.C., based on chariot-owning nobles, who played a part comparable to the horse-riding knights of the Middle Ages. Among the Hittites, for example, the king was now both the sun-god in person, following earlier belief, and the delegated representative of the nobility, which met in council to confirm or depose a king, as well as for other purposes. The nobility of the Horites (Hurrians) and the Cosseans (Kassites) received fiefs from the king and were thenceforth bound to fight for him when called on. The new society became sharply differentiated: nobles, serfs, and slaves formed its main classes.[12]

In the early Iron Age we find the same two general tendencies as we saw in the early second millennium: absolute royal power on the one hand and gerontocratic reaction against it on the other. Among Assyrians and Persians the king was in principle absolute, deriving his power from the direct command of the gods, as we are repeatedly assured in the royal inscriptions. Since the king

[10] See the literature cited above, n. 8.

[11] See above, n. 7.

[12] There are a great many partial studies of this subject but no comprehensive survey seems yet to have appeared. Meanwhile see R. T. O'Callaghan, S.J., *Aram Naharaim* (*Analecta Orientalia*, 26; Rome, 1948), pp. 64 ff. The situation was similar in Cossean Babylonia, where assignment of property to notables under feudal lien was very common, and where the great relative importance of chariot horses, with an Indo-Aryan hippic terminology, is well established; see Kemal Balkan, *Kassitenstudien: 1. Die Sprache der Kassiten* ("American Oriental Series," 37; New Haven, 1954), pp. 11 ff., and studies by W. von Soden, Manfred Mayrhofer, and others since 1957 (in part still unpublished).

generally obtained his authorization to act from priest-controlled oracles, this meant in practice that he was often controlled by the priests. Another check on arbitrary exercise of his power came from the fact that the king was surrounded in both Assyria and Persia by ancient and powerful noble families, which divided the principal functions of the complex bureaucratic state among themselves, either in rotation, as in Assyria, or by inheritance, as in Persia. Assyria was particularly fortunate in its system of checks and balances, which kept the state on a relatively even keel, with only the rarest change of dynasty, for some eight centuries or more.[13]

In the West, on the other hand, we find the period from 1200 to 300 B.C. characterized by constant oscillation between one-man rule (tyranny) and some form of gerontocracy or democracy.[14] In the Phoenician cities and colonies we find that rule by kings tended to be replaced by gerontocracy, the earliest and best example of which was Carthage. Tyre followed suit in the sixth century B.C. To this general picture belong also the rise and subsequent overthrow of the "tyrants" ("dictators" in modern parlance) of the Hellenic world. We need not dwell on such a well-known episode in world history, nor stress the fact that several dynasties of tyrants maintained power through the Hellenic golden age. The democracy of Athens was, however, comparable to the best Anglo-Saxon democracies of recent times: when slavery is cited against it, we must remember that slavery was part of the social framework of the southern United States, where democratic theory flowered first and best; we must also recall that industrial serfdom has been common in other parts of the Anglo-Saxon world in still more recent decades.

For some two hundred years, during the Age of the Judges, the tribes of Israel were governed by a loosely federated amphictyonic league, details of which are not known to us. Local organization was on a tribal basis, where nomadic traditions of freedom and religious ideals of equality and liberty for every Israelite, prevented the clan heads from achieving dictatorial power over members of their clans. Later Israel remembered this age as one in which

[13] It is not even certain that there was a real change of dynasty during this long period; the evidence is conflicting.
[14] See above, n. 7.

"every man did what was right in his own eyes." The menace of predatory neighbors led first to the temporary choice of leaders by the men of fighting age, and finally to the selection of a *nāgîd*[15] for life (Saul, David), who soon became a "king" to all intents and was later permitted to hand down his office to his son. Even after the establishment of the monarchy, antiroyalist rebellions were frequent: Yahweh was Israel's king—no other ruler was needed. Neither the Northern nor the Southern Kingdom ever became an absolute monarchy according to Ancient Oriental models; in both there was a standing quasi-democratic check on royal power. In Israel the reality of this check is shown by the fact that unpopular dynasties were invariably supplemented by others when a weak king appeared on the throne. In Judah, where the Davidic Dynasty lasted for over four centuries, there was a permanent body known as "the people of the land," whose exact constitution is not known. Our data make it certain that it was not a parliament, as has been suggested, yet that it was a recognized institution, presumably made up of representatives of the clans of Judah, who were convened whenever an emergency arose. The Lachish letters from about 589 B.C., just before the final conquest of Judah by Nebuchadnezzar, strikingly illustrate the account given in Jeremiah. King, royal officials, and representatives of the old clans created a triangular balance of power, to which the relative stability of the Jewish state may in part be attributed.[16] Neither stability nor democracy could easily have been maintained, however, without the extraordinary atmosphere of social and political reform created by the Prophets, whose freedom of speech puts Hyde Park and the best days of muckraking newspapers to shame. Protected by religious sanctions, the Prophets of Judah were a reforming political force which has never been surpassed and perhaps never equaled in subsequent world history.[17]

After the Jewish Restoration in the sixth century B.C., a semi-

---

[15] On this term and its meaning for the constitutional change in Israel during the eleventh-tenth centuries B.C., see the discussion in my Goldenson Lecture for 1961: *Samuel and the Beginnings of the Prophetic Movement*, Cincinnati, Hebrew Union College Press, 1961.

[16] The balance of power between hierarchic priests and charismatic prophets unquestionably formed an important factor in this stability; see *ibid.*, pp. 18 ff.

[17] See *ibid.*, *passim*, and for a general survey from a somewhat different point of view, see *From the Stone Age to Christianity*, 1957 ed., pp. 301-333.

autonomous ecclesiocratic state was set up under Persian political domination. A comparison of our fragmentary Biblical records with the Elephantine Papyri shows that the Jewish state was controlled by a gerontocratic body of some kind. At Elephantine, this body was made up of the chief priest and representatives of the leading priestly and secular families.[18]

As a result of the Macedonian victory over the Persian Empire, Hellenic civilization spread rapidly over the civilized world. Alexander himself, the pupil of Aristotle, seems to have tried to establish self-governing Greek cities over the whole empire, with a view to combining Hellenic ideals of personal freedom with imperial organization. The contest between democracy and absolutism was destined to failure, since the odds were heavily in favor of the latter. Not only were few of the Greeks accustomed to the exercise of democratic rights; they became a small minority in the vast conquered empire. The personal ambitions of the warring successors of Alexander became Orientalized with startling speed. If Greek philosophy could have raised its voice effectively against absolutism, some fragments of democracy might have been saved in the Hellenistic world. Unfortunately, both of the dominant new philosophical sects which arose in the wake of Alexander's career turned their backs almost from the start on the struggle for political liberty. The Stoics surrendered to astrology, which rapidly became the most popular aspect of their system. In the new faith, which spread from Babylonia in the third century B.C. and took definite form in Egypt during the second century, Babylonian ideas of absolute divine and human political authority were dominant. There was no escape from cosmic predestination, called *heimarmenē* by the Greeks; political activity became meaningless to the philosophically inclined man. On earth royal decrees were in their way just as immutable, following the popular conception of Persian law which is attested in the Bible. It is true that fate might be changed by magical means and that royal decrees might be superseded by legal fiction, but both alternatives were

[18] We may leave open the question of terminology. Here I have used the word "ecclesiocratic" where my survey in *The Biblical Period from Abraham to Ezra*, 1963, p. 95, has "hierocratic." The common "theocratic" is quite misleading, since there is no evidence that oracles or other means of ascertaining divine will were in use by Jews at that time.

irrational and could not appeal to thinking men. Epicurean thought was even more unfavorable to political reform, since it stressed the principle of detachment from the affairs of state, thus discouraging many of the most intelligent and public-spirited citizens from participation in political life.

Among the extremes to which increasing acceptance of the principle of absolute royal power led, was the deification of Hellenistic kings. As might be expected, it began in Egypt, where Alexander had already accepted identification with Zeus Ammon, and spread to Syria, where the Seleucids adopted it. As has been pointed out by W. W. Tarn, the idea was familiar to the Greeks from their own heroic legend; it must have shocked the native Aramean population of the Seleucid Empire. Under Antiochus Epiphanes the theory of the divinity of the king was pushed so far that he tried to abolish all faiths except belief in him and his Olympian colleagues.[19] Not unnaturally, the Jews rebelled and established a new ecclesiocratic state under the rule of Maccabean high priests, who later declared themselves also kings. Maccabean coins are very instructive, since they were issued by the incumbent high priest, whose name and title were followed by the words "and the commonwealth of the Jews." The expression, whose exact meaning was long doubtful, has been explained by recent discoveries; it corresponds closely to Greek *koinon*, "community, commonwealth." In the light of contemporary Greek usage in Greece itself, it is evident that the autonomous Jewish state was regarded by its citizens as an ecclesiocratic commonwealth, combining traditional Jewish features of great antiquity with ideas of recent Greek origin. Since the Hasmoneans were great admirers of Rome, some reflection of Roman republicanism is by no means unlikely. The ideals in question were, however, unseasonable; the enveloping Hellenistic climate of absolute royal power overcame nascent republicanism and the last Hasmonean princes ruled as arbitrarily as their Macedonian contemporaries.

The Greco-Oriental world was moribund. Never perhaps in history had mighty kings ruled with so few checks on their despotic power. As we saw previously, new ways of Hellenistic thinking

[19] On this development see in general C. W. McEwan, *The Oriental Origin of Hellenistic Kingship*, Chicago, 1934, and Elias Bickermann, *Der Gott der Makkabäer*, Berlin, 1937.

had so demoralized educated men that they had lost all faith in the old religious and ethical sanctions. Among them there were neither priests nor priestly oracles to hold the king in check, while the native population was mostly too abject to offer any resistance to tyranny. Only at Petra and Palmyra did freedom-loving Arab tribes form new states, toward the end of the Seleucid period, where autonomous gerontocratic organizations developed rapidly from a tribal background.

In the light of the picture we have just drawn, it is evident that the Romans did not really destroy freedom when they conquered the eastern Mediterranean basin. By this time civic freedom had almost completely ceased to be honored in the East except in literary tradition. Actually the Roman conquest gave new freedom and security to the common man—however little he might appreciate it when oppressed by publican exactions. For the first time in history a relatively uniform system of codified law—public law, not arbitrary royal decree or legal interpretation—spread over most of the civilized world. Under Augustus and the Antonines the Near East was probably more peaceful and more prosperous than ever before in history. But while republican forms were sedulously preserved in Rome itself, in the East the emperor became a real divinity both in official theory and in private belief. Jewish and Christian opposition to Rome was nearly always the direct result of irreconcilable hostility to emperor-worship.

The rise of the Sassanian Empire in the third century A.D. gave added impetus to the growth of royal power in the civilized world; authoritarianism reached a new climax in both East and West in the fourth century A.D. There were, of course, violent reactions, best illustrated by the communistic uprising led by a Persian named Mazdak. In the early Byzantine Empire the emperor was no longer identified with God, but his power as vicegerent of God on earth was unimpaired. The republican forms which continued as a legal fiction in Rome were abandoned almost entirely. Roman law remained in force, and its cultivation was never as sedulous as under Justinian in the sixth century; yet the influence of the archaic corpus of Roman law on the courts was clearly less than it had been. On the other hand, the increasing power of the Christian clergy, especially of monastic bodies, formed a practical check on imperial autocracy. In monastic circles democratic organization flourished, drawing many public-spirited men away from civic life. However, the rapid decline of the middle class and the absence of an autonomous nobility more than compensated for the stabilizing influence of Christianity. When the Moslem irruption burst over the Roman Empire, the latter was so lacking in patriotic spirit that effective resistance was no longer possible. Political and economic democracy had virtually ceased to exist in the Mediterranean world.

Democracy was, however, by no means extinct. Among the semicivilized peoples on the fringes of the Roman Empire, especially the Germans and the Arabs, quasi-democratic institutions flourished on a low political level. The Germanic tribes possessed more stable forms of gerontocracy, from which Anglo-Saxon parliamentary government was eventually to evolve, but the Arabs of the sixth and seventh centuries A.D. surpassed them in their concept of individual freedom. We must, of course, remember that the Arabs were not so much barbarians as nomadic folk on the fringe of a very old sedentary civilization, which had been affecting them directly for thousands of years. Their concept of individual freedom was consequently much more sophisticated than that of the Germanic tribes, which were still in an undeveloped corporative stage of society. Nothing like the democratic spirit of most extant pre-Islamic poetry is known in early Germanic literature, where tribal nobility was generally exalted at the expense of the commoner. The nomadic Arab submitted only with reluctance to any leader, and the concentrated force of Arab impact on the sedentary world of the seventh century would have been unthinkable without the religiously conditioned harmony and enthusiasm characteristic of early Islam under the Prophet and his immediate successors.

Iranian and Byzantine influences were not long in modifying the unstable Arab constitution of early Islam. First the caliph, or "successor" of Mohammed, became the "leader of believers" ("commander of the faithful"). By the eighth century A.D. the caliphate had become assimilated to the Iranian monarchic idea. However, there was one great difference: the absence of any real class of nobles and the equalitarian principles of Islam, which taught that there was no difference in the sight of God between caliph and slave, encouraged the development of a relatively classless society, in which the humblest peasant or shopkeeper's son might hope through good fortune or industrious application to become the highest official in the land. Though a true nobility developed during the Middle Ages, every strong Moslem ruler had taken care to suppress or to weaken it. In this respect the Turks carried out Abbasid tradition: a well-known example is Mohammed Ali's extermination of the Mameluke nobility of Egypt. In many ways the Turkish Empire of the past four centuries was only the continuation of the Arab caliphate of the eighth-tenth centuries. The Sultan of Turkey was also spiritual head of all believers in his empire, as well as of millions of pious Moslems outside his realm.

In surveying the history of Islam there can be no doubt that it has carried on the equalitarian traditions of its parent faiths, Judaism and Christianity. No matter how autocratic his government may be, every Moslem firmly believes that he is equal to every other believer before God. Every new Moslem religious movement at first exhibits pronounced equalitarian and even communistic tendencies; we need only point to such divergent types as the Carmathians and the Wahhabis, the Sufi and Mahdi sects. In recent generations such anachronisms as the low status of woman and the survival of slavery have acted as a barrier to reformation of Islam, which has remained stagnant while the Christian and Jewish West have gone on to reach much higher levels of social and political practice. Trends in 1944 were encouraging: polygamy and slavery were fast becoming extinct; Western liberal ideas were becoming acclimated. The most important step of all remained to be taken: a great religious revival of Islam which would discard the anachronistic principle of holy war and stress the social responsibility of the individual believer. Only in this way can we hope for the development of a really stable basis for democratic society in the Moslem world.

In 1944 it could be predicted with confidence that the Moslem peoples of the Near East would not long remain under foreign tutelage. It is true that only a few Arab minorities, such as the Lebanese and perhaps the Druze, are ready for democratic self-government; almost all larger groups are still in relatively primitive stages of tribal or patronal organization. Whatever happens, the minorities must be protected, since the democratic future of Syria and Egypt is absolutely dependent on preservation and encouragement of the industrious and literate Christian minorities. Particularly important for the political future of the Arab peoples is the flight of Jewish refugees from Europe to Palestine, which has brought hundreds of thousands of well-educated Europeans into the middle of the Arab world. The large-scale demonstration by the Jews of modern democratic and cooperative organization, both in civic and in economic life, is certain to exert tremendous influence on the Arabs. However much the Arabs may dislike this intrusion, its value for their future evolution is of the highest order. In their own interest they should welcome the Jewish example of democratic organization for the common good. The Near East faces one of the most critical phases of its entire history, a phase which will be of great significance for the future of mankind.[20]

Epilogue

Our rapid historical survey of changing concepts of political authority in the Near East exhibits a complex series of oscillations between democratic and autocratic tendencies. Democracy is as old as human society, but even in its most primitive known forms it exhibited relative instability when compared with other types of government. This lack of stability is inherent in the very nature of democracy, and should not be cited as a proof of its necessarily ephemeral character, as has become so popular in recent years. The most advanced biological organisms are often the most delicate and unstable in structure. As long as democracy can be maintained on an even keel, it is the safest of vessels, because of its multiple control and the machinery of checks and balances required to direct its voyage without disaster.

Like the clue of Ariadne, the thread of religion has run through our narrative, details of which show that there can be no question of a rigid functional relationship between form of political authority and type of religion. Nor can we accept a standpoint like

[20] I have allowed the preceding 400 words to stand with only appropriate stylistic changes, since I should still endorse them. To be sure, the attainment of independence by all the Arab countries and the successful establishment of a Jewish republic in Palestine have brought new problems impossible to foresee in 1944. Nor could the revolution in power politics resulting from the development of nuclear power and the great advances of world Communism have been predicted. The only safe prophecy today is that no prophecy is more than a guess!

that of Durkheim, according to which any religion reflects the sociological structure of the society which professes it. It is true that a given religion often does reflect *earlier* social or political structures. Yet a religion is often borrowed almost unchanged from other peoples with entirely different social and political forms. And a new religion may sweep a country without appreciably changing the dominant concept of sovereignty. In the Fourth Egyptian Dynasty, religion buttressed the absolute power of the king. In many other periods it held royal power in check and saved the country from the effects of drastic experiment, as in the Amarna age. In short, political and religious concepts and practices become adapted to one another and modify one another, but they are not functions of one another; no such constant reciprocal relation exists. It is clear that the role of religion was, on the whole, most beneficial to the body politic, since it kept crown, patricians, and demos in check, while maintaining moral standards and ethical sanctions. The innate conservatism of all organized religion made it exceedingly valuable as a balance wheel in ordinary times; the tremendous drive of a successful new religion made it a powerful force in inaugurating a new age. It can scarcely be a coincidence that the breakdown of Hellenistic government followed rapidly after the disintegration of long-accepted religious beliefs under the impact of unrestrained philosophical speculation. Nor should we forget that the most persistently democratic of all peoples, Israelites and Jews, have been of all the most tenacious of their ancestral faith and the most insistent on the moral purity of citizens as a prior condition for civic prosperity. We have yet much to learn from Hellas and Israel; we disregard their instruction at our peril.[21]

[21] For the following discussion by F. S. C. Northrop, Dugald C. Jackson, and Alfred C. Lane see the original paper, p. 16.

Chapter 8

Some functions of
organized minorities[1]

The general problem of the relationship between majorities and minorities has not attacted great interest until recently. Symptomatic of the attention now being paid to this basic problem is the series of conferences on "Group Relations and Group Antagonisms," held in New York last year [1943], under the chairmanship of Louis Finkelstein and Robert M. MacIver; its proceedings, issued a few months ago, are attracting many readers throughout the country.

At first thought it may seem rather curious that so fundamental a question should be so long neglected, but the reasons for this neglect are easy to find. Group tensions are by no means new; in fact they go back into the mists of our evolutionary prehistory. The problem of how to deal with refractory minorities or, conversely, how to maintain the existence of threatened minorities, is as old as civilization. Ethnic and national minorities are as ancient as imperial ambitions, which antedate the dawn of history in both the Old and New Worlds. Religious minorities may be traced back to the

[1] This paper was originally published in *Approaches to National Unity* (Fifth Symposium of the Conference on Science, Philosophy, and Religion in Their Relation to the Democratic Way of Life; New York, 1945), pp. 260-275. No changes have been made in the printed text except to correct two or three misprints and a few spellings. The Postscript and notes are new. I wish to thank Mr. Melvin Arnold of Harper & Brothers (now Harper & Row) for obtaining permission to reprint the paper here.

middle of the second millennium B.C. in the Near East, and our ignorance of earlier cases is doubtless due to the silence of our written sources. In antiquity, however, the usual method of handling minorities was to liquidate them by a general massacre or by forcible removal to other regions. In these ruthless practices the Assyrians excelled, and their ephemeral success has been copied by the Nazis of our day. Tolerance of minorities, ethnic and religious, was achieved—within limits—by the earlier Persian kings, as well as by a few Greek and Roman rulers, but it remained a rare exception. Pagan Roman emperors persecuted Jews and Christians, and their Christian successors persecuted pagans and Jews. Contemporary Iranian adherents of Zoroaster persecuted heretics and Christians. Farther east, Brahmans persecuted Buddhists, who retaliated in kind.

Coming down to more modern times we see the same melancholy picture. The first Moslems showed a type of clemency hitherto little known toward the Jews and Christians, recognizing their intimate kinship with them in matters of faith, but even these favored minorities had from the first to suffer under severe civil disabilities and fiscal exactions. As for the Zoroastrian "fire-worshippers," they were treated by the Moslems with extreme ferocity. Long before the Crusades, moreover, the Moslems became just as intolerant as their Byzantine predecessors, and this intolerance has continued with rare exceptions ever since. It is scarcely surprising that the relatively barbarous Christians of western Europe showed similar intolerance under Charles the Great and many lesser princes. While (contrary to frequent assertions) the record proves that the Christian Church in Europe was on the whole more tolerant than the civil authorities, it cannot be denied that it remained consistently more intolerant than the Moslem world through the Middle Ages. This is illustrated both by the fact that the Jews enjoyed relative freedom from oppression in southern Spain and North Africa between the tenth and the fifteenth centuries, and by the fact that strong Christian minorities continued to exist in most Moslem countries down to our own times, whereas the Moslems were extirpated from all European lands reconquered by Christians before the sixteenth century. Religious heretics were treated with approximately equal brutality by Moslems and Christians during the Middle Ages, as may be illustrated from the story of Albigenses, Lollards, and Hussites in Europe, and of several comparable Shiite sects in Moslem lands. The religious wars of the sixteenth and seventeenth centuries present a disheartening picture, comparable only to the events of the past generation in eastern and central Europe, with their reciprocal massacres of whites and reds. Ogpu and Gestapo have their prototype in the Spanish Inquisition, which in its turn was only a more efficient instrument than still older forms of crushing minority opposition. All share the same unholy methods: the use of informers, torture chambers, and special judicial tribunals for quick execution.

The liberalism of the Enlightenment was responsible for the first period of general religious toleration in the history of the world; happily it coincided with the formative phase of American constitutional history, thus ensuring the freedom of minorities, at least in theory. To be sure, the liberals of that age favored tolerance mainly because of their conviction that state religion was fundamentally hostile to democracy and could best be fought by encouraging the growth of dissenting sects. In a somewhat similar way the Nazis have encouraged the Methodists and Baptists at the expense of the state churches, both Protestant and Catholic, while the Soviet authorities until recently allowed smaller sects more freedom of action than was granted to the Orthodox Church. John Dewey seriously distorted the historical situation when he said [1944] in New York, ". . . The men who made the Constitution forbade the establishment of a state church because they . . . knew that the introduction of religious differences into American life would undermine the democratic foundations of this country." The Founding Fathers undoubtedly opposed a state church, but this was because they wished to keep the intolerance characteristic of such churches in Europe out of American life. Dewey's point of view is very different. His view, echoed more than once by progressive educators speaking at previous sessions of our own Conference, is that we must oppose the divisive and disintegrating influences of modern American life by making our school curricula more uniform and by restricting religious influence on education as much as possible, both inside and outside the cadre of the public-school system. This tendency, which is on a par with the efforts of progressive educators to create new federal agencies for education, aims primarily to consolidate the power already achieved by these educators. In other words, in their propaganda we find incorporated the same basic human drive for power at any price. Our current educational empire is thus quite as great a menace to American liberties as a state church might have been. These propagandists serenely disregard or gloss over the principle, recognized by many American statesmen of the past, that the ability of citizens to govern themselves and to take an intelligent part in solving the problems of society, will atrophy in proportion to their loss of control over the formulation of civic policy. Centralization of education is just as dangerous to democracy as any other kind of centralization.

Infinitely more in harmony with the American democratic tradition of popular government under a system of carefully fashioned and constantly corrected checks and balances, is MacIver's statement in his introduction to *Group Relations and Group Antagonisms:* "Where multi-group societies have developed the influences of democracy are most clearly manifest, and on the other hand, the fact of a multi-group society has tended to encourage democratic ways of life. In short, a democracy and a multi-group society belong together."

It seems that *soi-disant* liberalism, however well-intentioned, cannot rid itself of the universal human drive to compel other men to submit to one's bidding, to conform to one's pattern. The liberalism of a John Dewey is infused with such compelling missionary zeal that he cannot brook opposition, and his followers automatically imitate the *intransigeance* of their leader. Dewey and his followers have accomplished so many good things that one may well hesitate before registering one's conviction that in throwing out the baby with the bath, that is, in waging formal war against all religious organizations and against the humanistic tradition as a whole, the evil they now do outweighs the good they have done.

The evolutionary momentum of a dynamic new nation, like the United States, is so great that an extremely delicate steering mechanism is needed. Centrifugal and centripetal forces must be nicely balanced; tendencies and movements must be controlled before they run wild. The so-called "melting pot" is necessary in order to fuse a congeries of distinct minorities into a single great nation. There was a time when German parish schools stood in the way of rapid Americanization of German Catholic and Lutheran children. At the same time Polish and Ruthenian, Italian and Spanish parishes served by foreign-born clergy were foci of resistance to the action of the melting pot. In the First World War the Church learned the lesson that in the long run this plan weakened it by accustoming its younger members to naïve association of language with religion; the youth, deprived of their customary language of confession, drifted away from the Church. But the opposite tendency, to suppress differences as completely as possible and to replace organisms and crystalline structures by amorphous masses, has always been dangerous and is now a greater menace than the earlier centrifugal trend. When a population of heterogeneous origin loses its diverse ethical and spiritual traditions, it inevitably replaces the lost forms by a new national ethos on a lower level—a level corresponding to some common denominator of the separate types from which it has arisen. The very democratic character of the American school system, emphasizing the cultivation of specific mental and manual skills, is calculated to oust the diversified underlying traditions with their wealth of emotional, aesthetic, and spiritual values. As a well-known example we need only cite the decay of popular music in America since the melting pot began to boil in earnest. This same situation is also an important cause of the growth of juvenile delinquency with concomitant gangsterism.

Observations like these led one of the leaders of Protestant German nationalistic thought in the first decades of the Second Empire, Paul de Lagarde, to the conclusion that in order to preserve the traditional German ethos it was necessary to eliminate the Jews from German life. Actually, of course, this decay of the old traditions was primarily due to the combined onset of industrialism and rationalism. In characteristic majority fashion, however, Lagarde looked for an intrusive foreign body to serve as scapegoat; in his program for the conservative party of Prussia he wrote (1884): "The Jews as Jews are a serious misfortune for any European people. As far as Germany is concerned, it follows that the Jews must either emigrate from Germany or must become Germans. Otherwise Germany will become Jewish—in fact it has almost reached that point now. For decay is faster than growth, and much faster than the growth of a noble spirit. . . . Germany must be full of Germans and German ways of life, after which there will be no room for Palestine in it." In view of the fact that Lagarde was one of Germany's leading academic humanists as well as an influential publicist, these words were strangely ominous; it was only his personal combination of rationalistic humanitarianism with a Christian ethos that kept him from anticipating Hitler and denying the Jews the alternative of becoming good Germans. Scores of thousands of Jews followed this advice and became assimilated to German life by surrendering all specifically Jewish traditions—we all know how much good their cowardice did them. Lagarde's attitude toward the Jews was essentially emotional, reflecting instinctive majority reaction toward a disturbing minority: the Jews then constituted the only minority of which all urban Germans were acutely conscious, since French, Polish, and Danish peripheral minorities were eliminated from the picture by being Germanized as rapidly as possible—or simply by being labeled as German.

However, considerations of general character are not likely to influence any intellectual whose mind is made up and who is convinced that he knows the only right way. From the political intolerance of a Lagarde to the religious intolerance of a Dewey is an even shorter step than from the religious liberalism of a Lagarde to the political liberalism of a Dewey. Moreover, general considerations will not deeply affect less arrogant intellectuals or even intelligent people generally. We must have more precise and more cogent reasons for our faith in American cultural pluralism. I shall, accordingly, list some of the more compelling arguments for the encouragement of minorities under the following five categories.

1. Cultural and religious minorities tend to be more productive in proportion to numbers than the majorities among which their members live. The reasons should be rather obvious. As a rule, members of minorities find life harder than members of majorities. Their origin in a despised minority restricts their social intercourse and closes many doors of advancement. Since they must expend greater effort in order to reach any attainable prize within the power of the majority to confer, they become habituated to greater tension of latent capacity. This principle is called "the stimulus of penalization" by Arnold J. Toynbee in his monumental *A Study of History*, where there are many cogent illustrations from the life of individuals and groups. It will be recalled that Emerson long ago wrote a brilliant essay on the operation of the law of compensation in the lives of individuals. In modern times we have many examples of the superior achievements of minority groups; one need

only mention such outstanding cases as the role played by the Huguenots in the life of Protestant Europe after the revocation of the Edict of Nantes by Louis XIV, as the domination of Ottoman Turkish administrative life by the Greek Orthodox Phanariotes in the eighteenth century, or as the contribution of the Jews to the culture of central Europe during the half century preceding the triumph of Hitler. When we remember that the Jews numbered only about one per cent of the population of Germany but were represented by five to ten per cent of the faculties of German universities and were even more solidly established in the legal and medical professions, when we recall that the percentage of Nobel prize winners of Jewish origin was even higher, and that a steadily increasing number of Germany's leading musicians and artists were Jewish, we see the extraordinary effect of the stimulus of penalization on a dynamic minority. In this connection it is wryly amusing to note that Kurt Breysig, a German thinker belonging to the circle around Werner Sombart and, like the latter, a precursor of the Nazi movement, published a book in 1932 entitled *Vom deutschen Geist und seiner Wesensart,* in which he listed the four contemporary German thinkers who had influenced him most: the philosopher Husserl, the psychologists Köhler and Wertheimer (both later exiled in America), and the biologist Driesch. For all his antagonism to the encroachments of that mythical monster, the Jewish spirit, Breysig seems not to have noticed that two (Husserl and Wertheimer) of these select four were Jews! I may add that a leading American pro-Nazi at whose home I happened to see this passage in Breysig's book was actually ignorant of the fact that they were Jews. To these academic preachers of racial intolerance, a "good" member of a disliked minority is tacitly removed from that minority, whose average standard is correspondingly lowered in their prejudiced minds.

2. Energetic minorities are an invaluable stimulus to the majority, which always tends to become a more or less inert mass unless it is pricked or galvanized into action from an external source. Undisturbed humanity is unenterprising and its activity languishes without competition. By the very fact that most minorities would cease to exist soon after their members stopped flaunting their differences in the face of the majority, dynamic minorities invariably irritate a majority. This irritation may lead at first to direct refusal on the

part of the majority to accept any ideas or improvements originating in a despised minority. Ultimately, however, economic self-interest comes into play, or reform is effected through the intervention of a superior member of the majority, who appropriates what he wants from the minority and disseminates it among his fellows as his own contribution.

3. A corollary of the previous consideration is that progress and reform always spring from the initiative of individuals or of small circles, and are hence more likely to originate in organized minorities than among members of a recognized majority. Since few individuals are able single-handed to influence any appreciable number of their fellows, it devolves upon the small minority which accepts the leadership of any superior or indeed independent person to exert the requisite amount of influence on the majority. It would be most instructive to gather a list of the important advances in American civilization which we owe to members of minorities, whether recognized or unrecognized. Quakers, Unitarians, and Jews, for example, have all played outstanding parts in this respect. Among self-made Americans who have achieved distinction during the past generation there is a surprisingly high proportion of foreign-born, or of members of minorities already established abroad before being transplanted to America. Insignificant indeed would have been the social progress of Great Britain during the past century if it had not been for its Catholics and nonconformists.

4. Organized minorities are powerful balance wheels in any highly-developed society. This is just as true in the fields of education and religion as in the political arena. In Germany the Catholic Center Party played a most important role in keeping the Weimar Republic on an even keel; dominance by either right or left might have led it directly toward the chasm into which Germany fell as soon as the middle classes had been seriously weakened by unfavorable economic conditions. Somewhat similar, though less effective, were the roles of the German minority in Czechoslovakia and of the Jewish minority in Poland. In England and especially in America, Catholic minorities have repeatedly helped to prevent violent swings toward political reaction on the one hand and toward socialism on the other. After progressive educators had triumphed over their antagonists, they became overconfident and aggressive, whereupon the Catholic Church threw its influence against them and prevented

a number of extremely dangerous social and educational experiments from being put into operation. Even Freudian psychology may be counted among the minority intellectual movements which have, whatever their other shortcomings, been salutary in so far as they have acted as a brake on current American pragmatism and behaviorism; it has at least taught a generation of American writers to respect the significance of the nonrational forces underlying personality. In strictly religious territory, for example, the Neoorthodox minority among Protestants represents a very wholesome reaction against the shortsighted experimentalism of most religious liberals, as well as a badly-needed corrective to the obscurantism of many conservatives. Even more striking is the socio-political function of the Catholic circle represented by the *Commonweal*, which constitutes a small liberal minority within the large Catholic minority and which represents in many ways the most enlightened and the best balanced religious group in America.

5. Somewhat different in character from these positive functions of minorities is their negative function as touchstones of democracy. MacIver's correlation of democracy with multi-group society, which we have have quoted, furnishes a most practical test of the viability of modern democracy, which generally finds a home in a complex society, often one in which different languages are spoken, different religions coexist, and different social organisms flourish in symbiosis. It is no accident that Switzerland, with its two religions and three languages, represents the oldest extant republic. It is highly probable that Great Britain could not have developed its aristocratic parliamentary system into a representative democracy but for the fact that the Church of England had increasingly powerful competitors in the nonconformists and Catholics. It is equally probable that the early triumph of the Industrial Revolution in England had much to do with the ultimate development of successful political compromise between social classes, a process with which one may contrast the political chaos into which extremely retarded industrialization threw Russia. The first warning that German democracy was doomed came with the increasing success of Nazi propaganda against minorities. The most serious threat to the continued existence of our American democracy during the past generation has come from the Ku Klux Klan and similar organizations in more recent years.

In conclusion we may infer from the foregoing considerations that America's future success as a democracy depends less on its natural resources and military power, less even on its constitutional tradition, than on its continued protection and encouragement of minorities. America became great through the migration of minorities, and she will remain a great democracy by respecting the right of men and minorities to differ in all matters not affecting the traditional fundamentals of right and wrong!

Appendix

David Baumgardt, *Library of Congress:*

The last five points of Professor Albright's paper seem to me as constructive for the future as his historical review is instructive concerning the past.

Even if one takes into account cruelties of medieval German bishops and the terror of the Spanish Inquisition, it seems to me, too, that the Christian Church was on the whole more tolerant than were the civil authorities and there was relatively little oppression of the Jews in southern Spain and North Africa between the tenth and fifteenth centuries if one takes into account that, for instance, Miamonides could at least leave Cordova and successfully settle in Cairo.

The hot iron of liberal fanaticism and all-forgiving milksop liberalism can, I think, be satisfactorily handled only if as much skill is used as Professor Albright is showing and demanding. The interesting mixture of German agressiveness with slight humanistic, international, Christian, or philosophic inhibitions can indeed be best illustrated by references to such types of Germans as Lagarde, Treitschke, Stocker, and Schopenhauer.

Professor Albright's five motives for the encouragement of minorities are closely interwoven with each other so as to form almost one whole. All the more important is, I believe, his dissecting them into several distinguishable elements. The stand which he is taking above majority—and minority—chauvinism provides, in my view, the only basis of understanding and fertilizing group tensions.

There are only minor points on which I dissent. Wolfgang Köhler and Hans Driesch belong to the most internationally minded Germans. Evidence of this is a far-too-little-known essay by Köhler, published in April, 1933, in the *Deutsche Allegemeine Zeitung* in Berlin and Driesch's report on his travelings in China and the USA as well as correspondence and talks I myself and my father had with him. Professor Albright's main thesis, therefore, stands: Breysig pointed to four German thinkers none of whom is by any means a German nationalist. Of somewhat greater interest is perhaps my final point. Very many Zionists agree that all baptized "assimilated" German Jews were "cowards." I myself am a Zionist. But I should not call the Mendelssohns, Heinrich Heine, Gabriel Riesser, Ferdinand Lassalle, Eduard Lasker, and Walter Rathenau cowards. I believe that German-Jewish assimilation was a more subtle and complicated historical phenomenon.

Taraknath Das, *College of the City of New York:*
On the fundamental conclusions of Professor Albright I am in full agreement, about which I shall make a few comments later. At the outset I wish to mention that in India in ancient times tolerance toward minorities was probably greater than in Persia or Greece. The edicts of Asoka (see *Asoka* by Vincent Smith) indicate this beyond any doubt. Toleration of the minorities in India, often extending refuge to persecuted peoples who sought shelter in India, was due to the religious philosophy of the people which did not believe in "exclusive right of any religion" to provide "salvation," as has been claimed by the three Semitic religions— Judaism, Christianity, and Islam. In ancient India there was virtually no religious war between the Hindus and the Buddhists. I may venture to disagree with Professor Albright and say that there was virtually no religious war, like the Crusades, among the Hindus and the Buddhists. It may be of interest to note that when the Jews were persecuted in the Near East, a branch of the Jewish people took shelter in India and they were not only given refuge, but they enjoyed complete cultural autonomy. They still live in India as Jews and have contributed their share to the good of the country. When the people of Persia were overrun by the Moslem invaders, some Persians of Zoroastrian faith took refuge in India, and they were not only given shelter and aid but full cultural autonomy. The Parsees, though small in number, from a very important minority in India. Early Christians—tradition has it that St. Thomas and his followers came to southern India—established a Christian Church

and they were never molested. Hindu and Buddhist India had virtually no religious wars such as were common in Europe in the past and even in the twentieth century.

In support of Professor Albright's thesis, I wish to emphasize the point that immigrants (who come as members of a minority community) have in most cases infused new blood for the progress of a country. The part of immigrants in the development of the United States has been ably discussed by Professor Hansen of Harvard in his studies, as well as by Professor Wittke (of Oberlin College) in his work *We Who Built America*.

It often happens that minorities contribute much to the progress of the country, because they want to gain recognition and equal opportunity in the new community, through their service and sacrifice. This is the best way for their security. This is not only true of the Jews in Germany, as Professor Albright has shown in his paper, but of the Parsees in India. This minority community is the most cultured and has done a great deal, in proportion to its number in India, for industrial development of the country.

A minority community is generally more deeply attached to its adopted country and makes greater sacrifices for the good of the country—general public—than the older and settled communities, because by doing so its members demonstrate their patriotism and also remove the stigma of being "alien" in spirit. Furthermore, they wish to give expression to their appreciation of the opportunity they have had and provide greater opportunity for others. This is not only true of the Jews of America—note such educational foundations as the Guggenheim Foundation, Rosenwald Foundation, Heckscher Foundation, and others—but of other minorities in other countries. For instance in India, the Parsees have not only contributed vast sums for educational and scientific progress, but also have taken a leading part in the Nationalist movement—the names of Naoroji, Wacha, Mehta, Tata, and others are intimately connected with the Indian Nationalist movement. They have played roles in India's national life similar to those of Ballin, Rathenau, Haber, and others of the Jewish community in Germany, which was their country and homeland.

In a democratic country like the United States, a minority community plays a great role by contributions in the field of intellectual attainments, because by its intellectual attainments it removes some of the disabilities and asserts its equality or potential greatness. This is true also of Asian minorities in the United States. In spite of discrimination, on the percentage basis, the number of Hindus (the people from India) in the United States who have taken their Ph.D.'s, M.D.'s, and M.Sc.'s in Engineering, and as scientists are carrying on their professional activities, *is higher than any other* community.

It is only in a democracy that a minority community can give expression to its innate ability and its members hold their own as equals; thus an organized and enlightened minority becomes the bulwark of a democracy. When a democracy begins to enact discriminatory legislation against a minority group or practices discrimination under cover, it is the sure sign of the beginning of its decline. Such a practice begins to be the forerunner of cultural isolation, which brings about lack of social vision and decline.

In this connection I may say that Carey McWilliams in his *Brothers Under the Skin* has given us some food for thought regarding the minorities in the United States and the actual practice of democracy.

W. F. Albright:

I heartily agree with Dr. Das's remark on the role of minorities; I am particularly happy that he has emphasized the remarkable achievements of the Parsees in India—one of the most striking possible illustrations.

I may have overemphasized the amount of persecution of adherents of rival faiths which went on in India before the Moslem invasion. However, I think Dr. Das has just as clearly underemphasized it. In the first place, it must be remembered that we have incredibly little record of political and ecclesiatical history during this period; most of our direct information comes from inscriptions and historical tales of much later date than the events which they recount. It is quite true that the spirit of early Buddhism was tolerant and that there are many words of tolerance in the inscriptions of Asoka (third century B.C.). Dr. Das might also have mentioned the fact that, in the slightly earlier Arthasastra of Kautilya, toleration of religious differences is advised. However, since this work probably dates from the very end of Persian imperial times, it is likely that there is some indirect connection with the well-known tolerant attitude of the Achaemenid rulers, especially of Cyrus and Darius (Cambyses and Xerxes were much less tolerant). Moreover (to return to Asoka), he had been, according to his own statement, a very cruel monarch before his conversion from Hinduism to Buddhism, and later Buddhist tradition embellishes this fact. His edicts prohibit Hindu feasts and sacrifices, and go into detail on the appointment of special censors to see to the execution of his orders. The edicts expressly mention the continued use of torture and capital punishment in the execution of his wishes. Tradition tells many stories of Asoka's persecution both of Brahmans and of Buddhist heretics. In the Vitasoka story the king is said to have slain 18,000 Hindus in a single day because a statue of Buddha had been destroyed. Early Chinese sources give harrowing details about the bloody massacre of the Buddhists of Gandhara by Mahirakula, about the fourth century A.D., as a result of which this once Buddhist land was thoroughly Hinduized. Moreover, it is very hard to explain how the once largely Buddhist northern India can have been so completely rid of Buddhism without the use of bloody measures of suppression. Brahman sources themselves claim that as a result of the mission of the Hindu religious reformer, Kumarila, in the eighth century, one king issued a proclamation that he would execute any subject of his who did not participate in the slaughter of the Buddhists. These are only a few of the illustrations which have survived in spite of the paucity of relevant sources.

I do not recite these facts in order to discredit India, but rather in order to show that India was subject to the same human emotions and compulsions that Near Eastern and European countries were at the same time. Christians are very much to blame for their cruelties—but there is no religious majority which has been guiltless in this respect. Indeed, since tolerance generally turns out to be intimately bound up with an attitude of indifference, there is some justification for associating persecution with zeal, however misguided and self-defeating this zeal may be.

Clyde Kluckhohn, *Peabody Museum, Cambridge:*
   Professor Albright's paper seems to me an amazing combination of breadth and learning. I found it instructive, provocative, closely reasoned. My sole dissent is *in re* American education. I share some of Professor Albright's distrust of "progressive education," but I

should like to say a word about one issue in more abstract terms. Cannot an argument be phrased this way: a great and heterogeneous democracy can hardly hope to survive unless there is some core of common values. The churches are sectarian and hence, in practice if not in theory, make for divergence rather than unity as to fundamentals. Although the richness of diversity is generally to be encouraged, we need one "institution" which implants values and which touches all the people. Surely this unifying "institution" had best be the schools—so long as they are potentially controllable by all the people (which implies, of course, that minority groups can make their influence felt both locally and nationally).

Indeed, to an observer who has watched the educational process in other societies, one striking (and sometimes disturbing) feature of our American public school system is the extent to which the function of the schools is conceived to be only that of imparting subject matter. In many communities if teachers venture beyond arithmetic and beyond purely formal affirmation of allegiance (such as leading the recitation of the Pledge to the Flag) to the discussion of the American way of life, school boards are overwhelmed with protests. " 'Politics' are no business of a teacher. Let her stick to facts." Admittedly this whole problem is complicated by the fact that we Americans have been so little articulate about our dominant and unifying values. A vague appeal to *some* of the doctrines of the Founding Fathers is about the only rallying cry which will receive the verbal assent of a majority in the more conservative sections of our country. Possibly this inarticulateness as to "ideology" is our great strength. I can well see that a strong argument may be advanced for this proposition. But I do submit that no society in which—for better or for worse—the school has "usurped" many of the functions which have traditionally been left to the home can afford to disregard this grave question. If our schools are to be agencies for inculcating the values shared as a "minimum definition of the American way," let us see that this is done openly and systematically in such a manner that any citizens whose ancient beliefs are affronted or whose rights seem threatened by silence or by affirmation, may make their protests heard and regarded. If public schoolteachers are to be confined to purely intellectual instruction, let this issue first be publicly argued rather than decided by oblique pressures which take their tacit justification in sentiments which may have been appropriate only to earlier conditions in the American scene.

A query respecting the final sentence. Can "the fundamentals of right and wrong" be accepted as "traditionally" given or do they need explicit re-examination in the light of changed conditions, the empirical facts which face us from a cross-cultural perspective, and the fresh ways of thinking which seem forced by these new conditions and new facts?

Pitirim A. Sorokin, *Harvard University:*

Professor Albright admirably summed up the important positive functions of the minorities. To be quite accurate, however, his statements need a few reservations and qualifications. First, not all the minorities play these roles but only those who, under the existing circumstances, have these creative qualities. The minorities that culturally are too backward in comparison with the majority amidst which they live, may not exert these influences. The second, and most important, limitation of the adequacy of his statements is that these positive functions are performed by the minorities only when there is a *common fund of values* of the minorities with one another and with the majority. Only then they can play and do perform these positive functions in a "multi-group society." Otherwise, when and where each group in a multi-group society has its values different from those of the other minority groups and from those of the majority; when there is no common fund of the values, the result is an unintegrated (or disintegrated) large society in which each group fights only for itself and its own values. In such a society there will be an abundance of antagonisms between the different minority groups and between these and the majority group. Eventually, such a society is bound either to fall apart or its mechanical unity will be maintained only by a coercive force with the dominant masters and subjugated "underdogs," with all the other consequences of such a situation. This lack of the common fund of the values is the reason why all the hastily built empires of various conquerors, made up of different ethnic groups, have been so short-lived; why an excessive social differentiation has usually resulted in society overcharged with inner antagonisms, group tensions, and *anomie.* In brief, the common fund of the values is a necessary condition of the multi-colored creative functions of any multi-group society.

W. F. Albright:

I quite agree with Professor Sorokin's statement that my remarks "need a few reservations and qualifications." In fact I am prepared to go farther and insist that they need many modifications and improvements in detail, partly because of personal limitations of the writer, and partly because of the comparatively little-explored nature of the terrain in question. I agree that there are minorities which are too backward to exercise the influence which I attributed to "organized minorities." However, I am inclined to doubt whether such minorities can really be called "organized." It is surprising to what extent even "backward" minorities respond to the "stimulus of penalization"; our American Negroes are a really remarkable example of how it is working in a group which came to this country wholly unorganized and entirely ignorant of the elements of modern Western civilization.

I accept certain implications of Sorokin's emphasis on the danger of an "unintegrated (or disintegrated) large society." However, I cannot agree that a "common fund of values" is necessary before minorities can play a positive part in a large society. Surely there never was a minority which shared fewer ideological values with the environment than the early Christians in the pagan Roman world. I would rather stress the danger to stability which results from the emergence of any vigorous minority in a congeries of unintegrated elements. Sorokin has himself performed an exceedingly useful service by pointing out the fundamental distinction between social congeries and social organisms; I believe that emphasis on mechanical analogies rather than axiological factors is more instructive here, since there is nothing more confusing than heterogeneous axiology.

Pitirim A. Sorokin, *Harvard University:*

If the creative role of the minority does not lead to the disintegration and splitting of the majority's society and culture in which they act, there must be a common fund of values. Otherwise, such a minority becomes a center of the forces disrupting the larger society and culture. The case of the early Christians is a good example of this. If Gibbon's famous statement about the barbarians and Christians as the main forces of the perdition of the Roman Empire greatly exaggerates the real situation, it is nevertheless true that Christianity notably facilitated a disintegration of the predominantly sensate Greco-Roman society and culture. So also does any creative minority having no common fund of the values with the majority (Communist minority, the minority of the radical religious sects, etc.). Perhaps a disintegration of the society and culture of the majority is a good and desirable thing. Perhaps it is an evil. Leaving this evaluation, the fact remains that without the common fund of values, the work of an aggressive minority leads to the disintegration of the sociocultural universe of the majority.

Postscript

In evaluating my 1944 paper and the discussion which then took place from the vantage point of nearly twenty years later, it must be remembered that minority problems have always been of concern to me (see below, p. 316). My reactions are, accordingly, not without emotional overtones. Dr. Baumgardt[2] was quite justified in objecting to my use of the word "cowardice" in referring to the assimilation of German Jews under the pressures of nineteenth- and twentieth-century Germany.[3] Motives were undoubtedly varied, and in some cases assimilation may have actually been rather courageous. For most, however, no honest conversion was involved but simply an act of expediency or often of sheer desperation. On the other hand, there was no misunderstanding in my reference to Köhler and Driesch, about whom I agree entirely with Baumgardt. The point is that Breysig was as confused as most German intellectuals who espoused the Nazi side.[4]

My reply to Dr. Taraknath Das requires no further explanation; the facts speak for themselves. Even if the data I cited were not

[2] Dr. David Baumgardt was professor of philosophy at the University of Berlin when he was dismissed by the Nazis in 1933. He was already favorably known for his penetrating volume on eighteenth-century precursors of modern ethical and moral theory: *Der Kampf um den Lebenssinn unter dem Vorläufern der modernen Ethik*, Leipzig, 1933. In this country he has published several books and many papers on the philosophy and history of ethics, as well as on religious themes. He is one of the very few who combine a rigorous approach to philosophical problems and a thorough grasp of the history of thought with conservative religious orientation.

[3] For a sympathetic description of their dilemma see the brilliant volume by Solomon Liptzin, *Germany's Stepchildren*, 1944.

[4] See the discussion of Werner Sombart's views on the Jewish origin of modern capitalism in my *Archaeology of Palestine*, p. 252. After Hitler came to power, Sombart's initially favorable attitude is said, by acquaintances of his with whom

available, something of the kind would be demanded by the simple disappearance of Buddhism from India between the Himalayas and Ceylon at some time during the second half of the first millennium A.D. A sequel of our discussion was the fact that Dr. Das persuaded me to become a member of his committee for aid to Indian university students in this country, so my wife and I learned to know and esteem a good many of them.

Dr. Clyde Kluckhohn's comments are very interesting, since they clearly show the ambivalence existing in the mind of a brilliant American social and cultural anthropologist (whom I liked and admired) on the subject of American culture. As a typical functionalist of the modified type which goes back in some respects to the school of Franz Boas (see above, pp. 47-49), he was very reluctant to accept the implications of cultural pluralism, which I heartily espouse. Consequently the differences between our point of view could not be eliminated by discussion; they were built into our two approaches.

The discussion with Dr. Pitirim Sorokin again speaks for itself. I do not deny some validity to his point of view, but I cannot agree that Christianity was partly responsible for the disintegration of Greco-Roman society and culture. The latter were already disintegrating without any help from Christianity, which actually enabled them to survive longer than they would have otherwise (see above, pp. 4-5).

A remarkable confirmation of my general thesis with regard to the functions of *organized* minorities has come since 1944 from a quite unexpected direction. At that time it was possible only to speak of the effect of Toynbee's "stimulus of penalization" on American Negroes. Of course, this is merely one of many factors which have been involved in the advance of the Negro minority during the century since emancipation. It may safely be said that if the Negroes had been established in a new commonwealth—say in Georgia and Florida, as urged by many a century ago—they would not have made anything like their actual progress, but would

---

I have talked, to have changed rapidly. See also my comments in *Orientalia*, 8, 1939, p. 120. Apropos of the German author being reviewed, the editor of this journal, the late Alfred Pohl, S. J., remarked to me: "Er wird wütend sein, aber kann gar nicht antworten."

have remained on a level somewhat comparable to that of Haiti, where the old native cultures and tribal loyalties have emerged in new structures and patterns which have helped to prevent the development of a viable modern state.

But since the end of the Second World War, and especially since the desegregation order of the Supreme Court in 1954, the picture has completely changed. Now, thanks to the efforts of the National Association for the Advancement of Colored People and other bodies, especially the Negro churches, the Negroes are becoming one of the best-organized minorities in American history. Borrowing the Gandhian principle of nonviolence and applying it (when these lines were being written) with extraordinary determination, Martin Luther King and his associates seem likely to achieve results far beyond the expectation of most realists.

It must again be emphasized that it is nonsense to speak, as Carleton Coon does in his book, *The Origin of Races* (1962), of a lag of some 200,000 years in Negro evolution. There is absolutely no reliable evidence for any such conclusion. Actually, there were flourishing native Negro states and civilizations in both East Africa, south of the equator, and in West Africa, north of the equator, during the period between the third-fourth centuries A.D. and the end of the Middle Ages (see above, p. 39, n. 16). Furthermore, there was an independent Negro state in Sudan as early as the sixteenth century B.C., and in the eighth century B.C. the Negro Ethiopians conquered Egypt and established a mighty empire which lasted about half a century. It may take American Negroes some time before they can compete with other Americans as successfully in the intellectual arena as they already do in athletics, music, dramatic art, and literature, but there is no sound reason for doubting early success. It must be remembered that it has usually taken three or four generations for European immigrant groups of peasant origin to enter fully into the higher culture—aesthetic and intellectual—of America. We can scarcely expect Negroes, emerging somewhat earlier from much more depressed conditions, to surpass the Europeans.

PART THREE

SOME SCHOLARLY APPROACHES

Chapter 9

James Henry Breasted, humanist[1]

James Henry Breasted was born in Rockford, Illinois, on August 27, 1865; he thus belonged entirely to the generation which grew up after the Civil War. He sprang mainly from English and Dutch stock, as indicated by his name, which stands for *van Breestede*. Born in the heart of the Middle West, of old American ancestry, he was typically American in background as well as in reaction to the world in which he lived. Obliged to earn part of his way through North Central College (Naperville, Illinois) and the Chicago College of Pharmacy, he showed a blend of practicality and erudition with which we are relatively familiar but which seldom fails to astonish the European savant who comes into closer contact with an American colleague. Like Gibbon, who maintained that his experience as officer of militia was not without value to the historian of the Roman Empire, so Breasted observed that his pharmaceutical training was useful when he came to interpret Egyptian medical papyri. To Breasted's environment in formative years may also be

[1] The article was originally published in *The American Scholar*, 5, 1936, pp. 287-299; it is reprinted here with revisions only where made necessary by the flight of time or the exigencies of style and factual content. Several footnotes have also been added. Thanks are due the editorial staff for permission to reprint the article here. Compare also the writer's obituary sketch in the *Yearbook* of the American Philosophical Society, 1937, pp. 338 ff. In 1943 appeared a brilliant biography by Breasted's son, Charles: *Pioneer to the Past: The Story of James Henry Breasted, Archaeologist*, New York: Scribner's, which has been translated into German. The volume is beautifully written, and quotes extensively from Breasted's letters and journals.

attributed another trait commonly ascribed in Europe to Americans, that of a pronounced meliorism—of which more below.

After receiving his A.B. degree in 1888 he studied for the ministry in the Chicago Theological Seminary, where he became fascinated by the study of Hebrew. This interest led him to go to Yale where William Rainey Harper had developed a most remarkable department of Hebrew, superior both in size and devotion to any other graduate department at that university. Harper was one of the greatest teachers and academic organizers of his day and fathered a renaissance of the then almost defunct study of Hebrew which exerted tremendous influence on theological teaching two generations ago. In 1891 Breasted obtained his A.M. at Yale and was sent by Harper, who had become the first president of the new University of Chicago, to study Egyptology under Erman at Berlin.

The period of study at the University of Berlin proved to be decisive. Adolf Erman, grandson of the great astronomer, Friedrich Wilhelm Bessel, and of the eminent physicist, Paul Erman, had shortly before founded a new school of Egyptology, characterized both by use of systematic methods in the study of grammar and lexicography and by interest in all branches of Egyptian culture. He was then in his late thirties and both he and his students were full of enthusiasm for the rapidly opening field of Egyptology. With Erman, who was soon to be recognized as the foremost living Egyptologist, and with his brilliant pupils, Kurt Sethe (who later fell heir to Erman's place and rank as a scholar) and Georg Steindorff, Breasted always remained on the intimate terms of *Duzenfreundschaft*.

In 1894 Breasted received his Ph.D., with a Latin thesis on the solar hymns of Ikhnaton (Amenophis IV), the famous heretic king of the fourteenth century B.C. Shortly afterward he married Miss Frances Hart, paying his first visit to Egypt on the honeymoon. It is characteristic of his indomitable enthusiasm that, undeterred by a very light purse, he tramped all over Egypt on foot. This was only the first of a long series of visits to Egypt in the course of which he learned to know the country and its people thoroughly, mastering colloquial Arabic—in striking contrast to many of his colleagues in related fields.

From 1894 to his death Breasted remained a member of the faculty of the University of Chicago, rising in rank from assistant through the grades of instructor (1896), assistant professor (1898), associate professor (1902), professor (1905), to that of Burton Distinguished Service Professor (1930). In 1925 he was relieved of all responsibility for teaching in order to devote his full time to the direction of the Oriental Institute. For the last sixteen years of his life he was absorbed by the organization and rapid expansion of the Oriental Institute, one of the greatest single enterprises for humanistic research which has ever been organized—certainly the most important one to be established in America. In order to understand his purpose in founding it we must make a brief survey of his scholarly career prior to 1919.

Early in his professional life he formed the plan of publishing an English translation of all Egyptian historical texts and official documents. Thanks to the liberal policy of President Harper he received frequent leaves of absence for study abroad, in the course of which he copied or collated virtually all available Egyptain inscriptions belonging to these classes. Owing to his training at Berlin and to his continuous association with projects sponsored by Erman, such as the Berlin Egyptian Dictionary, on which he collaborated intensively from 1899 to 1901, he was in an exceptionally advantageous position. Previous attempts to edit parts of the Egyptian historical inscriptions and to make them accessible to non-Egyptologists were hopelessly antiquated by the philological work of the Berlin school, which introduced precision in copying, collating, and interpreting, making such precision worth-while by its systematic reconstruction of the Egyptian grammar and lexicon. In 1906 the five volumes of Breasted's *Ancient Records of Egypt: Historical Documents* appeared, containing nearly two thousand octavo pages. Not only did this great work antiquate all previously published translations of historical documents, but it so thoroughly covered the available material that it has remained standard to the present day [it was recently reprinted], though additional volumes, containing new texts and improved readings and interpretations, are now badly needed [see above, p. 108]. European Egyptologists and historians received the *Ancient Records* with unbounded enthusiasm and the author's reputation was made.

Just before the *Ancient Records* appeared, Breasted published his *History of Egypt* (1905), in which he utilized the documentary data, which he controlled so well, for a brilliant account of the history of the Nile Valley in antiquity. Leaving technical details of chronology and prosopography for treatment in his source book, and employing archaeological and literary materials to round out the picture, he gave here the first real history of Egypt, a history so well balanced and proportioned as to remind one of an Egyptian temple. It still remains unequaled in its field, and its scholarly superiority is illustrated by the fact that it has been translated into German, French, Russian, and Arabic, in two cases by distinguished foreign scholars. So clear is the presentation and so limpid is the style that it has been read by multitudes with pleasure, and has even been put into braille for the use of the blind.

After two long seasons of archaeological and epigraphical field work in Nubia (1905-1907), Breasted's attention was devoted for a number of years to three main branches of activity. He first had to publish the results of his two expeditions, which he did in two volumes. He then occupied himself more intensively with Egyptian religious literature, especially with the Pyramid Texts, dating from the middle of the Old Empire, and forming by far the oldest compact body of religious texts anywhere in the world. Sethe's publication of a complete critical edition of these documents in 1908-1910 made it possible to attack them with hope of success for the first time since their discovery nearly thirty years before. In 1912 was published Breasted's *Development of Religion and Thought in Ancient Egypt*, expanded from the Morse Lectures of the Union Theological Seminary in New York. Here he gave the first analysis of the religious evolution which can be traced from the Pyramid Texts of the third millennium through the Coffin Texts of the Middle Empire to the documents of the second and first millennia b.c. Simply and clearly written, this book was epoch-making in its significance for the history of human thought. His third line of activity lay in popularization, to which we shall now turn.

In the course of his early career Breasted gradually discovered that he possessed an unusual aptitude for popularization and that intelligent laymen enjoyed reading his books and listening to his lectures. In those years he had not attained the facility in expression or the charm of presentation which he later exhibited; there was still something stilted about his style and a lack of ease in his appearance. In fact when the writer first mentioned him to a University of Chicago man about 1910 the latter observed: "Breasted is a funny-looking chap, but you hardly ever see him." This was the total impression he had made upon one man in the classical field in those days! As early as 1905 he published a series of popular lectures entitled *Egypt through the Stereoscope.* Then from 1914 to 1921 appeared six textbooks on ancient history for high schools and colleges, three of them written in collaboration with James Harvey Robinson. These books were so good that they obtained immediate and lasting success and made multitudes acquainted with the author's broad perspective of history and his enthusiasm for archaeological research. The best one is undoubtedly *Ancient Times* (1916), which has delighted innumerable cultivated readers of mature years and has been translated into several foreign languages. In its enlarged form, which appeared in 1935 and which drew on the resources of the Oriental Institute for illustrative matter, it is still one of the best introductions to ancient history in any tongue.

For years, like many American specialists in various branches of the science of man's past, Breasted had chafed against the exclusion of these fields of research from participation in the common activities of science. Since psychology and cultural anthropology were grudgingly admitted to this charmed circle, and since there never was any doubt about the citizenship right of geology, palaeontology, and palaeobotany, in spite of their dealing with an even remoter past and with methods and data strikingly parallel to those of the archaeologist, this exclusion had seemed unreasonable. At last came his opportunity: he was invited to deliver the William Ellery Hale Lectures on Evolution at the annual meeting of the National Academy of Sciences April 28-30, 1919. The lectures were well received by many outstanding scientists and appeared in print, with lavish illustration, in *The Scientific Monthly.* It was not long afterward that the lecturer was himself elected to a place in the National Academy of Sciences—the first time that an Old World archaeologist Orientalist had been so honored.[2] Yet there were many scientists who were offended by the invitation to Breasted. The writer will

[2] Breasted was not actually the first member to be elected to the Academy (1923) from the ranks of humanistic scholarship, since the great Sanskrit scholar, William Dwight Whitney (1827-1894), was a charter member when the Academy was founded by President Lincoln in 1863. Whitney resigned after a short tenure, disappointed by the fact that the Academy followed the exclusive policy of the Royal Society and did not become an American counterpart of the great continental Academies, as he had hoped. Incidentally, the present writer is the third in this line to have been elected a member of the National Academy of Sciences (1955).

never forget how disgusted an able young zoologist of Johns Hopkins was when he returned from Washington after the meetings: an unknown archaeologist and "language man" had been asked to give the principal address—what was the field of science coming to when such a thing was possible! In any case Breasted's addresses were very much like the *vox clamantis in deserto;* the time was not quite ripe for further progress in this direction.

In the same spring Breasted's enthusiastic description of the prospects for research in the Near East bore its first fruit in the foundation of the Oriental Institute of the University of Chicago, with an annual grant of $10,000 from Mr. John D. Rockefeller, Jr. In the widened perspective of the past few years of the Institute's expansion this grant may seem small, and it was certainly insignificant in comparison with many contemporary gifts for research in the natural and social sciences. But it was so much more generous than previous donations in America for the purpose of archaeological correlation and planning that it seemed princely. We must remember that in the years from 1917 to 1921, when the first panic came, the United States was in the clutch of an irresistible wave of intellectual and academic utilitarianism. Before it all branches of research which could not be proved immediately useful for the increase of wealth and the "uplift" of society were in constant danger of being swept away. To react against the current tendency was an act of faith on the part of the donor, and happily one which was justified by the results.

After having met Breasted at several gatherings of the American Oriental Society and having been enthralled by his brilliant presidential address in 1919, the writer saw a good deal of him in Cairo and Jerusalem during the extended exploratory trip to the Near East which followed the establishment of the Oriental Institute. He will never forget the enthusiasm which possessed Breasted or the charm of his conversation. At the age of fifty-four he was in many respects like a youth just setting out on a great voyage of discovery. Through his later books runs the same melodic theme: a haunting sense of the mysterious unknown that beckons the explorer, linked with a thrilling consciousness of impending triumph. In the last sentence of his last book this is pregnantly expressed: "there is no reason to doubt the growth of that light to illumine realms of being that still lie all unrealized in the unfathomed ages toward which our limited vision of today looks out. . . ."

Thanks to munificent further gifts and grants from Mr. Rockefeller personally as well as from the Rockefeller foundations and to minor (but often large) gifts from other sources, the Oriental Institute developed rapidly. After the preliminary stage came two main phases, the first of which began in 1925-1926 with large gifts for the purpose of launching the Megiddo expedition and the epigraphic survey of Thebes, etc., while the second began in 1928. A very little later came Mr. Rockefeller's gift of $10,000,000 toward the expenses and endowment of the Institute.

In selecting projects for research and sites for excavation, Breasted must frequently have been faced by the temptation to sacrifice tedious and expensive but fundamental undertakings in favor of easy and sensational ones. All credit must be given him for having resisted this temptation and for having made his choices with such discrimination. The study of the representations and inscriptions on the walls of the temple of Rameses III at Medinet Habu has taken many years of hard work on the part of a large staff but it has yielded the first absolutely accurate reproduction of these valuable source-materials. Part of these records of the first known contact between Europeans and Africans has been irretrievably lost, but now the extant remains are preserved in stately folios which will last until our own civilization shall have vanished from the earth. There is nothing exciting in the laborious copying, collating, and interpretation of the Coffin Texts from the Middle Empire, but they form the needed link between the oldest Egyptian religious texts and the New Empire ones and make it possible to recognize the organic evolution of Egyptian thought. Nor can the Assyrian dictionary project be called sensational, but the millions of accumulated cards and the volumes which have appeared annually since 1956 will soon make it possible to explain nearly all the still obscure words in the languages and dialects of ancient Mesopotamia and will thus enable scholars ultimately to give correct interpretations of hundreds of thousands of inscriptions already discovered in the valleys of the Tigris and Euphrates. For world history the value of this great mass of documents is even greater than that of the Egyptian records. It is only a century and a quarter since the first sure steps in the decipherment of the hieroglyphic and cuneiform scripts were made and only half that long since the first measurably adequate grammars and dictionaries could be published. In spite of the small number of workers in the field, new successes in philological interpretation are being obtained every year, but we have now reached the point where the individual scholar can do little without the aid of such elaborate projects of collection and correlation as these which we have mentioned.

In excavation the same is true. At Megiddo in Palestine an ancient town of importance was cleared for the first time over its complete area, stratum by stratum, with illuminating results.[3] At Alishar the first systematic excavations in eastern Asia Minor were undertaken, and it is now possible to write an outline history of the cultural development of this vital link in the territorial chain connecting Western Asia with Greece. The excavations in Syria were almost equally significant, and Frankfort's expeditions in Mesopotamia then represented the high-water mark of sound archaeological method, with epoch-making results. At Persepolis, capital of the far-flung Persian Empire, Herzfeld made discoveries of primary importance for our knowledge of Persian art and architecture and incidentally found thousands of clay tablets which will presumably revolutionize our knowledge of the administrative, fiscal, and legal organization of that great empire. And thus we might continue, since we have by no means exhausted the list of major enterprises of the Oriental Institute, quite aside from the many minor undertakings. A detailed picture of these projects, with an impressive synthesis, may be found in Breasted's volume, *The Oriental Institute* (Vol. XII of the *University of Chicago Survey*), published in 1933.

It is an extraordinary fact that Breasted did not ship his oars as a scholar during the arduous years in which the Oriental Institute was being organized and expanded. Quite the contrary, he seemed to be spurred to new efforts, both in original research and in popularization. In 1924 appeared his remarkably competent publication of the

[3] Two reservations are in order here. The Reisner-Fisher method envisaged complete clearance of the site, proceeding from stratum to stratum. After the fourth main level had been dug, excavation proceeded in much more restricted areas, and the sounding down to bedrock (Stratum XX) was very small in extent. The second reservation is that the Reisner-Fisher method is now supplemented (not superseded, as often stated) by the Wheeler-Kenyon method. It is now evident that clearing sites entirely makes it impossible to check already completed work by use of improved techniques.

mural paintings at Dura on the Euphrates, recorded by him while in Babylonia in 1920, *Oriental Forerunners of Byzantine Painting;* in 1930 were published the two stately volumes of his *Edwin Smith Surgical Papyrus,* an *editio princeps* in which a very ancient and extremely important document was interpreted in a masterly way. In 1933 came his *chef-d'oeuvre, The Dawn of Conscience,* in which the ideas first expressed in his Morse Lectures twenty-one years before were further developed, with greater documentation and more mature insight. We find the leitmotiv of his thinking put into eloquent words in the last chapter, "The New Past," where he stated in terms of nonreligious teleology his view of man's place in the scheme of organic evolution.

Though Breasted's philosophy closely approaches the nonreligious humanism of Irving Babbitt, it is scarcely likely that he was appreciably influenced by Babbitt; the similarity is rather due in part to a natural reaction on the part of both against the extreme instrumentalism in which most American pragmatism had found its logical conclusion. Inquiry has failed to yield any hint that Breasted may have been influenced from this direction. To appreciate the development of his views we must turn again to his background. A child of the young Middle West, a member of the staff of the new University of Chicago, he matured in an atmosphere of the most pronounced meliorism. With nature and science vying with one another to bring about material advance, with political, social, religious, and humanitarian reforms constantly being advocated on all sides, it was impossible to escape the conviction that man's destiny is to improve steadily and irresistibly. In such remorseless progress a teleological goal is inevitable. But there was nothing theistic about this meliorism. Orthodox theism was increasingly excluded from consideration by the theological liberals of the Divinity School, who reacted more and more vigorously against the place attributed to the Bible by historical Protestantism and saw religion primarily as a social and ethical phenomenon, with individual reactions which took different forms in H. N. Wieman, Eustace Haydon, and Shailer Mathews. In Breasted's case, Marxism and socialism were excluded by the obvious fact that progress in the recovery of the past can be made only in a friendly capitalistic society where funds may be spent if desired on undertakings which are not for the obvious material benefit of the commonwealth.

Thus he necessarily arrived at an essentially individualistic meliorism, in which "character is man's destiny," to quote the Hellenic motto of another influential Chicago thinker, Paul Carus. But it is a creed in which character is socially conditioned, and remains unattained except by persons who fit into the social framework. To Breasted's trained historical imagination the newly discovered and interpreted documents of ancient Egypt provided confirmation of his philosophical creed. In Egypt one can trace the evolution of social obligations, one can see the gradual flowering of more and more ethical forms of religious consciousness—in short, one can follow the unfolding of the human conscience and can see how social organization conditioned its flowering. One may reasonably ask whether Breasted did not telescope the long process of the formation of conscience into far too short a time. However, attentive perusal of his book shows that the title is partly responsible for the false impression which numerous readers and reviewers have gained. A more accurate title might have been *The Emergence of Conscience*—but the actual title is far more vivid and effective. To the "unconquerable buoyancy of the human soul" he attributed continuing validity: "the process of human advance which brought forth character is still unfinished—the possibilities of its future are unlimited."

Breasted's hominism, which is so strong as to lead him in one place to assert that man "*has* raised himself by his own bootstraps," is, of course, only one way of looking at the phenomena in question, the teleological import of which it is hard to deny. The theist may with equal right contend that man has been raised in spite of his nature, by infinitely skillful tutelage on the part of a Higher Power. However, nothing can alter the fact that Breasted's observations and syntheses have made it much harder to share the pessimism of a Spengler or to accept the revolutionary doctrines of a Bertrand Russell (to neither of whom he refers in his book). Thanks to the very fact that Breasted was not a professional philosopher, much less a metaphysician, he was able to couch his thought in simple and vivid language.[4]

[4] In the 1936 text of this article I imprudently predicted that "his influence on the coming generation is certain to be strong, though it will hardly weaken orthodox theism. It is much more likely that after theologians and philosophers have appropriated his weapons it will have precisely the opposite effect." The

It is not easy to make a succinct appraisal of a man of Breasted's magnitude. We have seen that he was a great scholar to whom many honors came by right. Among them we may mention several gold medals, a Litt. D. from Oxford, and many honorary memberships in foreign learned societies and academies. After having been for years a corresponding member of the Académie des Inscriptions he had just been slated at the time of his death for promotion to the rank of *membre associé* in that exclusive body. Breasted was the first American Orientalist to be regarded by competent European judges as fully equal to their best men in the field; he was also the first American humanistic scholar to be so highly respected in Europe. With him American scholarship first became respectable in many foreign circles. It is particularly encouraging to know that our greatest American organizer of humanistic research was free from charlatanry and bluff, those traditional vices of American intellectual life (though in reality just as common in Europe). It is characteristic of the man that he devoted himself with whole soul to his work. Mr. Charles Breasted writes:

> Strangely enough, my father never had what might be called a hobby. He read voraciously; in his youth and up to middle age he played the flute; he was always a music lover. . . . He loved horseback riding and took a boyish pleasure in motoring. He very seldom took vacations; but when he did, they invariably included several hours a day of work either on a book he was writing or some phase of his incessant scientific endeavors. The content of his scientific life was so diversified and was for him so constantly a challenge, that it could be said that his work and his hobbies were one and the same.[5]

Investigators in the field of the humanities must not forget that Breasted made their studies respectable in the circles of the great foundations and in many universities where only scanty and reluctant support was previously forthcoming. His enthusiastic approval could always be counted on whenever a sound project for human-

---

first sentence has not been verified by events, and the second sentence—though in a sense the thesis of this volume—is scarcely supported by the public status of rational-empirical history today, with existentialists boring in from one side and ultraconservatives from the other.

[5] In a letter to the writer, not long after his father's death.

istic or scientific research was presented to him.[6] This service to the humanities may in the long run be just as important as his innumerable direct contributions to the recovery of the past. He came on the scene just when the humanities most needed a champion, and many circles which exhibit a tendency to belittle him owe much to his timely intervention. Breasted would certainly wish to be remembered as a great humanist, by whose instrumentality the "new humanism," as he liked to call it, emerged from the womb of a forgotten past, impregnated by the *élan vital* of humanity. When the first two-thirds of recorded human history shall have yielded most of its secrets, it will be James Henry Breasted whom we must thank for the largest single share in its recovery. Breasted would have been too high-minded to have applied the lines of Horace to himself, but their Egyptian inspiration makes their application to him particularly fitting:

> *Exegi monumentum aere perennius*
> *Regalique situ pyramidum altius,*
> *Quod non imber edax, non Aquilo impotens*
> *Possit diruere aut innumerabilis*
> *Annorum series et fuga temporum.*

---

[6] The writer was a member of the American Council of Learned Societies during the time of Breasted's membership on its Advisory Board (1931-1935) and he can attest from repeated observation that the latter was always an enthusiastic supporter of worth-while enterprises, though much too busy to devote himself systematically to the encouragement of specific projects outside of his field.

Chapter 10

Gerhard Kittel and the Jewish question in antiquity[1]

On July 11, 1948, Gerhard Kittel, youngest son of Rudolph Kittel, died of cancer in his sixtieth year.[2] This bald statement carries with it overtones of intellectual tragedy and spiritual damnation to those who know his story. For the deceased was a distinguished Protestant theologian, professor of New Testament at Tübingen and Vienna, and his father had been in his time the most eminent Old Testament scholar in Germany, whose Leipzig school led the way in pointing to a sound approach to Biblical history. Yet he became the mouthpiece of the most vicious Nazi anti-Semitism, sharing with Emanuel Hirsch of Göttingen the grim distinction of making extermination of the Jews theologically respectable.

The story of Kittel may seem to be an unimportant paragraph out of the nightmare history of the Nazi movement. Yet it is even

[1] I wish to thank the Macmillan Company for permission to reprint this article, originally published in *Freedom and Reason: Studies in Philosophy and Jewish Culture in Memory of Morris Raphael Cohen*, ed. Salo W. Baron, Ernest Nagel, and Koppel S. Pinson (*Jewish Social Studies Publication*, No. 4; New York: Conference on Jewish Relations, 1951). The text has been left intact except for a few stylistic corrections and a few additional footnotes.

[2] He was born in 1888, according to his own sketch in *Wer ist's*, not in 1889 as stated by Max Weinreich, in *Hitler's Professors*, New York: Yiddish Scientific Institute, 1946, p. 273. The latter volume is an admirable study of the available sources, and is invaluable to all who are interested in this sinister phase of history. The writer has found it exceedingly accurate as a rule, and has derived much help from it in preparing this article.

darker and more menacing than the more flamboyant stories of Goering and Goebbels, since Kittel was a trained scholar and a Christian theologian. He was born September 23, 1888, and he grew up to be a delicate lad with aristocratic predilections.[3] He studied theology, becoming a New Testament scholar of promise, characterized by unusual breadth of preparation, including rabbinics. In fact his early work was distinguished from that of other New Testament students of his generation mainly by his emphasis on the importance of rabbinic studies. After becoming professor at Tübingen he launched a theological dictionary of the New Testament (1931 ——), which was interrupted by the war but is to be continued under different editorship. His own task in editing the dictionary was mainly one of organizing the contributions of others, which he did very well, so that the *Theologisches Wörterbuch zum Neuen Testament* rapidly became standard in its field.

When the Nazi movement came into power, Gerhard Kittel immediately rose to prominence as one of its leading academic supporters and as one of its chief specialists on the *Judenfrage*. His first publication after Hitler seized power in 1933 was a little book, *Die Judenfrage*, published by a leading theological publisher that same year. When the official journal of the *Forschungsabteilung Judenfrage* of the Reichsinstitut für Geschichte des neuen Deutschlands was established in 1936 under the title *Forschungen zur Judenfrage*, Kittel became its chief supporter; in fact his contributions to it during the nine years of its sorry life were several times as numerous as those of anyone else, aside from its editor, Walter Frank. He also contributed vicious articles to two other journals, *Die Judenfrage* (previously *Mitteilungen über die Judenfrage*), which began to appear in 1940, and *Archiv für Judenfragen*, initiated in 1943. His last contribution to the first of the three unholy sisters appeared in 1944, just before they suddenly expired. The content of these papers shows that there was no essential change in his public attitude toward the Nazi movement and the Jewish question up to 1943.

During this decade Kittel had, however, vigorously opposed Rosenberg and other extreme Nazi theorists who demanded the suppression of Christianity as well as of its Jewish parent, and had thus

[3] This information was given me by Professor Georg Steindorff, for decades Rudolf Kittel's friend and colleague in Leipzig, as well as by other persons who wish to remain anonymous.

lost favor with the regime. After his transfer to the University of Vienna following the *Anschluss* in 1938, he is stated on excellent private authority[4] to have defended the religious value of the Old Testament and to have deplored certain Nazi "excesses" in dealing with the Jews. None of this, however, was included in the articles that continued to appear until 1944. It must be remembered that the wholesale massacre of Russian Jews began almost immediately after the German invasion of Russia in the summer of 1941 and that the first gas chambers were installed in the concentration camp at Auschwitz in the early autumn of the same year. While it took some time for the news of this ghastly program to percolate through Germany, virtually all Germans had some inkling of what was going on before the end of 1942. Yet there is no record of any protest of public nature by Gerhard Kittel, who continued for nearly two years longer to publish his inflammatory material.

At the end of the war Kittel was captured and sent to a camp for war prisoners in the French Zone of Germany. Later he was released and allowed to retire to the Benedictine Abbey of Beuron, where he resumed work on the *Theologisches Wörterbuch* already mentioned. Both from his prison camp and from the Abbey of Beuron he kept up a stream of statements and letters on his own behalf, several of which reached the present writer through private channels.[5] In these documents he was undoubtedly sincere, but his very earnestness is more terrifying in its vision of abysses within the human heart than the diabolical crimes of the Nazi leaders themselves. Like other ex-Nazis and Nazi sympathizers with whom the

---

[4] Especially an eminent German Protestant Old Testament scholar who wrote in detail to me, but wishes to remain anonymous, and an Austrian Catholic scholar whose letter I have read. Owing to the request of the former that his long letter on the subject be kept confidential, it is impossible to quote in detail, as I should like to do. So much may be said: my correspondent and Gerhard Kittel became friends as young men and remained in close touch thereafter until the end of the war; my correspondent is firmly convinced of Kittel's honesty and of the fact that he did not really know what was going on in the concentration camps after 1941; at the same time he found it impossible to understand how Kittel could support the Nazis as he did and take such continuous part in anti-Jewish propaganda. In such cases a stranger can often judge more impartially than a friend.

[5] For one of them (Kittel's *apologia pro vita sua*) see my article "The War in Europe and the Future of Biblical Studies," in *The Study of the Bible Today and Tomorrow*, ed. H. R. Willoughby, Chicago, 1947, p. 165.

writer has corresponded since the end of the war, Kittel was totally unable to admit any guilt of his own. Again and again he stressed the "fact" that his scholarly work had been absolutely honest and that there was nothing in it of which to be ashamed. He asserted that the Nazi party leaders had "betrayed" him by going farther than he had expected—first by promising to respect the religious values of the Old Testament and then rejecting them and forbidding the teaching of them, secondly by promising to support Christianity and then trying to suppress it, thirdly by promising only to remove the Jews from their "dominant" position in German life and then proceeding to liquidate them as a people. Many German and Austrian theologians, together with a few English and American scholars, defended Kittel between 1945 and his death in 1948, assuring the world that he was sincere (which was unhappily true) and that the content of his anti-Semitism had been exaggerated (which was not at all true). Among these defenders were some of the leading intellectual figures in both Protestantism and Catholicism, including some eminent scholars who knew him well. The most startling thing about this situation is that these men were not Nazis, though a few of them perhaps sympathized too much with the latter as against their victims.

In these periodical articles Kittel campaigned against Jewish elements in Christianity (which he distinguished from "Israelite") and especially against the alleged Jewish threat to Germanism, finding a striking similarity between the effect of Jewish infiltration into Hellenistic-Roman civilization in the time of Christ and the same process within Christian German culture. According to him the relatively pure Israelites of the Old Testament, to which Christianity owed its historical origin, had been replaced by a world Jewry (*Weltjudentum*) which represented a confused mixture of heterogeneous elements (*Rassengemisch*). This world Jewry, against which the early Christians reacted, he considered as substantially identical with modern Jewry, both of them parasitic growths constituting a fatal danger to their respective host civilizations.

To be sure, Gerhard Kittel was not the only Protestant New Testament scholar to affiliate himself with the Nazi movement and to write in support of its Jewish policy. We may, however, discount G. Bertram of Giessen, who was a relatively minor figure. The third of this triad, Emanuel Hirsch of Göttingen, was in some respects even worse than Kittel, since he taught a new theology (accepted by many *"Deutsche Christen"*), according to which the Old Testament and much of the New had at most only a vague sentimental interest for Christians, and the will of the German state was binding on the conscience of every Christian, regardless of its morality in pre-Nazi Christian terms. Hirsch was a strange fanatic who had been a specialist in the existential philosophy of Kierkegaard at the same time that he was a strong German nationalist in the Hegelian tradition. After Hitler's triumph he developed an unholy fusion of the Nazi program with existential metaphysics and Neo-Marcionite theology, which enjoyed a brief vogue in German Protestant circles.[6] Hirsch and Kittel were between them clearly responsible for much of the guilt resting on the German Protestant churches for their silence while the Nazis were carrying out the liquidation of the Jews. After all, the fact that they were sincere made them even more dangerous, placing them in the line of Saul of Tarsus and Tomas Torquemada.

In this paper the writer will analyze the last book by Gerhard Kittel, *Das antike Weltjudentum*, written in collaboration with Eugen Fischer.[7] The preface of the book is dated in April, 1942, a fact which clearly shows that the authors were conscious of what their propaganda foreshadowed. Kittel's collaborator was born in 1874 and in 1918 he became full professor and director of the Anatomisches Institut at Freiburg in Breisgau. Nine years later he was called to Berlin as professor of physical anthropology at the University and as director of the Kaiser Wilhelm-Institut für Anthropologie, Erblehre und Eugenik. In 1934 he became rector of the University of Berlin, having become a Nazi some time before. The writer owes to an eminent Swiss physical anthropologist,[8] himself a

---

[6] My information about Hirsch came from other German scholars and from study of his publications (at least one of which I reviewed); see my remarks in the book cited in n. 5, p. 165. Contrast the sympathetic and surprisingly naïve account of his work by Emil G. Kraeling, *The Old Testament Since the Reformation*, 1955, esp. pp. 239-250.

[7] Hamburg, Hanseatische Verlagsanstalt, 1943 (=*Forschungen zur Judenfrage*, Band 7), 256 pp. with 225 figures in the text and a map). I wish particularly to thank Professor Ignace J. Gelb of the Oriental Institute of the University of Chicago for his kindness in lending me this book for over a year.

[8] His name is kept confidential at his request; I shall say only that he is one of the most distinguished living specialists in his field.

strong anti-Nazi, the following characterization (much abbreviated) of Fischer's work:

"Fischer had a thorough training in anatomy and in much of biology, he was an outstanding pioneer in human genetics, and he combined originality with high scholarly standards according to all his strictly technical work. In his great many large and small papers (up to 1939, to my knowledge) on human morphology and genetics, Fischer's generalizations and conclusions were always carefully considered and well supported by ample and sound observations. His staff and pupils produced a mass of publications under his direction which represent further contributions of lasting value for the development of physical anthropology as a science. . . . Sharply contrasting with all this are Fischer's activities in 'Eugenik,' that premature and hence unfortunate attempt to apply anthropology in politics, etc. . . . Fischer was no longer a well-trained scientist, but a dreamer (with a nightmare) who talks verbosely and vaguely of generalized topics of eugenics, race hygiene, racial 'psychology,' and the 'Rassenseele' without ever as much as mentioning any facts. He did use such terms as 'minderwertige Rassen' as early as 1913[9] but, as far as I can determine, did not take an active, public, part in forming and preaching National-Socialist theories until about 1930, when he evidently became a popular lecturer in Berlin at the expense of his scientific integrity and international reputation. For instance, his *Rede bei der Feier—der Berliner Universität*—1933 . . . is as full of . . . nonsensical claims as his technical reports are full of worthwhile facts and modest, sound deductions . . ."

Das antike Weltjudentum is beautifully printed, with superb illustrations and elegant binding—obviously intended for wide circulation as popular propaganda. Almost the entire letterpress (pp. 9-108) was written by Kittel, only pp. 109-114 coming from the pen of Fischer. Kittel expressly states that he gathered and annotated all the illustrations, which were then classified and "interpreted" from the standpoint of human genetics and anatomy by Fischer. It is quite certain that Kittel's point of view had not yet changed when he wrote the preface in collaboration with Fischer in 1942. Nor did it change appreciably in the following two years before the begin-

[9] In the monograph which made his reputation: *Die Rehobotherbastarde und das Bastardierungsproblem bei den Menschen.*

ning of German collapse, since several offensive essays of Kittel's appeared between 1942 and 1944, the latest of them in Vol. IX of *Forschungen zur Judenfrage*, whereas *Das antike Judentum* constituted Vol. VII of the same periodical!

This book is divided into three parts, which will be briefly described in Kittel's own words:—In the first part we have "facts and texts . . . just those that clarify this Jewish question of world Jewry [sic!]. With one exception all the texts are drawn from the millennium between Ezra and the Merovingian period. They are sometimes reproduced in brief digests of their content, but generally in translation. For the specialist it will be self-evident that the most 'correct' reproduction demands a certain freedom of rendering, especially in the case of rabbinic texts . . ." (p. 11).

In the second part, "the Egyptian mummy portraits of the Hellenistic-Roman period are for the first time subjected to a systematic analysis with a view to determining the extent to which they are portraits of Jews. If we have here, as we hope to prove, a relatively large number of certain portraits of Jews from antiquity, it is obvious that very important material for the earlier racial history of the Jews is thus made available."

The third part of the volume is devoted to a study of the anti-Jewish attitudes reflected by the alleged caricatures of Jews preserved in the museum at Treves (Trier) in the Rhineland. These form a group of terra-cotta and bronze statuettes attributed to the second or third centuries A.D.[10]

In Gerhard Kittel's *Einleitung* (written entirely by him) he says (p. 9, first paragraph): "No one who scrutinizes the modern Jewish question can fail to recognize—especially during the present fateful struggle of Europe [!] for existence—that of all its underlying sources the fact of a world Jewry that spreads out over the world and everywhere maintains its bases of operation from which it infiltrates through the political, economic, and cultural life of the peoples, is the most threatening. Among the many problems which are raised by Judaism as a curious phenomenon of world history and which together constitute the Jewish problem, the fact of a world Jewry and its effects on its environment is by far the

---

[10] For details see G. Kittel (alone), "Die ältesten Judenkarikaturen. Die Trierer Terrakotten," in *Forschungen zur Judenfrage*, IV, pp. 250-259.

most sinister (*unheimlich*) in its implications for non-Jewish mankind." Kittel goes on to insist that this "extraordinary phenomenon" is not really new; it is, on the contrary, he says, a repetition and continuation of a similar phenomenon in Hellenistic-Roman times. Men have failed to recognize its menace, he writes, because "its peculiar characteristics were submerged or concealed for a thousand years, from the beginning of the ghetto to Jewish emancipation and assimilation." From this statement it is obvious that Kittel was bitterly hostile both to the democratic ideal of Jewish emancipation and to the liberal idea of assimilation. Hundreds of pages written by him since 1933 and especially since 1940 are devoted to the development of this thesis of his.

Kittel then goes on to describe the chief characteristics of his "ancient world Jewry." First, he writes, came its diffusion over the Roman world, "from Assuan to the Crimea, from the Persian Gulf to Spain, from Tunis to Treves, Cologne and Britain." However, this people was not really an energetic and creative "conquering and colonizing stock," but was "characteristically represented" by the ancient *Wanderjude*, the "clever trader" (*der geschäftstüchtige Händler*), the "opportunistic freedman" (*der einflusshungrige Freigelassene*). "Its task was not to create anything new, but to control already existing forces and cultures."

Our author goes on to say (p. 10) that there was a "peculiar double tendency" (a kind of polarity) which characterized Hellenistic-Roman "world Jewry." On the one hand it became assimilated to existing Greco-Roman civilization, its members trying to assimilate as completely as possible. On the other hand it became a vigorous missionary religion, which proselyted enormous masses of people (*ein riesenhaftes Proselytentum*). He points out that these proselytes ceased to be Greeks or Romans [so Kittel] and attached themselves to the Jewish national bloc as well as to Jewish faith. At the end of this paragraph he bursts out into the familiar pattern of Nazi anti-Semitism: "For this was the underlying meaning and the basic unity of that double tendency: assimilative adaptation and absorption of converts were both means for a single purpose—power!" In recent anti-Semitic parlance, the sinister Elders of Zion utilize both international capitalism and international Communism as tools for their own gigantic conspiracy against the non-Jewish world. Any group which one dislikes is damned if it does one thing and equally damned if it does the opposite. The fact that Kittel generally disguises such sentiments behind a screen of specious learning does not in the least alter their profoundly illogical, undemocratic, and thoroughly unchristian character.

Kittel then writes: "Whether a Jewish slave-woman with genuine or forged letters is intermediary between the wife of the Roman emperor and a Jewish princess; . . . whether the embassy of the Alexandrine Jews uses the empress to ingratiate itself with the emperor and works for the execution of the leaders of the anti-Jewish party; or whether the Jews of Alexandria and Cyrene and Cyprus take advantage of the fact that the emperor is occupied elsewhere in order to kill hundreds of thousands of non-Jews in their ferocious uprisings; or whether . . . —always, in all periods, whether in the first century or the twentieth, world Jewry means a dream of sole power in this world and in the next!"

It should go without saying that such distortions of the story of Josephus (regardless of whether his version happens to be right or not) and such uncritical acceptance of the wildest exaggerations are alone enough to disprove Kittel's right to be considered as a critical historian. Philological knowledge and historical learning are not enough; the trained historian is supposed to weigh his sources, assign them to their proper categories, and refuse to pass judgment on human motives. In these wild sentences Kittel violates the fundamental canons of good history just as flagrantly as Father Coughlin flouted the standards of honest journalism by the falsehoods with which *Social Justice* was crammed. Kittel's hatred for the Jews was so intense and so distorted as to make him quite incapable of justice. How his non-Nazi German contemporaries could for a moment judge him to be well intentioned is hard to understand. A fanatic may be honest and sincere, but he intends the worst to all unfortunate targets of his insane dislike.

Kittel's selection of texts in the first part of the book shows wide learning and the traditional *Akribie* of the trained German scholar. His sample texts are well calculated to prove that Jewish settlement was widespread in that age, and that many Jews were slaves or freedmen, that there was much proselyting and a consequent mixture of peoples. Of course, the notion of ethnic mixture carried with it for the Nazi an idea of decadence and plebeian crudeness which is most distasteful. To the average American, on the other hand, the melting pot is a process whose value has been demonstrated again and again by the amazing energy and vitality of our composite people. We are proud of the many nationalities to which our ancestors belonged. Not so the authors of this book!

As the selection of texts proceeds, the author shows his prejudice more and more by limiting himself to passages which prove his points, such as a careful collection of references to Jewish assimilation (pp. 49 ff.), to Jews in business and banking (pp. 53 ff.), to Jewish cheats and rascals (pp. 58 ff.), to Jewish officials and *arrivistes* (pp. 61 ff.), to Jewish resilience after virtual destruction [which becomes a crime against humanity with Kittel!], etc. As we go on, the arbitrary character of the selections becomes more and more evident, until the author closes (p. 92) with quotations from Tacitus ("the disgusting people"), Ammianus Marcellinus (attributing to Marcus Aurelius the statement that the Egyptian Jews were more contemptible than the German and Sarmatian barbarians), the Greek Esther (quoting without comment what purported to be the [false] accusations of Haman against the Jews), and finally quotes the following passage from the Babylonian Talmud (Abodah Zara, 10b): "An emperor who hated the Jews said to the grandees of his kingdom, 'If there is a swelling on anybody's foot shall he cut it off in order to save his life, or shall he let it be and suffer?' They answered, 'Let him cut it off in order to save his life!'"[11] It is perfectly obvious that Gerhard Kittel meant to suggest the complete liquidation of the Jewish people, though we may perhaps surmise that he would not have prescribed the gas chamber and general massacre, but would have found some slower and more conventional methods for attaining the same end if he himself had been in power.

When such a learned but warped mind as that of Kittel joins forces with an equally learned and equally warped scientific mind to produce a book like this, we expect an intellectual monstrosity to come into existence. And this is exactly what happens in the second and third parts of the book. In the second part the two authors combine efforts to analyze the alleged Jewish racial percentage in some eighty mummy portraits of the Roman period in Egypt.

[11] Kittel should naturally have taken this with its rather beautiful continuation in the Babylonian Talmud. As it stands the quotation is grotesque and, placed where Kittel puts it, horrible.

When we consider that most of the artists were conventional and distinctly unskilled in indicating features, and that all are *en face* instead of in profile, the probability of success seems slight. When we further bear in mind that Lower Egypt then teemed with Greeks, Anatolians, Phoenicians, Arameans, and Arab Nabateans, as well as with Jews, and that we have no contemporary Jewish portraits (labeled as such) for comparison, the prospect of success-ful analysis becomes much slighter. However, the two authors plunge rashly on, stopping only for frequent slurs—one portrait is said to show typical Jewish "insolence, not to say impudence" (p. 160). As a result of their collaboration they assert that twelve to thirteen per cent of the portraits from the Faiyum represent Jews, a figure which agrees (*eine besonders schöne Bestätigung*) with Kittel's independent estimate of the Jewish population of Egypt as one-eighth of the total. This estimate is based on uncritical accept-ance of a generalization of Philo (a million Jews in Egypt in his day) with the guess of certain papyrologists that the total popula-tion of Egypt in the Roman period averaged eight million. This entire part is a caricature of scientific archaeological and anthro-pological method, showing to what lengths the best minds will go when obsessed by a perverse dogma.

If Part II is disconcerting, Part III is stupefying. Devoted to "the oldest caricatures of world Jewry," if we are to believe the authors, it features a homogeneous group of terra cottas "found" shortly before the Nazi regime at Treves (Figs. 151-157) together with illustrative material from the Rhineland and other parts of the Roman Empire.[12] Kittel tries to prove from his comparative material that all such caricatures from the Roman period—generally char-acterized by exaggerated, often hooked noses—represent Jews. The improbability of such an inference is clear enough to any scholar who bears in mind that such noses were far more typical of Anatolians and North Syrians than of Jews in antiquity as today, and that Greco-Roman caricature tended to exaggerate the length of noses and to treat them as beaks—much like modern car-toonists.

In any event, no experienced archaeologist can doubt for a moment—unless blinded by prejudice—that the bulk (at least) of the Treves figurines are recent forgeries. This combination of

[12] Cf. above, n. 10.

caricature with gross obscenity is typical of forgers of antiques. Notorious examples are the figurines made by Salim el-Qari and sold by Shapira in the early seventies of the last century. Said to come from Moab, they combined grotesqueness with obscenity, and for a time many scholars regarded them as reflecting the abominations of Baal-peor (!).[13] In the twenties of this century a family of French peasants manufactured an entirely different kind of grotesque and obscene figurines which enjoyed much success among less critical scholars until the *affaire Glozel* was wound up with the unmasking of the deception.[14] This incredible Treves mixture of circumcised phalli with grotesque heads has never been found in any systematic excavation under a reputable archaeologist anywhere in the ancient world, and not a single reliable record of such a find can be produced by Kittel. It is fantastic nonsense from start to finish, and the inclusion of such horrors in the book before us is final proof that Gerhard Kittel intended at that time, in spite of his subsequent story, to whip up hatred against the Jews in Germany to the last terrible orgasm. Even Torquemada left no such testament as this to his misguided followers.

This grim story is also the tale of all intellectual defiance of the Ten Commandments and the Sermon on the Mount. In many ways Kittel and Fischer typified European intellectual activity at its best, since the two men were leaders in their philological and biological fields. Surrendering to the devil of intellectual overconfidence, they plunged into the uncharted depths between their respective islands of special skill. Selling themselves to Satan, they abandoned the Judeo-Christian tradition of the Fatherhood of God and the brotherhood of man. Worshiping at the shrine of the ancient pagan gods of *Blut und Boden*, they adopted the mark of Cain as their perpetual badge of dishonor. And what happened in Germany can take place wherever the human intellect turns its back on the spiritual traditions which we have inherited from their sources in ancient Israel.

[13] See esp. the convenient summary by Ch. Clermont-Ganneau, who unmasked these forgeries, in his delightful book, *Les fraudes archéologiques en Palestine*, Paris, 1885.
[14] For the latter see the *Rapport de la commission internationale: Fouilles de Glozel*, published by the Institut Internationale d'Anthropologie as a supplement to the *Revue Anthropologique*, no. 10-12, 1927.

Chapter 11

Arnold Toynbee and the interpretation of history[1]

"A Study of History," VOLUMES I-VI

Since 1934 a new movement has appeared on the horizon and has attracted such general interest, even among laymen, that we may safely predict extraordinary attention to the philosophy of history throughout intellectual circles in the coming generation. This is undoubtedly due in part to the crisis of international civilization through which we are passing, a crisis that urges thinking men to look for solutions, or at least to devise explanations and forecasts. This movement has been inaugurated by Arnold J. Toynbee (b. 1889) of the University of London, who has brought out the first six volumes of a great work, *A Study of History* (1934-1939), planned to include over a dozen volumes.

Toynbee began his career as a classical scholar, attaining some distinction in the fields of Greek and modern European history as well as in international relations, before he undertook the task of reducing historical data to a comprehensive system. It is not easy to appraise an incomplete system which is developed in nearly 3,500 pages, especially when the entire work is apparently intended to cover more than 5,000 pages! It is even harder to condense an

[1] This survey of Arnold Toynbee's work is drawn partly from my book, *From the Stone Age to Christianity,* 1957 ed., pp. 96-100 (with revisions and additions), and partly from three reviews in the *Baltimore Evening Sun* (also revised where feasible). I wish to thank the publishers of the *Sunpapers* for permission to reprint these reviews. Footnotes have been added in connection with the revision of the text.

adequate account of his system into a few paragraphs. He has collected an immense body of material, making the collections of illustrative data by Hegel and his successors seem insignificant and even futile by comparison. It must also be said that the data are seldom wrong in themselves, except where Toynbee has been misled by the specialists on whom he must rely, or when he has tried to "cut corners" in his simplification of complex processes. The work is admirably arranged, beautifully written, and is remarkably free from sloppiness in dealing with facts and citations.

The great work has been planned as follows:

I. Introduction
II. The Geneses of Civilization
III. The Growths of Civilizations
IV. The Breakdowns of Civilizations
V. The Disintegrations of Civilizations
VI. Universal States
VII. Universal Churches
VIII. Heroic Ages
IX. Contacts between Civilizations in Space
X. Contacts between Civilizations in Time
XI. Rhythms in the Histories of Civilization [Changed to "Law and Freedom in History"]
XII. The Prospects of the Western Civilization
XIII. The Inspirations of Historians.

This is a grandiose conception, and the author's courage merits commendation, even though the subject is so complex that no clear solutions could possibly be found. Yet to make the effort on such a majestic scale is one of the really great achievements of the individual spirit.

Toynbee's philosophy of history is essentially organismic, recognizing the importance of treating history as the life of societal organisms. He divides historical mankind into twenty-one "societies," which he schematizes as "wholly unrelated, unrelated to earlier societies, infra-affiliated, affiliated I, affiliated II, and supra-affiliated." Of these societies over half are extinct and seven have been discovered and reconstructed by modern archaeology. For the first time, then, the results of archaeological labor here receive proportionate attention in a treatise on the philosophy of history. Analysis of the individual societies shows that they are in some cases independent of all other cultures, in some cases successive phases in the history of a single culture (Sumeric, Babylonic; Mayan, Yucatec, Mexic), and in some cases a congeries of different racial, national, and cultural groups of very dubious coherence (Syriac, Western, Orthodox Christian, Far Eastern).[2] The task of distinguishing cultural groups of mankind is by no means a new one (Toynbee points to Count de Gobineau as an early predecessor) and it will probably go on for a long time to come. It is not unfair to say that such divisions really exist, but that they cross one another and change chronologically, geographically, and culturally to such an extent that they become rather useless as units of classification. The only sound method of broad classification is to employ the criterion of physical race for one category, that of linguistic grouping (in a very wide sense) for another, that of religion for a third, that of cultural facies for a fourth, and so on. An attempt to take a common material culture as the basis in one case and a common religious culture (Islamic, Christian) or even a racial background (as in dividing Islam into two separate modern societies, the Iranic and the Arabic) in another can lead only to confusion. The biologist has much more precise criteria at his command when he undertakes to divide living beings into families, genera, and species, but he does not employ the larger classifications as a rule except for taxonomic and phylogenetic purposes, limiting himself exclusively to individual species (and often to smaller units) for experimental research. This principle is as relevant in human culture as in zoology and botany; we are helpless in trying to define cultures unless we limit them, so far as practicable, to relatively small units within a complex (which would correspond roughly to Toynbee's "society"). In other words, if we take Egyptian cultural history as such a complex we shall find some difficuty in setting up generalizations (except perhaps in physical race) which would be true of all its phases. We can only approach satisfactory results when we divide it into its successive chronological phases, Old Empire, Middle Empire,

---

[2] The "Syriac" and "Orthodox Christian" civilizations are extremely unsatisfactory classifications; subsequent reviewers have had no trouble in demonstrating their lack of homogeneity and vagueness of outline. If the civilizations of the Maya, the Yucatecs, and the Mexican Indians are to be separated, there is no reason why we should not distinguish the Canaanites and Phoenicians, the Hittites, the Iranians, and the South Arabians.

New Empire, Saite, etc., and take each of these phases as our unit. The larger division or complex retains its classificatory and historico-genetic significance, but cannot be made a basis for detailed research.

While it is true that Egypt, for instance, did keep its external physiognomy intact through thousands of years, internal changes were very great in some respects. For example, there have been long periods in Egyptian history when the inhabitants gained a reputation for being so unwarlike that they were considered to be lacking in basic morale. Comparable differences may be observed between the reputation of the German people in the early and the late nineteenth century, or the Chinese under the Manchus and their offspring under the Communists.

The weakness of Toynbee's method does not end here. "The next step," he writes, "in a study of history is to put these twenty-one societies through their paces and compare their performances in their geneses and growths, their breakdowns and disintegrations, their universal states and universal churches and heroic ages, their contacts in Time and Space." In his first six volumes he does not follow out this challenging program, but limits himself to studying various principles which bear on the genesis and growth of civilizations. Here his method is fundamentally sound, since his concrete illustrations are drawn from specific episodes and processes in history. The number of examples is so great, they are so judiciously selected and so widely distributed among the twenty-one "societies," that the method may be fairly considered as inductive in principle, though on such a broad canvas that "analogical" would be a better term.[3] It is true that he supplements his historical examples

[3] I had originally planned to include a long chapter on "Historical Analogy" in the present volume. Needless to say, many illustrations would have been drawn from Toynbee's volumes. Let me refer provisionally to my discussion above in Chapter 2, pp. 73-76, 78-79, as well as to two concrete examples which I have discussed in my Goldenson Lecture for 1961: *Samuel and the Beginnings of the Prophetic Movement*, Cincinnati, Hebrew Union College Press, 1961, pp. 19 ff. and 22 ff. These examples depend on two different types of demonstration for each: (1) patterns which recur over and over again; (2) homogeneous bodies of evidence, grammatical and stylistic in one case, clear-cut oral tradition in the other. Not all of Toynbee's analogies fulfill such convergent requirements. In his valuable section on "The Explanatory Use of Analogy" (Vol. XII, pp. 30-41), he freely confesses (p. 39): "I plead guilty to having carried

by drawing freely from a vast store of mythological and literary lore as well as from the biographies of great men. Since mythology and literature reflect the empirical observation of many generations of primitive men (who were by no means blind to what went on in the world around them) and many centuries of reflection on the part of thinkers and poets, they may be cautiously used to supplement historical examples, though Toynbee sometimes oversteps the bounds of prudence in drawing upon unhistorical sources. Sometimes one can hardly regard all his examples as serious, as when he gives an impressive list of great men, ending with Polybius, Clarendon, Ibn Khaldun, Confucius, Kant, Dante, and—Hamlet.

The fundamental principles which he derives by his inductive methods are the following: "Challenge-and-Response" as a partial explanation of the genesis of civilizations; "Withdrawal-and-Return" as a partial explanation of the nature of their growth. Both principles are elaborately illustrated by examples. The former is divided into a series of special categories: *chalepá ta kalá* ("good things are hard"), the stimulus of hard countries, the stimulus of new ground, the stimulus of blows, the stimulus of pressures, and the stimulus of penalizations. He emphasizes, however, that while civilizations are born and progress by the aid of external stimuli, there is, none the less, a "golden mean." He further points out that a challenge or stimulus may be inadequate or it may be excessive. Aside from such points as the author's acceptance of Ellsworth Huntington's erroneous hypothesis of climatic change, which seriously vitiates certain parts of his treatment, we can only praise its conception and execution. To be sure, there is nothing at all new about the idea of the value of the "hard way" in human life, but it has been so consistently disregarded or denied by modern writers and thinkers that it is a matter of the greatest importance to have it presented as clearly and convincingly as has been done by Toynbee. Similarly,

---

my use of analogy to excessive lengths . . . I agree that analogies are not explanations but are heuristic devices for seeking explanations." In my opinion the real trouble lies in the fact that our grasp of the principle of analogy has lagged so far behind that of other mental habits and processes that few historians have a clear idea of what they mean by this multivalent term. Properly used, analogy is immensely useful, but there are so many kinds of analogy, at such different levels of thinking and with such varying degrees of applicability, that extreme caution is needed.

the principle of the "conditioned reflex" is almost a matter of common sense and everyday experience, yet its demonstration by Pavlov must be considered as one of the greatest psychological discoveries of modern times.

Toynbee's principle of "Withdrawal-and-Return" is not quite as significant as the one just discussed, but it is also important. This principle he illustrates mainly from biographical sources, extending his treatment by analogy and confirmatory examples to the field of history. Great men, especially men of prophetic type, often exhibit periods of action separated from one another by phases of complete inactivity or withdrawal into seclusion, after which they emerge with fresh and "demonic" energy. Sometimes nations, or cultures, instead of growing, reaching a climax, and declining forever, show periods of curious inactivity, often accompanied by withdrawal from participation in the international scene, after which they emerge, apparently strong as ever, for a fresh career of activity. The sensational resurgence of German power since 1933 (and again since 1945) is a striking illustration. This idea is again not really new, but it has likewise been disregarded by recent writers, who prefer to stress the merits of active, as against contemplative, life and to exalt the nervous energy of Europe at the expense of the quiescence of some other parts of the world. Toynbee thus appears in both approaches to the problem of history as an old-fashioned spirit, acquiring the reputation of a great innovator and even of a prophet because he presents old but neglected principles with elaborate logical proof of their salient reality. All honor to him for reinstating forgotten truths!

"*A Study of History*," VOLUMES VII-X[4]

Now that Toynbee's gigantic work has been completely published, in over 6,000 closely printed octavo pages, one may perhaps try to assay its value with some slight hope of being just. Nothing like it has ever been written, and it is most unlikely that there ever will be another. No estimate of this prodigious undertaking by a professional scholar has been quite fair to its amazing sweep and its equally astounding mastery of the historian's material.

[4] See the *Baltimore Evening Sun*, Oct. 14, 1954.

Born April 14, 1889, Toynbee reflects an afterglow of Victorian culture. Belonging to a highly cultivated English family, with several distinguished scholars and public servants among his immediate relatives, he was educated according to the finest British tradition of humane letters. Both in background and in political training (in the intelligence and diplomatic services during two world wars) he acquired the outlook of a liberal citizen of a world empire. From his childhood, he was saturated in good reading, especially of Greek and Roman literature. At Oxford, he came under the influence of Gilbert Murray's circle and his first wife was that eminent humanist's daughter. His academic career began with classical Greek at Oxford, and he later held a chair of Byzantine studies at London, where he subsequently became research professor of international history. Yet this recital of the most essential facts gives little idea of the extraordinary breadth of his education and experience.

In the tenth volume of *A Study of History*, Toynbee has described in detail his preparation for writing the work, dwelling particularly on incidents of childhood and youth. Even where these details seem trivial, they are most instructive, enabling the attentive reader to watch the formation of a great mind. Since Toynbee nowhere else explains his social, political, religious, and philosophical approach from the standpoint of method and world view, we need these details if we are to appraise the author.[5]

Perhaps the most remarkable aspect of Toynbee's undertaking is the single-mindedness with which he worked toward his goal, once it became clearly pictured in his mind during the summer of 1927 (as he tells us). He was then thirty-eight, and twenty-seven years were to pass before the last of the ten projected volumes came off the press. But for the Second World War, he would probably have finished his task ten years ago. With a single change (the title of Part XI), the plan of the finished work is the same as was announced in the first volume (1934).

Inserted at appropriate places are a multitude of "annexes," ranging from brief essays to elaborate monographs. A number of the essays must have been written during his student days in

[5] See also his later books, *An Historian's Approach to Religion*, 1956 and *Reconsiderations*, 1961, with my reviews below.

Oxford or Athens and might have been omitted without loss. However, the annexes tend to become progressively more impressive, and the 110 pages of "The Administrative Geography of the Achaemenian Empire" (written with the aid of two American Orientalists) in Volume VII form an original contribution to basic historical research.

No philosopher of history has ever availed himself so fully of the unexampled wealth of data from all ages and regions which we now possess, and Toynbee never tires of expressing his indebtedness to the indefatigable labors of archaeologists and philologians during the last century and a half. If he had attempted to utilize this enormous mass of new data without adequate historical training, he might have produced another *Decline of the West*, but scarcely *A Study of History*. Fortunately, he possesses a comprehensive first-hand knowledge of two historical worlds—the ancient and medieval Mediterranean (especially Greece and Byzantium) and modern Europe. To this he adds a specialist's familiarity with Islamic history and culture and a highly intelligent use of secondary sources in dealing with Chinese history. Recently he has been studying the ancient Near and Middle East intensively. Thanks to the aid of research assistants for bibliographical work, indexing, checking data, and reading proof, errors of fact and spelling are almost incredibly few.

In addition to this unequaled command of historical data, Toynbee possesses a literary taste and skill in writing which are increasingly rare among historians on either side of the Atlantic. *A Study of History* is beautifully written, with only occasional signs of haste; both style and vocabulary are superb, and the author has a knack for arresting phrases and figures of speech. While he also has a penchant for Latin terms which looks rather pedantic, and one is sometimes disturbed by a parade of not quite relevant erudition, such minor defects in no way detract from the impressiveness of his achievement.

Though Toynbee is unquestionably one-sided in his theoretical approach to the interpretation of history, it may well be that he gains more from his independence than he loses by not taking account (at least explicitly) of most literature of the last century in the same general field. Few philosophers of history are mentioned at all; exceptions are the German Spengler (whom he seems to rate far too high, perhaps because he was stimulated by *Decline of the West* to write his own immensely superior work), and the American F. J. Teggart (whose importance as a stimulator of ideas greatly outweighed his significance as an original thinker). The brilliant Oxford archaeologist and philosopher, R. G. Collingwood, is mentioned increasingly as the work progresses.[6]

However, Toynbee's weakness in technical philosophy is vividly illustrated by his failure to understand Collingwood's philosophical background when he criticizes the latter's *Idea of History*. It was partly the clash between Collingwood's vocation as practical archaeologist and his acceptance of the philosophical idealism of Dilthey and Croce which resulted in a kind of intellectual schizophrenia. Being neither a scientific excavator nor a trained philosopher, Toynbee failed to see the reason for the strange approach of Collingwood to the interpretation of history, which he justly criticizes.[7]

Yet our author is profoundly philosophical by taste and purpose; his metaphysical guides have been Plato and C. G. Jung, the great Swiss psychologist. From Plato and the Platonic atmosphere of Oxford in the heyday of Gilbert Murray, Toynbee draws his respect for intangible truth, for the recognition of basic concepts and the use of *Mythos* as a means of conveying ideas; from the Zürich psychologist, he derives a tendency to fuse literature with history, and religion with psychology. Whereas we cannot understand Toynbee fully without knowing much of Jung, it must be emphasized that Toynbee is no Jungian in any proper sense, so that it is perfectly possible to understand most of Toynbee's thought without any reference to Jung.

Probably the most provocative aspect of Toynbee's work from the standpoint of our agnostic and materialistic age is its outright theism, which oscillates between a High Church orthodoxy (at least in phraseology) and a quasi-Jungian psychologism. It must be emphasized that Toynbee is in no sense an orthodox Christian, either Catholic or Protestant, but that he is much closer to orthodoxy than he is to—say—typical liberal Protestantism in America. The orthodox creeds have a profound meaning for him, though he shows a tendency toward recognizing the fundamental identity of all world

---

[6] See Collingwood's discussion of Toynbee in *The Idea of History*, 1946, pp. 159-165, and Toynbee's analysis of Collingwood in Vol. IX, pp. 718-737.

[7] See preceding note and above, Chapter 1, n. 47.

religions, as well as an inclination to dissolve the boundaries between history and mythology.

What can we say of *A Study of History* as a contribution to our basic understanding of man's present and future? A just estimate is scarcely possible today. For one thing, the author is so original in his approach that it is impossible to compare him with any other historian, sociologist, anthropologist, or philosopher. He is not particularly interested in the problem of historical knowledge, and he has no respect at all for most contemporary historical thinking on the philosophical level. His contempt for scientism and positivism are both so pronounced that one is at first startled to find a profound respect for the scientific work which has accumulated such vast stores of historical knowledge for his use.

There are, of course, innumerable details of classification and interpretation, as well as statements of fact, from which this reviewer would dissent, and Toynbee's total picture is in some ways wholly at variance with the reviewer's own point of view. But no amount of disagreement should obscure the fact that *A Study of History* is one of the greatest intellectual efforts ever put forth by a single man. No serious future historical thought can fail to be influenced by it.

"An Historian's Approach to Religion"[8]

Two years after the completion of Toynbee's ten-volume work, *A Study of History*, he delivered the Gifford Lectures at Edinburgh in 1952 and 1953. This is the first adequate presentation of his mature views on the subject of religion. It is also the first extended treatment of any specific area of human activity in the light of the principles laid down in his major work. Whatever one may think of Toynbee's position on this or that, he remains one of the greatest historical thinkers of modern times, and his detailed analysis of such a controversial subject as religion is bound to arouse widespread interest.

As in *A Study of History*, he continues to dazzle the educated reader with the extraordinary sweep of his erudition and the elegance of his style (after making due allowance for various peculiar ways of putting things and a persistent love of Latin clichés).

[8] See the *Baltimore Evening Sun*, Sept. 11, 1956.

When the reader becomes captivated by the author's eloquence, he is likely to read on with less and less emotional and intellectual resistance. But it is very important to retain a capacity for independent judgment while reading such a brilliant survey, since one is otherwise in danger of being completely swept away—perhaps into a new horizon where values are transvalued until they lose their power to influence life, perhaps into an area of metaphysical speculation where logical categories cease to seem binding and where one ceases to think systematically. These are some of the dangers which inevitably accompany the reading of Toynbee.

For great as Toynbee's achievement undoubtedly is, it remains a *tour de force* rather than a solution. He is not sufficiently interested in problems of historical knowledge—how we know, what classes of knowledge there are, and how each type of knowledge should be used by an historian—to be a safe guide in matters of historical fact. His weakness here is not because he is sloppy or because he exalts some kinds of historical knowledge at the expense of others, but because he is often quite unaware of the pitfalls which lie before the historian as he ventures into unfamiliar areas. A historian who has been trained in "historical epistemology" and who has done firsthand work in such fields as archaeology, history of ideas, and history of religions, is much more likely to be a safe guide than Toynbee. Unfortunately, this historian would scarcely be a great writer, much less an original thinker of tremendous sweep, so we must be grateful for the fact that we have Toynbee, whether we agree with him or not.

The fact remains that Toynbee is a human being who is full of prejudices—some of them characteristic of a post-Victorian English patrician, some resulting from a successful attempt to break away from Victorian forms of bias, some stemming from the religious liberalism of the past generation, some perhaps representing too violent a reaction against it. Toynbee does not give an "historian's" view—based on judgments of fact—but his own personal view—based on value judgments derived from his own "pseudo-theology." The title and tenor of discussion are very misleading. Among these prejudices is a very low opinion of early Biblical religion, which he considers as tribal, parochial, war-minded, and intolerant, giving rise to impious notions about the uniqueness of Israel as the "Chosen People."

In fact he even traces the intolerance of Christianity and Islam to their origin in Judaism, and to the same source he refers the "totalitarian intransigence" said to have been shown by the Roman Catholic Church and most Protestants toward modern experimental science. His severe criticism of Old Testament religion leads further to violent attacks on modern Judaism and especially on Zionism and Israel (though less extended in this book than in his *A Study of History*).[9] The two dominant religions of Indian history, Hinduism and Buddhism, on the other hand, he almost invariably paints in bright colors. For instance, he asserts that the successive triumphs of Buddhism over Hinduism in India in the third century B.C. and of Hinduism over Buddhism nearly a thousand years later were "peacefully accomplished."

In a published debate[10] with an able Indian scholar some twelve years ago, this reviewer brought direct testimony from ancient Indian sources, both Buddhist and Hindu, to the contrary; the successive victories were only won after a great deal of bloodshed. It is quite true that Buddhist scriptures and some Hindus preach non-violence, but so do the Christian Scriptures, and practice in India, Burma, and other lands of Indic tradition has differed at least as sharply from theory as has practice in Christian countries. We all remember the bloody massacres which attended the breakup of the British Empire in India a few years ago. Human nature remains fundamentally the same in all periods and all countries, and Toynbee himself never tires of emphasizing the ubiquity of original sin, though he often seems to record it exclusively to the discredit of Christians and Jews.

There are basic fallacies in Toynbee's treatment of Hinduism and Buddhism as though they were on a logical par with Judaism and Christianity—and judging from many statements of his, even superior to them. In the first place, Hinduism is Ancient Oriental polytheism and nature-worship, with a philosophical facet which remains far more out of touch with reality (since the phenomenal world is simply *maya*, "illusion") than the Greek philosophical systems which developed in the soil of paganism during the last few cen-

---

[9] The best reply to Toynbee's singularly biased attitude toward Jewish history is Maurice Samuel's *The Professor and the Fossil*, 1956. Having been in Palestine myself from 1919 to 1936 and again on later visits, I should like to register my almost complete agreement with Samuel against Toynbee.

[10] See above, pp. 205-208.

turies B.C. There is indeed a post-Buddhist phase of Hinduism, which Toynbee often stresses, but there is also a post-Christian phase of Hinduism, illustrated on the practical level by Mahatma Gandhi and on the philosophical level by Sir Sarvepalli Radhakrishnan, which Toynbee fails to mention. Buddhism arose in the fifth century B.C. on the soil of Hindu paganism, and turned to pantheism because of the already developed metaphysical pantheism of the Upanishads.

When one thinks of the historical, ethical, and spiritual treasures of the Old and New Testament, and considers the long process by which the ancestral faith of the West developed from Ancient Oriental, Hebrew, and Greek sources, and when one then contrasts them with the relative poverty of Hindu and Buddhist scriptures, it scarcely seems fair to place them on a level. Christianity has developed through the ages in constant interaction with the complex Western civilization which is now sweeping the world, and it stands to reason that it would be better adapted to the new age of technology than the illusionist and escapist faiths of the East.[11]

Toynbee never mentions the fact that Christian missionary activity (deployed on a vast and generally altruistic scale by both Catholic and Protestant churches) had transformed much of eastern Asia before the Communist world revolution, or that the heads of four East Asian states are Christian, with strong Christian minorities in several other countries.

Another fallacy of Toynbee's is his view that "toleration" is a fundamental good in itself. This reviewer is a warm friend of minorities and insists on full toleration of different races and religions. But tolerance of antisocial activities, such as robbery, murder, and dope traffic, is not a good thing at all; and in some modern periods of the world's history it has proved impossible to differentiate between a tolerable religion and a terroristic revolutionary movement such as the fanatic leaders of the Peasants' Revolt in Germany, or between legitimate religious activity and human sacrifice, ritual prostitution, suttee, and thuggery—to name only a few antisocial practices with religious sanctions. Nor should it ever be forgotten that much so-called "tolerance" is sheer indifference,

[11] See below, p. 257, and my comments at the end of my contribution to *An Outline of Man's Knowledge of the Modern World*, ed. Lyman Bryson, 1960, pp. 319-321.

and that earnest souls are bound to be somewhat intolerant, whether they are Puritans, Dominican Friars of the Middle Ages, or professional liberals.

Still another fallacy of the author is that there is something inherently wrong in recognizing uniqueness, and that a religion which professes to be unique involves its adherents in self-centered egotism and impious challenge to the Almighty. While the author is not always consistent here, his repeated attacks on the religion of Israel, on Judaism, and on the Messiahship of Jesus nearly all follow this direction. Actually, Homo sapiens is the only animal endowed with capacity for making tools, speaking to his fellows, and thinking (within limits). *Terra* is the only planet of the solar system capable of sustaining life in any form known to us. The Greeks discovered logical reasoning, introduced philosophical speculation, and set up forms of literature, art, and science which are still substantially valid; in these respects they remain unique. Plato and Aristotle remain unique in the history of human speculative thought, and all subsequent thinkers must trace their pedigree back to one or both of them. Newton in macromechanics, Darwin in biological evolution, and Einstein in physics and relativity theory are all unique in their way. Rome, Great Britain, the United States have all been unique in their successive contributions to freedom under law. So why should we refuse a priori to grant uniqueness to Israel, Moses—and Christ? We admit at once that Toynbee is right in emphasizing the danger involved in recognition of national or individual uniqueness, but such an admission need not carry with it denial of elementary human insight into the facts of existence.

In my discussion of Toynbee's *A Study of History* in 1954,[12] this reviewer attributed to him an "outright theism, which oscillates between a High Church orthodoxy (at least in phraseology) and a quasi-Jungian psychologism." On the basis of his new book we must probably emphasize the latter, and we may add that he is much more strongly influenced by Hinduism and especially Buddhism than was then evident.

Like two other noted Western religious thinkers of today, Albert Schweitzer and Paul Tillich, Toynbee is a modern Gnostic, though each reflects a different point of view and though none of the three

[12] See above, p. 249.

seems to quote the other two. Schweitzer has grafted Hindu "reverence for life" on Christian altruism, with an essentially pantheistic philosophy. Tillich has grafted existentialism on Schelling's pantheism (itself influenced more than a little by Hindu ideas) and has produced a theological structure which resembles traditional Christianity only in superficial respects. Toynbee has adopted a pantheism which may be called a mixture of Platonizing Christianity with Hinduism under the influence of Jung.

All three preach Christian altruism, but all three have diluted their Christianity with some thoroughly refractory ingredients. This does not, however, mean that Jewish and Christian thinkers cannot learn a great deal from them—far more from Toynbee than either of the others, for he has by far the greatest originality and aptitude for intellectual synthesis.

"Reconsiderations (*A Study of History,* VOLUME XII)*"*[13]

The first ten volumes of Toynbee's great work devoted over 6,000 closely printed pages to an analysis of historical data, from which he derived many far-reaching conclusions. Magnificently conceived and brilliantly executed, *A Study of History* will retain its value for a long time to come. To be sure, it is an intensely personal undertaking, with whose methods and goals other students will no doubt continue to disagree. Yet the differences of opinion aroused by the publication of the first three volumes in 1934 and stirred up by the appearance of three more volumes in 1939 and of four additional volumes in 1954, have been both instructive and interesting to all alert intellectuals.

The numerous and greatly varying criticisms of Toynbee's work, primarily of *A Study of History*, have not gone unnoticed by him. In the 750 pages of his *Reconsiderations*, Toynbee ventures again to challenge opinion by confronting his critics on a hitherto unprecedented scale. In the bibliography he lists more than 200 criticisms by almost as many critics, and he certainly refers to many additional criticisms in the body of his book. He obviously enjoys his task, taking special pleasure in listing reviewers who have criticized him severely for his sins, followed by other reviewers who have praised

[13] See the *Baltimore Evening Sun,* May 4, 1961.

him for the same qualities, which now become virtues. For instance, many critics have spoken highly of his style, while others have damned it with equal fervor. Many have accused him of sacrificing principles to factual data, while others have scolded him for claiming to approach history from an empirical basis, a claim which they reject. To these critics he seems to select factual data arbitrarily for the purpose of establishing some a priori principle.

Toynbee is an unusual combination of classical scholar, modern historian, publicist, and idealistic reformer. To his background in humane letters he owes his style, which is occasionally too Johnsonian, but which is admirably suited for the matter with which he deals. There can be no doubt that his fame is partly—perhaps largely —due to American journalists who were fascinated by the brilliant combination of qualities which the best of them could admire wholeheartedly.[14] Professional historians have turned against him almost to a man, though their attitude is beginning to weaken under the impact of the mass of factual data which he pours out, fortified by his constant efforts to bring all relevant new facts into his picture. Where most historians dislike admitting their mistakes, Toynbee generally seems to take pride in making such admissions.

In the reviewer's opinion, Toynbee has succeeded in proving his respect for empirical data and in establishing himself as an essentially empirical thinker. That he has not completely succeeded is probably due largely to his lack of basic philosophical training. He is still remote from understanding the problem of historical knowledge, as is illustrated by his failure to come to grips with a single epistemological issue. At the very least he should have studied Maurice Mandelbaum's *The Problem of Historical Knowledge* (1938).[15]

Certain fundamental weaknesses in Toynbee's approach are, we think, the direct result of his zeal for international good will and religious unity. In the first place, he dissolves the barriers between religions and philosophies by applying points of view drawn chiefly from Plato, Plotinus, and C. G. Jung. Partly through the last-named thinker a strain of Gnosticism enters his work, which would have

[14] Having known a good many prominent journalists, I can testify to the truth of this statement. Many of us remember vividly the impact on the American public of articles in *Time* about Toynbee.

[15] See *From the Stone Age to Christianity*, 1957 ed., pp. 113 ff.; also above, pp. 23-27 f.

been unacceptable to both Platonists and Neo-Platonists. *A Study of History* needs to be supplemented by Toynbee's more recent *An Historian's Approach to Religion*, in which he spells out his ideas much more explicitly. Perhaps because he did not want to expand *Reconsiderations* even more, this book is passed over in silence, without even cross-references. Since there is actually a complete barrier between Hellenic-European philosophy, all of which is—or pretends to be—postulational (*i.e.*, rational and deductive), and Indian metaphysics, together with the derived or related East-Asiatic systems of thought, Toynbee's elimination of differences between East and West appears to be doomed from the beginning.

Another result of Toynbee's missionary zeal for unity is his constant and deliberate effort to minimize uniqueness in history. This tendency is, however, directly opposed to the facts. All known forms of the true tool-making man belong to one genus and a single interbreeding species,[16] human intellect is thus unique among living beings on earth. Systematic reasoning, with the resulting philosophy, science, and technology, all goes back to Hellenic genius between 600 and 200 B.C. Plato and Aristotle remain uniquely towering geniuses. So do Newton and Einstein. Hebrew monotheism, with its emphasis on a personal God, uniting creative power with strict ethics and love for humanity, is unique in world history; Christianity and Islam, with all their human weaknesses, are its direct offspring. All three monotheistic religions can be, and have been, welded into philosophical structures based on philosophical realism and rationalism. This is not possible for the great Asiatic religions, sprung from the ancient polytheistic beliefs of pre-Hellenic cultures and essentially devoid of postulational philosophy (except where imported in recent times from Europe and America.)

Not only is Toynbee's effort to eliminate uniqueness a failure in his own postulational structure, it also leads him to an otherwise irrational prejudice against the religion of Israel and subsequent Judaism as well as against modern Zionism and specifically against the state of Israel. Without in any way endorsing all that has taken place, or suggesting that the survivors of the Nazi holocaust should be judged by a measure different from that applied to their

[16] See below, p. 292.

enemies,[17] this reviewer would call attention to the fact that self-preservation remains the first law of life and that nationalism is a universal phenomenon of our time, bringing both evil and good in its wake. Furthermore, if the allegedly fossil culture of Judaism had not persisted into our time, we should have lost the contributions of tens of thousands of cultural leaders to our own world civilization. And the contributors include an astoundingly high proportion of Nobel prize winners!

[17] When Toynbee compares the slaughter of six million Jewish captives by modern Nazi methods of mass destruction with the slaughter of several hundred Arab noncombatants in the Jewish-Arab War of 1948, he is surely carrying analogy much too far. Besides, the massacre of the Arab villagers of Deir Yasin by adherents of a Jewish zealot group (the "Stern gang") sent a wave of revulsion through the Jewish world, whereas the extermination of Jews in the gas chambers of the Second World War delighted the Nazis, and few Germans dared protest anywhere in the Third Empire (see above, Chapter 10). A point which seems to have escaped Toynbee completely is that there are not only more than a million Arab refugees from Israel in Arab countries (including their offspring, of course), but there are also nearly a million Jewish refugees from Arab countries (counting their offspring) in Israel. Toynbee should have permitted the logic of history to fix the collective responsibility of entire peoples, without venturing to pronounce judgment himself. Who but Almighty God can fix the ultimate moral responsibility of nations?

Chapter 12

Eric Voegelin: order and history[1]

As the successive volumes of Eric Voegelin's work are published, it becomes clear that *Order and History*[2] is a major undertaking, which may ultimately be given a place beside the ten volumes of Arnold Toynbee's *A Study of History*. We shall have to include in the scope of our analysis the first chapters of Volume II, as well as the whole of Volume I, with which we are especially concerned in this article, since Voegelin's philosophical underpinning is nowhere so clearly stated as in the former.

Philosophical assumptions

The author's eclectic philosophy consists of three main strands: a modified Hegelianism, an Augustinianism, and an existentialism of rather indefinite type. These are certainly not the only sources of

[1] Three years before this review article was written, I accepted a request from *Theological Studies* to review this work. Owing to heavy pressure of work during my last active year at Johns Hopkins and the first two years of "retirement," I found it impossible to meet this obligation. Having accepted an invitation from the American Political Science Association to present a paper on the first volume of *Order and History* at a symposium on Voegelin held at the Association's annual meeting in September, 1960, I combined the two assignments. The paper subsequently appeared in *Theological Studies*, 22, 1961, pp. 270-279.

[2] The first volume of Voegelin's work is entitled *Israel and Revelation*, Louisiana State Univ. Press, 1956. The second volume appeared in 1957 as *The World of the Polis*. Other volumes have subsequently appeared.

his thinking, but they are the most obvious and probably the decisive elements.

After becoming more and more convinced of the basically Hegelian character of Voegelin's thought while studying Volume I, I found it explicitly stated in the Introduction to Volume II, where he describes the relation between Hegel and his own point of view. Voegelin does not, however, fully succeed in clarifying this relation, since in trying to explain it he resorts to some highly obscure metaphors, such as "the Eros of the transcendent Sophon." He should have started with his own surrogate for the *Geist* of Hegel, namely "order"[3]—order as the guiding principle of history, as well as the form taken by individual societies participating "in the order of being that has its origin in world-transcendent divine Being."[4] By substituting "order" for Hegel's *Geist*, Voegelin has avoided much of the vagueness and ambivalence attached to the German word, at the same time that he keeps the essential historical feature of *Geist* as the ordering principle underlying the evolution of human societies. There is a striking superficial resemblance between Hegel and Voegelin when they try to define the relation of organized society to the basic principle of historical evolution. Hegel wrote, for instance: "The state is the idea of *Geist* in the external manifestation of human will and its freedom. . . . History is the exhibition of the divine, absolute development of *Geist* to its highest forms."[5] Voegelin writes: "Human existence in society has history because it has a dimension of spirit and freedom . . . because social order is an attunement of man with the order of being, and because this order . . . can be realized in society with increasing approximations to its truth."[6] Yet there is a real difference between Hegel and Voegelin: the former fails to distinguish betwen the *Geist* as working in history and the transcendent Spirit of Christian theology, while the latter generally makes a sharp distinction between the historical

---

[3] Cf. Harald Höffding, *A History of Modern Philosophy*, II (trans. E. E. Meyer) p. 179: "At this point Hegel is close to the so-called historical school which regards the ordering of rights as the work of history, exalted above all individual reflection and will."

[4] Voegelin, II, p. 2.

[5] Trans. from Hegel's sentence in his *Vorlesungen über die Philosophie der Geschichte* (ed. Glockner, XI, 1949, p. 80).

[6] Voegelin, II, p. 2.

order of being and the divine Being. On the other hand, one may question whether Voegelin's tendency to combine religious and political manifestations of cosmic order will not lead to an essentially Hegelian historicism in the work of followers who disregard his theistic emphasis.

Another pronounced difference between Hegel and Voegelin is the latter's implicit rejection of the Hegelian dialectic, for which he substitutes such principles as the Kierkegaardian "leap of being,"[7] the concept of stimulus and response, and the transformation of historical experience into symbolical forms. The "leap of being" is a concept of questionable utility, especially since it must have originated in some sort of fusion of the Augustinian "leap of faith" with Hegelian notions. The idea of "stimulus and response" is again a kind of blending of Hegel's "thesis and antithesis" with Toynbee's "challenge and response." The survival of already experienced history in symbolic form is evidently influenced by the thinking of Ernst Cassirer, though by no means identical with it.

In this reviewer's opinion, Voegelin's strong espousal of an Augustinian approach to history helps greatly to save him from falling into the trap of historicism. Every exponent of this many-sided attitude to history inevitably rewrites empirical history to suit his particular principle of evolution, whether it is Hegelian, positivistic, or something else. In general, Voegelin tries very hard to follow the latest and best authorities in the successive fields of history through which he passes in his survey. As a philosophical theist, he does not try to find an ordering principle within history itself, but looks at it *sub specie aeternitatis*. It is precisely his theism which permits him to treat historical data as important in themselves. In other words, his recognition of the extrahistorical source of the ordering principle helps to give him a respect for the facts of history which is rarely, if ever, found among those students who try to derive an over-all principle of organization from the historical experience itself. A standard or measure of history outside of its own development helps greatly to avert a tendency to treat history as relative to the standpoint of a given thinker. One difficulty with any idealistic point of view is that a thinker who takes this position is likely to slip into the habit of identifying himself with the Deity

[7] This is one of the author's favorite expressions; cf. the index to Vol. I, pp. 522b and 528b.

from whom he theoretically derives his ordering principle. I do not mean to suggest that Voegelin himself is guilty of this fallacy.

Voegelin's existentialism is rather hard to pinpoint; there is certainly much less existentialist terminology in Volume II than in Volume I. At first he seems to have distinguished more or less systematically between pure being (*Sein*) and existence (*Dasein*), treating the former as basic and the latter as the situation of man in the phenomenal world, "immediate to God."[8] However, this distinction scarcely suits his use of the term "leap of being" to describe a great advance in the intellectual and spiritual life of man. In the reviewer's opinion, the existentialism of the author's language has little or nothing to do with his historical synthesis as such. So far it has, in fact, proved virtually impossible to employ any form of the "philosophy of being"—least of all current existentialism—to interpret history. It is no accident that most existentialists neglect or misuse history, since their systems are predicated on an individual approach to the problem of finite man pitted against the infinite, whether God or nothing. Kierkegaard's use of history was fantastically arbitrary, and the more logical Heidegger has consistently disregarded it. Karl Jaspers uses historical data only scantily, and then for his own speculative purposes. Rudolf Bultmann's recent excursions into history have abandoned existential philosophy almost completely, substituting the relativist Wilhelm Dilthey and the Neo-Hegelian R. G. Collingwood for Heidegger and Jaspers.[9] Paul Tillich treats historical data with sovereign arbitrariness. In short, existentialism and history are just as contradictory in practice as are Husserl's phenomenology and natural science, however much each pair may seem superficially to have in common.

Comparison and contrast between Voegelin and Toynbee[10]

The two leading philosophical historians of today balance each other remarkably well. In the reviewer's opinion, Voegelin is superior

[8] See esp. Voegelin, I, pp. 1 ff. E.g., on p. 1 he says: "Participation in being, however, is not a partial involvement of man; he is engaged with the whole of his existence." Here "existence" is "created being"—a typical existentialist distinction between "pure being" (*Sein*) and "empirical being" (*Dasein*).
[9] See the writer's discussion of Bultmann's *History and Eschatology*, below, Chapter 13.
[10] See my discussion of Toynbee above, Chapter 11.

to Toynbee in having a much wider and deeper philosophical background, in taking a greater interest in the history of ideas, and in showing a far profounder sympathy with the Judeo-Christian tradition, which lies at the heart of Western civilization—however much some may resent this fact or try to conceal it. On the other hand, Toynbee is superior in the vast sweep of his historical horizon in time and space; he makes more of an effort to be up to date in his information; he is much more precise in his language, not having Voegelin's conflict between underlying German idiom and the semantics of English. As a phenomenology of history Toynbee's work is superior, but he too often appears to marshal data to prove his theories rather than permit the principles to establish themselves. When Toynbee goes astray, his errors are thus compounded until they reach monumental proportions. Yet Toynbee relies much more than Voegelin on primary sources; his approach has a large element of induction in it, though it tends to dissolve into analogy. Voegelin's reliance on the constructions of specialists avoids the compounding of errors, but results in a lack of focus which often blurs the historical picture.

The use of empirical data in the philosophy of history

In view of the tremendous sweep of Voegelin's own survey, it would be absurd to expect him to be up to date throughout. He himself believed at the outset of his work that there were facts enough at his disposal to make such a majestic synthesis quite feasible. In fact, he wrote in the Preface to Volume I (p. xii):

> The work could be undertaken in our time. . . . The sources are ready to hand; and the convergent interpretations by orientalists and semitologists, by classical philologists and historians of antiquity, by theologians and medievalists, facilitate and invite the attempt to use the primary sources as the basis for a philosophical study of order. The state of science in the various disciplines, as well as my own position with regard to fundamental questions, will be set forth in the course of the study.

These are brave words, and the author has done his best to justify them. But he is much too optimistic; neither the state of knowledge in our time nor the convergence of interpretations is as great as the author suggests. This statement is not intended as a criticism of his effort, which is well worth while even though one may disagree in detail. Unless we have such syntheses from time to time, our historical thinking is immeasurably poorer. The writer will limit himself to a few examples, grouped under three heads: (1) the author's use of the term "cosmological order" with reference to the pre-Israelite and pre-Hellenic civilizations of the Near East; (2) his treatment of Israelite faith as paradigmatic and symbolic; (3) his view of the evolution of Greek philosophical thought from earlier Hellenic mythology. The reviewer's criticisms are throughout based primarily on archaeological discoveries and their interpretation in publications which were either unknown to the author or were passed over by him in silence.

Cosmological order

It is scarcely probable that Voegelin would have employed such a term as "cosmological" of the civilizations of the ancient East if he had been aware of the extent to which Pan-Babylonian speculation has been discredited by recent research. While he cannot be called a follower of this school, in view of his frequent use of the work of more recent scholars who had discarded the views of Winckler and Jeremias over a generation ago, he unfortunately does follow Jeremias and other members of the Pan-Babylonian school repeatedly.[11] According to these views, which he quotes without criticism, Babylonian astral symbolism had already developed into an elaborate astrology in early Babylonian times, and the other peoples of the ancient East, in particular the Hebrews, had been strongly influenced by it. This position has been shown by Otto Neugebauer of Brown University (who is never quoted) to be completely baseless.[12] In fact, astrology was much less important than half a dozen other forms of divination, all quite without astral significance, in early Babylonian times. It was not until the Persian and

[11] See esp. p. 15, n. 1, and pp. 29 ff.
[12] There is no reference to the epoch-making work of Neugebauer; see especially the latter's book, *The Exact Sciences in Antiquity*, 1952; 2d ed., 1957, and his more detailed papers: "The History of Ancient Astronomy: Problems and Methods," *Journal of Near Eastern Studies*, 4, 1945, pp. 1-38; "The Alleged Babylonian Discovery of the Precession of the Equinoxes," *Journal of the American Oriental Society*, 70, 1950, pp. 1-8; and "Babylonian Planetary

Hellenistic periods that astrology became paramount in Babylonia, and its development into the elaborate structure which we know today did not take place until the second century B.C.—in Egypt.[13] It is, to be sure, correct to stress the importance of cosmic myths in the mythology of all ancient nations, but the cosmos is here simply part of the environment in which man was involved. All parts of it were necessary to man's supply of food and his security as a social being. The reviewer would suggest some such term as "physiocentric," centered in nature, as more appropriate to ancient Near Eastern higher culture and religion. In any case, there was at best only a cosmography, not a cosmology, before the rise of Greek science after the sixth century B.C. (It may be observed, in passing, that the true cosmological age may have begun in A.D. 1957.)

Israelite faith

The four hundred pages in which Voegelin discusses the role of Israel in world history show very careful study of the available material. His use of Hebrew is almost impeccable, and he is extremely well informed on German and Scandinavian Old Testament scholarship. Many of his own contributions are original and penetrating. And yet he is definitely wrong in following the Alt-Noth-von Rad school so closely. He cannot be blamed, since Albrecht Alt was a great scholar;[14] and his pupils Martin Noth and Gerhard von Rad are first-class men, whose work shows learning and acumen. Alt and Noth have made very important historical contributions, and von Rad is surpassed by no one in his insight into certain problems of Old Testament religion. But after the middle 1930s Alt himself was cut off almost completely from direct contact with Palestine as well as from non-German research. His pupils were in much the same situation, and the attempt to replace the influx of

---

Theory," *American Philosophical Society, Proceedings*, 98, 1954, pp. 60-89. Since there is not the slightest concrete evidence for the twelve signs of the zodiac before Neo-Babylonian times, most of Jeremias' speculations are automatically refuted. The real value of the Pan-Babylonian movement lay in quite another direction.

[13] As demonstrated by F. Cumont, *L'Égypte des astrologues*, 1937.

[14] Cf. my survey of his contributions in *Journal of Biblical Literature*, 75, 1956, pp. 169-173.

empirical data from Palestine and the ancient Near East by systematic research along a priori lines led to increasing loss of touch with archaeological and philological fact. Today there is a very sharp cleavage between the dominant German school and the archaeological school, best represented in America and Israel. In order to avoid the necessity of citing chapter and verse, the reviewer will mention the two most significant histories of Israel, Noth's *Geschichte Israels* (now available in English as *The History of of Israel*) and John Bright's *A History of Israel* (1959), which reflect the opposing positions most ably.[15]

A few general remarks will serve to illustrate what is happening. Thanks to an unexampled flood of discoveries in Palestine and adjacent lands, we now have illustrative texts in many languages from every century of the second millennium B.C. We can now date Hebrew and early Israelite name lists, individual events, and especially successive phases of Hebrew linguistic evolution. It is now quite certain that, whatever refraction and rearrangement of oral tradition may have taken place, the Patriarchal narratives of Genesis fit the first half of the second millennium B.C. very well.[16] Owing to the rapid progress of research and discovery during the past five years, we can be sure that the career of Moses and the subsequent Israelite occupation of Palestine are to be dated in the thirteenth century B.C. Furthermore, it is no longer possible to separate early Israelite religion sharply from that of later Israel;

[15] See the lucid discussion of the opposing postions by G. Ernest Wright, in *Journal of Bible and Religion*, 28, 1960, pp. 182-193, and *Expository Times*, 72, July, 1960, pp. 3-7.
[16] When these lines were written I could not yet have any idea of the new material which was to become available within a year. See my paper, "Abram the Hebrew: A New Archaeological Interpretation," *Bulletin of the American Schools of Oriental Research*, No. 163, 1961, pp. 36-54. For a general survey of the Patriarchal age in the light of our sources see *The Biblical Period from Abraham to Ezra: An Historical Survey*, 1963, pp. 1-34, and for bibliographical material see *ibid.*, pp. 97-101 (revised to July, 1962). On the religion of the Patriarchs see the admirable paper by Frank M. Cross, Jr., "Yahweh and the God of the Patriarchs," *Harvard Theological Review*, 55, 1962, pp. 225-259. See also G. Ernest Wright, *Biblical Archaeology*, 1957, pp. 40 ff., and John Bright, *A History of Israel*, 1959, pp. 60 ff., as well as, for details, H. Cazelles' article "Patriarches" in *Supplement au Dictionnaire de la Bible*, VII, 1961, cols. 81-156. My new material on the 'Apiru/'Abiru (Hebrews), as well as on Jacob and Joseph, should be published soon.

explicit if nonphilosophical monotheism must go back to the age of Moses, and the other essential principles and institutions of Biblical religion also go back to Israelite beginnings.[17]

In view of the fact that German scholars are inclined to discount the evidence of archaeological stratigraphy and to close their eyes to linguistic arguments, it should be emphasized that we now possess direct *literary* evidence for the earliest period of Israelite religious history. This evidence consists of many poems and poetic quotations in the books of Exodus-Judges, Psalms, and occasionally elsewhere. These poems reflect vocabulary, grammar, and especially literary style characteristic of the Canaanite religious epics which have been recovered from Ugarit on the North Syrian coast since 1929. These epics are now extant in copies from the fourteenth century B.C., several generations before Moses. Since it can also be shown that most of these peculiarities disappear rapidly in Biblical literature dating from the tenth century B.C. or later, it should be obvious that the text of such early compositions is older than that of any later prose narratives from Israel, all of which date from the tenth century B.C. and later.[18] But these poems and poetic quotations throughout presuppose a religious situation which is entirely monotheistic, though sometimes quite archaic in comparison to later literature.

Since the importance of historical analogy is often forgotten in the clash of exaggerated claims and counterclaims, the reviewer would like to recall the position taken by Herder, Ewald, Delitzsch, and other Biblical scholars of the late eighteenth and early nineteenth centuries with regard to the age of Biblical poetry. These scholars recognized that Hebrew poetry began before Hebrew prose, since verse is the natural style of oral tradition, which normally precedes the oldest prose literature. Parallels are innumerable;

[17] To the literature emanating largely from the Baltimore school (including esp. the forthcoming first volume of my projected *History of the Religion of Israel*) must be added particularly the notable—and wholly independent—work of Yehezkel Kaufmann, *Toldot ha-Emunah ha-Yisre'elit* (since 1937), now available in a superb translation and condensation by Moshe Greenberg, *The Religion of Israel*, Chicago, 1960.

[18] My detailed study has not yet been published; cf. my paper on the Song of Moses in Deut. 32, in *Vetus Testamentum*, 9, 1959, pp. 1-10, and esp. p. 10, for the direction of my latest work, which has been strongly influenced by Otto Eissfeldt. For bibliography, see above, Chapter 1, n. 64.

among the best are Greek and Latin, Germanic and Romance, Indic and Iranian, Chinese and other national literatures. The same is true of Sumerian, Egyptian, Hittite, Canaanite, etc. It would thus be passing strange if the Israelites were an exception. Historical analogies do not constitute proof when taken alone, but when they fully agree with such evidence as was mentioned above, the historical tradition may be considered as secure.[19]

Another category of Biblical literature which has been consistently dated too late by most critical scholars of the past century is early Hebrew law. This category includes fragments of civil codes, such as the so-called Book of the Covenant, extensive remains of early ritual and ceremonial law, and condensed summaries of the contents of older religious compacts of the $b^e r \hat{\imath} t$ type. The surviving civil and religious laws of early Israel are partly in generalized case form, couched in the same conditional formula that we find in all the codes preserved in whole or in part from the second millennium— Sumerian, Accadian, and Hittite. Parallels are so close that there can be no doubt that customary Hebrew law of this casuistic type goes back well into the pre-monarchic and often into Mosaic or pre-Mosaic times. It has recently been demonstrated by George E. Mendenhall of the University of Michigan that the structure of the best-known compact, the Covenant of Joshua, is virtually identical with that of the suzerainty treaties of the fourteenth and thirteenth centuries B.C., recovered from the capitals of Bronze Age Anatolia and Syria.[20] Suzerainty treaties of the eighth and seventh centuries, recovered in the past few years from Syria and Assyria, have a much simpler structure.[21] To illustrate, the earlier suzerainty treaties have a historical prologue and often a statement that the text was to be deposited in a specified temple. The Covenant between the God and

---

[19] On the use of analogy in history see above, pp. 73-76, 78-79, 244-245.

[20] See particularly his brilliant survey of the material in *Law and Covenant in Israel and the Ancient Near East*, Pittsburgh, 1955, and his article "Covenant," in *Interpreter's Dictionary of the Bible*, ed. G. A. Buttrick *et al.*, Vol. I, 1962, pp. 714-723. See also Klaus Baltzer, *Das Bundesformular*, 1960.

[21] Against some recent criticisms cf. William L. Moran, S.J., in his review of Mendenhall (*Biblica*, 41, 1960, pp. 297-299), where he emphasizes the fact that recently published Aramean and Assyrian treaties from the eighth-seventh centuries B.C. lack such vital elements as the historical prologue (see Mendenhall, *Law and Covenant*, p. 30, n. 19)—though there are naturally some survivals from earlier times.

people of Israel described in Joshua 24 begins and ends with these features, while other parallels of equal significance appear in its structure.[22] Quite aside from the similar structural framework, we find in the Anatolian treaties the same mixture of casuistic and apodictic formulation that we find in the Book of the Covenant in Exodus.

The underlying historical and literary tradition of the books of Exodus, Leviticus, Numbers, and Joshua is thus throughout in general agreement with literary and historical facts as we know them today. Voegelin's instinct is therefore correct when he insists repeatedly on the antiquity and centrality of Mosaic tradition. On the other hand, he relies far too much on modern scholarly analysis and much too little on the rapidly increasing mass of archaeological evidence—using "archaeology" in its broadest sense. As a result, his many illuminating observations about the development and transformation of symbols are too often buried in a mass of erroneous critical dissection and reinterpretation of the sources. Where the author follows the Hebrew text itself, he is at his best. The reviewer is reminded of Eduard Meyer's reply to his question about the great ancient historian's method of research: "Ich habe meine eigene Forschung immer auf die Quellen gebaut, nicht auf moderne Hypothesen und Konstruktionen."

Greek philosophical origins

Voegelin's approach to the problem of Greek philosophical origins is definitely in need of revision. Neither the attempt to trace the evolution of Ionian science and philosophy from Homer through Hesiod nor the assumption that they arose spontaneously by unrecorded empirical stages or by a series of brilliant intuitions is now tenable. In the first place, the theogony of Hesiod has been shown conclusively by H. G. Güterbock[23] and Uvo Hölscher[24] to be derived with scarcely any essential change from the pre-Hellenic Aegean, which had derived it from Hurro-Hittite theogony—ulti-

[22] See Mendenhall, *op. cit.*, pp. 41-42; J. Muilenburg, *Vetus Testamentum*, 9, 1959, pp. 357-360; Baltzer, *Das Bundesformular*, pp. 29-36.
[23] See his *Kumarbi* (*Istanbuler Schriften*, No. 16; 1946), pp. 100-115.
[24] See his important study, "Anaximander und die Anfänge der Philosophie," *Hermes*, 81, 1953, pp. 257-277, 385-418.

mately in part Sumerian. We can therefore not derive Hesiod's theogony from the Homeric epics, directly or indirectly; it is much older.

We now know that the material culture of Phoenicia, Cyprus, southern Anatolia, and the Aegean was thoroughly syncretized during the seventh and sixth centuries B.C., following several centuries of interpenetration of Aegean and Phoenician civilization. The Greeks of these two centuries had a long line of colonies and trading stations extending from Cyrene through Egypt, Palestine, and Phoenicia to northern Syria and Cilicia. The Phoenicians had been colonizing different Mediterranean lands for centuries, and the Hellenes had already borrowed from them much of their art and architecture, as well as their alphabet. The Ionians were at that time the leaders of the Greek world in culture, and all the Eastern peoples derived their names for "Greek" from "Ionian." Uvo Hölscher has well put the case for Phoenician and Egyptian origin of Ionic science and metaphysics. The great contribution of Thales to mathematics, I might add, consisted in generalizing and formulating mathematical propositions according to the analogy of legal codes. Since all mathematical texts from both Mesopotamia and Egypt state propositions only in the form of concrete problems which embody specific examples, the generalization of problems in the form of abstract propositions or theorems was a tremendous step forward.[25] Logical demonstration of propositions in geometry came gradually during the fifth century and reached its climax in Euclid, who applied Aristotelian logic.[26]

To conclude, we congratulate the author on a monumental work,

[25] Thales was not only reputed by the Greeks to have been the founder of geometry, but is said by Herodotus (I, 170) to have been a highly respected authority on public law.

[26] For a contrary view see B. L. van der Waerden, "La démonstration dans les sciences exactes de l'antiquité," *Bulletin de la Société Mathématique de Belgique*, 9, 1957, pp. 8-20, but he has misunderstood Proclus, as will be pointed out elsewhere. There is thus not the slightest evidence for such a tremendous leap as the transition from pre-deductive to deductive logic in a single lifetime. Logic and philosophy remain the contribution of Greek genius, though it required several centuries for the attainment of the level represented by Aristotle and Euclid. On the whole question of the emergence of Ionian science and philosophy from its northeast Mediterranean background see my next volume in this series.

from whose inevitable errors we may learn as much as from its innumerable correct statements. Since both Voegelin's standard of historical value and the ultimate aim of his work are beyond history, he has escaped Hegel's fatal mistake of treating history as a self-contained system from which its own goal could be inferred by the application of his dialectic logic to the factual data which he then believed to be true. In saying this, the reviewer is not speaking *pro domo*, since his own syntheses—published and unpublished—are based on quite different postulates: (1) historical knowledge is identical with scientific knowledge in vast areas of research dealing with the past of mankind, and differences tend to be of degree rather than of kind; (2) the historian is obligated to use all the resources of modern scientific and philosophical analysis to reconstruct the steps by which men have learned to use their minds more effectively. In other words, the writer insists on basing historical research on a combination of empirical and rational methodology. Neither philosophical idealism nor the existentialist systems of our day can contribute much to the historian, except where he undertakes to assess their influence on historical thought and its consequences. Here the historian must agree with Voltaire: "Il faut écrire l'histoire en philosophe!"

Chapter 13

Rudolph Bultmann on history and eschatology[1]

Rudolf Bultmann holds a place of authority in Central European theological circles comparable to that of Paul Tillich in similar American circles today. He is justly respected for his great learning in New Testament (his primary field), patristics, history of religions, and philosophy (where he reflects the influence of his former close colleague and friend of many years, Martin Heidegger).[2] New Testament scholars have long since learned to know his exegesis of John and the Pauline Epistles in the light of a supposed Gnostic background. More recently he has become world-famous as leader of a movement to interpret the New Testament existen-

[1] The following is a considerable expansion of my review article on Bultmann's *The Presence of Eternity: History and Eschatology*, New York, Harper, 1957 in *Journal of Biblical Literature*, 77, 1958, pp. 244-248. The book represents his Gifford Lectures, given at the University of Edinburgh in 1955, and first published as *History and Eschatology*. The title of the first American edition is thoroughly misleading, but title and subtitle have fortunately been reversed in the Torchbook edition of 1961. In expanding the 1958 discussion I have greatly broadened the scope of my treatment, without changing my point of view in any respect.

[2] On the philosophy of Martin Heidegger (1889 ——) see esp. the sympathetic yet critical accounts by the distinguished Polish Dominican logician, I. M. Bochenski, *Contemporary European Philosophy*, 1956, pp. 161-172 (trans. of *Europäische Philosophie der Gegenwart*, 2d ed., 1951), and F. H. Heinemann, *Existentialism and the Modern Predicament*, 1953; (Harper Torchbook edition, 1958), pp. 84-108. The latter has been exploited without acknowledg-

tially by divesting its message of alleged "mythical" content (*Ent-mythologisierung*).

Bultmann's thought has become known for a clarity of expression which often makes the complexity and obscurity of the issues deceptively simple. His lectures are unusually easy to follow and, thanks to his constant "dialogue" with other thinkers, it is possible to grasp the direction of his current thinking much more easily than would otherwise be true. It is evident that he is trying to strike out along a new path, since he mentions his philosophical mentor, Heidegger, only once, and soft-pedals the Gnostics. Karl Jaspers is mentioned mostly to oppose his views.[3] The author is now strongly influenced by such earlier thinkers as W. Dilthey and even more by B. Croce and their disciple, R. G. Collingwood. He has also been deeply impressed by two refugee scholars, Erich Frank and Karl Löwith, especially the former,[4] although their influence on his views seems unimportant.

It is extremely difficult to summarize the views of such a complex and often elusive thinker as Rudolf Bultmann without misrepresenting his position on some topic or at some period in his career. The

---

ment; cf., e.g., p. 88 (middle) with the review of the English translation by John Macquarrie and Edward Robinson of Heidegger's *Sein und Zeit* that appeared in the *Christian Century*, Dec. 5, 1962, p. 1484 (upper left, second paragraph). We must remember that Heidegger was a pupil of Edmund Husserl, founder of philosophical phenomenology, and that he has in the past considered himself a phenomenologist rather than an existentialist. Presumably—at least in part—because of his strong dependence on Nietzsche for inspiration, his attitude has been characterized by Heinemann as "heroic defiance" (of the universe). It is scarcely surprising that he became a Nazi sympathizer—at least in the early years of the Third Reich—and was dismissed from his Freiburg professorship after the war. Heidegger's attitude toward religion has generally been rather hostile, and he has oscillated between a kind of deism and outright atheism (in which he was followed by his famous pupil, Jean Paul Sartre). See below for other observations on Heidegger.

[3] See also the interchange between Jaspers and Bultmann in *Myth and Christianity: An Inquiry into the Possibility of Religion without Myth*, New York, 1958.

[4] See esp. the illuminating autobiography of Bultmann, written in 1956 and translated by Schubert M. Ogden for his edition of selected shorter writings of Bultmann (trans. into English): *Existence and Faith*, New York, 1960, pp. 283-288.

following discussion will at least illustrate the general basis of his thinking; it will also indicate my reasons for differing.

1. Bultmann postulates acceptance of the "modern scientific world view" of the early twentieth century, as though Christianity were dependent for its spiritual impact on the cosmology of any age. He writes: "the cause-and-effect nexus is fundamental. Although modern physical theories take account of chance . . . in subatomic phenomena, our daily living, purposes, and actions are not affected."[5] In reply to this one may point out that our entire technological civilization is profoundly affected by advances in nuclear science, and that if one maintains (correctly) that human reactions remain substantially the same as they always have been in historical times, the fact is equally true of the impact on ordinary human reactions of nineteenth and early twentieth century mechanism, evolution, etc. The supposed "modern scientific world view" is itself fluid. Science is constantly changing; it may safely be said that the science of today is roughly just as far behind that of A.D. 2013 as it is ahead of the science of ca. 1913. A decade ago, when Bultmann wrote the words cited above, he could, for instance, have no conception of anti-matter or of fundamental "right" and "left" inequalities in the "nature of things" (as we optimistically say). Nor could he have any idea of Chandrasekhar's view that the physical regularities governing phenomena in remote (and therefore unimaginably large) galaxies may be—from our point of view as human beings—just as different from macrophysical regularities as the latter are from the apparent regularities of the nuclear world. Nor could he imagine scientists as suggesting that physical principles like gravity and electromagnetism are elastic deformations in the structure of space, or religious leaders as speculating about changes in Christianity in order to adapt it for "denizens of outer space."[6] It is frankly absurd to claim that any difference in "our daily living, purposes, and actions" results from the discovery that the world is not "structured in three stories, heaven, earth, and hell," when no one can point to any difference in "daily life" resulting from the discovery that the earth

[5] See his *Jesus Christ and Mythology*, New York, 1958, p. 15.
[6] I wish to thank my son Hugh (Brother E. Alban, F.S.C.), a trained mathematician and logician, for helping me to fill in the breaks in logical continuity which made the first draft of the preceding paragraph decidedly cryptic, not to say oracular.

rotates as it orbits around the sun. "Sunrise" and "sunset" are metaphors—and so are "heaven" and its congeners; ultimate mythological origin of the metaphors is just as irrelevant as the fact that the goddess Ceres is etymologically connected with our breakfast cereal.[7] Besides, the simple three-story structure of the universe had long been a metaphor in New Testament times, since for centuries intellectuals had been assuming a cosmos of eight to ten concentric spheres, often with many further complications. In other words, we know so little about ultimate scientific reality that we cannot base theological revolutions on consensus of cosmological opinion in any period. The teachings of Christ do not touch cosmology.

2. Bultmann is even more uncompromising when he deals with the sciences of man, history, and psychology in particular. There cannot be "any intervention of supernatural powers in the inner life life of the soul." Again, "nothing happens without rational motivation. Otherwise, responsibility would be dissolved." When one seriously reflects on the limitations of our present knowledge of man, one wonders at the bold assumption that analogies drawn from our extremely scanty information about the nature of man and the universe, can be extended so far beyond the limits of knowledge. One must not forget that some of the same modern men of science who have heaped scorn on Christian views of the centrality of man in the phenomenal world, insisting that these views have been disproved by modern astronomy, now paint glowing word pictures about the future triumphs of man in outer space! Some of the same scientific publicists who laugh at such antiquated notions as teleology in the life sciences, are the first to insist that man must start at once to direct the future evolution of his species. As though individuals belonging to a class could guide the cosmic evolution of the class! Again Bultmann demythologizes, just as though we really knew something of the relation between man as a "phenomenon" and the universe in which he lives. Our areas of ignorance are so vast and

---

[7] Somewhat paradoxically, Bultmann's philosophical mentor, Martin Heidegger, is responsible for a most adventurous etymological argument; he goes so far as to use a totally impossible etymology of Greek *alētheia*, "truth," as evidence for a view of truth which is basic to his concept of reality. For a discussion of this aberration see Paul Friedländer, *Plato: 1. An Introduction*, 1958, pp. 221-229. Of course, even a correct etymology, if the original sense of a word has changed radically, has no place in the logical development of an idea.

so fundamental that we have no right to dogmatize about the ultimate nature of things. There is more room for "miracles" in the stochastic and probabilistic age into which science seems to be moving than there was in the age of astral determinism about the turn of our era. As for Christology, it represents the best efforts of the Church Fathers to put into logical human language what New Testament writers recognized as the uncommunicable secret of divine relationship to man. To accept it in principle as man's offering to the transcendent God is not a *sacrificium intellectus* as asserted by Bultmann, but a recognition of man's complex nature as man and animal, as creature of God and as co-worker with God.[8]

3. Bultmann's next bundle of postulates is the philologico-historical methodology he took over from the "History of Religions School" (*Religionsgeschichtliche Schule*) of Reitzenstein and others, as well as the form-critical method which he and Martin Dibelius almost simultaneously described in 1919.[9] The outstanding points are these: John is supposed to be a Gnostic Gospel, reworked to some extent by an "ecclesiastical" editor. The Epistles of Paul are only in part genuine, and they show strong influence from both the mystery religions and the Gnostics. The Synoptic Gospels reflect the ramification of late oral tradition, the controversies raging between different Christian groups, and the history of the early Church. Bultmann picks out the most unconventional traditions as the most authentic, turning Jesus into a habitual breaker of Jewish religious law and a regular companion of men living by their wits and women of easy virtue. He rejects most of the tradition of the evangelists, insisting that we know extremely little about the historical Jesus of Nazareth. The Gospel of John is, of course, completely unhistorical according to him.[10] In passing let it be noted that the

---

[8] This is certainly the natural meaning of I Cor. 3:9 (*theou gar esmen synergoi*), but it is true that some theologians have tried to tone it down to mean: "for we are fellow-workers under God."

[9] For an appraisal from my point of view and for earlier literature (to 1939) see *From the Stone Age to Christianity*, 1957 ed., pp. 381 ff., and Pierre Benoit, *Revue Biblique*, 53, 1946, pp. 481-512 (reprinted in his *Exégèse et Théologie*, I, 1961, pp. 25 ff.).

[10] See Bultmann, *Das Evangelium des Johannes*, 1941; 2d ed., 1950, and for a detailed analysis of its content see Burton Scott Easton in *Journal of Biblical Literature*, 65, 1946, pp. 73-81, 143-156. At that time Easton thought that Bultmann was a follower of Barth! (p. 81).

Dead Sea Scrolls have utterly demolished Bultmann's "critical" analysis of John, proving that this Gospel reflects pre-Gnostic dualism of Essene type, and that by far the closest similarities to the language and imagery of John are to be found in pre-Christian Essene literature.[11] There is nothing specifically Gnostic in Qumran Essenism; even the dualism is radically different from Gnostic dualism. Furthermore, the almost simultaneous discovery of the Gnostic codices of Chenoboskion has shown convincingly that the tradition of the Church fathers about Gnostic origins and beliefs is substantially correct even in detail.[12] The Gnostics were specifically Christian heretics, deriving from sects founded by Simon Magus and a Nicolas who was probably Deacon Nicolas of Acts. There is nothing characteristically Gnostic in the thought of John and Paul. Even the so-called debt of the latter to the mystery cults of the eastern Mediterranean basin is completely imaginary;[13] the *mysterion* of the Pauline Epistles is Jewish in background, as predicted by Arthur Darby Nock[14] and demonstrated by Raymond E. Brown.[15]

4. Bultmann adopts the essentially anti-Christian existentialism of Heidegger and proceeds again to "demythologize" by interpreting John and Paul in the light of it. Our entire Christian heritage of

[11] See the sketch of the present situation given in my pamphlet, *The Bible after Twenty Years of Archaeology*, Pittsburgh, 1954, section VI, reprinted (with additional notes) from *Religion in Life*, 21, 1952, pp. 537-550, and for the Gospel of John see particularly my article in the Dodd Anniversary Volume, *The Background of the New Testament and Its Eschatology*, Cambridge, 1956, pp. 153-171. Bultmann himself thinks that the Dead Sea Scrolls confirm his hypothesis of a Jewish Gnosticism underlying John; see his remarks in his "Note to the Torchbook Edition" in Bultmann and Kundsin, *Form Criticism*, trans. F. C. Grant (Harper Torchbook ed., 1962), pp. 2-3, and against Bultmann see his former student, K. G. Kuhn, in his brilliant survey entitled "Johannesevangelium und Qumrantexte," in *Neotestamentica et Patristica*, Cullmann *Festschrift;* 1962, pp. 111-122.

[12] For the impact of the codices of Chenoboskion on New Testament studies see esp. the brilliant book by Jean Doresse, *The Secret Books of the Egyptian Gnostics*, trans. P. Mairet, New York, 1960, and read the "Epilogue" (pp. 324-326) with particular care. Against Bultmann see the fine article by Johannes Munck, "The New Testament and Gnosticism," *Studia Theologica*, 15, 1961, pp. 182-195. If Bultmann were correct in considering Essene theology as Gnostic, he would have to explain why not a single Gnostic myth or characteristic point of view appears in it!

[13] On this see Bultmann, *Theology of the New Testament*, Vol. I, trans. K. Grobel, 1951, pp. 298 f., and *Das Urchristentum im Rahmen der antiken Re-*

Johannine and Pauline thought is turned upside down and reduced to terms which appeal almost equally to existentialists who believe in God and to existentialists who deny that there is a God. Since existentialism (in the sense of Heidegger) finds theology incompatible, it cannot be turned into a theology without radical alteration of meanings and emphases. This many Christian existentialists are unwilling to do; instead they accept the introspective psychological affirmations of the *chefs d'école* and adapt them to Christian ideals. It is hard to do this successfully, because the essence of Christianity is love of God and of other human beings, whereas the essence of existentialism is a sense of responsibility for oneself and an attitude of challenge toward the universe. (One must always remember that the original "existentialism" of Pascal and Kierkegaard is not at all the same thing as that of Heidegger and Bultmann.)

5. The transmutation of Biblical eschatology into "existential decisions" carries with it a transfer of the Christian view of man's future to the "here and now," which is allegedly the only point at which God and man somehow touch. No more misleading a slogan was ever coined. There is never a true "here and now," since time and place are constantly shifting in the psychological life of any given human being, and there is little stability in interpersonal relations. Man's relation to the physical universe has no "here and now," since any action or reaction takes time and involves movement. (As a useful warning against worrying too much about the world and its problems, this slogan may have value.)

6. Nor is there a general human feeling of *Angst* in the face of death and extinction. To be perpetually in such a state is a sign of abnormality; it might be expected in the case of Kierkegaard and Nietzsche (Heidegger's two guiding lights), who were both psy-

---

ligionen, 1949, pp. 111, 140, as well as A. D. Nock's strictures in *Nuntius Sodalicii Neotestamentici Upsaliensis*, No. 5, 1951, col. 37. (See also n. 14.)

[14] See esp. his article, "Hellenistic Mysteries and Christian Sacraments," *Mnemosyne*, S. iv/5, 1952, pp. 177-213.

[15] See the published form of his Johns Hopkins dissertation, *The Semitic Background of the New Testament Mysterion*, which appeared as three papers: *Catholic Biblical Quarterly*, 20, 1958, pp. 417-443; *Biblica*, 39, 1958, pp. 426-448, and 40, 1959, pp. 70-87. Every type of Pauline *mysterion* appears in Qumran literature except the "mystery of salvation through Christ," which is purely Christian.

chotic, but normal human beings do not react this way. The existential decision is no substitute for the love of an ever-present God— a God who became flesh and died for man.

My own philosophical positions are very remote from the subjective relativism of most German philosophical idealists and their numerous followers in other lands.[16] In particular, I refuse to accept their relativistic position with regard to history, which they all too often dissolve into historicism, making the latter into a straw-man target for their onslaughts. In my opinion it is quite impossible to use *any* of the familiar postulates of philosophical idealism as a basis for reconstruction of any kind of history—even the history of philosophical idealism.[17] All historical data, whether written documents, archaeological objects, or material derived from ancillary disciplines, must be rigorously analyzed after classifying the different types of judgment involved (judgments of fact, value, typical occurrence, cause or result, etc.).[18] The reliability of historical data ranges all the way from the highest humanly attainable level of cognitive certainty to the lowest level of subjective conjecture (as when one tries to penetrate the personalities of historical figures and describe their motives, etc.).[19] History cannot, therefore, be distinguished from

[16] A good many phenomenologists and existentialists refuse to be called "philosophical idealists." In the case of Husserl, the logical ontologist who founded both the "philosophy of essence" and the "philosophy of being," a good case can be made out for this attitude, but it is hard to see how Jaspers and Heidegger can be clearly distinguished from Neo-Hegelians, Neo-Kantians, and other contemporary German philosophical idealists on this ground alone. A distinguished philosopher of science who belongs to the Vienna school of logical positivism, returned from a summer in Germany in the autumn of 1961, and reported on the (to him) extraordinary fusion of existentialism and neo-Hegelianism which has become the vogue in Germany. This same situation is illustrated by the present volume of Bultmann. Actually, some close resemblances between aspects of Plato, the father of all philosophical idealism, and modern existentialism were pointed out by Paul Friendländer in his brilliant *Platon: Seinswahrheit und Lebenswirklichkeit,* 1954, trans. into English as *Plato: 1. An Introduction,* 1958, pp. 230 ff.

[17] I do not, of course, mean that philosophical idealism has not influenced human history profoundly from Plato on, but simply that it is useless as a source of historical methodology. A classification of phenomena along idealistic lines *may* have some heuristic value, although I am not convinced that it does.

[18] See above, pp. 23-26.

[19] See above, pp. 26-27 f.

any other science or intellectual discipline on the objective-subjective plane alone.[20]

To identify "history" with the self-expression of the human "soul" or "psyche," following such Neo-Hegelians as Croce and Collingwood (cf. Bultmann, pp. 130 ff.) opens the door to unbridled speculation. One may doubt whether Bultmann really mends their fences by combining their "self-knowledge" with the "encounters which demand decisions" of his own existentialist theology (p. 137). I do not think that the "problem of historicism" is solved by drawing on Croce and Collingwood (pp. 142 f.) for two postulates, neither of which has any real meaning: 1) "History is understood as the history of man"; 2) "The relativity of every historical situation is understood as having a positive meaning." The first postulate is clearly tautological, since the word "history" is seldom used except in direct reference to some phase of human activity, which is Bultmann's own intention. The second is almost as obvious a tautology, since "positive" is itself merely a relational word (the opposite of "negative" and its synonyms) and the postulate is thus tantamount to saying that "relativity" is relative. From such meaningless propositions no binding conclusions can possibly be deduced, and no problem can be solved by their application.

I have discussed Bultmann's philosophical point of view first, since his Biblical and theological positions are increasingly based largely on it. His account of historiographic and eschatological tendencies in pre-Christian times (pp. 12-31) is correct as a rule, but sets up many dubious generalizations. It is quite true that the historiographies of Israel and Greece were "completely different" (p. 18), but no hint of what most scholars consider the basic reason for this difference is given. Bultmann distorts the chronological perspective by dealing with Greek historians first and then discussing Israelite historical writing against the background of Greek thought. The fact is that *all* Israelite writing of history precedes the earliest possible influence of Greek philosophical thinking. Even the Deuteronomist was an older contemporary of the first Greek philosophical thinker, Thales of Miletus, and no competent scholar today regards the historical approach of the Chronicler as in any way influenced by Greek thought. On the other hand, Greek historical writing began with Hecataeus

[20] See above, pp. 27-28 f.

a full century after the *floruit* of his fellow townsman, Thales. As a result of this complete chronological transposition, Israelite historical writing appears in a totally unhistorical setting; it should be placed between the Ancient Orient and Greece.

It is scarcely surprising that the author's survey of historiography misses the essential, from my point of view. In the Ancient Orient, history and cosmology were not clearly distinguished, since thinking on higher cultural levels was dominated by proto-logical (prelogical) habits. History and cosmology became fused in cosmogonic narratives. Moreover, Bultmann says absolutely nothing about the fact that both Egyptian and Babylonian literatures of the late third and second millennia B.C. contain definitely eschatological compositions, notably the Egyptian texts of Ipuwer and Neferty (22nd-20th centuries B.C.)[21] and the Babylonian Erra Epic (about the 13th-12th centuries B.C.).[22] The Erra Epic comes from a region which was much less historically isolated; it is more general than the Egyptian in its predictions of doom.

In Israel, on the other hand, there was a strong empirical reaction against the fusion of nature with God, who was Creator of nature and not immanent in it; cosmology was "demythologized" and was not blended with history. This point is mentioned by the author, but he fails to emphasize two basic features of Israelite religious thinking: the Covenant, and Prophecy before the event.[23] Successive Israelite forms of the Covenant between God and His human vassals warned of doom but promised ultimate mercy. The Deuteronomic (but even more ancient) alternation of punishment and welfare gave

[21] For a translation of these texts see J. A. Wilson in *Ancient Near Eastern Texts*, ed. J. B. Pritchard, 1950, pp. 441-446, and for the name and personality of Neferty (not Nefer-rohu) see G. Posener, *Littérature et politique dans l'Égypte de la XIIe Dynastie*, 1956, pp. 33 ff.

[22] For this text see S. N. Kramer in *Mythologies of the Ancient World*, ed. S. N. Kramer, 1961, pp. 127-135, and for the latest treatment, with bibliography, see W. G. Lambert, *Archiv für Orientforschung*, XVIII/2, 1958, pp. 395-401 (Lambert favors a date in the eleventh century). The epic is now generally dated even later, but the Babylonians themselves dated it much earlier, and I find myself unable to come down any farther.

[23] Cf., e.g., my remarks in *From the Stone Age to Christianity*, 1957 ed., pp. 2-3, which have been greatly expanded in the first draft of the manuscript of my "History of the Religion of Israel" (to appear in a series edited by Louis Finkelstein).

rise to a deep-seated feeling that doom was inevitable (given the basic wickedness of man), but that restoration would follow (given the inherent mercy of God). None of this will be found in Bultmann's survey, which never mentions Exodus or Exile and barely refers to the Covenant or the Prophets.

Equally weak is Bultmann's account of the development of the apocalyptic movement.[24] Ezekiel's visions of the early sixth century B.C. are nowhere mentioned, though they show a full-fledged eschatology of archaic type, without a trace of the Iranian or Hellenistic elements which appear in Daniel and Enoch (contrast pp. 27 f.). The author's sketch of intertestamental eschatology would have been greatly strengthened by use of the Dead Sea scrolls, which are nowhere even mentioned. And yet these original writings of the period between ca. 125 B.C. and A.D. 25 (the earliest and latest probable dates for the original composition of the published Essene literature) are of the greatest possible significance for his subject—note especially the War, the *Hôdayôt*, and the still mostly unpublished descriptions of the coming Jewish commonwealth, all from a purely sectarian Jewish point of view.[25]

In general Bultmann's approach to New Testament problems suffers because he everywhere presupposes his own highly crystallized system. For instance, it is very misleading to write as he does (pp. 36 f.) about the "negative ethics" of the New Testament, in which he *appears* to include "the Old Testament commands." Not only does he exaggerate what he calls the eschatological element in early Christianity at the expense of Christian community life, but he seems to blame the New Testament for lack of a "social program" and "concrete goals of acting" (pp. 36-37). We must remember that all the social teachings of the Old Testament prophets were still an integral part of Holy Scripture and that the whole New Testament shows a drastic extension in scope and deepening in spirit of the prophetic goals. What could be more "up to the minute" than the attempt to establish Christian community of property after the Cru-

---

[24] Since Bultmann transmutes all Christian eschatology into the existential decision of the individual (*hic et nunc*), he could not be expected to care much for Old Testament eschatology. But this scarcely justifies him in dismissing it so cavalierly.

[25] On Essene eschatology see esp. F. M. Cross, Jr., *The Ancient Library of Qumran and Modern Biblical Studies*, 1958, pp. 162-173.

cifixion? Nearly all social programs of modern times have turned out to be premature, so we have no right to sit in judgment on the early Christian community. Actually the radical demands of Jesus on His followers were not only socially ahead of subsequent centuries, but they were developed in opposition to the traditionalism of the Pharisees and the isolationism of the Essenes.

There is absolutely no foundation for Bultmann's assertion (p. 47, note) that the passages in John "containing the traditional apocalyptic eschatology . . . are later additions by the ecclesiastical redaction of the Gospel."[26] This is a perfect example of circular argument; it may now be directly disproved in part by the recently discovered fact that John 5:29 (one of the verses in question) reflects characteristic Essene phraseology and thus belongs with the large number of similar passages in the Gospel.[27] The Gospel of John is homogeneous and reflects the sectarian Jewish background of the last century B.C., not an imaginary early Christian or even pre-Christian Gnosticism. The fact is that the Dead Sea Scrolls and the Gnostic codices of Chenoboskion have combined to demolish the structure of Johannine criticism on which these speculations are based.[28]

In his final chapters the author transmutes Christian eschatology into the existential decision of the individual.[29] To be sure, there is an element of truth in this drastic solution, since each person is a mirror of human existence, but the solution itself is totally non-Biblical. Nor is it at all likely to arouse the conscience of our own generation.[30] The author's ideas reflect the intellectual confusion of the Weimar Republic; he passes over the Nazi Abomination of Desolation in complete silence, "wie ein römischer Senator" (to quote a letter from a Continental colleague written to me in the

[26] For details see his commentary, *Das Evangelium des Johannes*, 1941; cf. above, n. 10.

[27] On John 6:51-58 (the other passage cited especially by Bultmann), see K. G. Kuhn in *The Scrolls and the New Testament*, ed. K. Stendahl, 1957, p. 76.

[28] See above, n. 11 and 12.

[29] See above, p. 278.

[30] Existentialism unquestionably tends to dull moral and social conscience, since it concentrates on the reaction of the individual to his cosmic "predicament." The records of Max Scheler (private) and of Martin Heidegger and Friedrich Gogarten (public) are cases in point; more might be mentioned. In practice existentialism tends to merge into fatalism; this is certainly the effect of atheistic existentialism.

winter of 1945-1946, with specific reference to Bultmann).[31] Nor does he once refer to the contemporary fulfillment of eschatological prophecy in part, at least, by the realization of man's age-old dream of discovering how to destroy himself and the entire world as we know it. Biblical eschatology still towers above its modern interpreters, whatever their sect or school.

[31] This statement has been misunderstood as a personal criticism of the distinguished figure under discussion; no slur was intended, but rather an emphasis on the stoic neutrality toward the problems of others which Bultmannian existentialism fosters.

PART FOUR

MORE PERSONAL

Chapter 14

Return to Biblical theology[1]

During the heyday of the Conference on Science, Philosophy and Religion in New York, I tried to persuade the speakers to state their credo or at least to define their approach in terms intelligible to others. I was very seldom successful, since most thinkers of our time feel that "labeling" oneself or attempting to classify one's position is somehow improper, if not dangerous. In the 1951 Symposium on Freedom and Authority a more basic reason for this hesitation became evident: fewer than a third of the members of a panel on "Postulates of Freedom and Authority" understood the nature of postulational thinking. In fact, one of the most honest admitted that he had been forced to look up "postulate" in the dictionary. Under the influence of my Johns Hopkins colleagues, Arthur O. Lovejoy and his pupil, George Boas, I have become increasingly aware of the inadequacy of most philosophical postulation. Scarcely any systematic thinker really explores the background of his own thinking or tries to work out his "protophilosophy." For instance, a letter to

[1] This paper was published in *The Christian Century*, Nov. 19, 1958, as one in a series of articles by American and foreign theologians in honor of the fiftieth anniversary of the weekly. I wish to thank the Christian Century Foundation and Mr. Kyle Haselden for permission to reprint it here "in revised and annotated form." Aside from correction of misprints and stylistic improvements I wish to call attention to revisions in paragraph six and to the addition of seven paragraphs at the end of the article. The footnotes have all been added. I wish also to thank *Christianity Today* for permitting reprint of a letter written to its editor in connection with the book by Dewey M. Beegle on *The Inspiration of Scripture*.

a leading Protestant theologian on the Continent, inquiring about his intellectual background, evoked the honest reply that he knew of no special philosophical influence on his own thinking!

Under these circumstances, it is clear that the chaotic state of contemporary Protestant theology is not due primarily to a "breakdown in communication," serious as this can be, but to the unwillingness or inability of its exponents to analyze their own work and present it objectively. I fully realize that my own point of view is also strongly influenced by my background. This is obviously not the place to go into details, but a few indications may help.[2]

A background note

My father was a Methodist missionary in South America, where I spent my first twelve years. Owing to extreme myopia and a crippled left hand, I spent most of my time as a boy in my father's library, reading omnivorously and acquiring a permanent taste for history, science, and theology. I later became a student of Semitic languages, to which I devoted myself intensively for many years. There followed a decade in the Middle East, carrying on research in archaeology. I was then called back to Johns Hopkins, dividing ten more years between it and the Middle East. Since 1936 I have given increasing attention to historical synthesis, laying particular stress on scientific method and philosophical analysis.

Beginning with the evangelical Protestantism characteristic of the late nineteenth century I have attended, for a year or more at a time, Methodist, Baptist, Lutheran, Episcopalian, and Presbyterian churches. I married an Anglo-Catholic who joined the Church of Rome a little over a year later. Through my family, my colleagues, and especially through my students, my ties with Catholicism have continued to become closer. At the same time my Jewish associations have also become progressively closer, and I wrote the original article here reprinted while I was "visiting research professor" in the Jewish Theological Seminary of America, the leading conservative Jewish institution in this country. Until I was twenty-one I had never met anyone whom I knew to be Jewish, but after nearly half a century of friendly association I am in some ways more at home in Jewish circles than anywhere else.

[2] For further details see below, Chapter 15.

All my work has been dominated by enthusiasm for scientific research of all kinds, and through the years I have continued to read extensively in scientific fields. Friendship with men of science and study of scientific method have been decisive in fixing the character of my own research, culminating in election to the National Academy of Sciences in 1955.

Intellectual approach

After this summary outline of my background, I shall describe my intellectual approach today. I am opposed to all systems of thought based on arbitrary postulates and denying or disregarding the historical experience of mankind. All recognized philosophical systems are constructed by a more or less rigorous use of deduction from postulates which cannot be proved and which are often meaningless in their wording. Idealistic systems are by their nature removed from empirical control, so they must remain undemonstrable.[3] Of course, rigorously pragmatic and instrumental philosophical systems are just as dangerous as idealisms, since they reject anything that cannot be determined experimentally or mathematically. All exaggerated philosophical emphases are under suspicion: naturalism because it neglects the age-old aspirations of man and denies the need of religion; scientism because it leads to materialism or naturalism; historicism because it distorts the record of man's experience for the sake of hypothetical structures built according to a priori blueprints.

Essential though science is in the life of our world, it cannot suffice: man does not live by bread alone. Besides, few people quite realize how insecure the hold of scientific method on mankind actually is. Whole areas of psychology and sociology are built on foundations of sand. To be sure, such systems as Freudian psychoanalysis and Jungian analytical psychology have added notably to our stock of ideas, they have had salutary effect in checking mech-

---

[3] It must be strongly emphasized that idealistic philosophy is useless for the interpretation of history except, of course, where philosophical idealism has itself contributed to *making* history. An extremely interesting essay in this direction is Chapter V ("German Idealism") in F. S. C. Northrop's *The Meeting of East and West*, 1946, pp. 193-219. On the subject see also above, pp. 279-280.

anistic views, and they have even restored the "soul" to favor in wide circles; but from the standpoint of experimental validation they are little more respectable than astrology or alchemy. Since much current social anthropology is built on the assumption that psychoanalysis is true as it stands, societal studies are in no better case than psychology.[4] Nor is the insecurity of the biological and physical sciences adequately understood. Whole fields of biological science have been turned upside down by the Russian Communists, and some Asiatic countries have abandoned modern medicine in favor of time-honored native practices.[5] Even in the most advanced Western countries, established facts of human biology and ecology have been and are being rejected by authoritarian rulers and democratic majorities alike.[6]

Revolution in historical knowledge

On the other hand, the importance of history has tended to be greatly underrated in recent decades. While the educated public has become excited by the writings of philosophic historians like Arnold J. Toynbee,[7] few people grasp the significance of the tremendous revolution in our historical knowledge which has been in progress during the past century and a half. This revolution we owe partic-

---

[4] When these lines were first written the Rorschach ink-blot test (which must be interpreted by a Freudian psychoanalyst) was still in vogue in personality and acculturation research, though it had begun to lose ground. Since there is no experimental validation for it in the first place, such evidence is practically worthless. But many of the same basic assumptions still govern research in social anthropology and sociology.

[5] All *official* Communist academic theory bans Western genetics and psychology (except where the West has accepted Pavlovian methods) because of its dogma that a completely nonbourgeois Communistic psychology can be instilled by Pavlovian conditioning and that this new Communist personality must displace "reactionary" habits of thinking and acting completely, as a result of the alleged principle of inheritance of acquired characteristics (Michurinism, adopted by the infamous Lysenko). On the Communist line in many sciences see particularly *Daedalus* (*Journal of the American Academy of Arts and Sciences*, summer, 1960). In China, Western medicine has been almost completely displaced over large areas by official espousal of medieval acupuncture —puncturing with a needle according to elaborate astrological patterning of the human body—and a host of equally dubious practices of "national medicine" such as massive purging against appendicitis. This extraordinary development

ularly to archaeology and its ancillary disciplines, but professional historians have contributed enormously to consolidate it. By history I mean the record of man's entire past, including the reconstruction of civilizations as well as the record of events. In this essay the term "history" will never be used in a metaphysical sense.[8]

It is misleading to insist on any fundamental difference between the nature of historical and scientific knowledge. If the more important types of judgment are classified with care, there is far-reaching congruence. For instance, judgments of fact remain just that, no matter what their context, and the criteria for establishing them remain logically comparable. Historical judgments such as "typical occurrence" cover vast areas of civilization; they are on the same logical basis as similar judgments in the biological and some of the physical sciences. Judgments of cause are shared with the social and biological sciences. Historians are generally much too free in making "value judgments," which are therefore sometimes thought to distinguish history from other fields of knowledge. On the other hand, when history is applied for didactic purposes, value judgments are entirely proper—just as they are in agriculture, economics, and medicine.[9]

The center of history

In the center of history stands the Bible. The latter has suffered more in many respects from its well-intentioned friends than from its honest foes, but it is now being rediscovered by the labors of archaeologists and philologians. We are rapidly regaining our balance after generations of bitter controversy. I shall point out a few basic changes in the situation.

The long controversy over evolution has led to a widespread impression that there is direct contradiction between the Christian view of the Fatherhood of God and the brotherhood of man, on the one

---

has been very widely advertised by Communist China in propaganda literature and medical exhibits abroad.

[6] Examples are legion, but in the Western democracies it is a matter of simple cultural lag, not of official dogma.

[7] See above, Chapter 11.

[8] See above, pp. 16-28.

[9] See above, pp. 26-27.

hand, and modern biological dogma on the other. It is true that many scientists have multiplied species, have pushed back chronology, and have assumed an exceedingly slow and gradual type of development. It is, however, now becoming clear, thanks to the accelerated rate of new finds and the revolution in dating brought by radiocarbon, that only one true species of genus Homo has hitherto been discovered, and that the differences between known types of fossil man have been gravely exaggerated.[10] It is also certain that all known forms of fossil man made tools[11] and probably spoke in different tongues; it is equally clear that the earliest men were inventive and possessed aesthetic tendencies. The antiquity of true tool-making man is probably only a fraction of previous estimates, and may not have exceeded 200,000 years.[12]

Another important result of recent discoveries is absolute proof that the cradle of higher culture was in the Near and Middle East, where simple agriculture began some 12,000 years ago, and where fortified settlements were being built at least 9,000 years ago, some two millennia before the invention of pottery.[13] By the earliest cuneiform inscriptions, over 5,000 years ago, Near Eastern man had discovered or invented a host of crafts, arts, uses of material, proc-

[10] Among different "species" of genus Homo formerly distinguished by many physical anthropologists, only one can stand scrutiny, since excavations in Palestine have proved that Homo neanderthalensis interbred with Homo sapiens. Only a few serious specialists still deny this obvious fact, which has been stressed by anatomists like W. L. Straus and geneticists such as Theodosius Dobzhansky.

[11] There are two other genera of fossil hominids commonly distinguished today: *Pithecanthropus* of the Middle Pleistocene in East Asia and Indonesia; *Australopithecus* of the Early Pleistocene (Villafranchian) in Africa. The Australopithecines already used bones, horns, animal teeth, and pebbles as tools, as abundantly proved by Raymond Dart and L. S. B. Leakey. The evidence for *Pithecanthropus* and the related *Sinanthropus* is very uncertain, but since these hominids are much closer in type and time to man than *Australopithecus*, it seems reasonable to suppose that they also used tools of sorts, and could presumably modify them slightly by flaking, chipping, or abrading. There is no reason so far to credit any precursors of genus Homo with true tool-making.

[12] The question of chronology is controversial; there is a sharp difference of opinion between the followers of Harold Urey and Cesare Emiliani, who have set up the chronology which the writer follows, on the one hand, and the adherents of the potassium-argon chronology of the University of California, which has been accepted by Leakey and others. Though the Lamont Geologi-

esses, and devices. Many pre-Christian arts and processes were completely forgotten before modern times. Some of them have been rediscovered after great effort on the part of modern technicians, but others remain enigmatic.[14] The Near East was thousands of years in advance of any other focus of higher culture, and it is becoming more and more probable that other such foci (China, Middle America) owed part of their original stimulation to borrowing across continents and oceans. The tremendous advance of modern Western civilization when transplanted to Japan little over a century ago, is a vivid illustration of a process familiar to all serious historians. The great progress of the West in science and technology since the fifteenth century has come precisely because we stand on the shoulders of our Greco-Roman predecessors, not because we are in any way more gifted than the ancients.

The Bible is the heir of the civilizations which had preceded it: Egyptian, Mesopotamian, Syrian, Anatolian, and others. Israel preserved older values, but it also transfigured them by its own genius into a great spiritual culture which was passed on to Europe and has ever since been the guiding light of Western civilization. Thanks to modern research we now recognize its substantial historicity.[15] The narratives of the Patriarchs, of Moses and the Exodus, of the Conquest of Canaan, of the Judges, the Monarchy, Exile, and Restoration, have all been confirmed and illustrated to an extent that I should have thought impossible forty years ago. The faith of the

---

cal Laboratory of Columbia University takes a position roughly in the middle (on largely ambivalent evidence), there can be little doubt, in my opinion, that the Urey-Emiliani correlation of data from oxygen isotopes with radiocarbon counts is approximately correct. For one thing, it agrees entirely with the now certain date of the end of the last Glacial-Pluvial period about 11,000 years ago (less than half of former estimates in America). Another fact is that the Middle Mousterian chronology established by radiocarbon is also considerably less than half of previous dates. And, finally, the estimate of the length of time required to build up the Lisan Terrace of the Jordan Valley made by G. S. Blake in 1928 (some 50,000 years) agrees closely with the same figure obtained by De Vries and Emiliani for the duration of the contemporary Würm-Wisconsin glaciation; it is also considerably less than half of previous estimates.

[13] See above, pp. 18-19.
[14] See above, pp. 70-71.
[15] See above, pp. 28-46.

Patriarchs still shines through the stories of Genesis, handed down by oral tradition with surprising accuracy in detail—though this tradition cannot be used to reconstruct a chronological record of events. The background of Moses and his contributions to religion and law take definite form in the light of our present knowledge, and we may rest assured that his towering personality is fairly represented by tenacious oral tradition. We can now date the Exodus and the Conquest, and can understand the evolution of institutions—if not always of ideas—during the time of the judges and kings of Israel. Exile and Restoration have been rescued from the critical controversy of the past generation and appear again in the clear light of history.

There has been a general return to appreciation of the accuracy, both in general sweep and in factual detail, of the religious history of Israel. The practical monotheism of Moses and other early Israelite religious leaders is again being accepted, in the light of more penetrating study, though no serious scholar now considers it to have been a philosophical theism. Philosophical thinking was not introduced into the world until the sixth century B.C., and it scarcely began to influence Jewish religious ideas before the end of the Old Testament canon in the second century B.C.

The Prophets of Israel are now better understood; they stand out more brilliantly than ever. The critical school associated with the name of Julius Wellhausen recognized their outstanding significance as social and ethical reformers, but failed to grasp two vitally important principles: the place of the Covenant and related ties to the past in prophetic thinking, and the vital role of insight into the future, which shaped the attitudes of the Prophets themselves as bearers of the divine word and which validated (or discredited) them in the eyes of their hearers. It is just as impossible to understand the Prophets by eliminating prophecy as it is to understand Jesus of Nazareth without the eschatological allusions which recur so often in the Gospels.

The Dead Sea Scrolls

The sensational finds among the Dead Sea Scrolls since 1948 bring an even more complete revaluation of what has passed for historico-literary criticism of the New Testament. At long last we possess original Hebrew and Aramaic religious books from the century and a half before the Crucifixion. It used to be impossible to find enough data on which to build a solid structure of relevant literary and religious history between about 165 B.C. and A.D. 135. Now we know just what the Jews (especially the Essenes) were writing and thinking in this period. Two main lines of evidence emerge: (1) actual grammatical, lexical, and stylistic knowledge of the Hebrew and Aramaic then used by the Jews of Palestine, and the unexpected discovery that Hebrew was still the principal medium of religious composition and instruction; (2) recovery of the immediate sources underlying much of the thought, phraseology, and organization of New Testament Christianity.[16] The importance of the Essene movement as an immediate precursor of John the Baptist and Jesus has become clear. The internal evidence supposed to prove the late date of many New Testament books has vanished. There is no longer any concrete evidence for dating a single New Testament book after the seventies or eighties of the first century A.D.—though this does not mean that such an early date is already proved. The external evidence for late date has also vanished with partial publication (since 1949) of the epoch-making contents of the Gnostic library at Chenoboskion in Upper Egypt. Confrontation of all the evidence now available for the origin of Gnosticism confirms the accounts of the Church Fathers, according to whom it was a movement originating among Christian proselytes of the first decade or two after the Crucifixion.[17]

To sum up, we can now again treat the Bible from beginning to end as an authentic document of religious history. Innumerable clarifications of the text greatly improve our understanding, especially of the poetic books. No translation which has yet appeared gives an adequate idea of the increase in our knowledge of Hebrew grammar, vocabulary, and poetic style. It must be emphasized, however, that vindication of the substantial historicity of the Bible and clarification of its meaning do not involve a return to uncritical belief in "verbal" inspiration and do not support an "orthodoxy" which insulates the Bible from the real world of today. The Bible must be judged as literature and history by exactly the same canons as we use

[16] See above, pp. 37-39.
[17] See above, pp. 39-41.

in studying similar non-Biblical literature, but not by arbitrary standards imposed on it by dogmatic liberals or conservatives. Extreme views are alike unsatisfactory; the truth lies in the middle. In any case the Bible towers in content above all earlier religious literature; and it towers just as impressively over all subsequent literature in the direct simplicity of its message and the catholicity of its appeal to men of all lands and times.

The historical unity of the Old and New Testaments has been consolidated by the Dead Sea Scrolls. All the authors of the New Testament were certainly or probably Jews—even Luke, with his Aramaizing Roman freedman's name and his use of Hebrew sources.[18] The supposed Greek elements in the New Testament nearly all came into nascent Christianity from a Judaism which had already been strongly influenced by 350 years of Hellenistic culture. To the writers of the New Testament the Hebrew Bible was Holy Scripture and they were the direct heirs of its Prophets. It is, accordingly, quite impossible to understand the New Testament without recognizing that its purpose was to supplement and explain the Hebrew Bible. Any attempt to go back to the sources of Christianity without accepting the entire Bible as our guide is thus doomed to failure. Every important heresy of the early church and every splinter sect of today show the danger of seizing on individual passages (seldom understood) in preference to total acceptance (which does not mean uncritical acceptance of all parts of the whole).

Concluding observations

Since we now realize that normative Judaism did not arise before the Herodian period and was not finally shaped until the Mishnah in the second century A.D., we may, for practical purposes, treat Christianity and rabbinic Judaism as offshoots of the same spiritual root, which developed many of their specific ideas in conscious opposition but retained the same basic faith. For theological purposes (as distinct from historic intent) the Christian reads his Old Testament in the light of the New, while the Jew reads his Bible in the light of rabbinic literature. There are indeed fundamental differences between Judaism and Christianity, but the similarities far outweigh the

[18] See above, p. 37.

contrasts. We must approach both faiths at the highest common level of intellectual and spiritual life, not (like many religious liberals) at what amounts to the lowest level. We cannot expect Christianity and Judaism to unite, but we must never forget that they stand or fall together in an essentially pagan world.

Christianity stands today at one of the most critical junctures of history, facing in Communism its deadliest foe since the end of pagan Rome. Outside of the Iron Curtain it faces untold millions of increasingly critical, if not actually hostile, neutrals—pagans, Moslems, and Western secularists. It is not a pleasant prospect, with Protestants and Catholics wasting much of their effort in reciprocal attacks, with theological anarchy sapping the strength of the former and moral flabbiness weakening both. When leading Protestant thinkers tend to follow the example of Marcion and discard the Old Testament, or of Valentinus and correlate an eclectic Christian "theology" with some post-Platonic philosophical structure, it is clear that Protestantism is in peril of becoming engulfed by a new phase of Gnosticism, which may prove even more dangerous than the Gnostic heresies that almost destroyed the Christian Church in its early centuries. Still other prominent Neo-Gnostics imitate the Manicheans and Mandaeans, substituting for Zoroastrian ideas, notions drawn from Hinduism, Buddhism, or Jainism. If we flee from these perils, we are likely to find ourselves in the company of ultra-conservatives who turn their backs on the Christ they profess to worship and raise the idols of racism and spiritual pride in His stead.

There is only one way out of the apparent impasse: we must return again to the Bible and draw new strength from the sources of Judeo-Christian faith. Like John the Baptist and Jesus, who turned back to the Prophets of Israel for inspiration, and like the great Reformers, who sought guidance from the Word of God, so must we reconstruct our religious thought on Biblical foundations. To all who believe in the eternal value of the Old and New Testaments, it is clear that God has been preparing the way for a revival of basic Christianity through enlightened faith in His Word. It is no accident that archaeology and its ancillary disciplines have revolutionized our historical approach to the Bible. Nor is it an accident that Roman Catholic interest in the Bible has risen to wholly unprecedented levels, with a great many new vernacular translations and steadily increasing attention both to Biblical research and to Biblical theology. In this writer's opinion it would be most undesirable for the chief independent branches of Christendom to unite, but they can cooperate independently in the task of winning the world for the faith of Moses and Christ.

Afterthoughts

One of the worst aberrations of our time is the widespread notion that the Bible is too antiquated to be a reliable guide for the "modern" human spirit. This point of view may be said to dominate the entire secular academic scene today; it is almost equally prevalent in liberal religious circles, while conservative circles rarely pay much more than lip service to enlightened reliance on the Bible. Many want us to substitute for Biblical faith introspective psychological "insights"—which have neither empirical nor experimental validation—and existential philosophies based on these "insights." Without denying that an existential approach may be a useful corrective to excessive pragmatism or instrumentalism, we cannot establish a "modern" faith on a philosophy which rejects the operational use of both science and history at the same time that it arrogantly claims to be founded on them.

The charge that Biblical religion is "out of date" is just as unreasonable as similar criticisms in other fields of human higher culture. Everyone knows how long it took for the discoveries of Darwin and Mendel to be generally accepted in the Western world; it took decades even for some of the leading psysicists to accept the novel ideas of Einstein. Going back a few centuries, it required generations and even centuries for the great astronomical innovations of Copernicus, Kepler, and Newton to establish themselves throughout academic circles in Europe. In abstract thought, comparable situations are even more striking. Whitehead never tired of observing that all philosophy since Plato has consisted chiefly of "footnotes" to him. This is clearly true of both philosophical idealism and realism. Similarly, philosophical rationalists and empiricists cannot break away completely from the rational empiricism of Aristotle. Both Platonic and Aristotelian tradition have been rediscovered over and over again during the past 2,300 years, causing many major philosophical revolutions.

If the emergence of great figures in science has been followed by such lags, and if the careers of such towering thinkers as Plato and Aristotle have been followed by lags of far longer duration, what shall we say of the great figures of Biblical faith? The profound moral and spiritual intuitions of the Bible, which form a unique revelation of God to man through the channels of human experience, are just as true today as they were two or three thousand years ago. The world has scarcely begun to catch up with the moral and spiritual demands of Moses, virtually all of which are being flouted in the twentieth century. How much more improbable it is that we can ever—as human beings—catch up with the even more demanding example of Christ!

In the conservative Protestant fortnightly, *Christianity Today* (issue of January 18, 1963), there appeared a "feature interview" in which a selected panel of scholars submitted questions to the writer who replied to them *seriatim;* the "interview" was entitled by the editors, "Toward a More Conservative View." A number of the questions have to do with the subject of Biblical inspiration, and my intermediate position naturally did not satisfy many right-wing conservatives. In the issue of April 26, 1963, nearly thirty columns are devoted to reviews and review articles on Dewey M. Beegle's book, *The Inspiration of Scripture* (Philadelphia: The Westminster Press, 1963), in which Dr. Beegle deals systematically with the subject from every significant point of view. In the writer's opinion, Dr. Beegle's book is excellent in every respect except that he should have devoted more space than was allowed him by his publisher to a positive presentation of the material. The following letter was written at his request to the editor of *Christianity Today*, and was printed in the issue of Aug. 2, 1963; it stresses the vital importance of meaning, which is almost always disregarded, and stresses also the need for a "holistic" approach to the problem of inspiration.

I dislike the terms "error" and "inerrancy," since they now often mean "mistake" and "infallibility." "Error" formerly meant "losing one's way, wandering," and was applied to misguided deviation from sound doctrine; it is now used also for simple mistakes in oral and written transmission, editing, copying, translating, etc.—all inseparable from our human condition, to which God condescends (used in its proper meaning). Actually mistakes resulting from change of meaning are nearly as common as other classes of "error." For instance, many years ago I heard an address by the pastor of the Moody Church in Chicago, reputed to be a converted prize fighter. He stated with superb dogmatism (using this word in its current meaning) that God had created the world and had then destroyed and recreated it. The evidence? In Genesis 1:28 the King James Version says that God had commanded man to "replenish the earth." In current English this verb means "fill again," so it must have been filled once before! R.S.V. agrees with the Hebrew as well as with the Elizabethan sense of "replenish," rendering simply "fill."

There are many passages in the New Testament which appear to take opposite sides in doctrinal controversies: e.g., Romans and James on faith. Today there are few theologians who are disturbed by the superficial conflict between faith and works, which belong together in "dialectic tension," like predestination and free will, etc. Such tensions between opposites (now the basis of Niels Bohr's famous law of complementarity) is the glory of the Bible, which must be taken as a whole; the Old Testament stands in judgment on the antinomianism resulting from arbitrary choice of proof texts in the New, and the New Testament reminds us constantly to follow the spirit, not the letter (Romans 2:29, 7:6; II Corinthians 3:6).

Historical tradition in the Bible presents us with similar cases. Without different, even divergent, accounts of men and events we cannot see personalities and movements in perspective. In other words, we should not have the stereoscopic effects inherent in the very nature of Biblical tradition, which preserves differences, even when they seem to be in direct contradiction. In short, we cannot have an historical revelation of God without transmission through human channels. If we follow the trend today and replace such revelation by existential decisions of individuals, our loss is immeasurable. But we cannot deny the Bible its historical humanity without an equivalent loss in rejecting the humanity of "the Word made flesh."

Chapter 15

William Foxwell Albright[1]
(autobiographical sketch)

Biography will always remain one of the most fascinating and difficult branches of *belles lettres*. It is often said that biography bears a relation to factual history not unlike that of portraiture to photography. Both the competent biographer and the skilled painter are compelled to venture beyond the outposts of datable and measurable fact into the region of insight into character and personality. Here no amount of psychological or psychiatric training will help appreciably, since both are essentially statistical sciences and individual idiosyncrasies defy any law of averages. The careful historian is somewhat suspicious of biography, which deals not only with facts known to many observers, and with external habits and practices common to large groups, but also with happenings recorded only by a single person (often the subject himself) and with personal peculiarities which cannot be statistically controlled. Moreover, if it is hard for the historian to be sure of the dominant causes and group motives which sway multitudes, how can he appraise the hidden reasons for an individual's acts, especially if the latter

[1] This autobiographical sketch appeared in *American Spiritual Autobiographies,* ed. Louis Finkelstein, New York, 1948, pp. 156-181. The text is unchanged except for removal of stylistic infelicities, correction of words, addition of a bracketed sentence, and some cross references. I wish again to thank Mr. Melvin Arnold of Harper & Row for securing permission to reprint the sketch here.

possesses the complex personality frequently associated with outstanding figures? It is true that a sensitive biographer can often probe as deeply into the recesses of personality as a talented portrait painter, but here again the artistic imagination is more than likely to construct a figure endowed with qualities which satisfy the creative urge of the artist rather than the intellectual curiosity of the historian.

Successful autobiography is an even more difficult and delicate art than good biography. To be sure, the subject is generally well-acquainted with the external facts of his own life. However, the temptation to readjust them and color them to the autobiographer's own advantage is often irresistible, and even the most honest man is likely to see past events in the refracted light of subsequent developments. If this formidable obstacle to good autobiography is hurdled, a more serious one often lies before the man who undertakes to describe himself. This new obstacle is the lack of perspective, as a result of which nearly everyone fails to judge himself correctly. And the closer the focus of attention lies to the spiritual inwardness of life, the harder it is for anyone to draw a true picture of himself. An unbiased friend is very often better able to understand one's character than one is oneself. There is even such a thing as being too close to another person to understand him. Husbands and wives often lack the necessary perspective to understand their mates. The famous words of the German historian Treitschke, "Man can only understand what he loves," used as a slogan by Nazi educators who tried to force youth into an unreal mold of racial and territorial Germanism, are not true to the facts of experience.

In the following concise "spiritual autobiography," the subject will attempt to appraise his own development, in the light of the more pertinent facts of his education, following this sketch by a series of brief treatments of five interrelated themes where his present views have been most clearly influenced by the external facts of his education and experience. Couching the recital of his early years in the third person and omitting subjective judgments on his own development as far as possible, he will bear in mind that the reader will scarcely be interested in any biographical detail except in so far as it throws convincing light on the main theme.

Education

A LAD IN SPANISH AMERICA

It was a world of striking contrasts in which this lad grew up. Always there were the great Pacific stretching westward into the limitless distance and the lofty foothills of the Andes which prevented the morning sun from becoming visible until long after dawn. Years afterwards the lad was to live again in the Mediterranean climate of Palestine, which was in many ways so strangely reminiscent of his Chilean boyhood in La Serena and Antofagasta. Nor was this similarity limited to physical environment, since the social contrasts between urban and rural, landowner and peasant, were closely comparable in both. The *peon* of that day was very like the Arab *fellah* of today. Though thunderstorms, which form so striking a feature of the Palestinian winter, are unknown in those parts of Chile, the undying roar of the Pacific and its storm-driven billows was more than sufficient compensation for the imagination of a sensitive boy. In both, again, the alternation of rainy season with dry and the cruel proximity of the rainless desert represent hard facts against which man is powerless to contend.

As a child in a Methodist missionary family living among a hostile population, to which the terms *gringo* (Anglo-American) and *canuto* (Protestant) were equal insults, the lad never felt secure. He will never forget the severe—but thoroughly beneficial—spankings which were needed to force him from the adobe walls of the mission into the unknown terrors of the street in order to run his first errand at the age of seven. Insults were frequently interspersed with stones, and the sight of a black-cassocked priest was enough to send him fleeing home in terror. In the more cosmopolitan atmosphere of the busy seaport and mining town of Antofagasta, he felt much safer, but there he heard and saw the victims of majority persecution in Peru and Bolivia, where the life of a Protestant missionary was worth little in those days. There cannot be the slightest doubt that the lad's experiences prepared him to take the intense interest in minorities which has been characteristic of his subsequent development.

There was little formal education. This little was received in private schools run by British subjects for the children of European residents and in a tiny, but very successful, school run by his mother for the older children. As the eldest of the family he was always in the top class. Because of nearsightedness he had an accident at five which crippled his left hand. For years he was unable to use the hand at all. Owing to his extreme myopia and the useless hand, he played little with other children, but divided his time between his father's library and solitary games of his own contrivance. His reading was inevitably extensive, and ran largely to history and theology, particularly the former. He read everything which could be found or borrowed, both in English and in Spanish. Owing to the Victorian ideas of his parents, he saw little modern fiction, but devoured Shakespeare and *Don Quixote*, which fed his love of the humorous, and among books of more recent vintage, Tennyson and Becquer, which piqued his taste for the romantic and marvelous. At the same time he plunged deep into the fascinating pages of history, particularly ancient, ecclesiastical, English, and Chilean. From the age of six he spent much of his time constructing imaginary worlds in his mind, and telling himself interminable tales of the wars and adventure of their heroes, covering centuries of time and thousands of miles of space, thus unconsciously cultivating a pronounced bent toward historical synthesis. At the age of eight he became intensely interested in archaeology, especially in Biblical antiquities. Two years later he ran errands for his parents until he had earned five dollars for the purchase of the newly published *History of Babylonia and Assyria* by R. W. Rogers. The two volumes finally arrived and at Christmas he was allowed to dip into them. Thereafter his happiest hours were spent in reading and rereading this work which, fortunately, was written in beautiful English by a well-trained and accurate scholar.

The lad's religious environment was strictly evangelical Protestant; it was not until later that he became conscious of his Methodist background as such. An omnivorous reader of church history and theology, he became acutely aware of creedal distinctions. Coming in his father's library upon considerable Protestant polemic literature, in both English and Spanish, he became violently anti-Catholic, an attitude not lessened by his external contacts. It must also be remembered that the Catholicism of Latin America around the turn of the century was very different in everyday life from that of France or of England and America at the time, and also different from the Catholicism of South America today. At that time there was hardly a Catholic vernacular Bible in the whole of Latin America—a result of the traditional Spanish attitude well known from the Council of Trent. The clergy was still educated along strictly medieval lines, and native priests were in general quite ignorant. Moreover, comparatively few parish priests were commonly believed to obey the rule of celibacy. During the past generation, under the goad of Protestant missionary activity, there has been a remarkable transformation in all these respects, though American priests are still surprised by many features of the religious practice of Latin America. In those days modern European and American ideas of cleanliness and sanitation had scarcely penetrated into South America, and much of Protestant missionary work was directed along these lines, as well as against alcoholism, then a terrible curse in the coastal towns of Chile. It was not, therefore, surprising that the lad formed a concept of evangelical Protestant action which was almost half compounded of hygiene and anti-alcoholism.

YOUTH IN RURAL AMERICA

The lad's parents had grown up together in northeastern Iowa, in farm homes less than half a mile apart. His grandfathers, though not formally educated, were wide readers and each possessed a library of several hundred volumes. One was a zealous Methodist layman of German and North-Irish blood, with a French-Canadian wife; the other was a Cornishman who had migrated to this country in middle life and whose family had also been Wesleyan. The Foxwell and Humphrey relatives tended to be rather clannish, but they had a much richer cultural background than the Albrights. The home of his Cornish grandmother in Fayette County, Iowa, was an oasis in the otherwise rather dreary life of the teen-age lad, who moved yearly with his parents from one drab little parsonage to another in some equally drab prairie village. The rosy picture of American Protestantism which the lad had formed in Chile was rapidly dissipated when he came to a country where Protestants, despite their sectarian differences, were undeniably in the majority. In this village life there were many fine things, but the man remembers little but the drabness of it and the total lack of anything resembling intellectual life. In view of his bookish background and his physical handicaps it is not surprising that those years were so unhappy that they have almost faded from his memory today. He retired more and more into his shell, living in the world of his imagination which he had created years before.

In retrospect it was fortunate for the lad that his parents were excessively poor, supporting six children on a salary which seldom exceeded $400 in cash. Poverty compelled him to devote his hours out of school to manual labor. His crippled left hand developed unexpected strength and he was able to use it regularly even for milking cows, though probably never to the satisfaction of the cow. From the age of fifteen he spent the summers as a farmhand, learning a good deal about agriculture, and acquiring a wiry toughness which stood him in good stead in later years of archaeological research. When he was sixteen he entered the preparatory school attached to Upper Iowa University, Fayette, Iowa, where his father had received his A.B. in 1885. Five years later he received his A.B. and went into the field of high school teaching, which was then the principal vocation of bookishly-inclined college graduates. These years in college continued to be marked by the severest economy, since he had to work his way. Thanks to familiar acquaintance with poverty it lost its terrors, and in subsequent life he had many occasions for gratitude to Providence for having given him such wholesome training for the rigors of life.

The cultural horizon of a small Methodist college in the Middle West of those days was very narrow, but it was still possible to obtain a good education in Latin, Greek, and mathematics. Other subjects were seldom as well taught, and intellectual standards were so low in some that it was easy to pass by sheer bluff. Fortunately our student concentrated on classics and mathematics, in which he had first-class instruction. Otherwise he might have suffered permanently from the low standards in other subjects. As it happened, he was able to get through his courses in education and social sciences with virtually no study at all, freeing the daylight hours necessary for earning enough to put him through college. Thanks to this outside labor and to a small scholarship, he was able to go through college without interruption, something which would have been impossible if he had attended a more expensive institution, where intellectual standards might have been higher.

After graduation the young man spent a year in South Dakota, acting as principal of the village high school in a German-Russian (Volga German) community. Here his knowledge of German, begun in Chile and subsequently improved, was to prove invaluable.

The little town was almost solidly German-speaking in those days, and its life was controlled by three very conservative German Protestant churches. An exciting year was climaxed by a fight in school between his biggest student and the principal, after which a determined effort was made to oust him. That it failed was due partly to the desperation of the young principal, who threw prudence to the wind and shouted down the school board, and partly to the intervention of a kindly Providence. Providence was to intervene again before the end of that year, when it had become clear that the young man could not hope for a successful career teaching school, owing particularly to his physical handicaps. An application to Paul Haupt, then head of the Oriental Seminary at the Johns Hopkins University, for a scholarship arrived in Baltimore just before the deadline; by lucky chance the application was accompanied by the proof sheets of a paper to appear in a German learned journal. Though the paper was undoubtedly bad, it showed originality, and to its author's inexpressible delight he received the offer of a fellowship covering tuition and basic cost of living in Baltimore. As a last reckless gesture before settling down—he hoped—the young man spent a summer in the Northwest as a tramp farm laborer, riding on top of passenger trains and under freight trains in approved hobo style. It was undoubtedly a foolish waste of time from the standpoint of his studies, but the toughening of his fiber and experience of hardship which it brought, proved later to be very helpful when the bookworm turned archaeologist.

During the summers which followed the next six years as student and research fellow at Johns Hopkins, the young man went home to the family farm in sourthern Virginia (to which his father had moved soon after retiring from the active ministry). Here he labored on the farm and, during his free time, read Oriental languages and Greek. This transplanting and its consequent associations gave him a new perspective, bringing insight into the problems of the rural Southeast, which are in so many ways divergent from the problems of the Middle West and Northwest. Another minority question which imposed itself on his attention was that of the American Negro, which is in many ways the most difficult of all.

THE EDUCATION OF AN ORIENTALIST

Ever since my boyhood days in Chile I had kept up my interest in Biblical archaeology and Oriental studies. At sixteen I took the bull by the horns and began to study Hebrew on Sundays, using my father's old copy of William Rainey Harper's inductive introduction. Through my college course I continued to buy books, mainly from Germany, and to study them on Sundays. All this was done surreptitiously, since I mortally feared the ridicule which might reasonably be expected to follow discovery of such a futile hobby. Besides, since the family was partly dependent on my earnings, which were meager at best, my hobby could not be pursued without acute smartings of a Methodist conscience. It is probable that my mother was only slightly relieved on one occasion when she came to me, after hearing from one of the younger children that I had brought a book home from the post office, saying, "You know, William, designing men sometimes send boys debasing literature through the mails," to learn that the book was a Hebrew grammar! By the time I reached Johns Hopkins, at the age of twenty-two, I possessed a fair elementary knowledge of Hebrew and Assyrian, together with a considerable reading knowledge of ancient history and related subjects.

The next three years were devoted to concentrated study and research, which would almost certainly have cost me my eyesight (always bad) if it had not been for the months spent mostly in outdoor labor on the Virginia farm. Happily, my fellowship freed me from the necessity of earning money, so I was enabled to study almost uninterruptedly while in Baltimore. For three more years after receiving the doctorate I continued to hold research fellowships, thanks to which I began intensive research in a number of ancient Near Eastern fields, interrupted only by being drafted for "limited service" in the army toward the end of the First World War. Even this interruption proved to be wholesome, though exceedingly distasteful at the time, since it forced me to spend several months away from my books and improved my health considerably, in spite of the wretched food served in the labor battalions into which I drifted.

During the three years after receiving my Ph.D., I became increasingly interested in psychology, comparative mythology, and the history of religions. It is very probable that the direction then taken by my research would have led me into deep waters, where the subjective element becomes increasingly strong as the investigator leaves the familiar coastal landmarks behind. Fortunately I had won the Thayer Fellowship in the American School of Oriental Research in Jerusalem, and the end of the war made it possible to spend a year there. At first I devoted myself almost exclusively to modern Arabic and Hebrew, but after the initial year had imperceptibly lengthened and I had been made acting director of the School, I turned toward topographical and archaeological exploration. The following years brought opportunities to excavate, and after 1926 my principal interest shifted from surface exploration to excavation. The following ten years were devoted mainly to excavation and preparation of the results for publication. During these fifteen years my initially rather skeptical attitude toward the accuracy of Israelite historical tradition had suffered repeated jolts as discovery after discovery confirmed the historicity of details which might reasonably have been considered legendary. At the same time, my partial espousal of the Pan-Babylonian point of view of Hugo Winckler against the school of Biblical historians headed by Julius Wellhausen, which I had opposed since boyhood, brought a sharp reaction against the basic positions of current Old Testament criticism. Wellhausen's view that Israel was cut off from the great civilizations of the ancient Near East and did not form part of a great cultural continuum, as maintained by Winckler, seemed to me just as incredible as Wellhausen's theory of unilinear evolution, which was contradicted by all the facts of Egyptology and Assyriology. I was, accordingly, led increasingly to insist on the substantial historicity of Mosaic tradition and the antiquity of Israelite monotheism; these principles have remained basic to my teaching ever since.

Through my years in the Near East I remained faithful to my interest in cuneiform studies, and after my return to Johns Hopkins in 1929 I resumed research in both cuneiform and Egyptian. After 1936, when the outbreak of the Arab rebellion, followed without intermission by the Second World War, made excavation in Palestine a practical impossibility, my growing interest in the philosophy of history led me to intensive reading and research in this field.

During the decade ending in 1947 a number of my pupils began to pursue research along similar lines, until it became evident that my pupils' work, published and planned, would soon considerably outweigh my own in significance. This is a development toward which every original investigator should look forward eagerly;

only at the moment where his pupils lead him rather than he them can he feel confident that his work has not been largely in vain. At the same time I began to receive European academic distinctions, which bring a scholar solid comfort, since they help to assure him that his correct observations outweigh his errors in the judgment of unbiased foreign observers, few of whom know him personally.

The subject of this essay has always had the temper of a pioneer, interested in surveying new routes and in breaking new ground. In the course of such a career many mistakes are bound to be made, and many hypotheses will have to be revised or discarded entirely. As time passes, a prudent investigator gradually learns to avoid certain types of research either as too subjective to yield safe results or as relatively unproductive. Above all he learns to value sound method, following approved logical principles of induction, deduction, and experiment. Yet "sound method" must not be permitted to become an obsession, for at that point the scholar is likely to become intellectually myopic and his work is likely to lose its heuristic value. Moreover, due respect for the traditions of true scholarship, aiming at truth and rejecting temptations to expose one's wares at the market place, should never be allowed to obscure the primary fact that all scholarly research which is worthy of the name must have a definite plan, a plan which will fit into the investigator's world view and enrich it at the same time that it is ennobled by it.

Credo ut intellegam

SCIENCE AND THE HUMANITIES

Boyhood interest in archaeology (which included paleontology) led me to an increasingly intense curiosity about all kinds of scientific research. My attention became successively concentrated on the physical sciences (physics and mathematics were my favorite college subjects), on the biological sciences (owing partly to the fact that my closest friend was an ardent devotee of zoology), and finally on the history and philosophy of science. It was a keen disappointment to learn after coming to Johns Hopkins that I could not reasonably expect to pursue a minor in mathematics at the same time that I tackled a major in Semitic languages.

Deep-seated interest in science has made our subject restive under the intellectual stigma which the science-minded world of our day has attached to research in any field connected with the past of man's cultural life. This attitude, which is much more pronounced in America than in Europe, began partly as a natural reaction on the part of scientists of the nineteenth century to a humanistic education which tried to prevent science from assuming its rightful place, but is now conditioned largely by the increasingly utilitarian atmosphere around natural science. Half a century ago most scientific research had little direct "practical" value, and the non-intellectual was apt to regard it with the same amused or irritated tolerance now shown toward research in the humanities by the typical scientist. As a result of two world wars, accompanied by tremendous forward surges of technology, it is almost universally recognized today that all good scientific research has "practical" value, since its application to technology, agriculture, medicine, etc., usually follows immediately or with only a relatively slight time lag. Fields like psychology and cultural anthropology share to a certain extent in the new prestige of science, though the right to be called "sciences" is conceded to them only grudgingly by many scientists. The social sciences are as a rule not recognized as "sciences" by the natural scientists, but because of their relative pertinence to the current scene they are fully accepted by most of the public.

The inferior rating to which the disciplines connected with human culture, such as history, languages (especially the classics), and philosophy, as well as their ancillary fields, have been assigned inevitably brings with it a vicious circle of decline. The relative insignificance of these studies in America brings with it progressive weakening of the average quality of their representatives and still further decline in student interest. From time to time the decline of the humanities has been checked by outstanding educators and scholars, such as the late James Henry Breasted, through whose extraordinary combination of the highest scholarship with promotional flair great popular interest was aroused in archaeology and Oriental studies.[2] Unfortunately, however, Breasted's efforts were directed against the prevailing trend and could scarcely have

[2] See my sketch of James Henry Breasted, above, Chapter 9.

had far-reaching effect. Moreover, his work was undertaken in the spirit of a melioristic rationalism which was far too shallow to give it permanence. In any case, there can be no doubt that the decline of the humanities has been accelerated by recent events. The author of these lines is no unredeemed pessimist, since he is as firmly convinced of the permanent value of the humanities as ever.

After returning to the States in 1929, I took an active part for a decade in the affairs of the American Council of Learned Societies, but I became increasingly disturbed by the constant reappearance of academic politics both at the meetings and behind the scenes. In spite of the influence of some outstanding personalities, intellectual idealism was more honored in the breach than in the observance. Close association with prominent natural scientists in the American Philosophical Society, as well as in various universities, has gone far to preserve my faith in the basic intellectual idealism of the American academic mind. (Thanks to the friendships thus established, I was elected to the National Academy of Sciences in 1955—probably the greatest single surprise of my life.) On the other hand, there has been in recent years a steady decline in the intellectual idealism of the younger scientists, especially at lower academic levels. The young natural scientist of today tends to be more interested in salary and position than in the pursuit of truth or of human welfare; in this respect he has often ceased to be a thinker and has become a professional.

In my opinion, recent experiments in centering college education around the humanities, as in the University of Wisconsin and lately at St. John's, have been in general a failure, in spite of some useful by-products. Most of these attempts have been inspired by a rationalistic, antireligious mentality which has made a mockery of the old humanism. At Southwestern (Memphis), where there was a really intelligent attempt to center an adequate course in the humanities around a religious approach to history, it appears to have succeeded for a few years. Devoted teachers remain, however, an absolute prerequisite to success. Without religious inspiration, history has little practical meaning for life, and philosophy is in constant danger of becoming a sterile intellectual exercise or even a formal training in militant cynicism. Yet I am firmly convinced that the humanities must be strengthened to prevent American education from becoming purely vocational, and that an intellectual culture which does not reckon with all the higher values of mankind is doomed to progressive sterility. There is perhaps no better way to clarify my point of view than to apply it systematically in the following brief sections to some vital problems of our day. (In recent books and papers the interested reader can find additional material.)

ORIENT AND OCCIDENT: RACE AND CULTURE

Owing to the combination of circumstances which gave me a living experience of three continents, in all of which I was at home in the spoken languages of my entourage and in constant association with those who spoke them, I have always been intensely conscious of the evils of race prejudice. My parents' love for the people among whom they worked gave this attitude early religious validation, which it has never lost. Finally, my many years of research on the ancient and modern Near East have impressed on my mind an ineradicable tendency to view all racial and cultural problems in the light of both their history and their environment.

In our day, when previously separated peoples are being brought closer in war and peace, and when "colored" races are in open revolt against "white" domination in many parts of the world, the question of their future relationship assumes an immediacy scarcely dreamed of in the past. The physical and biological sciences are helpless to solve any such problems, which they can only make still harder to solve by imprudent experiments. Peoples of differing cultures and world views do not become more friendly by improvement of communications or by the wide diffusion of moving pictures and mechanical gadgets—quite the reverse. Improvements in medicine and agriculture increase the population of rival nations and races, making it inevitable for any wars which break out between them to destroy human beings in far greater numbers than before. Social science is more helpful; but economics is powerless to eradicate basic human instincts, which emerge essentially unchanged whenever economic or other stresses disturb social equilibrium, while sociology is powerless to do more than describe them and identify them as they emerge. Cultural anthropology has already taught us much about primitive peoples; but it, too, is relatively helpless before complex higher cultures. Social psychology can teach us a great deal about the motives which swing masses of men in response to stimuli, but the same knowledge which gives an enlightened and idealistic leader a powerful instrument for reaching the masses, offers an ambitious demagogue an even greater advantage, since the latter is quite devoid of scruples in choosing his means. Only with the aid of accumulated humanistic insights can the social scientist hope for real understanding to grapple with these dangerous tendencies at their source.

This last statement will doubtless sound rash, if not absurd, to some American social scientists. It ought, however, to be clear that the only way to understand such phenomena as Russian Communism or Islamic culture is to study them intensively, analyzing their current manifestations in the light of their past history and literature. Moreover, study of their own history is not enough; knowledge of their prehistory is also needed. The Russian form of Communism is not fully intelligible unless one knows both the life and the institutions of Tsarist Russia. Islam cannot be historically understood except in the perspective of the pre-Islamic Greco-Roman and Judeo-Christian worlds. Similarly, study of their literatures demands a knowledge of the necessary languages, as well as of the philological techniques which give precision to this knowledge. Out of personal experience the writer could recite many amusing and saddening examples of the pitfalls which await investigators with inadequate knowledge in these fields.

The study of these disciplines is far from being purely academic. During the past century racist theories have encroached steadily and insidiously on our religious heritage of belief in racial equality. It is true that the disastrous collapse of the Nazi movement has made large-scale promotion of such doctrines unpopular, yet almost every writer who has emerged from Central Europe since 1933 is tarred with racism in one way or another. This applies to Jews as well as to "Aryans," to anti-Nazis as well as to pro-Nazis, though naturally in less degree. All recent European literature swarms with unproved and unprovable distinctions between racial and national psychologies. Differences between a typical Englishman's way of thinking and that of a Frenchman or German exist, to be sure, but they are functions of complex cultural differences rather than basic to the mind of a given national group. Any one of these men, transferred at birth to one of the other countries, would automatically absorb the way of thinking normative to his adopted country. Compared with such differences of cultural origin, the basic psychological distinctions which may easily exist even between such closely related peoples as the English and French have no measurable significance and may safely be disregarded until vastly more accurate means of measurement are discovered—assuming that this is possible!

A danger inherent in these types of racism is that they cannot be disproved as easily as the gross forms popularized even in America by men like Lothrop Stoddard. Ellsworth Huntington's speculations are almost equally dangerous, since they are cleverly combined with climatic and other variables in such a way that direct disproof is almost impossible at present.

The alleged differences between Asiatic and European mentality are mostly imaginative constructions of Westerners. Most features of Hinduism are simply survivals of ancient polytheism, and even Hindu pantheism is not as unique as often thought. Hindu mysticism has close parallels in Islamic Sufism and medieval European mysticism, as has been pointed out repeatedly by specialists such as Ananda K. Coomaraswamy. Neo-Confucianism seems to have a special affinity for American instrumentalism, to judge from the many converts the latter has made among exponents of the former in China—not to forget the favorable attitude toward Confucian ethics held by several American instrumentalists (see above, p. 8). There is a great deal of exaggeration in F. S. C. Northrop's stimulating recent volume, *The Meeting of East and West* (1946). Even in such a thoroughly competent analysis as H. A. R. Gibb's *Modern Trends in Islam,* the distinguished British Arabist paints a quite arbitrary picture of the basic differences between Arab and European mentality. According to this picture the European mind tends to be rational, the Arab mind to be intuitive; the European thinks synthetically and congruently, whereas the Arab tends to think atomistically. In so far as this is a correct description of certain observable cultural differences, the latter are the result of the backwardness of the Islamic peoples, who were culturally at a standstill between the fourteenth and the nineteenth centuries. Gibb's illustrations would have applied almost equally well to Europe before the Renaissance.

THE MINORITY PROBLEM[3]

The problem of religious, national, and racial minorities has always existed, but it was not until the nineteenth century that statesmen and philosophers became fully aware of its dangerous potentialities. Early in that century the liberalism of the Enlightenment, rein-

[3] See "Some Functions of Organized Minorities," above, Chapter 8.

forced by religious sanctions as the principle of toleration gained ground, had made the ruthless suppression of dissident groups unpopular in most Western lands. Released from oppression, however, the minorities grew rapidly and inevitably became a target for the increasing hostility of the majorities. Growing nationalism proved to be even more inhospitable to the idea of tolerating minorities than religion had been in previous centuries. When freed from inherited religious and ethical controls, the suppression of minorities became incredibly barbaric, as demonstrated by events in Europe during the past thirty years.

I have always been sensitive to the minority question, as noted in the first part of this essay. As a boy I was a member of a Protestant minority in Latin America; in the Near East I was a member of a Christian minority in a Moslem country and closely associated by ties of friendship with a Jewish minority; since I returned to this country my wife and family have been members of a Catholic minority in a Protestant country. Moreover, after 1933 I took a passionate interest in the fate of the Jewish minority in Central Europe. At the same time my wife and I began to take an intense interest in the Negro and other minorities in this country.

There is no easy recipe for the solution of the minority problem, which is extremely complex and is further complicated by the frictions and stresses within any majority. In my opinion it is wiser at present to emphasize the often overlooked—and more often unrecognized—positive aspects of the minority problem. Any nation which has organized national or religious minorities within its territory possesses assets of extraordinary value. As a rule, members of such minorities find life harder than do members of the majority; they are despised, restricted in their opportunities for social and professional advancement, and often actively persecuted. Under such difficult conditions they react according to Toynbee's principle of "the stimulus of penalization." The law of compensation proceeds to operate, and individuals of a minority work harder and cooperate better among themselves than do members of the majority. The Germany of the late nineteenth and early twentieth centuries affords an exceedingly fine illustration of the way in which this principle works. In the twenties of this century the Jews formed only about one per cent of its total population, but over five per cent of the faculties of its universities was Jewish, while the proportion of Jewish Nobel prize winners was considerably higher still. Energetic minorities form an invaluable source of stimulation for the majority, which tends to stagnate unless it receives such stimulation from outside. Progress and reform in a majority show a tendency to be initiated by members of minorities or of small groups which react similarly to their environment. Moreover, such minorities form powerful checks on excesses of the majority, thus serving as balance wheels. As soon as minorities become targets for open persecution and repression, democracy is imperiled. The continued presence and relative prosperity of minorities is thus the best possible test of the viability of a democracy.

HISTORY AND THE JUDEO-CHRISTIAN TRADITION

Through my long study of problems connected with the historical origins of our European civilization, I have come to devote particular attention to the higher culture which emerged within this civilization. In studying this higher culture I have become profoundly convinced of its necessary place in our civilization. Without sharing the strictly functional approach of the Malinowski school of cultural anthropologists, developed as a result of close preoccupation with "primitive" cultures, I am, nonetheless, convinced that it is difficult and often dangerous to experiment with cultures, since we know far too little about their basic factors to determine what can safely be eliminated and what cannot be excised without destroying both the culture in question and most of its bearers. It is a curious fact that members of the functional school tend to surrender their own logical premises as soon as they deal with Judaism or Christianity, appearing to feel, like the instrumentalists from whom they differ so radically in other respects, that these religions are somehow exceptions and that they can be safely discarded by modern representatives of their cultures, whereas the religious faiths of other cultures must be carefully guarded against disruption (see above, pp. 47-49). Another even more curious fact is that many contemporary social scientists seem to think that the religious culture of man is a kind of excrescence, to be cut away as some rash surgeons would remove tonsils or vermiform appendix, regardless of whether these organs are diseased or not. Since these same scholars would undoubtedly accept the verdict of biologists with reference to the physical organization of man, and would, accordingly, accept the fact of its amazingly complex structure and delicate balance, which cannot be upset without danger, they would presumably deny the applicability of evolutionary principles to the higher culture of man. In view of the well-known fact that they actually do hold evolution to be applicable to all life and history, they are guilty here of an inner contradiction so drastic and fundamental as to make their pertinent speculations a mere *reductio ad absurdum*.

Our knowledge of history is governed, in the writer's opinion, by the same logical principles, inductive, deductive, and statistical, which control our knowledge of the "natural" sciences. It is quite true that there are different kinds of knowledge. Thus physics is a body of knowledge which reckons in principle only with experimentally determined facts fitting into some recognized mathematical framework. Historical knowledge may be analyzed as consisting of three or four principal categories of judgment: judgments of fact, judgments of value, judgments of typical occurrence, judgments of cause and effect, etc.[4] The first and third of these judgments are subject to normal scientific methodology; the second and fourth are too complex and subjective to be regarded as the common intellectual property of scholars, even where the latter possess equal competence. They are, however, no less important on this account; in the hands of historians professing the same philosophical or religious creed they may yield a high proportion of agreement. The picture of history which emerges from application of the first and third kinds of judgment to the data accumulated by philologists, archaeologists, and other students of the past, does not consist of a relatively isolated sequence of individual occurrences, but rather of a succession of cultural patterns, elaborately crisscrossing one another in all directions and at many levels; isolated occurrences are like the survey points which serve the topographer as the basis of his charts. To call a chain of such occurrences "history," is like reducing a topographical map to nothing but surveyors' points.

In the writer's opinion, the history reflected by the Old and New Testaments is, humanly speaking, the outcome of normal processes of evolution, operating faster and more effectively in the complex world of the ancient Mediterranean and the Near East than in such

[4] See above, pp. 23-27.

isolated foci of civilization as India, China, or Middle America. Babylonian material civilization was easily two thousand years ahead of Chinese in most respects; Egyptian culture was a good four millennia in advance of that of Middle America in most matters. Moreover, with so many relatively independent hearths of civilization in close proximity to one another, the ancient Near Eastern world was able to develop much more symmetrically and with far less one-sidedness than was true of remoter centers. It was physically impossible for any Near Eastern culture to develop in isolation and thus to evolve such abnormal, "orthogenetic" growths as the Indian caste system or the rigid Chinese family system.

In the Near and Middle East the proto-logical ways of thinking which characterize most primitive higher culture were early replaced by empirical logic, a logic of experience implicitly developed for lack of tools of formal logic.[5] It was in this stage of logical thinking that the faith of early Israel came into being: in the monotheism of Moses and the Prophets there was no proto-logical magic or mythology (except in poetic symbolism); their beliefs were not classified or analyzed, but were just as logically consistent in most respects as are the ideas of modern Jews and Christians. Then, toward the end of the Prophetic age, formal logic was discovered and developed by the Greeks. Both Judaism and Christianity adopted the powerful new tools of thought and gradually formed their beliefs into systematic theological structures influenced strongly by Plato and Aristotle. Whatever may have been the individual weaknesses of this or that theologian, or of this sect or that, the theology and ethics of the Judeo-Christian tradition are basic to our modern Western way of life. The Ten Commandments cannot be violated with impunity by any people or by any ideological group. The attempts of Nazis and Communists to set them aside and to replace the Commandments by their own party-line practices have resulted in orgies of slaughter almost unparalleled in history. The doctrines of the Fatherhood of God and the brotherhood of man are basic; both are denied by the atavistic teachings of Nazis and Communists, a fact which illustrates the colossal danger inherent in the nature of arbitrary postulational structures which disregard the cultural heritage of mankind.

[5] See above, pp. 70-72.

THEOLOGY, CATHOLIC AND PROTESTANT

From history we turn to theology, from the development of Christian faith to its contemporary aspects. In dealing with this subject my views are powerfully affected by the circumstances of my personal life. Born an evangelical Protestant, reared by missionary parents in Latin America, where Catholicism was at its lowest level two generations ago, I became increasingly "liberal" after beginning my Oriental studies. Married in 1921 to a highly intelligent woman, only a year my junior and herself a Ph.D. in the related field of Sanskrit, I might have remained a "liberal," had it not been for two unforeseen developments. The first was the cumulative effect on me of archaeological confirmation of Biblical tradition and increasing disproof of the isolationist theory of Israelite history held by critical scholars; the second was my wife's conversion to Catholicism about a year after our marriage. Brought up an Anglo-Catholic, with a liberal "Protestant" attitude toward theology but with a "Catholic" sense of the meaning of ritual, the transition was relatively easy for her, but it brought with it a completely new piety and feeling for the realities of faith. After becoming a Dominican tertiary, she rapidly acquired a grounding in Thomistic theology, which consolidated her beliefs on logical lines, preventing her faith from dissolving into emotionalism or sentimentality. My wife's influence was slow in making itself felt, owing partly to the wall of indifference or active hostility which it had to breach, but in the long run it has doubtless been even more effective than the other development which we have sketched. Thanks to my wife's intellectual background, the house was kept filled with the best Catholic literature, mostly of Scholastic origin or inspiration, which I have read for many years. At the same time I continued to be a Methodist and to read Protestant, especially Neo-orthodox, literature with equal interest. The outcome could scarcely be in doubt; with powerful forces pulling in opposite directions at all times, one's position is likely to become more or less stabilized in the middle. Points of view common to both Neo-Thomists and Neo-orthodox are likely a priori to be adopted, except where they are contradicted by one's scholarly convictions. Where the opponents differ, one is likely to adopt an attitude divergent from both, however similar it may be to one or the other. The following paragraphs will illustrate certain critical features of the resultant attitude.

Religion is just as real and necessary a part of a complete life as food or social intercourse. It rises above the level of "matter" and "energy" into a higher world which cannot be controlled by quantitative experiment or mathematical logic, a world to which our emotions and our intuitive imagination give access. To assert that this world is not real because it cannot be measured quantitatively is a vagary of modern scientism. Qualitative experience tells us that there is a Higher Power, with whom we can come into direct personal relationship through spiritual means and that this Higher Power has actively participated in the molding of our lives, either through providential intervention or through continuous action, or both. The task of the theologian is to generalize the individual experience of God and to put it into a conceptual frame intelligible to our logically conditioned minds. In this task the theologian continues the work of a multitude of precursors, building on the foundations of historical revelation and experience which are imbedded in the Bible and other religious literature. The theologian is further aided in his difficult task by comparative study of different philosophical and religious systems, pre-Christian and non-Christian as well as Christian. His materials are proto-logical, empirico-logical, and logical; each form of logic has its own applicability to the mysteries of God, which remain beyond human understanding. In other words, the theologian is trying to reduce the profound experiences of religion and the paradoxical contradictions of the metaphysical world of values into a consistent scheme which will not offend the earth-bound reason of men. Such questions as that of evil are too profound to be answered by any human mind, no matter how logical or how broadly informed; they will always retain something of their essentially paradoxical nature.

It follows, accordingly, as emphasized effectively by Neo-orthodox thinkers, that the profoundest truths of religious intuition and revelation cannot be logically defined or analyzed without sacrificing part of their truth. To call them "myths," as has become so popular among theologians, is highly misleading, since nearly all ancient or primitive myths have to do with physical phenomena and with the sexual and economic bases of human life. On the other hand, they cannot be formulated as logical "dogmas" without an elastic use of obscure or ambiguous metaphysical words such as "substance." To discard fundamental Christian doctrine because of the fact that we cannot fully understand its meaning goes much too far. During the past two thousand years the churches have had to abandon doctrines and interpretations of doctrines once popular in the Christian world but shown by experience to be dangerous to the delicate balance of spiritual effectiveness. Orthodox Christian theology has crystallized certain basic principles of life without which mankind cannot be saved from its own exaggerated drives and powers of mechanical creation: there is a God who is infinitely above us, but who is also the Being in whom we have our being; God is not only one and indivisible but is also divisible within His own Being and as close to any man as that man's own being; evil is a real and terrible force in the world, but love is still more powerful; suffering is a necessary part of experience, and without it there can be no true greatness or holiness. These are samples of the rich body of truth with which only historical theology is prepared to deal, and which no other discipline can teach adequately.

I profoundly respect both the great Catholic Church and my rich personal heritage from many forms of Protestantism. I am revolted by attempts on either side to denounce the heroes of the other wing of the universal church as diabolical figures or as misguided leaders of the blind. Yet I am not so naïve as to believe that my own peculiar brand of tolerance will—or can—be accepted by either side. I am angered by cheap attacks on Catholicism or Protestantism, no matter where they originate. The not-too-remote flood of violent onslaughts on the Catholic Church in American Protestant periodicals was as degrading to the religious spirit as unscholarly in its command of the facts. Catholic and Protestant attacks on the Jews and Judaism deeply disturb me. I hold that Christianity penetrates more deeply than Judaism into the meaning of life; it is far better equipped to give the world a frame of mind necessary for life in the atomic age; yet, in the words of a great Pope, we are spiritually all Semites.

The profoundest intuitions of faith are not subject to logical proof —but neither are the axioms on which all science and technology are erected. We end as we began, with the humble scholar's *credo ut intellegam!*

Appendix

1891   Born in Coquimbo, Chile, May 24, eldest son of Reverend Wilbur Finley Albright and Zephine Viola (née Foxwell).

1903   Came in June with his parents to the United States (Iowa).

1907–08   Entered preparatory department of Upper Iowa University (Fayette, Iowa). Began private study of Hebrew, using inductive method.

1909–10   Entered Upper Iowa University as sophomore.

1912   Received A.B. from Upper Iowa University (June).

1912–13   Principal of high school, Menno, South Dakota. Joined Vorderasiatische Gesellschaft. First scholarly paper ("Dallalu") accepted by *Orientalistische Literaturzeitung*. Received fellowship at Johns Hopkins University on the strength of it.

1913–14   University Fellow, Oriental Seminary, Johns Hopkins University. Passed French and German, second minor.

1914–15   Rayner Fellow, Johns Hopkins. First lot of original ideas accepted by Paul Haupt. Read first paper ("Balaam") at meeting of American Oriental Society.

1915–16   Reappointed Rayner Fellow. Presented successful paper on misunderstood cuneiform passages at American Oriental Society. Admitted to Phi Beta Kappa. Won Thayer Fellowship at American School of Oriental Research, Jerusalem (held in 1919-1920). Received Ph.D., June, 1916 (dissertation: "The Assyrian Deluge Epic").

1916–17   Rayner Fellow and titular Instructor, Oriental Seminary, Johns Hopkins.

1917–18   Johnston Scholar, Johns Hopkins. Several papers published.

1918–19   Spent five months as private, limited service, U. S. Army (August-December). Returned to Johns Hopkins in January. Engaged to Ruth Norton in May. Prepared elaborate papers which appeared later in *Revue d'Assyriologie*, *Journal of Egyptian Archaeology*, as well as monograph on Egyptian vowel system (accepted for *Beiträge zur Assyriologie* but lost —sketch of conclusions published in 1923 in *Recueil de Travaux*).

1919–20 Thayer Fellow, American School of Oriental Research, Jerusalem.

1920–21 Acting Director, A.S.O.R. Member, Archaeological Advisory Board, Palestine Government.

1921–22 Director, A.S.O.R. Married to Ruth Norton, August 31. President, Palestine Oriental Society. Litt.D., Upper Iowa University.

1922–23 First excavation (Tell el-Ful).

1923–24 First organized archaeological exploration (Dead Sea Expedition).

1924–25 First book (*Gibeah*). Reached No. 100 in bibliography.

1925–26 Trip with R. P. Dougherty to Iraq. First campaign at Tell Beit Mirsim.

1926–27 Hamburg Orientalistentag. Sabbatical year in America; gave 125 lectures. Elected Professor of Semitic Languages at Johns Hopkins, but not appointed.

1927–28 Appointed professor at Johns Hopkins. Second campaign at Tell Beit Mirsim.

1928–29 Bonn Orientalistentag, Oxford Congress of Orientalists. Elected member of American Philosophical Society. Hon. Member, Institute of Oriental Studies, Hebrew University.

1929–30 Professor at Johns Hopkins and Chairman of Oriental Seminary. Member, American Council of Learned Societies (elected to Executive Committee). Member, Executive Committee, A.S.O.R.

1930–31 W. W. Spence Professor of Semitic Languages, Johns Hopkins. Third campaign at Tell Beit Mirsim. Chairman, Committee on Mediterranean Antiquities, A.C.L.S. Richards Lecturer, University of Virginia. Reached No. 200 in bibliography.

1931–32 Leiden Congress of Orientalists (Member, Consultative Committee). Carew Lecturer, Hartford Seminary Foundation. *The Archaeology of Palestine and the Bible* published.

1932–33 Fourth campaign at Tell Beit Mirsim. *Tell Beit Mirsim I* published. Elected director, A.S.O.R., on half-time basis.

1933–34 Director, A.S.O.R. (second time) and professor at Johns Hopkins, half-time each. Elected Laffan Professor of Assyriology and Babylonian Literature and head of Semitic Department at Yale. Declined offer and remained at Johns Hopkins. Member, Nominating Committee, American Philosophical Society.

1934–35 First campaign at Bethel. President, Palestine Oriental Society (second time). *The Vocalization of the Egyptian Syllabic Orthography* published.

1935–36 President, American Oriental Society. Rome Congress of Orientalists (Chairman, U.S. delegation; Member, Consultative Committee). Director, A.S.O.R. (eleventh and last year). Trustee, A.S.O.R. and Chairman, Jerusalem School Committee; Editor of Old Testament book reviews, *Journal of Biblical Literature*. D.H.L., Jewish Institute of Religion, Jewish Theological Seminary of America. Th.D., University of Utrecht on tercentenary.

1936–37 Member, Academic Council at Johns Hopkins, five-year term. Member, Committee on Research and Membership (Class of Humanities), Am. Philos. Soc.

1937–38 Vice-President, A.S.O.R. Member of Council, Am. Philos. Soc. (three-year term). *Tell Beit Mirsim II* published.

1938–39 Brussels Congress of Orientalists and Oxford meeting of Society for Old Testament Study. President, Society of Biblical Literature; Vice-chairman, A.C.L.S.

1940–41 Co-chairman, Conference on Science, Philosophy, and Religion. Member, Committee of Three to select executive officer of Am. Philos. Soc. Vice-president, Linguistic Society of America. Ayer Lecturer, Colgate-Rochester Theological Seminary. *From the Stone Age to Christianity* published.

1941–42 Strook Lecturer, Jewish Institute of Religion. *Archaeology and the Religion of Israel* published. *Indexed Bibliography of the Writings of William Foxwell Albright* appeared.

1942–43 Member of Faculty, Linguistic Institute, University of Wisconsin. Associate Editor, *American Journal of Archaeology*. Hon. Member, Glasgow Oriental Society. *Tell Beit Mirsim III* published, completing the work.

1943–44 Haskell Lecturer, Oberlin Graduate School of Theology.

1944–45 Hon. Life Member, Catholic Biblical Association of America. Member, Committee on Revision of the American Standard Old Testament.

1945–46 Visiting Professor of Ancient Oriental History, Oriental Institute, University of Chicago (winter term). Th.D. Honoris Causa, University of Oslo. Member, Governing Council, School of Asiatic Studies (New York).

1946–47 Hon. Member, Société Asiatique (Paris) and Society for Old Testament Study (Great Britain). Foreign Member, Royal Danish Academy of Sciences and Royal Flemish Academy of Sciences. Corresponding Member, Finnish Oriental Society. Member, Executive Committee, Archaeological Institute of

America (two-year term). Member, Advisory Council, African Expedition of University of California. LL.D., Boston College.

1947–48   Archaeological Advisor to the University of California African Expedition and member of Sinai exploration party. Corresponding Member, Académie des Inscriptions et Belles Lettres (Institut de France). Lowell Institute Lecturer, King's Chapel, Boston; L. P. Stone Lecturer, Princeton Theological Seminary; D.H.L., Hebrew Union College. Paris Congress of Orientalists (Chairman, U.S. delegation; Member, Consultative Committee; Chairman, Semitic Section).

1948–49   Vice-president, Archaeological Institute of America and Asia Institute. Sprunt Lecturer, Union Theological Seminary, Richmond. First foreign lecture tour (England and Scotland). Pelican edition of *Archaeology of Palestine* published. Hon. LL.D., University of St. Andrews.

1949–50   First Vice-president, American Foundation for the Study of Man; Chief Archaeologist, American Foundation Arabian Expedition. First German translation: *Von der Steinzeit zum Christentum;* first Hebrew translation: (*Archaeology of Palestine*). D.H.L., College of Jewish Studies (Chicago).

1950–51   Messenger Lecturer, Cornell University. Litt.D., Yale University.

1951–52   Second foreign lecture tour (Scandinavia and Germany). Member, Honorary Committee, International Congress of Orientalists, Istanbul. Th.D., University of Uppsala; Litt.D., Georgetown University. First French translation: *De l'âge de la pierre à la Chrétienté.*

1952–53   Received Lord and Taylor award ($1,000). Litt.D., University of Dublin (Trinity College).

1953–54   Third foreign lecture tour (Israel). LL.D., Franklin and Marshall College. Socius Ordinarius, German Archaeological Institute; Hon. Member, Royal Irish Academy.

1954–55   Member, National Academy of Sciences (Section of Anthropology); Corresponding Member, Austrian Academy of Sciences.

1955–56   Fellow, American Academy of Arts and Sciences (Cambridge). Vice-president, American Philosophical Society. Corresponding Member, School of Oriental and African Studies, University of London.

1956–57   President, International Organization of Old Testament Scholars. State Department Exchange Professor, Turkey. Hon. Dr. Phil., Hebrew University in Jerusalem; D.C.L., Pace College.

1957–58 Ph.D., La Salle College (Philadelphia). Last year of active teaching at Johns Hopkins University.

1958–59 Visiting Research Professor, Jewish Theological Seminary of America. Hon. vice-president, Leeds University Oriental Society. Litt.D., Loyola College (Baltimore).

1959–60 Litt.D., Loyola University (Chicago).

1960–61 Visiting Professor, Graduate Department of Philosophy, Harvard University (two months). Hon. Correspondent, Department of Archaeology, India. A.C.L.S. Award "for Distinguished Scholarship in the Humanities" ($10,000). Celebrations of seventieth birthday in Cincinnati and Detroit. *The Bible and the Ancient Near East* (*Festschrift*) published, with bibliography. L.H.D., Manhattan College; HH.D., Wayne State University.

1961–62 Visiting Professor, University of Minnesota (one term), University of Iowa (one term). Litt.D., Harvard University; HH.D., Brigham Young University.

Index of Names and Subjects
(see also Contents)

DATE DUE